THE TRUE LIFE OF

CAPT. SIR RICHARD F. BURTON

K.C.M.G.   F.R.G.S.   ETC.

CAPT. SIR RICHARD F. BURTON, K.C.M.G., F.R.G.S., ETC.

Ætat 69

THE TRUE LIFE OF

Capt. Sir Richard F. Burton

K.C.M.G., F.R.G.S., ETC.

WRITTEN BY HIS NIECE

GEORGIANA M. STISTED

WITH THE AUTHORITY AND APPROVAL OF THE
BURTON FAMILY

DARF PUBLISHERS LIMITED
LONDON
1985

FIRST PUBLISHED 1896
NEW IMPRESSION 1985

ISBN 1 85077 049 2

Printed and bound in Great Britain
by A. Wheaton & Co. Ltd, Exeter

PREFACE

My object in compiling this Memoir is twofold. First, to tell the truth concerning one who can no longer defend himself; secondly, to supply a want often complained of—the story of the great traveller's life in a popular form. Having disproved tales so flimsy that no unbiassed person failed to see through them, though knowing Richard Burton ever so slightly, and having succeeded, thanks to the cordial assistance of my publisher, in issuing a "Life" for the masses as well as for the classes, whilst regretting no abler pen than mine was ready to perform the work, I feel that an imperative duty to the memory of a hero, to the public, and to ourselves, is now fulfilled.

Grazeley, Upper Norwood, S.E.

December 1st, 1896.

CONTENTS.

CHAPTER I

CHAPTER II

CHAPTER III

CHAPTER IV

CHAPTER VIII

CHAPTER IX

CHAPTER X

PAGE

CHAPTER XIV

CHAPTER XV

CHAPTER XVI

THE TRUE LIFE OF

CAPT. SIR RICHARD F. BURTON

K.C.M.G. F.R.G.S. ETC.

CHAPTER I

RICHARD FRANCIS BURTON was born on the
19th March, 1821, at Barham House, Herts, the
home of his maternal grandfather and grandmother, Richard
and Sarah Beckwith Baker. His mother, one of three co-
heiresses, had married the earliest; and he, her first child,
became the darling of the household. Baptized in due course
at Elstree Parish Church, he spent most part of his infancy
with these relatives ; and, as often happens even with very
young children, who have passed two or three perfectly
happy years, and never quite forget them, he could just
remember being brought down after dinner to dessert,
seated on the knee of a tall man with yellow hair and
bright blue eyes.

His grandfather on the paternal side he never saw. The
Rev. Edward Burton, Rector of Tuam, was educated in
England for the Church ; and, on being presented with his
Irish benefice, left the Lake Country with his brother
Edmond, afterwards Dean of Killala, and settled in Ireland
for the rest of his life. These brothers, originally of Barker's
Hill, near Shap, Westmoreland, were related to the Burtons
of Longnor, like Lord Conyngham and Sir Charles Burton
of Pollacton ; and were, in fact, collateral descendants of

Francis Pierpoint Burton first Marquis of Conyngham. The notable man of the family, Sir Edward Burton, fought so bravely during the Wars of the Roses, that he was made a Knight Banneret by Edward IV after the second battle of St. Albans.

The rector who, besides his living, possessed private means, had not been long in Ireland before he purchased the property of Newgarden, near Tuam, where he seems to have combined, according to the easy-going fashion of the day, the duties of squire and parson. Like most clergymen he married young and had a large family; but his wife, Maria Margaretta, daughter by a Lejeune of Dr. John Campbell, Vicar General of Tuam, long survived him.

Concerning the ancestry of the said Maria Margaretta there exists an interesting legend, one which also affects several well-known Irish families, to wit, the Nettervilles, Droughts, Graves, Plunketts and Trimlestons. More than one document exists to prove that Louis Lejeune, father of Sarah, Dr. Campbell's wife, was a son of Louis Quatorze by the Comtesse de Montmorenci. The mother, a Huguenot, having repented of her error and fearing her child would be educated as a Papist, had him secretly carried off to Ireland at an early age, where his name was translated to Young, and where he became eventually a doctor of divinity in the Anglican Church. This romantic story, familiar to widely scattered members of the families already referred to, is curiously corrobated by the striking resemblance between the Bourbons and certain of their supposed descendants. A miniature of Maria Margaretta preserved amongst the family treasures, depicts the peculiar Bourbon traits so vividly that no one fails to remark the pear-shaped face and head that culminated in Louis Philippe.

Either the rector had proved an unusually good husband, or the widow found her position almost intolerable after his death, for it is said, she never ceased to regret

his loss, until she was laid beside him in the old cathedral
at Tuam.   As four sons and four daughters were the result
of their union, her house was not left desolate; but in those
days the lot of a widow residing in County Galway must
have been far from pleasant.   Not that she was wanting
in courage.   On one occasion Newgarden was broken
into by thieves.   Her sons seem to have been absent,
so Madam Burton, as her tenantry called her, lighted
a candle, went upstairs to fetch some gunpowder which
was kept in a barrel, loaded her pistols, and hastened down
to the hall, to find the robbers decamped.   She then
remembered the dip which, in her hurry, she had left
standing on the barrel in disagreeable proximity to the
explosive contents, and at the risk of being blown to atoms,
she coolly re-entered the room and removed the guttering
wick from its perilous position.

Joseph Netterville, her third and handsomest son, was
the father of the traveller.   He had too many brothers and
sisters to remain idle at home, and as obtaining a commission in the army was a far easier matter then than it is
now, he decided to become a soldier.   On being gazetted to
the 36th Regiment, he insisted upon several of his tenants
enlisting at the same time, and so cleared his mother's
property for a while, from some of the wildest and most
dangerous characters.   But his military career proved
a short one.   After he had seen a little service in
Sicily, his regiment was ordered to England, where it
remained in inglorious idleness during the stirring times
on the Continent.   Finally, in 1819, he obtained several
months' leave and married Martha Beckwith Baker, one
of the three co-heiresses already mentioned, a descendant
on her mother's side of the Macgregors and Macleans.

Of this marriage were born three children,—Richard
Francis, Maria Catherine Eliza, who married in 1845
Lieutenant-General Sir Henry William Stisted, K.C.B.,
and Edward Joseph Netterville.   After the birth of the

last, Colonel Burton gave up soldiering for ever. Although a stalwart, broad-chested man, he was seized in the prime of life by bronchial asthma, a complaint which, appearing in one of its severest forms, utterly incapacitated him for active service. A faint hope of being able to rejoin his regiment at some future time prevented him from selling out, so he went on half pay, as it proved, for the remainder of his life. Thus young Richard's migratory instincts were early fostered : during many years the family roamed incessantly over the Continent in search of health, or at least some alleviation of the father's sufferings.

Hoping to breathe more freely in the comparatively dry air of Touraine, Colonel Burton pitched his tent at Tours. The Château de Beauséjour, his first house, stood on the right bank of the Loire, half way up the heights that bound the stream. It commanded a lovely view, was surrounded on three sides by a charming garden and vineyard, and proved quite an ideal home. The children revelled in country pleasures, eating grapes in the vineyard and working in their own little private gardens ; the father, whose health for a time improved almost miraculously, indulged in boar-hunting in le Forêt d'Ambroise; and the mother, a veritable Martha, looked after her house and her little ones. She had other duties, for Beauséjour was no hermitage. Tours then contained some two hundred English families, attracted by the beauty of the place and the facilities of education ; and as the Burtons enjoyed a comfortable income (Mr. Baker had died suddenly just before they left England), they kept an excellent *chef* and cellar, and were noted for their hospitality.

They were popular, and not merely on account of keeping open house. To begin with, they were pleasant-looking people. Colonel Burton, once the handsomest man of his regiment, had a clear, olive complexion, delicately modelled, slightly arched nose, and bright piercing eyes. His wife, with her luxuriant brown hair, large grey eyes, tall, graceful figure, and tiny hands and feet, was, if not so regular in feature, quite as attractive as the husband. The children followed suit. Richard, a dark, clever-faced boy, showed every indication of equalling his sire's good looks; his sister was a lovely pink-cheeked girl; and Edward had the profile of a Greek statue. But this was not all. Most of us have been taught somewhat erroneously that looks matter little: the truth is, form and feature often convey a true idea of character. It was so in this instance; for the Burtons were not merely sociable, courteous and generous, but thoroughly well principled. Steady, old-fashioned Church folk, free from the rabid Evangelicalism then at its height, and the Tractarianism which later became so general, they were as true to what they thought right as the needle to the pole. Richard Burton said, in after days, that his father was the most moral man he had ever known; and would often add, in his curious, abrupt way, "Nice to be able to feel proud of one's parents!" It must be allowed that the Colonel's line of conduct with respect to the education of his boys, was not the most sagacious that could have been followed, but clairvoyance is given to few. The wife was gentle, intensely unselfish; the daughter possessed all the family virtues, marred by none of the faults; and Edward was noted for lavish generosity.

Richard, owing perhaps to weak health, for as a child he showed no indication of his future herculean strength, was the least amiable, Rough in manner, mischievous as a monkey, and subject to outbursts of temper, he often called down upon his head the vials of his father's wrath. But, on the other hand, he was brave and affectionate in the highest degree. When he had the toothache it was known only next day—by the swelling of his face. But where his affections were concerned his stoicism vanished. He adored his mother, thinking nothing in heaven or earth too good for her; and one of the earliest stories recorded of him is that he was found rolling on the floor, howling

with mingled rage and anguish because some women had
carriages to drive in while for a time his parent had to go
on foot. He was nearly as much attached to his sister.
Some years later he was amusing himself, boy fashion, by
throwing stones, one hit the little girl by mischance and
cut her forehead so severely that she could not help crying
out. Aghast at what he had done, he rushed up to her,
flung his arms around her neck, burst into a paroxysm of
sobs and tears, and not for some time did he recover his
composure. Pets of all kinds he delighted in, often spending hours trying to revive some unlucky bird or beast
which, like pets in general, had come to a sad and untimely
end ; in fact, it is said he did once succeed in resuscitating
a favourite bullfinch which had nearly drowned itself in a
water jug. To sum up, all his relatives agreed that though
often most troublesome and disagreeable, " Dick " was one
of the warmest-hearted boys that ever breathed.

As all three children were more or less fond of reading,
their father began their education early. One morning
when " Dick " was only six years old, he and his brother
were conveyed to Tours and introduced as pupils to a
lame Irish schoolmaster named Clough. These Liliputian
learners spent their time at first wondering at their novel
surroundings, and after a pretence at lessons, took advantage
of their hours of freedom by playing with pop-guns, spring
pistols, and tin and wooden sabres, so realistically too, that
small " Dick " quite longed to kill the porter because he
dared to gibe at the *sabres de bois* and *pistolets de paille*.
Unfortunately it was soon found that the Château de
Beauséjour was too far from the town for the boys to
trudge to and fro every day, so the family moved to the
Rue de l'Archévêché, the then best street in Tours, but
unsuitable for delicate parents and young children.

Here the Burtons remained until 1829. Then the father,
whose complaint had become fairly bearable, resolved to
return for a while to England. An uncomfortable sus-

picion appears to have crossed his mind, that a foreign education might not be the best thing in the world for his boys. Sons of sundry cronies at Tours were turning out distinctly badly ; their example might be dangerous, and it seemed more prudent to remove his lads from so disturbing an influence. On arriving in London with a half-formed intention of sending Richard and Edward to Eton, to prepare for Oxford and Cambridge, he unluckily met a blundering friend who recommended a preparatory school at Richmond ; and as the latter place was pleasantly get-at-able, and his wife was anxious to remain near her mother and sisters in Town, he ultimately decided on settling for a year in this romantic suburb.

Opening upon the famous Green stood the school, a handsome building with a paddock which enclosed some fine old elm trees. Rev. Charles Delafosse, the master, a bluff and portly man with an aquiline nose, looked a model pedagogue ; he was assisted by a large staff of ushers, and at first matters seemed most promising. But there must have been something radically wrong both with the management and the mode of teaching. The Burton boys learnt next to nothing except a certain facility of using their fists ; quarrels were so incessant that the playground was turned into a miniature battlefield every day, when the boys were allowed to beat each other black and blue; and the fare was limited in quantity and detestable in quality. Finally, scarlet fever of a very malignant type broke out and put an end to the Richmond scheme for ever. Some lads died, the rest were sent to their respective homes. Richard and Edward went straight to their grandmother's house in Cumberland Street, to avoid conveying the infection to their sister ; and it was well they did so, for the elder sickened a few days after his arrival. He was tenderly nursed by his aunt, Georgiana Baker, and a friend, a Miss Morgan. Edward, though intensely anxious to fall ill too, and so come in for some of the nice things going—he was caught more than once inhaling the air through the key-hole of his brother's bedroom to ensure so desirable a piece of luck—remained in excellent health; and the two little chaps were soon taken by their kind relative to Ramsgate.

Meanwhile their father had become thoroughly disenchanted with Richmond. The school from which he had hoped so much had turned out an expensive failure; worse still, his family had been attacked with fever and influenza, he felt ill and miserable, and fairly recoiled from the prospect of spending another winter on the green. So marching orders were again issued, and for the Continent. It would have been wiser to leave the sons at Rugby or Eton, but he was a warm-hearted Irishman, and distances in those comparatively steamless days were much more formidable than now. So he squared matters with his conscience by engaging a tutor for his lads and a governess for his daughter, and thus reinforced, the family left Richmond, and went to Blois.

There education began in real earnest, the young people working hard to make up for lost time. The boys, under their tutor, M. Du Pré, of Exeter College, Oxford, made rapid progress in dead and living languages: local masters taught them swimming, fencing, and, after some slight opposition, dancing. Fencing was their pet occupation. They spent most of their leisure in exchanging thrusts, either with or without the old French soldier who taught them; and after Richard had passed his foil down his brother's throat, nearly destroying the uvula, they learned not to neglect the mask. " Dick " also spent many an anxious hour in attempting to train a falcon. The poor bird on whom the " 'prentice hand " was tried soon died, worn out like a mediæval saint, by austerities, especially in the fasting line, and so bitterly mourned was it by its affectionate young owner, that he never tried the experiment again until later in life, when success attended his efforts.

At times the wild lads must have been very troublesome

neighbours. It was about as easy to confine them to their own premises, as to prevent cats from roaming. An elderly French maiden who lived next door, tired of ceaseless irruptions into her prim, well-kept grounds, at last complained to the parents. Punishment had followed, not meekly borne, and Richard, the chief offender, after deep cogitation and frequent consultations with his brother and sister, determined on revenge—revenge which should prove difficult to detect. He searched his own garden and the surrounding neighbourhood, wherever he could gain access, for fine, fat snails—so delightful to think of them devouring the old wretch's flowers!—secured a goodly number over night in a sack, and at early dawn before the enemy was abroad, climbed the wall with his burden and scattered the contents over her most promising plants. A closer acquaintance with the mysteries of French cooking would have spared him the disappointment that ensued. When the old lady, unaware of the three pairs of eyes anxiously awaiting her arrival, did come out for her daily walk, her countenance brightened. Hastily fetching a basket, she picked up as many snails as it would hold, and vanished into her kitchen with her *bonne* to make soup.

That year the winter at Blois was very severe. Water froze in the drawing-room. Colonel Burton had a fearful attack of asthma, which he insisted on leaving to run its own course, one of his peculiarities being that he would never send for medical advice, until death stared him in the face. Change of air and scene was his only remedy. And as he had to spend night after night propped in a chair, utterly unable to lie down, his laboured breathing audible half over the house, it seemed about time to try it. So no sooner had spring set in, and the milder weather rendered it possible for him to move, than he proposed going to Italy. His wife, poor thing, who only moderately enjoyed a migratory existence, was aghast ; but the young people, all three rovers at heart, were wild with delight on hearing of this

exciting project. It seemed almost too good to be true
when the yellow travelling chariot, a luxury indispensable
to well-to-do folk of that period, was taken out of its
coach-house and furbished up for the journey. This
equipage contained all the funny old-fashioned receptacles
then in vogue, some of whose very names are unfamiliar
—imperial, boot, sword-case, and plate-chest—a sort of
miniature home on wheels. And during such leisurely
progress—it took a month to get to Italy—comforts were
required, for the posting and country inns were at times
far from agreeable. Of course, everybody could not
squeeze into the chariot, roomy though it was, so it
was occupied by the father, mother, and daughter, while
a chaise drawn by an ugly horse known as Dobbin, driven
by young Richard, accommodated the rest of the family.
The boy delighted in acting Jehu, though at the close of
each day his father very rightly insisted on his attending to the watering, feeding, and rubbing down of the
steed in question, before he got his own dinner. At
Marseilles, chariot, chaise, horse, and family were shipped
to Leghorn, a spot which proved so utterly uninhabitable
that, after a few days' rest, the colonel and his belongings
transferred themselves to Pisa.

Although they often returned to it, the Burtons' first
sojourn under the shadow of the Leaning Tower was a
very brief one. Next summer found them at Siena, and their
stay in that venerable town, one of the dullest places
under heaven, was far from exciting. Hitherto Italy
had certainly not realised expectations; but, by the end
of September, the father determined to visit Rome, so
with hopes once more raised to their highest pitch, the
children watched the chariot—which, by the way, was
drawn by post-horses—Dobbin, and the chaise being made
ready for the march.

Travelling in vetturino was not without its charm. It
is true one seldom progressed more than five miles an

hour; if uphill still less; and in some parts of Italy the fear of brigands was a distinct bar to perfect enjoyment. Moreover, the harness was perpetually breaking; and often a horse fell lame; and the inns were too far apart to render such accidents easily remedied; but one saw the country thoroughly, and went along slowly enough to impress everything on the memory. Food consisted chiefly of omelettes, pigeons, and ill-fed chickens, the latter being killed unpleasantly soon before dinner; but bread, wine, and oil were excellent, and adulteration was then unknown. Taking it altogether, it is doubtful whether we have changed for the better, rushing along in hot, crowded railway carriages, hustled over our meals, and catching so fleeting a glimpse of the fairest scenes, that we often return home feeling decidedly hazy as to what we have seen and what we haven't.

At Rome, sight-seeing was pursued with peculiar ardour. The young Burtons were wild with delight at visiting all the celebrated sites of which they had so often heard; for, be it remembered, they were well-read youngsters, and would have turned up their noses at the mawky story-books, so popular nowadays amongst our boys and girls. They roamed with " Mrs. Starke " under the arm, for " Murray " and " Baedeker " were not then invented, from the Vatican to the Capitol, from church to palazzo, from ruin to ruin. Little did they care that the Ghetto was a disgrace to civilization, that the Trastevere was filthy as an African village, that the Tiber flooded the lower town. Sufficient that it was the Tiber. When they tired of the city, they made long excursions into the country; Richard even ascended Mount Soracte. And when the Holy Week came round, its ceremonies presided over by that very jovial old pontiff, Gregory XVI, we may be sure not one was shirked by the active young people. Being staunch Protestants, they were much amused to hear the Romans cracking small jokes upon the mien and demeanour of the Vecchierello,

while the Pope stood in the balcony delivering his benediction—*urbi et orbi*—in strong contrast with the English
and Irish Romanists, who straightway became almost
hysterical with rapture.

From Rome our migratory family proceeded to Naples,
fixing on Sorrento as summer quarters. Here Richard,
excited perhaps by the immense variety of excursions—
travels on a small scale—became more than usually troublesome. First he crept over the Natural Arch, merely
because an Italian lad had said: "*Non è possibilé, Signorino.*"
Next he insisted on taking the dog's place in the Grotto del
Cane, instigated rather by inquisitiveness than sympathy
for the ill-used animal, and was pulled out just in time to
avoid suffocation. And on another occasion he was caught
in an attempt to descend the crater of Mount Vesuvius,
apparently on a wild goose chase after Satan, who, so the
neighbours declared, had been seen vanishing therein, clawing fast to the soul of a usurer. But in spite of these
occasional shocks to the parental nerves, everybody enjoyed
the years passed at Naples and its lovely environs.

Education went on briskly. The celebrated Cavalli was
engaged as fencing master. In those days the Neapolitan
school, which has now almost died out, was in its last
bloom. It was indeed such a thoroughly business-like
affair, that whenever a Neapolitan and a Frenchman fought
a duel, the former was sure to win. The Burton boys
worked at their favourite art, heart and soul, and generally
managed, by rising early, to devote several hours a day to
it. Young Richard determined even at that age to produce
a combination between the Neapolitan and the French
school, so as to supplement the defects of the one by the
merits of the other; and, although a life of very hard work
did not allow leisure enough to carry out the whole plan,
one large volume of "A Book on the Sword" was published in 1880.

The sojourn at Naples was temporarily interrupted by the

terrible cholera visitation in the winter of the early thirties. It caused a fearful mortality, sometimes twelve hundred deaths a day. Colonel Burton had soon to decide between remaining in a comfortable palazzo on the Chiaja, wherein people lay dead above and beneath his apartments, or removing to Sorrento, where there was little sickness but no doctor. Characteristically he chose the latter, and very dismal did he find a place then only suitable for summer quarters. To wile away the time he devoted himself to chemistry, and nearly drove his Italian servants mad with superstitious terror by performing before their horrified eyes, an excellent imitation of the miracle of St. Januarius, using as a main ingredient the blood of the bird beloved by Æsculapius. They quite expected so sacrilegious an act would at once bring down upon the family the pestilence raging in the neighbourhood ; but the Burtons, in common with many of their fellow country people, escaped unharmed. It was a curious circumstance, one which excited much comment at the time, that the British colony at Naples led almost charmed lives throughout the course of an epidemic of unparalleled severity, although so many persons had fallen victims to it in England.

In the spring of 1836, Colonel Burton having had enough of Naples, removed with his family to Pau in the Pyrenees. Some crony who had preceded him thither, had written such glowing accounts of the climate and society, that he was only too glad of the excuse for a thorough change. M. du Pré was still one of the party, so there was little interruption to the studies. At Pau, Richard began mathematics, varied by boxing lessons from an Irish groom. His interest in every branch of the noble art of self-defence threatened to become almost a monomania, owing perhaps to a day-dream indulged in by both lads, but kept for the present profoundly secret—thrashing their tutor. To prepare the more thoroughly for this dashing exploit, they passed hours in the barracks fencing with the soldiers, a

familiarity tolerated by the *piou-pious* on account of the
largesse bestowed on these occasions; for the Burton boys
were handsomely supplied with pocket-money, and Edward
was especially generous in the manner of spending it. But
although a good deal of time was spent in boxing and
fencing, Richard never became a loafer; at Pau he mastered the Béarnais *patois*, a charming *naïve* dialect which
considerably assisted him in learning Provençale. And he
tells us how later in life he found these studies useful in his
official capacity, even in the most out-of-the-way corners of
the world: nothing goes home to the heart of a man so
much as to speak to him in his own tongue.

At last, after sundry summer trips to Bagnières de
Bigorre and Argélés, the poor asthmatic father again found
a change imperative. Two winters at Pau with its windy,
rainy, snowy climate, had by no means improved his health;
and when the mountain fogs began once more to roll down
upon the valley, and a third cold season was approaching,
he ruefully confessed the little capital of the Basses-
Pyrénées, so far as he was concerned, had proved a
failure. So he issued marching orders for Pisa, a place
for which during many a year he cherished a somewhat
unreasonable affection. No one except his wife objected
to the long, weary journey, and she very mildly; and before
autumn had waned the family were safely established in a
house on the south side of the Lung' Arno. A number of
old acquaintances were yet living in the queer old town,
and a few new ones were added to the list.

Richard now diligently applied himself to drawing;
and it was lucky for him he did take so much pains with
this art, as it enabled him to illustrate his own books.
Traveller-authors who have the misfortune to be indifferent
draughtsmen, and bring home only a few scrawls to put
into the hands of professionals, have the pleasure of seeing
strange anomalies depicted in their pages. Even though
Burton could draw, once, when sending to London a

sketch of a pilgrim in his correct costume, the portable Koran, worn under the left arm, narrowly escaped becoming a revolver. In music, his brother and sister left him far behind. Perhaps with him the sense of harmony was lacking, for he seems to have devoted some time to an accomplishment which might have increased his fascinations with the fair sex.

For, like Byron, he soon fell a victim to the tender passion. One, Signorina Caterina, a tall, slim, dark girl, with the palest possible complexion, and regular features, was the first of a long procession of beloveds. Proposals of marriage were made and accepted; but, as parental consent had not been requested on either side, and would certainly have been withheld even had that dutiful preliminary occurred to the enamoured pair, it was impossible to get the ceremony performed. The days of Romeo and Juliet and their accommodating old friar were past; and even then had Romeo been a heretic there might have been a hitch. Vainly the lovers racked their brains; the difficulties proved insurmountable. Their adieux were heartrending; but history hath it that Caterina was soon forgotten and replaced, while it maintains a discreet silence as to whether Ricardo long retained undisputed possession of her heart.

The love affair reached the good old father's ears; he was not best pleased, and it was easy to see that a family break-up was approaching. The young Burtons had grown very unruly; they made close friendships with Italian medical students, they smoked incessantly; they *had* thrashed the tutor, so he could do nothing towards keeping them in order. Recognising the unpleasant fact that his lads had become unmanageable, Colonel Burton bore with their wild pranks for only a very short time, and then, accompanied by the luckless M. du Pré, marshalled his sons to England.

Richard had passed his nineteenth birthday, and if he

was ever to go to College the time had arrived. That he did not care to lead a semi-mediæval existence mattered little: neither his nor his brother's inclinations were consulted, for it was well known that both lads wished to enter the army. His father, who like many Irishmen, ran from one extreme into another—from allowing his sons too much liberty abroad to almost cloistering them at home—had set his heart upon their taking honours, one at Oxford, the other at Cambridge, and later becoming parsons. While this programme betrayed very little knowledge of character, it showed a great deal of affectionate solicitude for their future welfare. His health had been ruined by his short campaign in Sicily, his private fortune diminished rather than increased by his profession, and it was but natural that, remembering the comfortable home at Tuam and his uncle's luxurious house at Killala, he should desire for his clever sons a career which might secure them a competence. In those days the army was considered hardly suitable for men with brains; moreover, commissions in crack regiments were expensive, and the pay was, as it is now, beggarly. Certainly Richard and Edward Burton did not evince much of a vocation for the priestly calling, but their parent fondly trusted that university life might foster latent pious proclivities which might never have seen the light under less favourable conditions.

His hopes at first seemed doomed to disappointment. A certain professor, a well-known Grecian, put young Richard through his paces in the classics, and found him lamentably deficient. While as to his religious studies, he broke down ignominiously in the Nicene Creed, and knew next to nothing about the Thirty-nine Articles. Evidently pretty severe coaching was required before he could appear in the character of a sucking parson at Oxford.

Fortunately it happened to be Long Vacation, and a Doctor Greenhill, who had then little to do, agreed to lodge and coach this most unpromising youth until the opening

term. Colonel Burton accompanied his son to the very
door of his future abode, consigned him personally to the
new tutor, and then returned to his wife and daughter in
Italy. Edward was already studying with a clergyman at
Cambridge.

Stern though the old man was, Richard confessed later
that when the last familiar face had disappeared he felt too
lonely and miserable even to get into mischief. Ashamed
of the poor appearance he had presented to his first ex-
aminer, he worked hard with Dr. Greenhill to make up his
deficiencies ; and, thanks to his excellent memory and
great power of concentration, he began residence in Trinity
College no worse equipped for his future studies than quite
two-thirds of his brother collegians. But any trace of
enthusiasm regarding his romantic environment seems to
have been lacking. His quarters he described as a couple
of dog-holes; chapel was a bore; the lectures which succeeded it either incomprehensible or useless; and the dinner
at 5 p.m. was uneatable. At that time beer was the only
drink allowed, and the food consisted of hunches of meat
cooked after Homeric fashion, plain boiled vegetables, and
stodgy pudding. In fact, this cannibal repast so disgusted
him, that he found a place in the town where, when he
could escape " Hall," he was able to order some more
appetising viands.

There were real annoyances besides. Ignorance of the
customs of the place gave rise to quarrels ; and, as he had
not the least idea how to manage his limited allowance, he
speedily outran the constable. With regard to his studies,
he soon found that University honours required harder
work and stricter self-denial than he was disposed for; a
truth made disagreeably plain by his trying for two scholarships, and failing to win either. Presently a bright idea
struck him. As the desire of his heart was to become a
soldier, why not leave the unattainable classics, and look
round for means of furthering his own designs ? It was

2

the Indian army he wished to join, attracted by its opportunities of mastering Oriental languages, and of studying all
sorts and conditions of men; so, after this lucky thought,
he kept a sharp look out for any chance of grounding himself in Hindustani or Arabic. At last, tired of waiting for a
regular class, he attacked the latter language, and was soon
well on in Erpinius's grammar; and, by and by, Don
Pascual de Gayangos, whom he met at Dr. Greenhill's,
showed him how to copy the alphabet.

Strange that in those days, though England was then,
as now, the greatest Mohammedan Empire in the world,
learning Arabic at Oxford was next to impossible. A
Regius Professor existed nominally, but he had no other
occupations than to profess. When Burton required assistance in mastering the language, and applied to the learned
gentleman in question, he was told a Professor would teach
a class and not an individual. *Nous avons changé tout cela,*
but none too soon.

As time went on Richard's spirits improved. He
amused himself by taking long walks to Bagley Wood,
where a pretty gipsy sat in state to receive the shillings and
the homage of the undergraduates, and when less romantically disposed, spent his leisure hours in the fencing-room.
Riding was too expensive, as he objected to a cheap and
nasty "monture," but on Sunday afternoons he often drove
a tandem to Abingdon, about ten miles off—an excursion
not without a spice of excitement, tandems being forbidden.
As he was rather shy, and his brother collegians did not
like his half-foreign appearance, he made few friends—
Alfred Bates Richards was, perhaps, the most intimate.
But he did associate occasionally with some of the young
men at Exeter and Brasenose, preferring, however, Oriel,
both as regards fellows and undergraduates; and at times
he dined with various families in the town, meeting at their
houses some of the celebrities of the day. Once Dr. Arnold
and Dr. Newman were amongst the guests. Much was

expected from the conversation of the two learned and reverend men ; but as it was mostly confined to discussing the size of the apostles in the Cathedral of St. Peter's in Rome, and as both divines showed a very dim recollection of the subject, the said feast of reason and flow of soul must have been to say the least, disappointing.

Autumn term over, and very long it seemed to the lonely young fellow, he went to stay with his grandmother and aunts in London. It proved a memorable visit, for he met at their house the three sons of a Colonel White of the Third Dragoons, who were all preparing for military service in India. There is little doubt that the society of this trio of embryo soldiers strengthened Richard's resolution to choose the army as a profession ; many an exciting talk must they have had together on the subject ; for our dominion in India had entered upon a critical stage of its history, or as the four young fellows would have expressed it, conditions there were remarkably favourable for rapid promotion. Presently he was able to discuss the all-absorbing subject with his brother. Edward came up from Cambridge, and the two chummed together in Maddox Street, Mrs. Baker's house not being large enough to take them both in. They could not come to any conclusion how best to escape from their trammels ; but from all accounts they seemed to have followed the advice of a certain cheerful-minded sage—to enjoy the present, and let the future take care of itself.

But their "high old time" appeared only too short. Spring term arrived, and all the delightful chats about India with the Whites, and larking about London with a congenial companion—the brothers' tastes were very similar—had to be given up for a dismal existence in two frowsy rooms. To console himself, Burton played a few pranks, but they were neither original nor numerous ; and by-and-by he settled down to the various kinds of work that suited him best.

He was certainly not idle, for about this time he invented a system of learning lauguages, peculiarly his own. As Burton became one of the greatest linguists of the day, this system evidently suited him. It may be valuable to students, so I give it in his own words.

"I get a grammar and a vocabulary, mark out the forms and words which I know are absolutely necessary, and learn them by heart by carrying them in my pocket and looking over them at spare moments during the day. I never work more than a quarter of an hour at a time, for after that time the brain loses its freshness. After learning some three hundred words, easily done in a week, I stumble through some easy book-work (one of the Gospels is the most come-at-able), and underline every word I wish to recollect, in order to read over my pencillings at least once a day. Having finished my volume, I then carefully work up the grammar minutiæ, and I then choose some other book whose subject most interests me. The neck of the language is now broken, and progress is rapid. If I come across a new sound like the Arabic *Ghayn*, I train my tongue to it by repeating it so many hundred times a day. When I read, I invariably read out loud, so that the ear may aid memory. I am delighted with the most difficult characters, Chinese and Cuneiform, because I feel that they impress themselves more strongly upon the eye than the eternal Roman letters. This, by the bye, made me resolutely stand aloof from the hundred schemes for transliterating Eastern languages, such as Arabic, Sanscrit, Hebrew, and Syriac into Latin letters. Whenever I converse with anyone in a language that I am learning, I take the trouble to repeat their words inaudibly after them, and so to learn the trick of pronunciation and emphasis."

Thanks either to his natural facility, or to the system in question, Burton made considerable progress in Arabic; a language which was to be of the greatest service to him in after days. His Greek and Latin seem to have done him more harm than good. The English pronunciation of Latin vowels, then universal, happens to be the worst in the world, because we have an O and an A which belong peculiarly to English. A boy educated abroad would naturally speak real (Roman) Latin ; Richard adhered with tenacity to his original style, and when he insisted on spouting Greek by accent and not by quantity, as they did and still do at Athens, and refused to be corrected, he was looked upon as a very conceited and unruly youngster.

Burton was right, only he was not in the position to give an opinion. An undergraduate just over twenty could not reasonably expect to introduce so great an innovation amongst bald-headed seniors ; and his line of conduct, which they ascribed solely to vanity and stubbornness, was not calculated to make him a favourite with the authorities. It mattered little in this case, as the sooner he began his military career and finished his University one, the better for all concerned; but the lack of tact or worldly wisdom, the habit of telling the truth whether timely or not,—that veracity which Carlyle declares is the root of all greatness or real worth in human creatures,—sadly hindered him at times in his struggle with the world.

Meanwhile, his family had not forgotten him, and a happy meeting made amends for past annoyances. Colonel Burton had brought his wife and daughter from Lucca to Wiesbaden in order to be nearer England; and the " boys," as they were still called, were sent for to spend the Long Vacation in Germany. There was no larking in Town this time; the brothers did not lose a day after receiving their letters, but started at once for the Continent. Great was the delight of both mother and sister at seeing the bright, good-hearted young fellows again. It is a common saying in the family that Burtons understand only each other ; and while this peculiarity has drawbacks as regards their friendships and marriages, it makes them very happy and united at home. Richard, who had just succeeded in exciting a fair amount of enmity at Oxford in an exceeding short space of time, was so loving a son that his mother, then almost invalided with heart complaint, exclaimed when he left her, " Just as if the sun itself had disappeared ! "

Wiesbaden, which, in those days before railways, was intensely German, he described as a kind of Teutonic Margate with a *chic* of its own. The gaming tables were still in all their glory, and as they were forbidden, of course, Richard lost no time in trying his luck. But after a few furtive visits, and the winning or losing of a few sovereigns, he soon wearied of them. Gambling never seems to have possessed any attraction for him. Games of hazard he considered mere waste of time; horse-racing only moderately amusing; and of the Stock Exchange he had a positive horror.

Play was not the sole entertainment at Wiesbaden. There were often dances in the evening, and Burton, who waltzed exceedingly well, enjoyed these mild festivities intensely. The girls liked him as a partner, not only because he could steer them skilfully round the room, but for his good looks. He had grown tall and broad-chested; his shapely head was plentifully covered with curly brown hair; and his large, lustrous brown eyes, whose lashes owed their surprising length to having been cut by his mother in infancy, were singularly beautiful. A thick moustache, which, much to his indignation, he had been compelled to shave at Oxford, had grown again, and completed a *tout ensemble* of manly grace very rarely surpassed. His sister, who, during a brief season at the Baths of Lucca, was known by friends and admirers as the Moss Rose, had become a lovely girl; the father, in spite of his asthma, was nearly as upright and good-looking as ever; and there is little doubt these handsome Burtons attracted no small notice whenever they appeared.

From Wiesbaden they moved to Heidelberg. This

charmingly picturesque place then harboured a little English colony, which, as usual, warmly welcomed the new comers. Richard's attention, however, was almost entirely absorbed by the students' methods of fighting. He haunted the fencing rooms, and delighted in a new kind of play with the Schlager, a straight, pointless blade with razor-like edges, the favourite weapon used to settle affairs of honour. Both he and his brother, egged on by a young Irishman who was studying at the University, were most anxious to enter one of the so-called brigades, carefully choosing the Nassau, the most quarrelsome of all. But this fancy did not last. The appearance of the combatants was so ridiculous with their thick felt caps, their necks swathed in enormous cravats, their arms and bodies padded, and the students seemed so uneasy at the young Englishmen's superior knowledge of their art, that the project fell to the ground.

The delightful holiday was drawing to an end ; and Richard made one more attempt to persuade his father to let him enter the army. He pointed out almost with tears that the training he had received while fitting him for a soldier's life in India, rendered a successful career at Oxford impossible. Reminding the old man of his two failures in the matter of the scholarships, he declared further that the course marked out for him was utterly unsuitable, and the prospect of taking orders most distasteful. Edward also chimed in and begged for a commission, Cambridge being nearly as obnoxious to him as the sister University was to his brother. But the father was inexorable. Dazzled by the prospect of a comparatively luxurious life for his sons, and convinced that a vocation for the Church must declare itself before long, he turned a deaf ear to all prayers and arguments, and insisted on his odious programme being carried out to the bitter end. And, lest the dear old man be blamed not only for a certain density of comprehension, but for too ardently coveting a share of ecclesiastical loaves and fishes for a pair of lads who would never do anything to deserve them, I must hasten to add that, at that time, the young Burtons were perfectly " orthodox " in their views. Their faith, though limited in quantity, was genuine in quality ; and we hear of no doubts or changes until another year or two.

So, as their father was inflexible, the boys took a doleful leave of their mother and sister, and with heavy hearts returned to England. Edward went back to Cambridge, dutifully resolved to do his best. But Richard, a more determined character, was goaded to despair. Again inside his wretched little rooms at Trinity, he felt like a rat in a trap, his one thought being how to escape. For all hesitation had vanished, get away he must and would. What he was born to do was neither preaching nor teaching ; and he knew that unless the whole of his future life was to be ruined, the moment for action had arrived. Had he been a year or two younger, he might have worked for a good place amongst the crowd that do not go in for honours, and so left the University with a certain amount of credit ; but to make matters yet more desperate, the age for entering the army was passing by. Finally, after many a sleepless night spent in forming first one plan then another, he decided to get rusticated. A youth may be rusticated in consequence of the smallest irregularity ; but to be expelled implies ungentlemanly conduct, and was not to be thought of. Having come to this decision, Richard now waited for an opportunity.

One soon presented itself. A celebrated steeple-chaser, Oliver the Irishman, came down to Oxford, and the more sporting of the undergraduates were desperately anxious to see him ride. The collegiate authorities with questionable wisdom, forbad the youngsters to be present at the races ; and to make obedience certain as they thought, they ordered all the students to attend a lecture at the identical hour when the exciting event was to come off. This created a small mutiny. A number of high-spirited young fellows, Burton at the head, swore they would not stand being treated like little boys, and that go they would. So sundry tandems, those proscribed vehicles, were directed to wait in a secluded position behind Worcester College, and when the truants should have been listening to and profiting by a lecture in the tutor's room, they were flying across the country at a rate of twelve miles an hour. The steeplechase was a delight, and Oliver a hero; but next morning for many of the culprits came the eating of humble pie.

Summoned to the green room, they were made conscious of the enormity of their offence. Some, no doubt, took their moral drubbing quietly enough, only too anxious to have their prank overlooked and forgiven. But this was Burton's opportunity of freeing himself from his odious University trammels, and he did not fail to take the fullest advantage of it. Instead of expressing the slightest contrition for what was after all an act of disobedience, he boldly asserted that there was no moral turpitude in being present at a race—a truism which did not happen to be quite to the point, *mais n'importe*. With amusing audacity he placed himself on an ethical pinnacle, announcing, as if no one had heard the axiom before, that trust begets trust, and complaining in pathetic terms how collegiate men had been treated like naughty children. Probably his learned and reverend censors were nearly struck dumb with amazement, otherwise this flow of eloquence would have been arrested sooner ; but when they did speak, it was indeed to the purpose. While all the culprits were rusticated forthwith, Burton was singled out by a special recommendation not to return to Oxford. His end gained, with a courtly bow, perhaps a trifle exaggerated, he retired from the scene.

His mode of leaving his *Alma Mater* was no less characteristic. One of his brother collegians on whom sentence had just been passed, proposed they should "go up from

the land with a soar," and as no balloon happened to be
at hand, the nearest approach to this sky-rocket mode of
progression could be attained, figuratively anyhow, by
one of the identical vehicles which had so often proved
a bone of contention with the authorities.   There
being now no need for it to hide behind Worcester
College, the tandem was driven boldly up to the door,
bag and baggage were stowed therein, and, with a cantering leader and a high-trotting shaft horse, which, unfortunately went over some of the finest flower-beds, Richard
Burton started for the nearest railway station artistically
performing upon a yard of tin trumpet.[1]

By this bold step he freed not only himself from a
profession wherein he would have never excelled, but his
brother also.   Colonel Burton, whose prejudices were
cruelly shocked by what he considered nothing less than his
elder son's disgrace, ceased to press the younger to persist in studies for which he had no inclination.   Edward
was plodding on steadily enough in spite of his disappointment about the army ; but his filial duty and endurance
were to be tried no longer.   As soon as his father had
recovered from the dreadful news of Richard's rustication,
he received a kind letter from home, giving him full permission to choose his own career.   Overjoyed by this
unexpected deliverance from his distasteful environment,
he left at the end of the next term, with his parents'
full consent, and presently obtained a commission in the
37th Regiment, a gift from Lord Fitzroy Somerset, afterwards Lord Raglan.

---

[1] He had got his own way, but I have often heard that beneath all
this bravado lay a deep sense of regret that such a course had been
necessary.

CHAPTER II

IT was fortunate that Richard Burton preferred the Indian Army to the Queen's, for after his Oxford escapade, no alternative remained. His father, much too irate to exert himself very actively in helping forward a youth, whom he looked upon as an undutiful scapegrace, considered John Company's service quite good enough for the elder son, and reserved what little interest he possessed for the benefit of the younger. There was no difficulty in obtaining a commission after the recent wholesale slaughter of officers and men by Akbar Khan; and before long Richard was duly sworn in at the India House, a dull, smoky old place long since numbered amongst the things that were. Bombay was the Presidency of his predilection, not because, as he jocularly remarked, he had two relatives, one a Judge, the other a General, living at Calcutta, but for the more cogent reason that it afforded the best conditions for studying languages and people.

Notwithstanding his indignation, Colonel Burton provided a very liberal outfit. An unusual item was a wig from Winter's in Oxford Street. Some old campaigner had recommended the use of this venerable coiffure, as enabling its wearer to shave the head and keep it cool when disposed to get heated by study in a tropical climate. Another odd addition to the ordinary stereotyped list was a bull terrier of the Oxford breed, destined as companion to the outward bound, by whom it was regarded with unmingled satisfaction. In fact, outfits in those days being notorious for including everything that was not wanted and nothing that

was, the dog and the wig happened to be the solitary items
mentioned by their owner with unqualified approval.

On the 18th June, 1842, young Burton bid farewell to
friends and relatives, and embarked at Greenwich in the
sailing ship *John Knox*, bound for India *viâ* the Cape. His
hopes ran high. The Afghan disaster in the beginning of
that year, when out of sixteen thousand men only Dr.
Brydon escaped to tell the dismal tale, was to be amply
avenged; and our cadet expected to be employed on active
service as soon as he arrived. If the campaign lasted a
little longer, how glorious it would be to assist in the
punishment of the murderers of Burnes and MacNaughton;
besides—a secondary consideration—what unlimited prospects of promotion lay stretched before him! His military
fellow-passengers, cadets likewise, were equally sanguine.
Afghans were to be slaughtered wholesale; medals, stars,
crosses gleamed in the future like so many will-o'-the-wisps.
But Richard was far too sensible to spend all his time in
day-dreams. Three native servants were on board, and, as
he had learnt a little Hindustani before leaving London, he
took every opportunity of talking to these men in their own
tongue. Besides this, he read up stories from old Shakespeare's text-book and every other work in the language the
ship possessed. In preparation for the much desired brush
with the Afghans, he kept up his sword exercise by teaching his brother cadets; while shooting birds, catching
sharks and flying fish filled up the lighter hours of a four
months' voyage to India half a century ago.

Hardly had he arrived before his airy castles vanished
into space. When the *John Knox* was about to lumber into
port and the Government pilot sprang on board, a dozen
excited voices called out " What of the war ? What was
doing in Afghanistan ? " At the answer the cadets' faces
lengthened. Lord Ellenborough had succeeded Lord Auck-
land; the avenging army had done its work, and begun its
return march through the Khaybar Pass—the campaign was

over. No chance of medals or stars for newcomers that year at any rate !

Other illusions melted away on the morning of October 28th, 1842. Many times during the voyage had Burton pictured his destination, misled by those truly deceptive lines:

> " Thy towers, Bombay, gleam bright, they say,
> Against the dark blue sea."

The much praised bay he thought a great splay thing too long for its height, the bright towers were nowhere, unless the blotched cathedral buildings might stand for such; and although the rains had just ceased, the sky seemed never clear, while the water was always dirty.

Fifty years ago Mombadevi Town presented a marvellous contrast to the present Queen of Western India. In those days passengers had to land in wretched shore-boats at the Apollo Bunder, and the dirt and squalor that greeted their eyes was well nigh indescribable. As to the poor cadets, under the slovenly rule of the Court of Directors, the scantiest arrangements were made for their comfort. Usually they were lodged at a Parsee tavern dignified by the high-sounding name of the British Hotel, which was not merely filthy, but excessively expensive. To crown all the disappointments of that day, Burton caught sight of a Sepoy, type of the creatures he was about to command ; and this figure of fun, with its shako planted on the top of its dingy face, its wasp-like form clad in a tight-fitting scarlet coat, so damped his ardour for his new profession, that he felt sorely disposed to return to England by the *John Knox*.

After a week, the cadets were drafted into so-called sanitary bungalows—thatched hovels facing Back Bay. These buildings were semi-detached, and so small that the accommodation seems to have been limited to a butt and a ben, or an outer and an inner room. Both apartments swarmed with lizards and rats, a depressing smell of roast Hindoo wafted in from a neighbouring burning-ground when the wind blew that way, and all the boasted luxuries and comforts of Indian existence were conspicuous by their absence.

As society at Bombay was apt to turn up its nose at cadets, Burton, seeing there was little chance of amusement, devoted his attention to work. Western India then offered two specialities for the Britisher — first, sport ; secondly, opportunities of becoming acquainted with the people and their languages. The latter were practically unlimited, and required no small amount of time to turn to full advantage. Diligent though our student was, seven years elapsed before he could distinguish the several castes, and feel thoroughly familiar with their manners and customs, religions and superstitions. That it is only prudent not to remain in utter ignorance of the character, and habits of the millions under our rule, was just beginning to dawn upon the Anglo-Indian mind. The truth glared at once into Burton's, and, grudging every hour wasted amongst people with whom he could not fluently converse, he engaged a venerable Parsee, Dosabhai Sohrabji, who had coached many a generation of griffs, and under his guidance plunged at once into the Akhlak-i-Hindi and other such text books. Burton remained friends with this old man for life ; and the master always used to quote his pupil as one who could learn a language running.

At the end of six weeks orders arrived to join the 18th Bombay Native Infantry, then stationed at Baroda in Gujarat. At that time even a subaltern was expected to keep six or eight servants, and one or two horses; so, before leaving Bombay, Burton engaged a domestic staff of Goanese, presided over by one Salvador Soares; and instead of a so-called Arab, which would have cost an extravagant price, he purchased a Kattywar nag. The happy family, including the bull-terrier, none the worse for her voyage, started by "pattymar," a native craft with

huge lateen sails, which sometimes took six weeks over
what a steamer now does in four days.

The voyage, slow though it was, delighted our young
traveller. Every evening he made a point of landing to
enjoy a very novel sort of sight-seeing,—Diu, once so
famous in Portuguese story, holy Dwarka, guarded outside
by an efficient police force of sharks, Bassein, the ruins of
Somanáth, Surat, then slowly recovering from her combined
disasters of fire and flood, and many other places equally
interesting. In a fortnight the pattymar reached the
Tunkaria-Bunder, a small landing-place in the Bay of
Cambay, famous only for its Ghorá or bore. Then followed
a four days' march even more enjoyable than the sail.
Mounted on his Kattywar nag, a gallant little beast with
black stripes and stockings, Burton rode about fifteen miles
a day over country green as a card-table, and flat as a
prairie. Gujarat in winter presented many charms to the
newcomer. The rich black earth was covered with that
leek-like verdigris green which one associates only with
early spring in the temperate zone, while the atmosphere,
free from wind or storms, felt soft and pleasant. Every
little village was surrounded by hedge milk bush of the
colour of emeralds, and shaded by glorious banyan and pipal
trees, or topes of giant figs; and during the quiet evenings
when a sheeny mist hung over each settlement, and the
flocks were slowly wending their way home, and all manner
of strange and beautiful birds were preparing to roost in
the giant branches high overhead, it must have been difficult
to imagine a more quaint and charming scene.

On arriving at Baroda, Burton found his corps in a
somewhat skeleton condition. One wing containing the
greater number of officers, was stationed at Mhow, not to
mention several who were on the Staff or in Civil employ.
Major James, then in command of the 18th, formally presented the new comer at mess, which, though meagrely
attended, was so neatly served in the large, cool regimental

dining room, the table decked with clean napery and bright silver, that the young subaltern seemed to have thoroughly enjoyed his first well-appointed dinner since leaving England.

Baroda, the second city of Gujarat and third in the Presidency of Bombay, now boasts of a railway and an enormously increased population. Fifty years ago, it was a jumble of low huts and tall houses grotesquely painted, its principal buildings being a shabby palace and a bazaar. The dingiest of London lodgings would have been luxury compared with the wretched accommodation afforded within the precincts of the camp. Burton described his bungalow as a thatched article not unlike a cow-shed, which, while it kept out the sun, too often let in the rain; an unfortunate failing, as the tropical downpours in that part of the country were closely related to water-spouts. However, he made himself as comfortable as possible with his servants, horse, and bull terrier, and then applied himself with frenzy to his studies. Military work was slack just then, his environment uninviting, society almost nil; so he had plenty of leisure. While keeping up the Arabic acquired at Oxford, he devoted eight or ten hours a day to a desperate tussle with Hindustani; and so fierce was his ardour, that two munshis barely kept up with him.

A sketch of a military day at Baroda, will account for the enormous amount of spare time this young subaltern was able to give to languages.

Men rose at the first glimmer of light, dressed, and drank a cup of tea. Then the horse was brought round, saddled, and carried its rider to the drill-ground. Work there usually began at dawn, and lasted until shortly after sunrise. Parade over, the officers met at what was called a coffee shop, where they breakfasted on tea, café-au-lait, biscuit, bread and butter and fruit; then duty being done, each was practically free to occupy himself as he best could until dinner-time. As Burton abjured the heavy tiffins indulged in by most Anglo-Indians, contenting himself with a biscuit and a glass of port, he retired to his studies for the rest of the day, while the other officers played at billiards or went shooting or pig-sticking.

In the evening all dined together. Dinner consisted of soup, a joint of roast mutton at one end and boiled mutton or boiled fowls at the other, with vegetables in the side dishes. Beef was never seen, because the cow was worshipped at Baroda; nor was roast or boiled pork known at native messes, where the manners and customs of Indian bazaar pig were familiar to all, and where nauseous stories circulated as to the insults his remains were exposed to on the part of the Mohammedan scullions. The substantial part of the meal concluded with curry, Bombay ducks, and a peculiar kind of cake. Coffee was unknown, beer was the favourite drink, ice rare, and tinned vegetables had only just been thought of. After cheese each man lighted his cigar, invariably a Manilla, costing twenty rupees a thousand. Havanas were never seen, pipes but seldom used, and the hookah was going out of fashion.

Of course, Burton did not spend every day over his books. Sport in the neighbourhood of Baroda was excellent. In the thick jungle to the east of the city, tigers abounded, and native friends would always lend their elephants for a consideration. Black bucks, large antelopes, birds in countless numbers, from the huge adjutant crane to snipe equal to any in England, afforded an endless variety of "something to kill," and an exciting change occasionally from the Munshis, and the Hindustani studies; for, though kind-hearted to tame animals, Burton was an ardent sportsman, sparing only monkeys when he was shooting, because their manner of dying is too horribly human.

Besides these holidays there were the annual reviews, when the General came over from Ahmedabad to inspect the corps, and the yearly races. At the latter, on one occasion, the Kattywar nag, ridden by its owner, succeeded in carrying off all the honours.

Had matters been as quiet in all parts of India as they
were at Baroda, Burton might have found his profession
somewhat tame.   But before long the whole cantonment
was aroused by the news of the battle of Meeanee, fought
on February 21st, 1843.   Sir Charles Napier, a truly Grand
Old Man, had shown that with a little force of mixed
Englishmen and Sepoys he could beat the best army that
any native power could bring into the field.   On March
22nd followed the battle of Dubba ; Sind fell into the power
of the English, and the eagle-faced old conqueror rose to
the pinnacle of his fame.

A sense of mortal injury at being kept in inglorious
idleness, seems to have spurred on our young soldier to
prepare himself and his men for the field, in the event of a
turn of luck.   He now devoted only half his time to his
studies.   Having passed his drill and been given the
charge of a company, he proceeded to teach not merely
what he had just learnt, but a great deal besides.   His aim
was to encourage personal prowess, gymnastics, and the
practice of weapons in which our forefathers took such pride,
knowing but too well how many a brave man has lost his
life during our wars with uncivilised races, in consequence
of having neglected the use of the sword, which alone can
insure success in single combat.   So he encouraged his
Sepoys in this exercise, and would get his most promising
pupils to his own quarters for a good long bout every day.
Once a month he gave a prize, usually a smart turban, to
the ablest swordsman or wrestler.   His brother subalterns,
who did not take life quite so seriously, wondered at such
enthusiasm, which presently took the form of learning from
a native jockey the Indian art of riding and training the
horse.   This was also of importance : men rode mostly
half-broken Arabs, and at many reviews it was no uncommon spectacle for the commanding officer to be bolted
with in one direction, and the second in command in another.
Surely, he reasoned, there are quite enough dangers in the

field, even when perfectly equipped, without the extraneous one of an unmanageable animal.

In April, 1843, Burton obtained two months' leave for the purpose of passing an examination in Hindustani at the Presidency. It was a most prosperous trip. Travelling in the same way as before, he was not delayed by contrary winds, and the sail, despite the heat, was charming. The north-east monsoon about drawing to a close, alternated with a salt sea breeze known as the Doctor, and delicious spicy land zephyrs ; while the deep blue sky unsullied by a single cloud was reflected in the still, clear water. During his stay at Bombay, he escaped the horrors of the hotel and Sanitorium, by hiring a tent and pitching it in the Strangers' Lines, which then extended southwards from the Sanitorium along the shore of Back Bay. With the assistance of his old Parsee coach he worked up the last minutiæ of the language, and on the 5th of May passed first of twelve. Although, as he modestly remarked, this was no great feat, as he had begun Hindustani in London, continued it on board ship, and studied from eight to ten hours a day at Baroda ; still the little triumph must have afforded an agreeable contrast to his disastrous exams. at Oxford. Leaving Bombay, May 12th, he rejoined his regiment just before the burst of the south-west monsoon, and when this began we hear no more about the charms of Gujarát.

The discomfort of this season in those days must have been almost unbearable. Inside the bungalow it was impossible to keep dry, while outside the aspect of nature, as poor Buckle used to say, suggested a second deluge. The rains, exceptionally heavy at Baroda, sometimes last without intermission during seven days and seven nights; a meteorological feature common enough in the lowlands of India and other places where the Gháts approach the coast. To reach mess and dine in comfort, Burton had to send on clothes, put on a mackintosh, and gallop at full speed through water above and below. There was no duty: there could be none, for the parade ground was turned into a pond only fit for ducks. Moreover, the air became full of loathsome insects—beings apparently born for the occasion—flying horrors of all kinds, ants and bugs, which persisted in forcing their way into meat and drink, until at last it was necessary to protect each tumbler with a silver lid, and hardly safe even to open the mouth.

Having mastered Hindustani, Burton, with the assistance of a Nagar Brahmin named Him Chand, next attacked the Gujarati language. He took besides, elementary lessons in Sanscrit from the regimental pandit, a sort of half priest half schoolmaster, who read prayers and superintended the native festivals, with all their complicated observances. Under this pair of teachers, he became as well acquainted as an outsider can be with the practice of Hinduism, and eventually Him Chand officially allowed him to wear the Janeo, or Brahminical thread of the twice born. It is said our versatile soldier occasionally varied his Sundays by attending a Romish chapel served by a berry-brown Goanese padre; and it is possible he did profit by this opportunity of studying the effect produced by the Church of Rome on the semi-civilised people around him. But the foolish tale that the said chocolate coloured divine received him into the communion in question was utterly refuted by the fact that at his marriage nearly twenty years later, the presence of a registrar was required in the chapel; a functionary called in only when the contracting parties belong to a different religion.

Another visit to Bombay, in August 1843, for an examination in the Gujarati tongue was again crowned with success. And his industry was further rewarded by an appointment as interpreter to his regiment, which added a trifle to his income. Returning to Baroda, this indefatigable man was just in time to join in the farewell revels of " the 18th," which had been ordered to Sind ; and after the usual slow march and equally slow sail were safely over, he and his corps embarked for Karáchi on board the H.E.I. Company's steamship " Semiramis."

Green Gujarát in winter had excited something like enthusiasm in our young traveller's breast : this sentiment was wholly lacking when first he looked upon Sind. " Oh ! the barren shore ! a regular desert ; a thread of low coast, sandy as a Scotchman's whiskers ; a bald and dismal glaring waste with visible and palpable heat playing over its dirty white, dirty yellow, and dirty brown surface, something between a dust-bin and an oven ! " In such terms did he apostrophise the Unhappy Valley and Karáchi its port town. Nor did his opinion become more favourable on closer inspection. Karáchi in 1844 was little more than a village ; streets there were none, the wretched houses almost meeting over the narrow lanes that formed the only thoroughfares ; and nothing could exceed the filth, for sewers were non-existent, and the harbour when the tide was out was a system of mud-flats like the lagoons of Venice.

But in the cantonment just outside the town British energy had already got things ship-shape. Here were large, roomy barracks, stables, two churches, mess-houses, every convenience for lodging a number of troops ; and when " the 18th " had settled down in camp they had a lively and far from unpleasant time. Sir Charles Napier was staying in the place for a short time, accompanied by a large staff, and the garrison consisted of some five thousand men, European and native. Foremost among the regiments for pluck and spirit were the 78th Highlanders and the 86th, or " County Down Boys." Such boisterous jollity, such incessant larking as Burton writes of in his " Sind,"[1] seems almost incredible in such a climate. A favourite resort, a

---

1 " Scinde ; or, the Unhappy Valley," two vols., Bentley, 1851 ; and " Sind Revisited," Bentley, two vols., 1877.

short distance from Karáchi, was a huge tank or pond
tenanted by some hundreds of alligators, sacred animals
guarded by a holy Fakir.   One day our subaltern and a
party of officers, accompanied by a scratch pack of rakish
bull dogs, determined to have a bit of fun with the huge
saurians, some of which were splashing in the water, others
basking on the bank.   But first the keeper had to be pro-
pitiated with a bottle of Cognac, a gift that so delighted
him that he retired at once to partake of it, begging his
kind, generous young friends to remember the beasts were
very ferocious, especially one, Mor Sahib, the grisly
monarch of the place.

Hardly had he departed before Lieutenant Beresford, of
" the 86th," proposed to demonstrate by actual experiment
" what confounded nonsense the old cuss was talking."

He looked to his shoe-ties, turned round to take a
run at the bog, and charged the spot right gallantly, now
planting his foot upon one of the tufts of rank grass which
protuded from the muddy water, then sticking for a moment
in the black mire, then hopping dexterously off a scaly
back or a sesquipedalian snout.   Many were his narrow
escapes from lashing tails and snapping jaws; many a time
did he nearly topple into the water from the back of the
wobbling startled brute he was so unceremoniously using
as a bridge; but he did reach the other side with a whole
skin, though with ragged pantaloons.   The feat of crossing
the pond on the alligators' bodies does not seem to have
been repeated; but often the youngsters, in the fakir's
absence, would muzzle one of his sacred pets by means of a
fowl fastened to a hook and a rope, then jump on its neck
and enjoy a wriggling, zigzag ride, which usually ended in
the morass.

At other times the subs. on their Arabs, formed line upon
a bit of clean, hard beach, which separates the sea from
the cliff some two miles from Karáchi.   A prick of the
spur, a lash with the whip, and on dashed the horses like

mad towards and into the Arabian Sea. A long hollow breaker, on one occasion, curled as it neared the land and burst into a shower of snowy foam. Of twelve cavaliers only one weathered the storm, kept his seat and won the bet. Eleven were seen in various positions, some struggling in the swell, others flat upon the sand, and others scudding about the hillocks vainly endeavouring to catch and to curb their runaway nags.

Perhaps the most comical of Burton's experiences at that time was an attempt to ride a baggage camel. After considerable difficulty in getting on the roaring, yelling beast, he found it necessary to draw his sword and prick its nose each time that member crept round near his foot. Finding all attempts to bite unavailing, the beast changed tactics and made for every low thorn tree, as close to the trunk as possible, in the vain hope of rubbing off the rider. This exercise was varied by occasionally standing still for half an hour, in spite of persuasive arguments in the shape of heels, whip and point with which the stubborn flanks were plied. Then it would rush forward, as if momentarily making up its mind to be good. At last this desert craft settled upon the plan of bolting, arched its long bowsprit till its head was almost in contact with its rider's, and in this position indulged in a scudding canter, a pace which felt exactly like that of a horse taking a five-barred gate every second stride.

Fortunately the road was perfectly level. Soon snap went the nose-string ! The amiable *monture* shook its head, snorted a little blood, slackened speed, executed a *demi-volte*, and turned deliberately towards the nearest jungle.

Seeing a swamp in front, and knowing that a certain spill was in prospect, for these beasts always tumble down on slippery mud, Burton deliberated for a moment whether to try and chop open his property's skull, to jump off its back, or to keep his seat until it became no longer tenable. And his mind was still in doubt when, after sliding two or three yards over the slimy mire, the brute fell plump upon its sounding side.

Apparently the Arabs' superstition about the camel is not without foundation ; they assure you no man was ever killed by a fall from these tall louts, whereas a little nag or donkey has lost many a life. The cause, of course, is that the beast breaks the fall by slipping down on its knees; still, I find no mention of any attempt on Burton's part to steer this utterly unmanageable " Ship of the Desert " again.

Presently " the 18th " was moved to Ghára, a melancholy village some thirty odd miles by road north of headquarters, just within hearing of the evening gun. Here were neither barracks nor bungalows, only dirty heaps of mud-and-mat hovels close to a salt-water creek, bone-dry in March, a waste of salt flat, barren rock, and sandy plain, where eternal sea-gales blow up and blow down a succession of hillocks, warts on the foul face of a hideous landscape. At first the entire corps had to live under canvas; one long, weary, hot season Burton spent in a single-poled tent, where to escape suffocation when the temperature approached 120° F., he had to cover his table with a large wet cloth and sit underneath it for the best part of the day. Difficulties notwithstanding, he wrote a portion of his " Sind," and worked up for an examination in Maráthi, which he passed successfully in October, 1844.

On his return to Karáchi he found himself gazetted as Assistant in the Sind Survey, with special reference to the Canal Department. This piece of luck was partly the result of his own talents, partly the good offices of a friend, Colonel Walter Scott. The old Commander-in-Chief, like most clever men, admired genius in others, and had kept an eye on his promising young soldier, so when, through Colonel Scott, he heard how Burton could read and translate the valuable Italian works on Hydrodynamics, he presented him with the vacant appointment. On the

10th December, 1844, highly gratified by this mark of recognition, our hero departed with a surveying party and six camels to work at the Phuléli and its continuation, the Guni river.

His own words best show what a pleasant break in the monotonous regimental duty his friend's kindness had afforded him.

"It is a known fact that a Staff appointment has the general effect of doing away with one's bad opinion of any place whatever. So when the Governor of Sind was persuaded to give me the temporary appointment of Assistant in the Survey, I began to look with interest on the desolation around me. The country was a new one, so was its population, so was their language. My new duties compelled me to spend the cold season in wandering over the districts, levelling the beds of canals, and making preparatory sketches for a grand survey. I was thrown so entirely amongst the people as to depend upon them for society; and the dignity, not to mention the increased allowance, of a Staff officer, enabled me to collect a fair stock of books, and to gather around me those who could make them of any use. So, after the first year, when I had Persian at my fingers' ends, sufficient Arabic to read, write, and converse fluently, and a superficial knowledge of that dialect of Punjaubee which is spoken in the wilder parts of the province, I began the systematic study of the Sindian people, their manners, and their tongue."

Now began some of the most romantic adventures of Burton's life. After the winter of 1845, during which he had enjoyed some sport, notably hawking—the latter enabling him to collect material for a second book, „Falconry in the Valley of the Indus"[1]—he returned northwards, found his corps at Hyderabad, passed through deserted Ghára, and joined the headquarters of the Survey at Karáchi in April. Here he made acquaintance with

---

[1] " Falconry in the Valley of the Indus," Van Voorst, 1852.

one Mirza Ali Akhbar, who owed the rank of Khan
Bohádur to gallant conduct at Meeanee and Dubba,
where he did his best to save the lives of many Beloch
braves. This man lived just outside the camp in a bungalow which he had built for himself, and where he lodged
a friend, Mirza Daud, a first-rate Persian scholar. With
these two Persians, and a Munshi, Burton became very
friendly; and their assistance proved invaluable in enabling
him to study the manners and customs of the country,
much in the same practical way as some of our enthusiasts
work the London slums, namely, by dressing like the
people and living amongst them. Possessing in a rare
degree the faculty of imitation, he soon began to model
himself on his companions, and presently disguised himself
as a native and opened a shop at Karáchi. When tired of
his booth in the dirty town, and very close and ill-smelling
it must have been, he assumed the character of a semi-
Arab, semi-Iranian pedlar, and roamed about the country
followed by servants carrying his pack. His own description of these experiences is well worth quoting.

" With hair falling on his shoulders, a long beard, face
and hands, arms and neck stained with a thin coat of henna,
Mirza Abdullah of Bushiri—your humble servant—set out
upon many and many a trip. He was a bayzaz, a vendor
of fine linen, calicoes and muslins,—such chapmen are sometimes admitted to display their wares even in the sacred
harem, and he had a little parcel of *bijouterie* reserved for
emergencies.

The timid villagers collected in crowds to see the
merchant in Oriental dress riding, spear in hand, and
pistols in holsters, towards the little camp near their
settlements. When the Mirza arrived at a strange town,
his first step was to secure a house in or near the bazaar
for the purpose of evening conversazione. Now and then
he rented a shop and stocked it with clammy dates, viscid
molasses, tobacco, ginger and strong-smelling sweetmeats ;

but somehow or other the establishments in question throve not in a pecuniary point of view. Crowded though they were, the polite Mirza was in the habit of giving the heaviest possible weight for their money to all the ladies, particularly the pretty ones, who honoured him by patronising his concern.

Sometimes the Mirza passed his evening in a mosque listening to the ragged students who, stretched at full length with their stomachs on the dusty floor, and their arms supporting their heads, mumbled out Arabic from the thumbed, soiled and tattered pages of theology upon which a dim oil light shed its scanty ray ; or he sat debating the niceties of faith with the long-bearded, shaven-pated and stolid-faced *genus loci*, the Mullah. At other times, when in merrier mood, he entered uninvited the first door whence issued sounds of music and the dance ; or he played chess with some native friend, or visited the Mrs. Gadabouts who make matches among the Faithful, and gathered from them a precious budget of private history and domestic scandal.

Under these light-hearted adventures a tragedy lay hid. Even in Burton's own family, only his sister knew of his passionate and ill-fated attachment in Sind, a love which occupied an unique place in his life. During one of the many romantic rambles just described, he met a beautiful Persian girl of high descent, with whom he had been able to converse by means of his disguise. Her personal charms, her lovely language, the single-hearted devotion of one of those noble natures which may be found even amongst Orientals, inspired him with a feeling little short of idolatry. The affectionate young soldier-student, separated by thousands of miles from kith and kin, expended the full force of his warm heart and fervid imagination upon his lustrous-eyed, ebon-haired darling ; never had he so loved before, never did he so love again. She worshipped him in return ; but such rapture was not to last. He would have married her and brought her home to his family,

for she was as good as she was beautiful, had not the fell
foe that ever lurks in ambush to strike or divide when for
awhile we dare to be happy, snatched her from him in the
flower of her youth, and the brightest hours of their joy-
dream. Her untimely end proved a bitter and enduring
sorrow; years after when he told the story, his sister perceived with ready intuition that he could hardly bear to
speak of that awful parting, even the gentlest sympathy
hurt like a touch on an open wound. From the day of the
death of his best beloved he became subject to fits of
melancholy, and it seems as if the conception of his fine,
but pessimistic poem, the " Kasidah,"[1] dated from the great
grief of his life.

" Mine eyes, my brain, my heart are sad,—sad is the very core of me ;
All wearies, changes, passes, ends ! alas the birthday's injury."

In November Burton started with Colonel Walter Scott
for a three months' tour to the north of Sind. They
travelled by high road to Kotri, the station of the Sind
flotilla, and then crossed to Hyderabad. After a week
spent in the ex-capital, they resumed their way up the
right bank of the Indus towards the extreme western
frontier, where the Beloch herdsmen existed in their
wildest state. Presently came exciting tidings. At
Larkhana a letter arrived from John Napier announcing
that as many of the assistant surveyors as could be spared
might join their regiments if ordered on service. This,
beyond bazaar reports, was the first notice of the great Sikh
War which added the Punjaub to our Indian possessions.
We know Richard Burton was a most unwilling carpet
soldier, so, although the good appointment in the Survey
would have to be given up, the news made him wild to take
part in the fighting: not even the advice of his practical
Scotch friend could restrain him from a step which, while

---

[1] Published originally by Bernard Quaritch in 1880, reprinted by
H. S. Nichols, 1894.

plucky and chivalrous, seemed somewhat imprudent. He applied himself at once to preparations for the campaign, persuaded Colonel Scott, after some difficulty, to send in his resignation, and, on the 23rd of February, 1846, marched with his corps from Rohri.

Unfortunately, his post was sacrificed to no purpose. The battle of Sobraon had already been fought, and a patched-up peace which divided the Sikh State, depleted the Sikh treasury, but left intact the Sikh army, was most unwisely concluded. Burton thus summarised the un-pleasant episode.

"Ours was a model army of 13,000 men, Europeans and natives and under old Charley it would have walked into Multan as into a mutton pie. We had also heard that Náo Mall, the Hindu Commandant under the Sikhs, was wasting his two millions of gold, and we were willing to save him the trouble. Merrily we trudged through Sabzal-cote and Khánpúr, and we entered Bahául̄púr, where we found the heart-chilling order to retire and march home. Consequently we returned to Rohri on the 2nd of April, and after a few days' halt there, tired and miserable, we made Khayrpur, and after seventeen marches reached the old regimental quarters in Mohammad Khanká Tanda on the Phuleli river."

The hot season of 1846 was unusually sickly even for Sind, and the white regiments stationed at Karáchi, not-ably the 78th Highlanders, suffered terribly from cholera. Burton escaped this scourge, but in early July he was attacked by one of the fevers peculiar to the country, and laid low for nearly two months. Like his father, he be-lieved firmly in the sovereign virtue of change of air and scene, while by no means tabooing the doctor ; so, when he had recovered from what was undoubtedly a most critical illness treated in the drastic fashion now happily obselete, he determined to allow himself a holiday. Assisted by a friend, Henry J. Carter, he obtained two years' leave of

absence to the Neilgherries ; and, turning his back for
awhile on pestiferous Sind, right joyfully scrambled over
the sides of a pattimar.

With such ample time before him, and with health
mending fast, there was no need to hurry to his destination—
those Blue Mountains about which he writes so entertain-
ingly in his " Goa."[1] On the contrary, he planned to visit
Goa and Calicut, then follow the route along the sea-shore
to Poonanee on horseback, and finally strike inland to the
hills. The Goanese servants and the Kattywar nag accompanied him, but the dog was dead. The servants were
in a frantic state of excitement at the prospect of seeing
their native land once more, and Burton himself, his
imagination fired by the romantic story of the old Portuguese settlement, shared their enthusiasm when his sable
butler, ecstasied by propinquity to home, sweet home, and
forgetting self-possession in an *élan* of patriotism, abruptly
directed his master's vision towards the whitewashed
lighthouse which marked the north side of the entrance
into the Goa creek. Owing to sundry delays, the pattimar
did not reach the landing-place before dark, and Burton
had to curb his impatience to enjoy the celebrated view
of the Rio until next morning. A last night was spent
on the quaint old craft, and on the following day he
secured a house with six rooms, kitchen, stable and courtyard for the ridiculous sum of fourteen shillings a month.
Here he remained while exploring the city and its neighbourhood.

Panjim, the present capital, situated on a narrow ridge
between a hill to the north and an arm of the sea, contains
many respectable looking buildings, usually one storey
high, solidly constructed of stone and mortar, with red
tile roofs, and surrounded by large courtyards overgrown
with cocoanut trees.

----

[1] " Goa and the Blue Mountains," one vol., Bentley, 1851.

But it is old Goa that possesses all the historic associations; and travellers at once strain their eyes towards the dim view visible from the Rio, of steeples, domes, huge masses of masonry, some standing out from the deep blue sky, others lining the edge of the creek. Hardly was Burton settled in his new lodgings before he started by canoe to inspect the remains of the once wealthy and magnificent city. A couple of hours' row landed him at his destination, while the crimson rays of the setting sun were lighting up the scene; and in order to see the ruins to perfection, he went no further than the Ajube, or ecclesiastical prison, where he intended to pass the night. When the moon, then at its full, had risen, he sallied forth to view the romantic spectacle under her silvery beams. One solitary gateway towered above the large mass of *débris* flanking the entrance to the Strada Duetta, the arch under which the newly appointed viceroys of Goa used to pass in triumphal procession ; but, churches and monasteries excepted, the once populous town appeared a veritable city of the dead. About thirty buildings were still standing, and even of these some were being demolished for the sake of their material, for the poverty-stricken Portuguese preferred to carry away cut stone than to quarry it. Everything that met the eye or ear seemed teeming with melancholy associations ; the very rustling of the trees and the murmur of the waves sounded like a dirge for departed grandeur.

Beyond the gateway a level road, once a crowded thoroughfare, led to the Terra di Sabaio, or large square, fronting St. Catherine's Cathedral. In this huge pile some twenty natives were performing their devotions ; and in monasteries built for hundreds of monks a single priest was often the only occupant. The site of the Viceregal Palace, long since razed to the ground, was covered with a luxuriant growth of poisonous plants and thorny trees ; while on the remains of the vile Casa Santa a curse seemed to have fallen—not a shrub sprung between the fragments of stone which, broken and blackened with decay, were left to encumber the soil as unworthy of the trouble of removal.

After vainly trying to save the life of an old Jogi discovered in an expiring condition by the roadside, and who very sensibly begged to be left to die, Burton spent the remainder of the night inside his gloomy lodgings. By the light of day he found Old Goa had few charms, and having visited several churches, including that of Bom Jesus, containing the tomb of St. Francis Xavier, about which he flippantly remarked that "his saintship was no longer displayed to reverential gazers in mummy or scalded pig form," our traveller betook himself to the more cheerful modern capital.

During a stay of three or four weeks at Panjim, Burton met with a curious adventure. While visiting a convent for the sake of some books contained in its library, he remarked a very pretty nun, who, judging from her expression, seemed far from contented with her dreary lot. She evidently aroused his pity, and he soon conceived the plucky project of carrying her off to some place under English rule, where she could lead a less dismal and unnatural existence. By dint of sundry presents of Cognac, labelled medicine, to the prioress and sub-prioress, two holy personages rudely described as more like Gujurát apes than mortal women, and of pretending, naughty man, to be deeply interested in the Life of St. Augustine, he managed to visit the nunnery pretty frequently. At first the black-eyed, rosy-lipped sister seemed hopelessly bashful, gradually she became less shy, and finally, after receiving a note from him enclosed in a bouquet and containing full instructions how to escape, she consented to trust herself to her deliverer.

A swift-sailing pattimar was in readiness. Burton and two servants disguised themselves as Moslems, and one night opened the garden gate and that of the cloisters by means of false keys. Unfortunately, in the hurry of the moment, the three men took the wrong turning, and found themselves unawares in the chamber of the sub-prioress, whose sleeping form was instantly raised and borne off in triumph by the domestics.

Alas! shrill shrieks and tiger-like claws soon revealed the fatal mistake. Two rolling yellow eyes glared into Salvador's face, two big black lips began to shout and scream and abuse him with all their might. It was an utter failure. Not daring to remain another moment, the three men deposited their ugly burthen in the garden to make her way back at her leisure, and decamped with all possible speed. The poor nun had to be left to her fate, but, owing to Burton's admirable disguise, her knight-errant was never found out.

Still, he thought it prudent to bid adieu to Panjim without delay. Four days later he landed at Calicut, no longer the " Cidade nobre e rica " described by Camoens' tuneful muses. Some travellers even think it is not the one alluded to in the " Lusiads "; and a tradition exists amongst the natives of the land that ancient Calicut was merged beneath the waves. Of monumental antiquities there are none; still, as the surrounding country has changed but little since the poet's time, and it must have been somewhere on that coast that old De Gama first cast anchor and stepped forth from his weather-beaten ship at the head of his mail-clad warriors, the visit proved of value when, many years after, Burton translated the great Portuguese poem.

Wishing to see as much as possible of the Malabar coast, he preferred the longer route to the short mountain cut up the Koondah range. The roads were bad and the ferries incessant on account of the lakes, rivers and breakwaters that intersect the country; but the brave little nag did his work valiantly, and when it was too hard, his master walked. As they plodded along, our traveller admired the substantial pagodas, the pretty little villages that crown the gentle eminences rising above the swampy rice-lands, and noted that the country seemed both prosperous and fertile, each tenement having its own croft planted with pepper, plantains, and the betel vine, with small tufts of cocoas, bamboos, and the tall feathery areca. At Maty-polliam, situated at the foot of the Neilgherries, a short delay occurred, the Bhawani river having battered down her bridge, no uncommon disaster; but afterwards he proceeded steadily along dark ravines, up parapetless roads, over torrents and apologies for bridges that made even his strong brain reel, until at last he came within sight of the cantonment of Ootacamund.

Everybody who has read anything about India is familiar with Ootacamund. So the three chapters in "Goa" describing the place and its customs, may be condensed into a few sentences. Burton's visit was far from a pleasant one. He would have enjoyed the exhilarating air, the varied, almost English food, had not the sudden change of temperature from hot, dry Sind to the damp, chilly hills, brought on an attack of rheumatic opthalmia that confined him to dark rooms for a fortnight at a time. True, these spells of inactivity alternated with excursions to adjacent places of interest; but one of these rides cost him the life of his favourite horse, a painful shock to a lonely man who loved his little beast and could ill afford its loss. Then the Goanese servants, disgusted with the climate and thinking solely of their own skins, deserted in a body; and some Madrassees engaged in their stead, proved very indifferent substitutes. So at last, in spite of painful memories of sickness and death connected with Karáchi, Burton determined to throw up his remaining leave and go back to his regiment.

The return journey did him good. His eyes mended so rapidly that on the 15th October, 1847, he passed in Persian at Bombay, coming out first of some thirty with a compliment from the examiners. It is probable his proficiency in this language was a result of his intimacy with his poor dead love, for, although he had worked at it on and off ever since his arrival in India, he had had no leisure to study very hard before the examination. His linguistic achievements were beginning to attract notice; this particular triumph was followed by an honorarium in the shape of a thousand rupees from the Court of Directors.

Forthwith he concentrated his attention upon Arabic. Thrown more and more into Moslem society, he presently conceived the idea of performing a pilgrimage to Meccah and El-Medinah. His knowledge of these hitherto mysterious penetralia of Mohammedan superstition was of the flimsiest, for since the days of William Pitts of Exeter, in 1678, no European traveller with the exception of Burckhardt, in 1811, had been able to enter the holy cities and send back an account of their travels. There was no chance of carrying out this project for some time to come, but it was not too early to prepare for what would certainly prove a difficult and dangerous expedition.

Under the tuition of Shaykh Háslim, a half Bedawin, who had accompanied him from Bombay to Karáchi, he investigated practical Moslem divinity, learnt about a quarter of the Koran by heart, and became a proficient at prayer, or rather those " vain repetitions " which seem so strangely attractive to many of the religions of the world. To gain a more thorough insight into this faith in all its phases, he added a sympathetic study of Sufi-ism, the Gnosticism of El Islam, a Master Sufi ranking high above a mere Moslem.

" I conscientiously went through the Chillá, or quarantine of fasting and other exercises, which, by-the-bye, proved rather too exciting to the brain. At times, when overstrung, I relieved my nerves with a course of Sikh religion and literature; and, at last, the good old priest, my instructor, solemnly initiated me in presence of the swinging ' Granth,' or Nának Shah's scriptures. As I had already been duly invested by a strict Hindú with the

Janeo or ' Brahminical thread,' my experience of Eastern faiths became phenomenal."

And now, as often happens with deeply-read and widely-travelled men, Burton found the views of his youth no longer tenable. During these studies of alien faiths, Christianity dwindled in his mind to what he considered her true proportions—not the one religion, but one amongst many religions. A God he believed in, Unknowable and Impersonal; for, too thoughtful a man to deny what he couldn't prove, he never drifted into Atheism. While by no means an optimist, he held that absolute evil is impossible, because it is always rising up into good, and the theory of a maleficient power is a purely superstitious fancy, contradicted by human reason and the aspect of the world. Man he considered a co-ordinate term of Nature's great progression, a result of the inter-action of organism and environment working through cosmic sections of time. As regards the future life, while admitting that absolute certainty on that point is unattainable, he was inclined to think all ideas of another existence copies more or less idealized of the present :—

" Then, if Nirwânâ round our life with nothingness, 'tis haply best ;
    Thy toil and troubles, want and woe, at length have won their
        guerdon—Rest."

Of practical advice he had the best to give—to uproot ignorance, avoid self-tormenting, do good because good is good to do, and lastly to

" Abjure the Why and seek the How."

From these convictions, arrived at in the prime of manhood, and after the profoundest study, Richard Burton never swerved. No mystery was affected ; he spoke and published but too openly. His beautiful poem the " Kasidah," written about this time, his Terminal Essay in the original as also in the Library edition of the " Thousand Nights and a Night," almost his last work, would satisfy any reader that his views differed not

merely from those of any Christian Church, but also
from the invertebrate eclecticism of the day. Towards
the Church of Rome he had a positive aversion, declaring she has added a fourth person to the Trinity.
While believing our own the purest form of Christianity
extant, he had lived so long amongst the teeming popu-
lations of the East, that he was disposed to award the
palm to El Islam as the faith best fitted to civilize
the wretched creatures known under the comprehensive
name of heathen. Moreover, to a rigid Monotheist,
the religion promulgated by Mahomet, appealed by
virtue of its fairly pure Deism; to a Humanitarian,
by the practical work effected amongst its converts by
enforcing cleanliness, sobriety, and the nearest approach
to morality which their physical and mental condition
admit of. But while he admired Mohammedanism for
sundry of its attributes, he states in clearest language
that the rewards it offers for mere belief, reducing every
virtue to the scale of a somewhat unrefined egotism, has
produced demoralising effects that become more distinct
in every progressive age. To sum up, there is not the
shadow of a doubt amongst those who knew Burton best
and who had no reason for not speaking the truth concerning him, that he looked with somewhat cynical eyes
upon the conflicting religions of the world.

His first visit to India was now drawing to a close.
The spring of 1848 brought the news of Anderson's murder
by Nao Mall of Multan. A campaign seemed imminent,
and a report circulated that Sir Charles Napier, then in
England, would return to take command. Colonel Walter
Scott and many other brother officers were ordered to be
in readiness for the field, and Burton, again inflamed by the
war fever, applied to accompany the force as interpreter.
Examinations in six native languages had been passed
successfully; he was studying two more: but he had
neglected to curry favour with men in power; worse,

indeed, he had expressed his opinion of some amongst them a little too openly. So, in answer to his request, he was informed that another man had already been appointed, one who possessed exactly *one-sixth* of his linguistic knowledge.

This last misfortune disheartened him. Rheumatic ophthalmia, which the exciting prospect of a campaign had nearly cured, came on again with redoubled virulence, and a change to Europe was recommended almost as a final resource. Sick and depressed, Burton began to long for home, for the sight of dear familiar faces; and with strength fast failing, he managed to get as far as his Presidency. At Bombay his health broke down completely, and in a well-nigh insensible condition he had to be carried on board the brig *Eliza*, where, but for the assiduous care of a Moslem servant, one Allahdad, he would most probably have died before reaching England.

CHAPTER III

THE voyage soon re-established Burton's health. When he sailed, his fellow-passengers believed he would never reach home alive, and it was with considerable difficulty that he contrived to write a few words of farewell to his mother and sister. But within less than a fortnight a marked improvement took place. For some constitutions sea air is the best of remedies; in Burton's case it almost always produced such a magical effect, that, when indisposed, he frequently arranged to travel by water, even though the sea route were twice as long as the overland. Nor was it an unpleasant mode of treatment. He was never sick, never even uncomfortable during the roughest weather; and he often dined *tête-à-tête* with the captain in the height of a gale which had prostrated every other landsman on board.

As he grew stronger and the *Eliza*, favoured by fair winds, scudded on her homeward way, his thoughts became entirely centred on the fast approaching meeting with his relatives. Seven years had gone by since he sailed for Bombay in the *John Knox*. A chapter of accidents had prevented his seeing Edward Burton, stationed at Ceylon with " the 37th," although the two brothers had been most anxious to spend some time together, and, with this end in view, had made plan after plan; while, as for other members of his family, those were days before cheap winter trips to the Presidencies enable us to visit our friends in India, whenever affection or restlessness prompts us thus to expend our money and our energies. Happily, as yet death had made no gaps in the home circle. His mother, though ailing, lived some years longer, his father's health was no worse, while his sister, married in 1845, had two children.

By the time he landed, his longing for the sight of a familiar face had grown so utterly uncontrollable, that, on his arrival in London, regardless of the unearthly hour, he went straight to the house of the aunt who had nursed him through the scarlet fever, and knocked her up at 2 A.M. After a short stay in town, he went on to see other relatives, notably two pretty Burton cousins and their mother ; and finally, having attended to various business matters which had accumulated during his long absence from England, he travelled night and day to Pisa, where his parents, sister and nieces were to spend the winter.

It was a very happy meeting. All the more so, perhaps, as it took place in his still beloved Italy. He went over old scenes with interest, rubbed up his Italian, which had done him such good service in the matter of the Sind Survey, and revelled in the mild climate and comparative luxury of Pisa. Its drawbacks, once grumbled over, must have seemed trifles indeed after his stifling tent at Ghára, with the wet cloth dangling over its one table, or the leaking bungalow at Baroda, where not even a mackintosh and an umbrella could keep its solitary tenant dry.

Allahdad, clad in picturesque costume—turban, baggy trousers, etc., accompanied his master, and was most kindly received by the family, who were exceedingly grateful for the care and attention he had shown the invalid on board the *Eliza*. At first the Mussulman adapted himself very graciously to his novel environment, devoting himself so assiduously to the children that they would cry to be dandled in his arms. But soon, like most Asiatics absent from their own country, he grew home-sick, consequently quarrelsome. On one occasion, Sabbatino, the Italian cook, showed him, as a joke, a ham boiling in a big kettle. Allahdad promptly avenged his insulted creed by

seizing the man in his strong brown arms, and attempting
to seat him upon the charcoal fire, an *auto-da-fé* with
difficulty frustrated by the bystanders. Then, from his
slender stock of English, he selected the forcible phrase,
"God damn Italy," and repeated it, parrot fashion, to every
Italian he met. The two last words were fairly intelligible,
the tone in which they were uttered was yet more so, for
the Mussulman with ready vanity had taken a violent
dislike to a people, who evidently considered him a soulless
monster; fights innumerable ensued, and once he tried to
stab his opponent. At last even his master, whom he still
cared for in a way, failed to manage him, and he had to be
discharged. But not until he had accompanied the family
back to England, whence his passage was taken for
Bombay.

Next year's leave was spent between Leamington and
Dover, with occasional trips to Malvern for the hydropathic
treatment, then in its infancy. Burton gave the latter a
fair trial, and considered the " cure " in a modified form—
minus the semi-starvation, plus the use of warm water in
certain cases instead of cold—a very valuable one.[1] Well
for him had the harmless water cure always been within his
reach, for, unlike his father, Medicine and her professors
attracted him strongly. He had acquired a smattering of
pathology and therapeutics, useful enough during his wanderings, but which, at other times, was apt to take the form
of experimenting upon himself. While far from blind to
the mistakes made by the faculty, aud unpleasantly conscious
of real injury inflicted by the drastic drugs then in vogue,
he was never without some pet surgeon or physician.
Possibly this fancy was a result of a sanguine disposition;
when he found himself decidedly the worse for the well-
intentioned but not very skilful efforts of one of these professors of the healing art, he would comfort himself with

---

[1] Since 1850 both modifications have been adopted.

the reflection that " Medicine was still guess-work, but that no one could tell what great discovery might be made before long ; " and then proceed to try some other doctor with no better success.

Wearying after a time of the formality of England, and yet more of her dismal climate, which never thoroughly suited him, Burton crossed over to Boulogne in 1851. One great attraction to that shabby little town was a celebrated salle d'armes, kept by a M. Constantin, of which more anon. However, living alone at an hotel did not long suit a man who still possessed the affectionate heart of a boy, so presently various relatives received dismal letters complaining of dulness and low spirits. The first to come to the rescue was Burton's sister, then in England expecting the return of her husband from India, a return delayed by the approaching troubles ; and shortly after she came with her two children, Colonel and Mrs. Burton arrived from Pisa.

Burton did not recover his spirits immediately. He had fallen in love with one of his handsome cousins. There was real liking on her part ; she was lively, amiable, well-dowered—in short, so far as he was concerned, an excellent choice. Unfortunately *his* prospects were dismal in the extreme. Still merely a lieutenant of a John Company's regiment which obliged him to spend most of his life in India, he reluctantly bowed to the wise decision of her nearest relations who, sincerely as they cared for him, could not sanction an engagement. The affair fell through, to the great regret of his parents and sister, for he would have secured an excellent wife. But, strange to say, his affection for his cousin lacked the intensity of his love for the dead girl in Sind ; and before long the fencing school, and a manual he was just bringing out, a new system of bayonet exercise,[1] absorbed all his energies. About a year later there was another love affair, a very evanescent one, which, like the last, soon came to an untimely end.

[1] " A Complete System of Bayonet Exercise." Clowes & Sons, 1853.

That Burton had a great many *affaires de cœur* is no secret. They were mostly of an ephemeral nature, and may be attributed to a variety of causes. A very sociable man, with nothing of the hermit about him, he thoroughly enjoyed women's society, though pretending at times to look down upon it. Then, possessing in almost the highest degree the love of the beautiful, he found a fair face an irresistible attraction. Besides, as he was not merely a handsome but a powerfully magnetic man, women fell in love with him by the score, often careless whether their affection was returned or not. It is certain that many of his amours were not originated by himself; and in these cases, some of a delicate and troublesome nature, he was at a distinct advantage. He was easily cajoled, easily deceived, and his kind heart quailed at tears and scenes which a sterner, colder man would have taken at their real value. Sometimes he rode away; perhaps he should have followed that prudent course more frequently. But he was no rake. Ever courteous and honourable, he would emerge safely from embarrassing straits where another man similarly circumstanced would have plunged into serious trouble. And it speaks greatly in his favour that, with an amative and somewhat fickle temperament, he made several attempts to marry a virtuous woman and settle down as a Benedict before he reached his thirtieth year.

His passion for beauty had one disadvantage, a grave one. Unlike some eminent men of our day, he loved women rather for their good looks than for their moral qualities. So long as a girl was handsome it never seemed to matter how narrow, how vain, how supremely silly she might be. While keenly appreciating talent in his own relatives, when he fell in love he actually preferred a doll. Not that he never cared for a sensible or clever woman, he did so more than once, as in the case of his cousin, but on the whole he preferred the Eastern ideal of a wife—an ideal described in " Vikram and the Vampire," [1] a sort of dog-like being whom no Englishwoman, clever or stupid, could possibly imitate. Perhaps, as he somewhat cynically remarks in the pages just quoted, " because she has no fear of losing her nose or parting with her ears."

It has been said Burton could look through a man, and gauge him in a moment. Now in my description of his character I aim most anxiously at accuracy in every detail. Give a man qualities foreign to his nature, and his life straightway becomes unintelligible. Had powers some-what similar to the Röntgen rays been his, would he have made the blunders he did ? He confesses in one of his books to not understanding the fair sex, but there is little doubt that in knowledge of character generally he was deficient. With Asiatics and Africans his judgment was oftener correct, partly because his very life depended upon his observing them accurately, and partly because education and environment often obscure Nature's handwriting on the face of a European, whilst amongst the less artificial chil-dren of the East, physiognomy rarely errs. A studious habit of mind, a good-natured inclination to think well of persons who appeared kindly disposed towards him, may have prevented him from centring his attention on cha-racters purposely veiled. Often have I heard him speak of a woman as harmless and amiable, when in truth she was neither, often seen him associate with men whom he considered right good fellows, and heard the same right good fellows abuse him roundly as soon as his back was turned, and they thought no one was listening. Naturally, this lack of insight into the dispositions of those about him involved him in many troubles. Ill-chosen friends usually turn into ultra virulent enemies.

At that time the influences surrounding Burton were all thoroughly wholesome. Colonel Burton paid only

---

1 " Vikram and the Vampire," 1870. See the Vampire's eleventh story.

flying visits to Boulogne, as the keen air disagreed with his complaint ; besides, he had long since given up any attempt to interfere with his son's views and plans, and contented himself with setting a good example of what a man's life ought to be. His wife, who remained with her son and daughter during the whole of their stay at the French port, had become quite an invalid, but continued, unlike most invalids, as affectionate and as unselfish as of old. It was Burton's sister who resolutely set herself to study his character and views, and assist him with the best of advice. A talented woman, high principled, gifted moreover, with excellent judgment, she not only took the keenest interest in all his plans, but she never failed to tell him when, as often happened, he went the wrong way to work to further them. With characteristic good sense she encouraged the most promising of his love affairs, and only the most promising. She saw that her brother's roving temperament and Eastern ideas would not content the ordinary British matron, and the ordinary British matron, after a year or so, would certainly not have suited him. Still, since his life seemed destined to be spent in distant countries, it was well to marry, if he could find someone who could really make him happy. With regard to minor matters, she vehemently discouraged eccentricities in dress, roughness of manner, the disposition to wage war against harmless prejudices, and, above all, Burton's almost suicidal practice of telling horrible tales against himself. This last foible, by the way, was almost maddening. He usually selected some unfriendly nonentity as audience, and then proceeded to relate a ghastly story of having eaten a boy, or shot two or three men for no particular reason, or run away with at least a dozen of other people's wives, all of which nonsense was duly treasured up and brought against him years afterwards. It can only be accounted for by an almost monkey-like love of fun and mischief ; but his sister, divining the danger of his thus heaping up slander against himself, very properly warned him of the folly of such unsuitable jokes. In short, possessing as she did that rarest of combinations, talent and common sense, it is probable that had she been afforded more frequent opportunities of influencing him even in trifles, his would have proved a less chequered career, for, be it said to his honour, when kindly counselled by anyone whom he respected, he not merely listened to advice with perfect temper, but what is more uncommon, he often followed it.

Second only to the blunder of, for mere fun, actually starting calumny against himself, was his inveterate habit of fighting harmless prejudices. Burton's tolerance had not attained to the perfection defined by George Eliot as tolerating the intolerant. That pride of ignorance, which so far exceeds the pride of science, was not treated with the patience or silent contempt with which colder or more prudent men regard it. There is little doubt Burton made a needlessly large number of enemies, not by injuring people—he had nothing malicious or cruel in his character—but by offending their vanity—worst grievance of any. Unlike most "sensible men" he did not keep his views to himself. Familiar with the Arabic precept, "Conceal thy travels, thy tenets, and thy treasure," he failed to profit by it. Of course his opinions, so far as Boulogne could understand them, ranked as utter infidelity; no matter, he scorned to hide them; and, as flashing a light into an owl's eyes usually induces that reverend bird to fly at your face, so did Boulogne resent any attempt to illuminate the obscurity in which she contentedly squatted. It was of great depth. People were still holding up their hands and exposing the whites of their eyes over the impiety of the " Vestiges of Creation ; " Sir Charles Lyell's "Antiquity of Man " was not yet written, and Darwin was still busy in his study thinking out his wonderful " Origin of Species."

Also in smaller matters, Burton was wanting in tact and

patience; if people bored him, he would take up a book, or even leave the room with scant ceremony. Probably his great broad mind could not take in the infinite stupidity, and the infinite littleness of most dispositions, for he never made an enemy intentionally. Dowered, like most deep and sensitive natures, with the love of love, he felt the insults of the most contemptible foe so keenly that we used to say of him, the meanest insect drew blood. Very indignant was he when sundry members of the English clique at Boulogne crossed the road when they saw him approaching; and ruefully surprised did he look on hearing how one elderly and somewhat rancorous dame had declared, with singular vehemence, " she would not and could not sit in the room with that fellow Burton."

On the other hand, he made many warm friends. These he never lacked wherever he went, friends who stood by him and took his part manfully throughout life. If a person, unrepelled by the little failings just mentioned, was attracted towards him, had time to know him well, and was noble minded enough to appreciate him, I may fitly use Shakespeare's forcible phrase, he was grappled to his soul with hooks of steel. And since there was nothing mean, or spiteful, or envious about his nature, time and propinquity only deepened mutual esteem and affection. Even now I have the pleasure of reading the enthusiastic letters of those who still remember him, and who declare that they have never met his like again. It is a touching trait that nearly every dedication affixed to the numerous volumes published during his lifetime was to a friend or relative; seldom to one of the many powerful patrons who more than once assisted him by their influence, and whose noble names another man, even at the expense of his affections, would have been only too delighted to honour.

In his family circle he was adored. The asperities of his early boyhood had all worn away. Marvellously sweet-tempered about trifling annoyances, he never grumbled

or swore when the household, kept on moderate means,
occasionally creaked on its hinges. Unlike many an unreasonable " he-thing," he did not expect every comfort on
a limited income. Besides, he could always amuse and
occupy himself, he could bear pain and sickness without
making everybody miserable, even when suffering from
his fits of melancholy which no study of his namesake's
great work could ever cure, he generally succeeded by a
heroic effort in concealing much of his depression. And no
sooner had his naturally high spirits once more gained the
day, than friends and relatives were kept continually
amused by his delightful witty sayings, until at last,
excited by the general hilarity, he became fairly uproarious,
and no one could imagine he had ever known sorrow in the
world.

In 1851-2 a good French painter was staying at
Boulogne. François Jacquand had attained distinction
partly by his monk pictures, but principally through a
large historical tableau representing the death chamber of
the Duc d'Orléans, which he executed by order of Louis
Philippe shortly after the sad accident that destroyed the
life of the popular heir to the throne. The earliest portrait
of Richard Burton is the work of this artist. It belongs
to the writer of these memoirs, and helps to confirm the
impressions and recollections of childhood. A pale young
man, heavily moustached, with large brown eyes still
bright and piercing, is seated, clad in the not unbecoming
uniform of the Bombay Light Infantry, his head supported
by his left hand, with a large folio open before him.
Jacquand was no flatterer, rather the other way, and the
family thought he had hardly done justice to his handsome
sitter ; but with the exception of Lord Leighton's magnificent portrait—Burton's living image—it is far superior to any
painted since. Some I have seen are simply hideous ; the
skin the colour of a brown monkey's, the features, coarsened
and exaggerated, wearing the expression of a Bill Sykes.

With Burton's marked look of race, he never could have been taken, unless purposely disguised, for other than an English gentleman; these intensely unpleasant caricatures might stand for a pugilist, a brigand, or, as already suggested, for poor Nancy's swain. That a man who, like most active natures, particularly objected to the restraint inevitable when sitting for a portrait, should have tolerated these ugly and repulsive likenesses, some of which have re-appeared as prints or photographs in various books written by himself or his wife, can be explained only on the score of that eccentricity which his good sister tried so hard to discourage.

Jacquand had rendered with his usual scrupulous fidelity a worn, wan look on the face of his model. A plentiful crop of ailments, engendered by the climate and hardships of India, kept breaking out again and again, to the intense discomfort of their victim. Though interested in medical lore, Burton ignored that branch now well nigh paramount —the prevention of disease; careless of his health, he would either make some desperate attempt to harden himself, as he called it, which generally brought on bronchitis, or bear with unwise stoicism premonitory symptoms, which, neglected, ended in a sharp attack of illness. Liver trouble, chest affections, internal inflammation prostrated him for many a weary hour during the earlier part of his furlough. Imprudent folk are not always brave when confronted with the results of their rashness; but his fortitude in sickness was extraordinary, often actually misleading the bystanders with respect to the gravity of the case. On one occasion, when seized with inflammation of the bladder, a fact he tried to keep to himself, he continued to joke and laugh much as usual. Pain rather stimulated than depressed the action of his powerful brain, so he went on with his reading and writing as if little were the matter. At last the agony became too atrocious, and he remarked in a fit of absence, " If I don't get better before night, I shall be an angel."

Questions followed, consternation reigned around, and the doctor was instantly summoned.

Life at Boulogne was not all play. The lessons of such a capable instructor as M. Constantin afforded Burton an opportunity of perfecting himself in that noble art which he had studied with such enthusiasm even as a boy. Few men delighted more in fencing than he; and his admiration for the sword, which he called the "Queen of Weapons," was almost romantic. In his monograph on its origin, genealogy and history, published many years later, he writes of it in these glowing terms:

" The best of calisthenics, this energetic educator teaches the man to carry himself like a soldier. A compendium of gymnastics, it increases strength and activity, dexterity, and rapidity of movement. Professors calculate that one hour of hard fencing wastes forty ounces by perspiration and respiration. The foil is still the best training tool for the consensus of eye and hand, for the judgment of distance and opportunity, and, in fact, for the practice of combat. And thus swordsmanship engenders moral confidence and self-reliance, while it stimulates a habit of resource; and it is not without suggesting, even in the schools, that curious, fantastic, very noble generosity proper to itself alone."

And later he regrets that it has come down from its high estate as tutor to the noble and the great. As soon as the sword ceased to be worn in France, the politest people in Europe suddenly became the rudest. That gallant and courteous bearing, which in England during the early nineteenth century so charmed the fastidious Alfieri, lingers only amongst a few. Courtesy and punctiliousness, the politeness of man to man, and respect and deference of man to woman, the very conception of the knightly character, have to a great extent been removed from the face of the earth.

Of course, when Burton once devoted himself to any

art, he was never satisfied until he had thoroughly mastered it. So he soon earned his *brevet de pointe* for the excellence of his swordsmanship: and the Salle d'Armes used to be thronged when it was known he was going to play. A friend, Lieutenant Colonel Arthur Shuldham, kindly sent me the following anecdote illustrating the prowess of the new Maître d'Armes.

" In the year 1851-2 I met the late Sir Richard Burton at Boulogne, and he asked me to accompany him to the Salle d'Armes where he was going to have a fencing bout with a sergeant of French Hussars, a celebrated player. The sergeant donned his guard, to protect his head, and a leather fencing jacket, while Burton bared his neck and stood up in his shirt sleeves ; on my remonstrating with him, he said it was of no consequence. They performed the customary salute and set to work. It was a sight to see Burton with his eagle eye keenly fixed on his adversary, shortly followed by a very rapid swing of his arm and a sharp stroke downwards when the Frenchman was disarmed. He did this seven times in succession, when the sergeant declined any further contest, saying that his wrist was nearly dislocated by the force with which the Englishman struck his weapon. The spectators, mostly French, were astonished at Burton, who, with the exception of a prod in the neck, was otherwise untouched.

" To me it was a marvellous display of fencing skill and the strange magnetic power that he seemed to possess over everybody present was equally surprising."

Before leaving the subject, I will quote from a letter to Captain Low, for many years in the Indian Navy, another old and valued friend, to whom he wrote about the " energetic educator."

" You know the single-stick was never my favourite weapon, and in handling it I always considered it a derogation. My system of ' point ' will be out before very long ; it is a mixture of the French and Italo-Spanish

schools, which ought to make a sensation amongst swords-
men." [1]

Besides fencing, Burton had fierce fits of literary industry, during which he brought out three books already
mentioned.   He also published a " Complete System of
Bayonet Exercise," printed in pamphlet form in 1853, and
which after a time created no little stir.   One might have
imagined that anything tending to increase the efficiency of
the Service would have been welcomed at once by the
Horse Guards; but in pre-Crimean days red tape and
routine had obtained a complete ascendency, and the present rage for novelty was as yet unknown.   That the
author received a severe reprimand because " bayonet
exercise might make the men unsteady in the ranks,"
seems an exaggeration, but there is no doubt he was
mildly snubbed.

The sequel to the story is curious.   The importance of
the said system had already been recognised throughout
Europe, and even in the United States; England alone
refused to consider it.   When the terrible lessons of the
Crimean War had impressed upon our military authorities
the absolute importance of training our men according to
the latest methods, the pamphlet written by the despised
" lieutenant of blacks " was taken down from its pigeon-
hole, and a " Manual of Bayonet Exercise for use in the
British Army " was compiled from his system, with merely
a few modifications.   Which last, by the way, were considered by competent persons hardly in the light of
improvements.

What reward, then, was bestowed upon the man who
had detected the weak point in our military system, and
shown how to remedy it ?   Burton was too proud to ask
for any pecuniary recompense; but he did hope for a compliment, or a few words of thanks.   Instead, he received a

---

[1] " New System of Sword Exercise," Clowes & Sons, 1875.

letter from the Treasury with a most imposing seal : within was the permission to draw upon this department for the sum of one shilling.

In spite of the disappointment, there was an irresistible drollery about the whole affair which so keen a humourist was the first to appreciate. Perhaps it might have been better, so far as his popularity with his seniors was concerned, had he failed to enjoy it quite so thoroughly. Clutching his warrant, he proceeded to the War Office and requested with great politeness to be paid his shilling. Such a thing having never been heard of before, he was referred by the utterly bewildered clerks from one room to another for nearly three-quarters of an hour, still demanding his money. At last his perseverance was rewarded, and having succeeded in claiming his own, he bestowed the coin on the first beggar he met on leaving the building.

Unluckily, it was not only the manual that brought in nothing ; his other works failed to pay for some time. Critics were hostile, or loftily patronising; the public was shy; the publishers were stingy. Writing rather added to his expenses than otherwise, as he required a fair stock of books of reference, and volumes of this nature are not to be had for nothing. Cheap as Boulogne then was, he found it almost beyond his means. His father and mother, ailing and ageing, required more comforts, and although they did add a little to his wretched half-pay, they could not do much, for their income had not increased since the days at Tours, while their expenses had. Burton was not an extravagant man, but he was a very active one, and most victims of a limited income know full well how every pursuit, every amusement, creates a more or less heavy demand upon the purse. Books, the fencing school, society, such as it was, ran away with money which he could ill afford, and for a while he racked his brains in vain how to make both ends meet. It has been said his was not a generous character, but it is not easy to be liberal when, first from one cause and then from another, one has hardly enough money to supply one's own requirements.

As time went on he began to tire also of his position and environment. With comical imprudence, considering the state of his finances, he had again fallen in love, this time with a pretty but penniless girl of eighteen, whose mother was unpleasantly outspoken about his daring, with his prospects, to propose to *her* daughter ; and the snub, though a blessing in disguise, helped to make him discontented with his commonplace surroundings. By some bold achievement he yearned to raise himself above them, to leave behind for a time the petty cares of civilisation, and to help in that great work, the increase of the knowledge of our earth and of our brother man. His family having removed to England and settled at Bath, he was free to centre his energies on his future plans.

The project conceived in Sind of a pilgrimage to Meccah and El-Medinah, and half-forgotten during the four years spent in Europe, now revived, and gradually occupied all his thoughts. If the fates were kind, it seemed capable too of being extended and improved. By spending three years in Arabia, landing at Maskat, a favourite starting place for the interior, he could apply himself, slowly but surely, to the task of spanning the Deserts. To cross the unknown Arabian Peninsula in a direct line from either El-Medinah to Maskat, or diagonally from Meccah to Makallah on the Indian Ocean, would have been of course a far greater feat and one more valuable to geography than a mere visit to the two holy cities. So in the autumn of 1852, through the medium of an excellent friend, the late General Monteith, he offered his services to the Royal Geographical Society, for the purpose of removing what he called that opprobrium to modern adventure, the huge white blot which, in our maps, still notes the Eastern and the central regions of Arabia.

Sir R. J. Murchison, Colonel P. Yorke, and Dr. Shaw,

a deputation from the said Society, forthwith supported in a personal interview with the Chairman of the Court of Directors, Burton's application for three years' leave of absence on special duty from India to Maskat. But for some cause never ascertained, Sir James Hogg refused his consent, merely remarking that the contemplated journey was of too dangerous a nature. Thus the larger plan was frustrated, and our traveller had to content himself with his original one. Even this the authorities would not formally sanction, but an additional furlough of twelve months was accorded to him, in order, it was cautiously worded, "that he might pursue his Arabic studies in lands where the language is best learned." And where could it be acquired in such perfection as in the cities of Meccah and El-Medinah?

This concession gained, Burton had to prepare himself for going absolutely alone into a new country, mingling with strange companions, conforming to unfamiliar manners, and living for many months in the hottest climate in the world. After a four years' sojourn in Europe, during which many things Oriental had faded from his memory, he was to suddenly appear as an Eastern upon the stage of Moslem life. Had it not been for his experiences in Sind as Mirza Abdullah the Bushiri, recollections of which he diligently revived, he could never have made the attempt with any hope of success. He had to attend besides to innumerable little details, all important in their way, for in such strangely perilous circumstances, neglect of the smallest trifle might lead to death. Amongst many other useful things, he learned the process of shoeing a horse, taking lessons from a blacksmith not merely how to nail on the shoes but how to forge them.

While making his preparations for this expedition, Burton stayed mostly in London, occasionally running down to Bath to see his parents and sister. The last visit was the longest, for he spent the very latest hour he could with them, just leaving himself time to catch the steamer at Southampton. Of course, they all knew of his determina-tion to undertake this most dangerous journey, and heartily wished him God-speed; but the subject having been almost too painful to talk about, he had managed to conceal the date of his departure. Burton had a deep-rooted horror of farewells ; the word "good-bye" produced some strangely-disturbing effect upon his nerves, his hands turning cold and his eyes filling with tears before even a short separation. On this occasion no hint was given that the hour for parting had arrived. One evening all retired to rest as usual, and on the morrow he was gone, having left behind a farewell letter to his mother, and his small stock of valuables to be divided as keepsakes between her and his sister. The Arabian Knight, as his friends were afterwards wont to call him, had started on his wonderful travels.

CHAPTER IV

ON the evening of April 3rd, 1853, Burton started for Southampton. By the advice of a brother officer his Persian disguise was called into requisition, and all his impedimenta were made to look exceedingly Oriental. Early next day Mirza Abdullah, accompanied by Captain H. Grindley of the Bengal Cavalry, embarked on board the P. and O. Company's steamer *Bengal*.

A fortnight was profitably spent in getting into the train of Eastern manners. For example, to drink a cup of water seems to us simple enough ; with an Indian Moslem the operation includes no less than five novelties. In the first place, he clutches his tumbler as though it were the throat of a foe ; secondly, he ejaculates before wetting his lips, " In the Name of Allah the Compassionate, the Merciful !" thirdly, he imbibes the contents, swallowing them, not sipping them as he ought to do ; fourthly, before setting down the cup, he sighs forth, " Praise be to Allah !" and, fifthly, in answer to his friend's polite " Pleasure and health," he replies, " May Allah make it pleasant to thee " . . . . Recalling to mind a hundred other similar customs, which, in fact, were being practised on board the good ship *Bengal* by her dark-skinned passenger, Burton passed his time to such advantage that, on landing at Alexandria, he was recognised and blessed as a True Believer by the Moslem population.

The only person who shared his secret was a friend, John Wingfield Larking, at whose house, on the Mahmudijah Canal, our traveller stayed a month—lodged, how-

ever, in an outbuilding, the better to blind inquisitive eyes
of servants and visitors. He lost no time before securing
the assistance of a Shaykh, with whom he plunged once
more into the intricacies of the Faith, revived recollections
of religious ablutions, of the Koran, and of the art of
prostration.   His leisure hours were no less profitably
employed in lounging about the baths, coffee houses and
bazaars, attending the mosque, visiting sundry venerable
localities, in which Alexandria abounds; in short, studying
the natives amongst all the haunts wherein they most did
congregate.

Moreover, always a dabbler in medical lore, this versatile man practised as a doctor, with such success that one
grateful elder offered his daughter in marriage, and a
middle-aged personage of the feminine gender proposed
to disburse the munificent fee of one napoleon provided
Dr. Abdullah would remain at Alexandria and superintend
the restoration to sight of her stone-blind left eye.   Besides
the character of physician, Burton assumed that of a wandering Dervish, but we shall see presently for good reasons
he did not retain it long.

During this comparatively quiet interval he thoroughly
matured his plans.   After a short stay at Cairo he intended
to push on to Suez, thence to embark with a horde of
pilgrims for Yambu, the port of El-Medinah.   A more
luxurious way of travelling would have been to charter a
vessel for himself and servants, but when on the march
comfort was the last thing Burton considered.   Further,
after much deliberation, he decided to pass through the
Moslem's Holy Land as a born believer, not as a renegade.
Had he declared himself a Burma, or 'vert, his co-re-
ligionists would have suspected and catechised him to such
a degree as to seriously obstruct the aim of his wanderings,
i.e., to see everything and to go everywhere.   The 'vert is
always watched with Argus eyes; men do not willingly
give information to a new Moslem, especially a Frank:

they suspect his change of faith to be feigned or forced, look upon him as a spy, and let him into as little of their life as possible.

The month at Alexandria having elapsed (Burton mentions leaving with regret his little room in the flowery garden), he procured a pass-book from H.B.M. Consul, describing him as a British Indian, bade adieu to friends and patients, and started for Cairo by a Nile steamer. His baggage was light. A coarse bag containing a tooth-stick, a piece of soap, and a wooden comb, replaced the silver-mounted dressing case of past days. Equally simple was his wardrobe; two or three changes of clothes. Bedding consisted of a Persian rug, a cotton-stuffed, chintz-covered pillow, a blanket in case of cold, and a sheet which did duty for tent or mosquito curtain during hot nights. These luxuries were supplemented by a huge umbrella, brightly yellow, suggesting a gigantic sunflower, a dagger, a brass inkstand and penholder stuck in the belt, and a mighty rosary, which on occasion could be converted into a weapon of defence. With regard to money, small coins were carried in a cotton purse secured in a breast pocket, gold and papers in a substantial leathern belt strapped round the waist under the shirt. A pea-green box, capable of standing falls from a camel twice a day, served as a medicine chest; saddle-bags contained the clothes; and the bed-furniture was readily rolled up in a bundle.

The wretched steamer, whose name, the *Little Asthmatic*, seems to have described her correctly, took three mortal days and nights in puffing her way to Cairo. A fiery sun pierced her canvas awning like hot water through a gauze veil, and our pilgrim, having taken a third class or deck passage, the evils of the journey were exaggerated. Squatting as far from the crowd as possible, he smoked incessantly, with occasional interruptions to say his prayers and tell his beads on the huge rosary. The dignity of Dervish-hood did not permit him to sit at meals with infidels, nor to eat the food they had polluted; so he drank muddy water from the canal out of a leathern bucket, and munched his bread and garlic with desperate sanctity.

Two fellow passengers, who, in spite of the holy man's evident unsociability, insisted on making his acquaintance, were destined to play a part in the comedy at Cairo. One, Khudabakhsh, a native of Lahore, entertained Burton for a fortnight, and would have extended his hospitality even longer, had not his guest, wearied out of the wily Hindi's somewhat burdensome society, fled to the comparative liberty of a Wakalah, or inn. The other, Haji Wali, a burly Alexandrian merchant, happened to be staying at the identical hostelry wherein our traveller took refuge, and he soon became a fast friend. Constituting himself Burton's cicerone, he guarded him against cheating trades-people; and, having in the course of his wanderings thrown off many of the prejudices of his people, he was able to give some valuable advice.

The most important step suggested by the Haji, was to make choice of a new nationality. " If you persist in being an Ajemi," said he, " you will get yourself into trouble; in Egypt you will be cursed; in Arabia you will be beaten because you are a heretic; you will pay treble what other travellers do, and if you fall sick you may die by the roadside." Nor did the *rôle* of Dervish find greater favour in the shrewd merchant's eyes than the pretended connection with Persia and the Persians. " What business," he asked, " have those reverend men with statistics or any of the information which you are collecting?" After some deliberation he recommended his friend to assume the character of a Pathan or Afghan. Presumably born in India of Afghan parents, and educated at Rangoon, the pilgrim would be well guarded against danger of detection by fellow countrymen, as any trifling inaccuracy would be attributed to a long residence in Burmah. To support the part, a

knowledge of Persian, Hindustani and Arabic, was necessary, in all of which languages Burton was proficient.

No objection, however, was made to the *rôle* of an
Indian physician. The practice of physic is comparatively
easy amongst dwellers in warm latitudes, uncivilized people,
where there is not that complication of maladies which
troubles more polished nations ; and the doctor, if fairly
prudent and not too grasping, is sure of being popular.
Burton appears to have treated his patients with singular
care and tenderness, attending alike some miserable Abyssinian slave girls, who suffered from many complaints on
first arriving in Egypt, and a pasha who had been a
favourite with Mohammed Ali. Perhaps good luck had
something to do with it ; anyway, his success at Cairo
rivalled that at Alexandria.

The following is a specimen of his prescriptions. The
ingredients have the merit of being harmless, the regimen
is strict, and the religious phrases, liberally interspersed,
introduce an element of faith all potent amongst a nervous
and excitable people.

A.[1]

" In the name of Allah the Compassionate, the Merciful,
and blessings and peace be upon our Lord the Apostle, and
his family, and his companions one and all. But afterwards
let him take bees' honey and cinnamon and album græcum,
of each half a part, and of ginger a whole part, which let
him pound and mix with the honey and form boluses, each
bolus the weight of a Miskal, and of it let him use every
day a Miskal on the saliva. Verily, its effects are wonderful.
And let him abstain from flesh, fish, vegetables, sweetmeats,
flatulent food, acids of all descriptions, as well as the major
ablution, and live in perfect quiet. So shall he be cured
by the help of the King, the Healer. And the peace (*w'as-
salam*, i.e. adieu)."

---

[1] A monogram generally placed at the head of writings, the initia
letter of Allah, and the first of the alphabet.

It was necessary to engage a servant to look after the baggage, &c., and the choice was not made without trouble. Indispensable on such a journey were good health, readiness to travel anywhere, a little skill in cooking, sewing, and washing, a fair amount of pluck and a habit of regular prayer. Berberis, Saidis, Egyptians were tried in succession, and all found wanting; while the last, a long-legged Nubian, after a stay of two days with his new master, dismissed *him* for expressing a determination to go by sea from Suez to Yambu. None suited even tolerably except a Surat lad, Nur by name, a docile but eminently commonplace character, and one Mohammed el-Basyúni, a Meccan. The latter, who became a sort of companion, did not join Burton until later. He is described as a beardless youth of about eighteen years, chocolate-brown, with high features, a bold profile, and a decided tendency to corpulence. Meccah had taught him to speak excellent Arabic, to understand the literary dialect, to be eloquent in abuse, and profound at prayer and pilgrimage. From him, while at Cairo, our traveller purchased the pilgrim garb, el-Ihram, and the Kafan or shroud, a festive article of attire wherewith the Moslem usually provides himself before starting on such a prolonged journey.

The next thing to do was to lay in stores for an eighty-four mile ride across the Desert to Suez, and for the voyage to Yambu. These consisted of tea, coffee, loaf-sugar, rice, dates, biscuits, oil, vinegar, tobacco, lanterns, cooking pots, a small bell-shaped tent, and four water-skins. The provisions were packed in a hamper and enclosed in a huge wooden box about three feet each way, covered with leather, and provided with a small lid. The green medicine chest and the saddle-bags were to hang on one side of the baggage camel, and the big wooden box on the other. Atop was a place for a Shibriyah, or cot, useful in case of hard night travelling. A second animal, with saddle and all necessary accoutrements, was hired for riding, and a third for the Indian lad and surplus luggage. Before

starting Burton renewed his stock of ready money, providing himself with eighty pounds sterling in gold and
silver coin.

Nur was sent on in advance, as his master wished to
make a forced march, accompanied only by the camel
drivers, in order to ascertain how much a four years' life
of European effeminacy had impaired his powers of endurance. Haji Wali, helpful to the last, recommended his
friend to start at about 3 p.m., so that he might arrive at
Suez the evening of the following day. Accordingly, at the
hour named, Burton, wearing the crimson cord attached to
the Hamail or pocket Koran over his shoulder in token of
pilgrimage, mounted his beast and rode along the street
which leads towards the desert.

As he emerged from the caravanserai all the bystanders,
except the porter, who believed him to be a Persian, exclaimed, " Allah bless thee, Y'al Hajj, (O Pilgrim), and
restore thee to thy country and friends !" And, passing
through the Bab-el-Nasr, where he addressed the salutation
of peace to the sentry and to the officer commanding the
guard, both gave him God-speed with great cordiality—the
pilgrim's blessing in the East, like the old woman's in
Europe, being supposed to possess peculiar efficacy.
Outside the gate his friend took leave of him, and he
confessed to a tightening of heart as Haji Wali's burly
form disappeared in the distance.

Burton journeyed on till near sunset without ennui. In
such a weird scene every slight modification of form and
colour rivets observation ; the senses are sharpened, and
the perceptive faculties, prone to sleep over a confused
mass of natural objects, act vigorously when excited by the
capability of embracing every detail. In 1853 the Suez
road had become as safe to European travellers as that
between Highgate and Hampstead, so our pilgrim had
nothing to divert his attention from the fantastic desolation
of the wilderness east of the Nile.

As evening drew near he was surprised at hearing an

" As Salamo Alaykum " of truly Arab sound. The salutation emanated from Mohammed, the Meccan. This youth, happening to be short of money, and recognising a good opportunity of living at someone else's expense, had determined to constitute himself Burton's companion ; and after he had cooked a tempting supper, lighted the pilgrim's pipe, and become generally useful, he was graciously permitted to form one of the party.

Thus reinforced, the travellers reached the Central Station about midnight, and straightway lay down under its walls to rest. The dews fell heavily, wetting the sheets that covered them, the breeze blew coolly, and a solitary jackal sang a lullaby which in this instance lost no time in inducing soundest sleep. As the Wolf's Tail (the first brushes of grey light which appear as forerunners of dawn) showed in the heavens, Burton rose and watched for a few moments the grey mists, which, floating over the hills northwards, gave the Dar el-Bayda, the Pasha's palace, the look of some old feudal castle. Presently his companions awoke, and, mounting their camels, all resumed their march in real earnest. Dawn passed away with its delicious freshness, sultry morning came on, then day glared in its fierceness, and the noontide sun made the plain glow with terrible heat. Still, except for one short halt, they pressed on.

It was late in the afternoon when their destination appeared in sight. From afar were visible the castellated peaks of Jebel Rahah, and the wide sand-tracks over which lies the land-route to El-Hejaz. In front lay a strip of sea, gloriously azure, with a gallant steamer ploughing its waters. On the right were the broad slopes of Jebel Mukattam, a range of hills which flank the road continuously from Cairo. It was at that hour a spectacle not easily to be forgotten. The near range of chalk and sandstone wore a russet suit, gilt where the last rays of the sun seamed it with light ; while the background of the higher hills, Jebel Taweri, was sky-blue streaked with the lightest plum colour.

Night had closed in when Burton passed through the tumbledown old gateway of Suez, and the task still remained of finding his Indian servant. After wandering in and out of every Wakalah in the place, he heard that a Hindi had taken lodgings at a certain hostelry, whence, after locking his door, he had gone with friends to a ship anchored in the harbour. It looked unpleasantly as if Nur had decamped—no slight disaster, as he had taken charge of all the silver money. However, nothing more could be done until next day ; so Burton turned into an empty room of a squalid inn, where, as he had merely a square of carpet for a bed, and his eighty-four mile ride had made every bone ache, he passed an unrefreshing night.

Joy came in the morning in the form of Nur with money and goods intact. Moreover, Burton, up and about again, fell in with a party of men who were returning to Medinah, and who were fated to do him no small service. They numbered four—Umar Effendi, a Circassian ; Saad, his servant, nicknamed the Demon ; Shaykh Hamid el-Samman, with whom our traveller afterwards lodged at Medinah, and Salih Shakkar, a Madani dandy, who, after being, for pecuniary reasons, extremely civil en route, cut his friend at home as pitilessly as any " town man " does a continental acquaintance accidentally met in Hyde Park. All four asked almost simultaneously for a loan, which all duly received. The sums were not large, and it was well worth while to keep fellow-travellers in good humour.

Although Burton and his new friends lodged together in the same Wakalah, only once was the would-be Haji suspected of being an infidel. The four Moslems had looked at his clothes, overhauled his medicine chest, and criticised his pistols ; they sneered at his copper-cased watch, and remembered having seen a compass at Constantinople. Therefore, he imagined they would think little

6

about a sextant. This was a mistake : the instrument aroused grave suspicions, and at last a council was held to discuss the case. Fortunately, Umar Effendi, an ultra-serious person, had at various times received from his obliging creditor categorical replies to certain questions in high theology, and so, as a judge on spiritual matters, felt himself in a position to certify to the good faith of the owner of the mysterious article. While Shaykh Hamid, who looked forward to being host, guide, and debtor in general, and probably cared scantily for catechism or creed, swore that the light of El-Islam shone on Burton's counten-ance. However, the sextant had to be left behind, and its possessor was obliged to be more than usually circum-spect for several days afterwards.

Many a wearisome delay occurred before everything was ready for departure. Passports alone would have wearied out the patience of most men. Burton's had not been *visé* at Cairo, and but for the kindness of the English consul, Mr. West, who, at his own risk, issued a fresh document, describing the pilgrim as a British subject travelling from Suez to Arabia, he could not have proceeded any further for some time to come. At last the pilgrims embarked *en masse* on board the *Golden Wire*, bound for Yambu on the Arabian coast of the Red Sea.

The *Golden Wire* (I spare readers the Arabic names wherever possible) was a Sambuk of about fifty tons, with narrow, wedge-like bows, undecked except upon the poop, which was high enough to act sail in a gale of wind. She carried two masts, raking imminently forwards, the main being considerably larger than the mizzen ; the former was provided with a huge triangular latine, but the second sail was unaccountably missing. Of compass, log, spare ropes, or even an elementary chart, she had not a trace. Still more dangerous was the over-crowding. Her greedy owner had originally bargained to carry sixty passengers, but had stretched the number to nearly a hundred. On the poop alone, a space not exceeding ten feet by eight, were three Syrians, a married Turk with his wife and family, the Rais, or captain, with a portion of his crew, Burton's own party of seven, composing a total of eighteen human beings. Luckily, our traveller spied a spare bed-frame slung to the ship's side, which, after giving a dollar to the owner, he appropriated, preferring any hardship outside to the condition of a herring in a barrel.

Never did a Holyhead packet in the olden time display a finer scene of pugnacity than did this pilgrim craft in 1853. The first thing thought of after gaining standing room, was to fight for greater comfort; a general scramble ensued, which was quelled by the simple expedient of dashing sundry jars of cold water upon the combatants. Quieted for awhile, they fell to praying and reciting the Fatihah, or first chapter of the Koran. It being a very short one, they soon quarrelled again. At times nothing was to be seen except a confused mass of humanity, each item indiscriminately punching and pulling, scratching and biting, butting and trampling. The Rais was powerless, his crew worse than useless; in short, a more disorderly scene than the *Golden Wire* and her pious cargo could hardly be imagined.

In such a craft and in such company Burton voyaged from Suez to Yambu, a distance in a straight line of six hundred miles, but protracted by detours to double that space. Cruising along the coast by day, the Sambuk generally lay to in the nearest cove by night. The first evening while still within sight of Suez, she anchored in classic waters; for the eastern shore was dotted with the little grove of palm trees which cluster round Moses' Wells ; and on the west, between two towering ridges, was visible the mouth of the valley down which, according to some authorities, the Israelites fled to the Sea of Sedge.

Next morning preluded a fearfully trying day, type of many another. The sun's rays reflected by the glaring

sea were a very fiery ordeal; even the native passengers
seemed more dead than alive. Shade there was none, and
the crowded state of the vessel heaped horror on horror.
Lying in his cot, plentifully besplashed by the waves
beneath, Burton, with blinded eyes, blistered skin, and
parched mouth, could only count the slow hours which
must minute by until the blessed sunset. At night the temperature became bearable and the passengers, still sick and
dizzy from their sufferings, began to prepare the evening
meal, a very spare one, for in such circumstances a single
good dinner would justify long odds against the eater seeing
another morning.

Had our Haji been cooped up in this "Shippe of Helle"
during the whole voyage, it is unlikely that even his iron
constitution could have survived the strain. Luckily, when
the Sambuk anchored at sunset, he was usually able to
spend the night on shore. During one halt, which, in
consequence of bad weather, lasted twenty-four hours, he
visited Moses' hot baths, and duly venerated the marks of
that prophet's nails, deep indentations in the stone, probably
left by some extinct Saurian. Great excitement prevailed
at another landing place on account of the grounding of the
Sambuk, which was not floated off again without much
noise and trouble. Her Rais on this occasion was forgiven, but a few days later, when he nearly let her strike
on the razor-like edges of a coral-reef, he got well thrashed
for his carelessness, a precedent worthy of the consideration
of more civilised nations.

A serious disaster, so far as our pilgrim was concerned,
occurred at Marsa Mahár. While wading to shore he felt
a sharp object penetrate his foot. After examining the hurt
and extracting what appeared to be a bit of thorn, he
dismissed the matter from his mind, little guessing the
trouble this accident would cause him. The injury was
inflicted by an Echinus, common in those seas, generally
supposed to be poisonous. It seemed so in his case, for

by the time the *Golden Wire* arrived at Yambu, he had become quite lame, and months elapsed before the wound healed.

Yambu afforded a pleasant surprise. It boasted of a Hamman, priceless luxury to weary travellers, and of what in those lands represents a good water supply, viz., sweet rain-water, collected among the hills in tanks and cisterns, and brought on camel-back to the town. Nor was the accommodation bad. Burton and his friends lodged at a Wakalah near the bazaar, where they secured an airy upper room opposite the sea, tolerably free from Yambu's plague, myriads of flies. But the nearer they approached their goal, the more eager they became to press forward. No time, therefore, was lost before treating for camels with an agent, without whose assistance it would have been difficult to hire the animals. The usual squabble over, a bargain was struck. Three dollars were to be paid for each beast, half in ready money, half on reaching their destination; and it was arranged to start next day with a grain caravan guarded by an escort of irregular cavalry. Our pilgrim hired two camels, one to carry his luggage and Indian servant, the other Mohammed and himself. Sundry purchases, too, were indispensable; a Shugduf, or litter, and a plentiful supply of provisions for self and friends; for, although with his usual good taste he did not parade his hospitality, it was very evident that he fed, and fed liberally, the whole of his party.

By the advice of one of his friends he temporarily changed his nationality, this time to avoid a capitation tax extorted from strangers by the natives. So he dressed himself as an Arab, the costume in which he is most familiar. Every reader of the " Pilgrimage " will remember the large square kerchief of mixed silk and wool bound round the head with a twist of cord, the cotton shirt of ample dimensions with its handsome sash, the long-skirted cloak of camel's hair, perhaps the most picturesque raiment in the world.

At about 7 p.m. next day the caravan left Yambu. Burton's own little band numbered twelve camels, each pacing in Indian file, and headed by Umar Effendi in smart attire on a dromedary. Altogether there were six hundred animals attended by their proprietors, truculent-looking fellows, armed with heavy sticks, and an escort of seven soldiers, tolerably mounted and well armed. One might think robbers would have respected so numerous a gathering. Such, however, was not the case. As evening approached and the procession emerged from a scrub of acacia and tamarisk, and turned due east, traversing an open country with a perceptible rise, the cry of " Harami " (thieves) rose loud in the rear. Ensued no small confusion ; all the camel-men brandished their huge staves and rushed vociferating in the direction of the Bedawin. They were followed by the horsemen, and truly, had the thieves possessed the usual acuteness of their profession, they might have driven off the camels in the van, which was left utterly unprotected, with perfect safety and convenience. However, the contemptible beings were only half a dozen in number, and when a bullet or two was fired in their direction, they ran away.

At Said's Well all stopped to rest. No pastoral scene was this, as the name suggests, merely a sort of punch-bowl with granite walls, upon whose grim surface a few thorn bushes of exceeding hardihood braved the sun for a season. Further on lay a country fantastic in its desolation, a mass of huge bare hills, barren plains, and desert vales. Even the sturdy acacias here failed, and in some places the camel grass could not find earth enough for its roots. The road wound monotonously among mountains, rocks and hills of granite, over broken ground, flanked by huge blocks and boulders, piled up as if man's art had aided Nature to disfigure herself. Vast clefts seamed, like scars, the hideous face of earth ; here widening into dark caves, there choked with glistening drift sand.

El-Hamrá, so called from the redness of the sands near
which it is built, is the middle station between Yambu' and
El-Medinah. It is, therefore, considerably out of place in
Burckhardt's map ; and those who copy from him make it
much nearer the sea-port than it really is. Burton described
it as a long, straggling village, a miserable collection of
stunted hovels, with walls of unbaked brick, roofed with
palm leaves and pierced with air-holes to represent windows.
Here he spent a very uncomfortable day. The far-famed
Arab hospitality was conspicuous by its absence ; for while
huge flocks of sheep and goats were being driven in and
out of the place, their surly shepherds refused to give a
cup of milk even in exchange for bread and meat.   Moreover, a depressing rumour circulated that Saad, the great
robber chief, and his brother were in the field ; consequently, further progress would be delayed. These banditti,
the pests of El-Hejaz, then had a following of some 5,000
men, who seized every opportunity of shooting troopers,
plundering travellers, and closing the roads. Before proceeding further it was necessary to muster a stronger party,
and, luckily, just as this was decided upon, a caravan from
Meccah came in with an escort of two hundred irregular
horse.

Thus reinforced, our procession once more set forth.
But they found to their cost the Bedawin did worse than
merely threaten. The Old Man of the Mountains proved
no bugbear, but a very unpleasant reality.   One night the
caravans travelled up a Fiumara, or dry torrent-bed, and at
early dawn reached an ill-famed gorge called Shuab-el-Hajj,
the Pilgrimage Pass. The loudest talkers became silent as
they neared it, and their countenances showed apprehension written in legible characters. Every excuse existed
for faint-heartedness. Pent within the walls of the ravine,
travellers were entirely at the mercy of the marauders,
who, hidden behind the rocks, could fire away at their
convenience.

Presently from a high cliff on the left thin blue clouds of smoke rose in the air, and instantly afterwards rang out sharp cracks from the hillmen's matchlocks. A number of Bedawin were to be seen swarming like hornets over the crests of the hills, boys as well as men carrying huge weapons, and climbing with the agility of cats. They took up sheltered places on their cut-throat eminence, and directed a sharp fire on the pilgrims. It was useless to challenge the Bedawin to come down and fight like men upon the level; and it was equally unprofitable for the escort to fire upon a foe ensconced behind stones. So there was nothing to do except to blaze away as much powder as possible, in order to veil the caravans in smoke; and, meanwhile, to hurry along the gorge, each man at the height of his speed. The cowardly assailants were distanced at last; but the raid cost the lives of twelve men, besides camels and other beasts of burden.

There remained but one more night before the pilgrims came within sight of their goal. In the most auspicious circumstances this part of the way, up rocky hills, and down stony vales, would have been most fatiguing; but the result of a quarrel which had broken out between young Mohammed and his camel-drivers, rendered it almost intolerable. This youth lost his temper, no uncommon occurrence, and remarking that the men's beards were now in his fist, meaning he was out of reach of their wild kinsfolk, he proceeded to abuse them in language which sent their hands flying in the direction of their swords. At last, goaded to madness, the fellows disappeared, taking with them their best animals. A stumbling dromedary, substituted for the usual monture, tottered or tumbled at least once every mile during the long dark hours; and the Shugduf, already ricketty, became such an utter ruin, that its tenants had to perch bird fashion on the only bits of framework which remained. Add to this the pain of an inflamed foot, and one wonders how Burton retained suffi-

cient strength to take part in the exciting scenes of the
following day.

For, at dawn, July 25th, every man was hurrying his
beast, regardless of rough ground; not a soul spoke a word
to his neighbour.

" Are there robbers in sight ? " was Burton's natural
question.

" No," replied Mohammed, " they are walking with
their eyes ; they will presently see their homes."

Rapidly the pilgrims marched through the " Blessed
Valley," and soon came to a huge flight of steps, roughly
cut in a long, broad line of black scoriaceous basalt.   The
summit reached, they hastened along a lane of dark lava,
with steep banks on either side ; and, after a few minutes,
a full view of the city suddenly opened upon them."

" O Allah ! this is the Sanctuary of Thy Apostle; make
it to us a Protection from Hell Fire, and a Refuge from
Eternal Punishment !   O open the Gates of Thy Mercy,
and let us pass through them to the Land of Joy.   Live
for ever, O Most Excellent of Prophets !   live in the
Shadow of Happiness during the Hours of Night and the
Times of Day, whilst the [1] Bird of the Tamarisk moaneth
like the childless Mother, whilst the west wind bloweth
gently over the Hills of Nejd, and the Lightning flasheth
bright in the Firmament of El-Hejaz ! "

Such were some of the poetical exclamations that rose
around, showing how deeply tinged with imagination
becomes the language of the Arab under the influence of
strong passion or religious excitement.   Besides, it *was* all
very beautiful.   Burton now understood the full value of a
phrase in the Moslem ritual, " And when the pilgrim's eyes
shall fall upon the trees of El-Medinah, let him raise his
voice and bless the Apostle with the choicest of blessings."
In all the fair view before him nothing was more striking,
after the desolation through which he had passed, than the

---

[1] The dove.

gardens and orchards about the town. For some moments
the enthusiasm of our English Haji rose as high as that of
his companions; then the traveller's instincts returned
strong upon him, and he made a rough sketch of the scene
in order to fix the details on his memory.

In front stretched a spacious plain bounded by the
undulating ground of Nejd. On the left rose a grim pile of
rocks, the celebrated Mount Ohod, with a clump of verdure
and a white dome or two nestling at its base. Rightwards,
broad streaks of lilac-coloured mists floated over the date-
groves and gardens of Kuba, which stood out emerald green
from the dull, tawny surface of the earth. Distant about
two miles lay El-Medinah, appearing at first sight a large
place, but closer inspection proved the impression erroneous.[1]
A tortuous road starting from the ridge whereon Burton
stood, wound across the plain and led to a tall rectangular
gateway, pierced in a ruinous mud wall which surrounded
the suburbs. This, the Ambari entrance, was flanked on
the left by the domes and minarets of a pretty Turkish
building erected for Dervish travellers, and on the right by
an ugly imitation of civilised barracks. Outside the *enceinte*,
among the palm-trees to the north, peeped the picturesque
ruins of an old public fountain; nearer was the Governor's
palace. In the suburb, El-Manakhah, or kneeling-place
of camels, the new domes and minarets of the Five Mosques
stood brightly out from the dull grey mass of houses and
grounds. And behind, in the most easterly quarter, remarkable from afar, soared the gem of El-Medinah, the four tall
substantial towers, and the flashing green dome under
which the Prophet's remains are said to rest. Dimly visible,
besides, were certain white specks upon a verdant surface,
the tombs that occupy the venerable cemetery of El-Bakia.

After a short rest Burton remounted and slowly rode
onwards with his companions. Even at that early hour the
way was crowded with an eager multitude coming forth to

---

[1] Its population, exclusive of the garrison, numbers only 16,000 souls.

meet the caravans. Friends and comrades greeted one another, regardless of rank or fortune, with affectionate embraces, and an abundance of queries which neither party seemed to think of answering. Passing through the Bab Ambari, our travellers proceeded along a broad, dusty street, and traversed the principal quarter in the Manakhah suburb, a thoroughfare wider and more regular than those of most Eastern cities. They then crossed a bridge, a single arch of brown stone, built over the bed of a torrent, turned to the right, and presently found themselves at the entrance of a small corner building, Hamid el-Samman's house.

While Burton is introduced to innumerable relatives who have crowded to meet their kinsman—the Samman is a great family, in numbers anyway—let us take a peep into Hamid's abode. The ground floor seems merely a vestibule, in which old Shugdufs, mats, and bits of sacking are lying about. We cannot blame Mrs. Hamid, poor thing, as, unlike our irrepressible British matron, she is confined mostly to her own apartments, in the congenial company of her mother-in-law, sundry children, and two black slave girls. Dark and winding stairs of rugged stone lead to the first floor, where the men live, a space divided into one large, windowless room used for bathing, and two others looking on the front, one the parlour. The latter, with its spacious window-sills garnished with cushions, whereon an occupant can lounge and contemplate the varied views outside, its quaint ceiling of date-sticks laid across palm rafters stained red, is the most cheerful spot we have yet visited, though the only signs of furniture are a divan round the sides and a carpet in the centre. The kitchen and rooms on the second floor, given over to the women, we won't intrude upon, lest we wax prosy and pragmatical, as even the cleverest Englishwomen will do on the subject of the harem—a subject of which some travellers have dared to tell us we know next to nothing.

Perhaps these apartments are superior to the rest of the
house; certainly, with the exception of the parlour, it seems
rather mean, and hardly spacious enough to contain Hamid,
his wife, or wives, mother, sundry youngsters, two African
slaveys, and the guest.

Travellers, however, are not particular as to their
lodging. Burton appears to have thoroughly enjoyed his
stay in this Medinite household. At dawn he rose, washed,
prayed, and broke his fast upon a crust of stale bread,
afterwards smoking a pipe and drinking a cup of coffee.
Then it was time to dress and visit one of the holy places.
Returning before the sun became intolerable, he sat and
chatted with his host, coffee and tobacco whiling away the
interval until dinner, which appeared at the unfashionable
hour of 11 A.M. The meal, served on a large copper tray,
consisted of unleavened bread, meat, and vegetable stews,
with a second course of plain boiled rice, followed by fresh
dates, grapes and pomegranates. During the hottest hours
he indulged in a doze or a smoke, lying on a rug spread in
a dark passage behind the parlour. Sunset was the time
for paying and receiving calls. Prayers, a supper similar
to dinner, a stroll to a café, or an hour or two spent in the
open, concluded the day. The men all slept on mattresses
spread just outside the front door, perhaps a necessary
arrangement, but certainly not conducive to sound slumbers,
for incessant quarrels between the horses and pariah dogs
made night hideous.

Tired though our traveller was on the afternoon of
arrival, he would not defer his visit to the Prophet's tomb.
Having performed the usual ablutions, used the tooth-stick
as directed, and attired himself in white clothes, he mounted
an ass, and, accompanied by Shaykh Hamid and the young
Meccan, started on his way. His beast, one of the sorriest
of its kind, lacked an ear, and during the ride he heard the
Bedawin, who, like the Indians, despise poor Neddy, ask
each other " What curse of Allah had subjected them to

ass-riders." But our Haji was too excited to pay much heed to their rudeness. With every thought absorbed in the famous but mysterious mosque he was about to visit, he jogged along several muddy streets which had been recently watered, and, when least expected, came suddenly upon the building. Like that at Meccah, the approach is choked up by ignoble hovels, some actually touching the *enceinte*, others separated by a lane compared with which the road round St. Paul's is a Vatican Square. There is no outer front, no general prospect ; consequently as an edifice it has neither beauty nor dignity.[1] And on entering the Bab el-Rahmah —the Gate of Pity—by a diminutive flight of steps, he was yet more astonished at the mean and tawdry appearance of a place so universally venerated in the Moslem world. Unlike the Meccan Temple, grand and simple, the ex-pression of a single sublime idea, it suggested a museum of second rate art, an old curiosity shop full of ornaments that are not accessories, and decorated with pauper splendour.

But Shaykh Hamid hastily warned our disappointed pilgrim that this was not the time for lionizing, and en-quired loudly if he was religiously prepared. Burton at once assumed the posture of prayer, and, pacing slowly forward, beginning with the dexter foot, the Shaykh on his right side, recited :—

" In the Name of Allah and in the Faith of Allah's Apostle! O Lord, cause me to enter the Entering of Truth, and cause me to issue forth the Issuing of Truth, and permit me to draw near to Thee, and make me a Sultan Victorious ! O Allah ! open to me the Doors of Thy Mercy, and grant me Entrance into it, and protect me from the Stoned Devil ! "

During this preliminary prayer they had traversed two-thirds of the Muwajihat el-Sharifah, or the " Illustrious

---

[1] It measures 420 ft. in length, 340 in breadth, is hypaetural in struc-ture, with a spacious central area,—El-Sahn, El-Hash, and El-Ramlah, surrounded by a peristyle with numerous rows of pillars.

Fronting," which, divided off like an aisle, runs parallel
with the southern boundary of the mosque. On the left is
a dwarf wall, about the height of a man, painted with
arabesques, and pierced with four small doors. Within this
barrier are sundry erections, including the Mambar, or
pulpit, a graceful collection of slender columns, elegant
tracery, and inscriptions admirably carved. Arrived at the
western door in the dwarf wall, they entered the celebrated
spot called El-Rauzah, or the Garden, after a saying of the
Apostles, " Between my tomb and my pulpit is a Garden
of the Gardens of Paradise." Here, after reciting the
afternoon prayers, Burton performed two bows in honour of
the Temple, and intoned the 109th and the 112th chapters
of the Koran, concluding with a single prostration of thanks
in gratitude to Allah for permitting him to visit so hallowed
a spot.

El-Rauzah, the most elaborate part of the mosque,
decorated so as to resemble a garden, is about eighty feet
in length. The pediments are cased with green tiles, the
carpets are flowered, and the columns adorned to a man's
height with gaudy and unnatural vegetation in arabesque.
It is further disfigured by branched candelabras of cut
crystal, the production of a London firm. The only admirable feature of the view is the light cast by the windows
of stained glass in the southern wall. Its peculiar background, the railing of Mohammed's tomb, a splendid
filigree-work of green and polished brass, gilt or made to
resemble gold, looks more picturesque near than at a
distance, when it suggests the idea of a gigantic bird-cage.
But at night the eye, dazzled by countless oil-lamps suspended from the roof, by huge wax candles, and by smaller
illuminations falling upon crowds of visitors in handsome
attire, with the richest and noblest of the city sitting in
congregation when service is performed, becomes less
critical.

After pacing round the outer courts, our pilgrim was

conducted to the Mausoleum, known as the Hujrah, or Chamber, which is supposed to enshrine the remains of Mohammed and his first two successors. Space is left for a single grave where, according to popular superstition Isa bin Maryam[1] shall be buried after a second coming in the flesh. This Hujrah, so called from its having been Ayisha's room, is an irregular square of from fifty to fifty-five feet, in the south-east corner of the building, and separated on all sides from the walls of the mosque by a passage about twenty-six feet broad on the south side, and twenty on the east. The Green Dome rises directly above the Chamber, surmounted by a large gilt crescent springing from a series of globes.

Standing about six feet or so from the railing already described, our pilgrim prayed in "awe, fear, and love," calling down blessings innumerable on the Prophet in a tautological style affected by many creeds. After sundry recitations on the same spot, including the "Fatihah," which has the merit of brevity, our Haji was permitted to look through the three windows of the Chamber, holes about half a foot square, placed from four to five feet above the ground. The most westerly is said to front Mohammed's tomb. Straining his eyes, Burton saw a curtain, or rather hangings, with three inscriptions in long, gold letters, informing readers that behind them lie Allah's Apostle and the two first Caliphs.

The exact place of Mohammed's supposed tomb is, moreover, distinguished by a large pearl rosary, and a peculiar ornament, the celebrated Kaukab el-Durri, or constellation of pearls suspended to the curtain, breast high. This is described by Moslem writers as a brilliant star set in diamonds and pearls, placed in the dark that man's eye may be able to bear its splendours ; the vulgar believe it to be a jewel of the jewels of Paradise. The *coup d'œil* of

---

[1] Jesus, son of Mary.

this portion of the mosque has little to recommend it by day; but, like El-Rauzah, by night, when the lamps suspended in the passage between the outer and inner walls of the mausoleum, shed their dim light on the mosaic work of the marble floors, upon the glittering inscriptions and the massive hangings, the scene is more impressive.

Rather disappointing, after all this misplaced devotion, is it to hear it is by no means certain that Mohammed's remains repose under the great green dome at El-Medinah. For after visiting the spot and carefully investigating its history, Burton believed the true site of the prophet's grave to be as doubtful as that of the Sepulchre at Jerusalem. His reasons for so concluding are as follows:

From the earliest days the shape of the Apostle's tomb has never been generally known in El-Islam. Moslem graves are made convex in some countries, flat in others; had there been a Sunnat, such would not have been the case.

The accounts given by the learned of the tomb are discrepant. El-Samanhudi, perhaps the highest authority, contradicts himself. In one place he describes the coffin, in another he declares he saw merely three deep holes. Either then the mortal remains of the Prophet had crumbled to dust, or they had been removed by the Shiah schismatics who for centuries had charge of the sepulchre.

And lastly, the tale of the blinding light which surrounds the tomb, current for ages past, and still universally believed upon the authority of its guardians, looks like a priestly gloss intended to conceal a defect.

To resume. Our Haji now proceeded to the south-eastern corner of the Hujrah and paused at the place of Gabriel's Descent. Prayers were said and progress made to the sixth station, the sepulchre of Fatimah; (three localities claim the honour of containing her mortal spoils), and here, in spite of the uncertainty, a florid blessing was invoked. Then, turning to the north, Burton recited orisons in honour of Hamzah and other martyrs buried at the foot of Mount Ohod; revolving to the east, he blessed the Blessed of El-Bakia; with another turn to the south, he breathed a general prayer for himself; and this done, he returned to the Apostle's Window and prayed again. Finally, he retraced his steps to El-Rauzah, where a two-bow supplication terminated worship for that day.

Sundry fees and alms cost about one pound sterling. Beggars are allowed to infest the mosques in Moslem countries, just as they are permitted to haunt the churches in Roman Catholic lands. But, when we remember the guardians of the tomb, the water-carrier of the well, and an assortment of mendicants, all had to be paid, it seems that our pilgrim got off very cheaply.

There were other places of pious visitation which it behoved Burton not to neglect. The principal were the mosques of Kuba, Hamzah's tomb, and the cemetery of El-Bakia. Moslems affirm that a prayer at Kuba is of great religious efficacy; a number of traditions testify to the dignity of the principal mosque begun by the Prophet's own hands; sundry miracles took place there, and a verset of the Koran descended from heaven. Burton, who journeyed thither on a dromedary, through palm plantations, where the splashing of tiny cascades from wells into wooden troughs, and the warbling of innumerable birds charmed the ear, described his visit as most delightful. Jebel Ohod owes its reputation to a cave which sheltered Mohammed when pursued by his enemies, to certain springs of which he drank, and especially to its being the scene of a battle celebrated in El-Islam. His relative Hamzah, and other Moslem dead, were interred where they fell; and although the scenes about this holy hill could not have been wholly pleasant to remember, the Prophet declared, "Ohod is a mountain which loves us and which we love; it is upon the gate of heaven!"

El-Bakia, redolent of the odour of sanctity, requires a longer notice. This venerable spot, frequented by the pious every day after prayer at the Prophet's tomb, and especially on Fridays, owes its reputation as a cemetery to the extraordinary number of saintly personages to whom it has afforded a resting place. There is a tradition that a hundred thousand saints, all with faces like full moons, shall cleave its yawning bosom on the last day.

The first person interred in the " Place of many Roots " was Usman bin Mazun, a fugitive from Meccah, and a friend of the Prophet's. Mohammed wished the body to be buried within sight of his own abode, and as in those days the present grave-yard was merely a field covered with trees, the latter had to be cut down before the place was suitable for a burial-ground. Ibrahim, the Prophet's infant second son, was laid in time by Usman's side, after which El-Bakia's renown was assured.

The shape of this celebrated spot is an irregular oblong surrounded by walls, which at their south-west angle are connected with one of the suburbs. The space is small considering that all who die at El-Medinah, strangers as well as natives, heretics and schismatics only excepted, expect to be interred therein. It must be choked with corpses, which it could never contain did not the Moslem style of burial favour rapid decomposition. The gate is small and ignoble ; inside there are no flower-plots, no tall trees, nothing to lighten the gloom of a place of sepulture ; the buildings are simple even to meanness, and almost all are the common Arab mosque shape, cleanly white-washed, and looking quite new. For it must be remembered that the ancient monuments were levelled by Saad the Wahhabi and his Puritan followers, who waged pitiless war against what must have appeared to them magnificent mausolea, deeming, as they did, a loose heap of stones sufficient for a grave. In Burckhardt's time the whole place was a confused accumulation of heaps of earth, wide pits, and rubbish, without a single regular tombstone. The present erections owe their existence to the liberality of the Sultans Abd el-Hamid and Mahmud.

Our pilgrim, accompanied as usual by Shaykh Hamid and the young Meccan, entered the cemetery right foot foremost, as though it were a mosque. He began with the general benediction :—

" Peace be upon Ye, O People of El-Bakia! Peace be upon Ye, O Admitted to the Presence of the Most High! Receive You what You have been promised! Peace be upon Ye, Martyrs of El-Bakia, One and All! We, verily, if Allah please, are about to join Ye! O Allah, pardon us and Them, and the Mercy of God, and His Blessings!" After which he recited a chapter of the Koran, and the Testification, then raised his hands, mumbled the Fatihah, passed his palms down his face, and went on.

Praying in this dismal place never ceased. Prayer and almsgiving were obligatory at the mausoleum of Caliph Osman ; a benediction was invoked at a tomb erected to the memory of the Bedawi nurse who suckled the Prophet. Fronting northwards, our pilgrim recited noisy supplications before a low enclosure containing ovals of loose stones, marking the site of sepulture of the Martyrs of El-Bakia, who received their crown of glory at the hands of El-Muslim, the general of the arch heretic Yezid. Then came the turn of the grave of Ibrahim, the Prophet's youthful son, and of the tombs of the Prophet's wives, all of whom, except Khadijah,[1] are interred in this populous burial-ground. Nor might the tombs of his ten daughters, nor those of many, many holy personages be passed by without the most florid and wearisome orisons.

What, however, rendered this Visitation so peculiarly exhausting was the crowd of beggars. These pests mustered their strongest. Along the walls, at the entrance of

[1] She was buried at Meccah.

7—2

each building, squatted ancient dames engaged in anxious contemplation of every approaching face. Loudly they demanded largesse, some promised to recite Fatihahs, and the most audacious seized visitors by the skirts of their garments. At the doors of sundry tombs which had to be entered bare-footed, old women and young ones also, struggled with our Haji for his slippers as he doffed them, and it was with no slight amount of wrangling, expense, and delay that these useful articles were recovered. In all, his purse was lightened of three dollars, money un-deniably mis-spent, for he added with his usual dry humour, "although at least fifty female voices loudly promised for the sum of ten paras each to supplicate Allah on behalf of my lame foot, no perceptible good came of their efforts."

At last the general benediction concluded the function. There still remained a visit to the burial-place of the Prophet's aunts, northwards of El-Medinah; but here Burton, quite worn out, hurried over his devotions, and after a brief stoppage for refreshment at a little coffee-house near the town gate, rode home with his companions.

CHAPTER V

I T will be remembered that Burton had wished not merely
to visit the holy cities of El-Hejaz—interesting enough
in their way, but of little value to geographical science—
but to cross the almost unknown Arabian peninsula.
Besides treading in the footsteps of the famous Swiss
traveller, he desired to obtain information concerning the
great Eastern Wilderness, marked in our atlases Ruba'
el-Khali (the empty abode); to determine the hydrography
of the Hejaz, its watershed, the slope of the country, the
existence or non-existence of perennial streams; and, finally,
to make certain ethnographical enquiries concerning the
Arab race.

But even had Sir James Hogg given the required leave,
this vast design must have been abandoned. Unexpected
obstacles had arisen. Part of the route had become
impassable in consequence of the furious quarrels between
the tribes of the interior. For some days the sound of
musketry could be heard even in El-Medinah, and many
parties of Bedawin were seen hurrying to the fray, matchlock in hand, or with huge staves on their shoulders.
Nobody could leave the town on one side, even to get as
far as Khaybor, much less Muskat. Besides these more
serious difficulties, the sextant had been left at Suez. All
that remained in the way of instruments was a watch and
a pocket compass; so the benefit rendered to geography
would have been scanty, even supposing our explorer had
escaped with his life.

Seeing that his original scheme had become impracticable, he centred his attention on his approaching journey to Meccah. At El-Medinah every visitation had been performed ; notes innumerable concerning the city, its history, climate, population, had been duly taken and hidden away, and now it was time to seek fresh adventures. There was a fair chance of stirring ones too, for a lucky chance enabled our Haji to travel along the wild eastern frontier, instead of by the ordinary route.

The Damascus caravan was to set out September 1st. Burton had intended to accompany one which usually left two days later, and reached its destination about the same date. Suddenly arose the rumour that there would be no " Tayyarah," and all pilgrims must proceed by the former or await the Rakb, or dromedary caravan, a sort of express, in which each person carries only his saddle-bags.

Early on the morning of August 31st, Shaykh Hamid returned hurriedly from the bazaar, exclaiming, " You must make ready at once ! All Hajis start to-morrow. Allah will make it easy to you ! Have your water-skins in order. You are to travel down the Darb el-Sharki, where you will not see water for three days ! "

Hamid appeared horror-struck as he concluded this fearful announcement, and probably wondered why no dismay was reflected on his guest's face. On the contrary, Burton looked delighted. Here was some consolation for the failure of his original design. Burckhardt had visited and described the Darb el-Sultani, the road along the line of coast ; but no European had as yet travelled by the celebrated route which owes its existence to the piety of Zubaydah Khatun, wife of Harun el-Rashid.

Evidently there was not a moment to lose. Mohammed, who had invited our pilgrim to lodge at his mother's house at Meccah, and who already began to feel all the importance of a host, went and bought a new Shugduf, or litter, and a cot for the Surat lad. Rats had made considerable rents in two of the water-skins, which Burton proceeded to carefully patch up, while Nur was sent to lay in supplies for fourteen days. The journey to Meccah by the slower caravans is calculated at eleven days, but provisions are apt to spoil and the camel-men expect to be plentifully fed. The stores consisted as usual of wheat-flour, rice, turmeric, onions, dates, unleavened bread, cheese, tobacco, sugar, tea, and coffee.

Hamid himself hurried away to attend to the most important business. Faithful camel-drivers are required on a road where robbers are frequent, and stabbings occasional—where there is no law to prevent desertion or to limit extortionate demands. He soon returned, accompanied by a boy of about fourteen, and a short, well-built old man with regular features and a white beard, " Masud of the Rahlah," who bound himself to provide, for the sum of twenty dollars, two camels, which were to be changed in case of accidents. He also agreed to supply his beasts with water, and to accompany his employer, after reaching Meccah, to Arafat and back. Aware of the nature of the journey before him, he absolutely refused to carry Burton's large chest, declaring that the tent under the shugduf was burden enough for one camel, and the green box of medicines, the saddle-bags, and sundry provision sacks surmounted by Nur's cot were amply sufficient for the other. On his part, Burton promised to advance ten dollars at once, to feed the old man and his son ; and on the return from Mount Arafat, to repay the remaining hire with a discretionary present.

These arrangements concluded, Hamid turned to the old Bedawi and exclaimed, " Thou wilt treat these friends well, O Masud ! " To which the prudent ancient replied, " Even as the Father of Mustachios behaveth to us, so will we behave to him." Most men of the Shafei school clip their mustachios exceedingly small. Burton had neglected to do so, and as his were naturally bushy, they won for him the nickname above mentioned.

Spiritual matters also had to be attended to.   The correct thing was to repair to the mosque for a farewell visitation, to give alms, vow piety, repentance and obedience,
and finally retire overwhelmed with grief.   But this waste
of time our Haji objected to so vehemently, that he was
permitted to perform the ceremony at home ; and even then
it was quite long and wearisome enough.

Then began the necessary process of paying off little
bills.   Hamid had treated Burton so hospitably, that the
latter presented his host with the money borrowed at Suez.
Three " Samman " brothers received a dollar or two each ;
and one or two cousins hinted to good effect that such a
precedent would meet with their approbation.   The luggage was then carried out and disposed in packs before the
house-door, to be ready for loading at a moment's notice.
Late in the evening arose a new report, that the body of
the caravan would march about midnight ; but after sitting
up until 2 a.m. and hearing no gun, our traveller lay down
to sleep through the sultry remnant of the hours of darkness.

Early next day Masud and his camels arrived in hot
haste.   No time was lost in final preparations, and at 9 a.m.
Burton, surrounded by his friends, who took leave with
marked cordiality, mounted his beast and shaped his course
towards the north.   At first his attention was completely
absorbed by the extraordinary appearance of the caravan of
which he was a unit.   The morning sun shone brightly on
some seven thousand souls, upon the scarlet and gilt con-
veyances of the grandees, on men on horseback, in litters,
or bestriding the splendid camels of Syria.   Not the least
charm of the spectacle was its wondrous variety of detail.
The pauper pilgrims, almost naked, hobbled along with
heavy staves, then came the riders ; women and children of
the poorer classes sat on rugs spread over the two boxes
which form a camel's load.   Nothing was stranger than the
contrasts—a band of nearly nude negroes marching with

the Pasha's equipage, and long-capped, bearded Persians conversing with Tarbush'd and shaven Turks. The Sultan's Mahmal, or litter, surrounded by the glittering arms of the soldiery, had for convenience sake been stripped of its embroidered cover, and did not appear in its full magnificence until it reached its destination.

At the Well of Rashid the caravan halted and turned to take farewell of the Holy City. All the pilgrims dismounted and gazed once more on the venerable minarets, the Green Dome; and at least an hour elapsed before they again pursued their way over the rough and stony path which leads out of the Medinah basin. The air was full of simoom, cold draughts occasionally poured down from the hills, causing alternations of temperature trying in the extreme. The road was strewn with stones and dotted with thorny acacias; and after a tedious march many a wretched, unseasoned beast of burden sank under the strain. Carcases of asses, ponies, and camels lay by the wayside; those that had been allowed to die peaceably were abandoned to carrion birds, while all whose throats had been religiously cut — a pious attention which the poor creatures must doubtfully appreciate — were surrounded by groups of Takruri pilgrims, negroes who make the pilgrimage on alms. These half-starved beings cut steaks from the choicer portions of the dead animals, and slung the meat over their shoulders till an opportunity for cooking might arrive.

The camp was pitched that evening in excellent order; the Pasha's pavilion surrounded by his soldiers and guards disposed in tents, with sentinels regularly posted, protecting the outskirts. One of Burton's men, who had gone on a little in advance, led him to an open place where the camels were unloaded, after which the tent was erected, and every preparation made for rest and refreshment. Before long our Haji had supped, smoked, and turned in for the night.

Unluckily, a night halt was the exception, not the rule.

Bitter were Burton's complaints of nocturnal marches, a point on which the Arabians are inexorable. It was of course impossible even by moonlight to observe the country to any advantage ; the day sleep became, from fatigue, a kind of lethargy, and it was out of the question to preserve an appetite during the hours of heat. On such roads as the caravan had to traverse, the physical danger was increased tenfold ; the camels had often to feel their way from one basalt block to another, the poor beasts en-livening the scene by keeping up in their terror an incessant piteous moaning. Sometimes an invisible acacia would catch the shugduf, almost overthrowing the hapless bearer by the suddenness and tenacity of its clutch, and shaking the inmates with unpleasant violence out of their uneasy slumber. But the Prophet had said " Choose early dark-ness for your wayfarings, as the calamities of the earth (serpents and wild animals) appear not at night," and right or wrong, whenever practicable, he has to be obeyed.

In spite of this wearisome practice, which, however, could not invariably be adhered to, Burton saw many a curious phenomenon. One day appeared the pillars of sand described by Abyssinian Bruce. They scudded on the wings of the whirlwind over the plain, huge yellow shafts, with lofty heads, horizontally bent backwards, in the form of clouds ; on more than one occasion camels have been thrown down by them. It required little stretch of fancy to enter into the Arab's superstition, that these sand columns are Genii of the Waste, which cannot be caught, a notion arising from the fitful movements of the electrical wind - eddy which raises them. As they advance, the pious Moslem stretches out his finger, exclaiming, " Iron ! O thou ill-omened one ! " The mirage our traveller had already seen in Sind ; but one evening a long thin line of salt efflorescence appearing at some distance on a plain below, when the shades of coming night invested the view, completely deceived him. Even the Arabs were divided in opinion, some thinking it was the effects of rain which had recently fallen; others were more acute. So far as our traveller was able to judge, animals are never taken in by this refraction, probably because most of them recognise the vicinity of moisture by smell rather than sight.

Procuring fresh supplies of water was a great trouble. Under the fiery Arabian sky thirst is incessant, and the water-skins are soon emptied. It was necessary, too, to supply the camels with a sufficiency; and, as often the wells were situated two miles from the halting-place and strictly guarded by soldiers, who exacted hard coin in exchange for the precious fluid, the task of refilling the awkward leathern receptacles was an unending source of quarrels and anxiety. And after all the fatigue and worry, it usually proved either brackish or bitter.

Never were the wells more nauseous than at El-Sawayrkiyah, about ninety miles from El-Medinah. Burton had bought some fresh dates, and paid a dollar and a half for a sheep destined to furnish a dish of liver and fry for himself and a plentiful meal for his servants. Vainly did he attempt to enjoy himself; what dinner could please if washed down with cups of a certain mineral-spring found at Epsom? It was especially disappointing, as this townlet boasted of a bazaar well supplied with meat, particularly mutton, while wheat, barley and dates were brought in every day fresh from the neighbourhood.

The caravan left El-Sawayrkiyah on the 5th September and travelled over a flat country thinly dotted with desert vegetation. At 1 p.m. they passed a basaltic ridge, and then, entering a kind of valley, paced down it five tedious hours. The simoom, as usual, was blowing hard, and it seemed to affect the pilgrims' tempers. Presently occurred an incident which revealed the innate ferocity of the Arab nature. A Turk, who could not speak a word of Arabic, began a violent dispute with an Arab, who could not understand a word of Turkish. It was all about nothing:

the former insisted on adding to the camel's load a few
dry sticks, such as are picked up for cooking, and the
camel-owner as perseveringly threw off the extra burthen,
one the animal could have hardly felt. They screamed
with rage, hustled each other, and at last the Turk
imprudently dealt the Arab a heavy blow. That night
the pilgrim was mortally wounded by the revengeful
Bedawi, and, wrapped in his shroud, was left to die in
a half-dug grave.

Burton commented with horror on this atrocity, one of
not unfrequent occurrence. The poor friendless wretch's
fate appealed peculiarly to his sympathy, for an uneasy
doubt must have flashed across his mind whether he too
might not be attacked by one of these wild children of
the desert and abandoned while yet alive to the jackal
and the vulture. Fortunately, his attention was soon
diverted from the tragedy by one of the most curious of
the Moslem ceremonies. At El-Zaribah, some forty-seven
miles from their destination, the pilgrims prepared to assume
the Ihram, or peculiar garb in which they enter Meccah.
Between noontide and afternoon prayers, a barber attended
to shave their heads, cut their nails, and trim their
mustachios ; then, having bathed, they donned their new
attire, merely two new white cotton cloths each six feet long
by three and a half broad. One of these sheets, which, by
the way, is ornamented with red stripes and fringes, is
thrown over the back, and exposing the arm and shoulder,
is knotted at the right side ; the second is wrapped round
the loins from waist to knee, and, tucked in at the middle,
supports itself. The head remains bare, a barbarous practice in such a climate, and nothing is allowed on the instep.

After their toilet the pilgrims with their faces towards
Meccah were ordered to say aloud, " I vow this Ihram of
Hajj (the pilgrimage) and the Umrah (the little pilgrimage)
to Allah Almighty ! " Then without rising from the sitting
position, they repeated, " O Allah ! verily I purpose the

Hajj and the Umrah, then enable me to accomplish the two and accept them both of me, and make both blessed to me!" Followed the Talbiyat,[1] or exclaiming:

"Here I am! O Allah! here am I—
No Partner hast Thou, here am I:
Verily the Praise and the Beneficence are Thine, and the Kingdom—
No Partner hast Thou, here am I!"

And they were warned to repeat these words as often as possible until the conclusion of the ceremonies.

Then a certain namesake of our traveller's, Shaykh Abdullah, a reverend elder who acted as director of consciences, preached a little sermon. They must be good pilgrims, avoiding quarrels, immorality, bad language, and light conversation. They must reverence life, avoid killing game, and even pointing out an animal for destruction; nor might they scratch themselves save with the open palm lest vermin be destroyed. They were to respect the Sanctuary by sparing the trees, and not to pluck a single blade of grass. They were to abstain from oils, perfumes, unguents, from washing the head with mallow-leaves, from dyeing, shaving, or vellicating a single hair; and, though they might take advantage of shade, and even form it with upraised hands, they must by no means cover their shaven pates. For each infraction of these ordinances they must sacrifice a sheep; and this command, together with the wholesale slaughter at Muna, furnishes, when we recall the tender care enjoined for fleas and other vermin, an instance of glaring inconsistency which, however, is not peculiar to the Mohammedan creed.

In the middle of all this monotonous praying and preaching, Burton enjoyed a hearty laugh. The wife and daughter of a Turk assumed the Ihram at the same time as himself. After a short absence they reappeared dressed in white garments sorely resembling roomy shrouds; and, by way of rendering themselves yet more hideous, they had exchanged the coquettish fold of muslin which veils the

---

[1] From the word Labbayka—here am I.

lower part of the face for an ugly mask made of split, dried, and plaited palm leaves, with two holes for light. While our pilgrim could not restrain his merriment when these strange objects met his sight, the objects themselves, to judge by the shaking of their shoulders, were no less tickled by the passing ugliness of their pious garb.

This important function over, the caravan again started on its way. The ceremony had added fuel to the general fervour; crowds hurried along in their scanty attire, whose whiteness contrasted strangely with their dark skins, and the rocks rang with shouts of " Labbayk! Labbayk! " Presently they fell in with a horde of Wahhabis, those Puritans of El-Islam, wild-looking mountaineers who were accompanying the Baghdad caravan, and who, in the same state of religious ecstasy, responded by yells of " Here am I! " They were too strict, however, to be altogether pleasant companions; whenever they saw their brother Moslems smoking they cursed them aloud for infidels and idolaters, and what they might have done had any thirsty soul indulged in Raki, they alone could tell.

Gradually amongst the huge multitude a rumour circulated that the Bedawin were " out." This gave rise to no small anxiety, which increased when the caravans entered a veritable Valley Perilous, one which strongly reminded our Haji of the Pilgrimage Pass on the way to El-Medinah. On the right was a stony buttress, on the left a precipitous cliff, grim and barren, while opposite, egress seemed barred by piles of hills, crest rising above crest into the far blue distance. Day still smiled upon the upper peaks, but the lower slopes and the dry bed of a torrent were already curtained with grey, sombre shade.

The voices of women and children sank into silence, and the loud " Labbayk " of the pilgrims was gradually hushed. Burton was still speculating upon the cause of this sudden lull, when it became brusquely apparent. The Bedawin were in sight and preparing to fire. Simultaneously with the echoing crack of a matchlock, a high trotting dromedary in front of our Haji rolled over upon the sand—a bullet had split its heart—throwing the rider a goodly somersault of five or six yards.

The Wahhabis were unpleasantly puritanical, but they had the redeeming virtue of bravery. During the terrible confusion which ensued — vehicles, animals, and human beings jammed into a solid mass, whilst the missiles from the heights whistled into their midst—these mountaineers alone retained their wits. They rallied at once, kept their camels well in hand, and, taking up a well-selected position, one body began to fire upon the robbers, and two or three hundred, dismounting, swarmed up the hill to dislodge the foe. Presently firing was heard far in the rear, and, as usual, the caravans hurried along their perilous path until all danger was left behind. It was said the bandits numbered only a hundred and fifty, and that their principal reason for attacking the harmless pilgrims was to boast how, on such and such an occasion, they had delayed the Sultan's Mahmal one whole hour in the Pass.

The scene that night was truly Stygian—one hardly calculated to calm nerves shaken by the late assault. On either side grim precipices towered above till their summits mingled with the darkness, and, between, formidable looked the chasm down which the host hurried with yells and discharges of matchlocks. The torch-smoke and night fires of flaming Asclepias formed a canopy, sable above, and lurid red below : here flames flashed fiercely from a tall thorn-tree, that crackled and shot up showers of sparks into the air ; there they died away in uncertain gleams ; while the moaning of affrighted camels, the shouts and cries of their riders, distracted the ear on every side.

Delightful was the contrast next morning — Wady Laymun, or the Valley of Limes. From remote ages this charming spot, celebrated for the purity of its air, has been a favourite resort of the Meccans. Nothing could be more

soothing than the dark green foliage of its trees and the
sweet sound of a bubbling stream which, issuing from the
base of a hill, flowed through its gardens, filling them with
the most delicious of melodies, the gladdest sound which
Nature in these regions knows. Burton would fain have
lingered in this pleasantest of pleasant places, but Masud,
the camel owner, was inexorable. It was the next station
to the Holy City, and the wily old Arab knew that by
preceding the main body, already augmented by the arrival
of the Sherif and his attendants, who had come to greet
the Pasha, he would get his animals attended to sooner,
and secure more easily lodgings for himself. So, exactly
at noon, he seized the halter of his foremost beast and
marched off.

As evening approached, our party halted, and strained
their eyes to catch sight of Meccah. But the town, which
lies in a winding valley, was still invisible, and the pilgrims
betook themselves to prayer. After repeating sundry
formulæ, prescribed on nearing the Sanctuary, they again
mounted their camels and journeyed through the darkness,
until about 1 a.m., when loud cries of "Labbayk! Labbayk!"
not unfrequently broken by sobs, warned our traveller he
had reached his goal. Peering from his shugduf, he beheld
by the light of the southern stars a large city dimly out-
lined. A winding pass, flanked by watch-towers which
command the road from the north, leads into the northern
suburb where stands the Sherif's palace, a large, whitewashed building, with numerous balconied windows. After
this, on the left hand, appeared the deserted abode of Sherif
bin Aun, now said to be haunted. Thence, turning to the
right, our party entered the Afghan quarter, turned off the
main road into a by-way, ascended the rough heights of
Jebel Hindi, and finally, after threading sundry dark streets
crowded with rude cots and dusky figures, drew up in
safety at the door of young Mohammed's house.

For a few minutes the youth forgot his duties as host.

With scant ceremony he rushed upstairs to embrace his mother, and the shrill cry, or Lululú, which in these lands welcomes the wanderer home, broke the stillness. Though our pilgrim elsewhere compares this cry peculiar to women in the East to the notes of a fife, he confessed that while lingering outside, a stranger in the dark street, it sent a chill to his heart.

Presently Mohammed returned. He now remembered what was required of him, his jaunty manner had changed to one of grave and attentive courtesy. He led his guest into a sort of hall, seated him on a carpeted platform, and told his servant to bring lights. Meanwhile, a shuffling of slippered feet upstairs informed hungry ears that the mistress was on hospitable thoughts intent ; and before long appeared a dish of fine vermicelli, browned, and powdered with loaf sugar. After his meal Burton procured a cot from a neighbouring coffee-house, and lay down, anxious to snatch an hour or two of repose during what remained of the night. At dawn he was expected to perform his " Circumambulation of Arrival " at the Meccan sanctuary.

Scarcely had the first smile of morning beamed upon the rugged head of Abu Kubays, a hill which bounds Meccah to the east, than our Haji rose, bathed, and proceeded in pilgrim garb to the Great Mosque. Entering by the principal northern door, he descended two flights of steps, traversed a cloister, and stood in sight of the Kiblah of El-Islam,[1] the place to which the Moslem turns in prayer from all quarters of the globe.

This far-famed Kaabah, the most interesting feature of the Meccan mosque, is an oblong structure, eighteen paces in length, fourteen in breadth, and from thirty-five to forty feet in height. Constructed of grey granite, it stands upon

---

[1] The Great Mosque consists of a large quadrangle, surrounded by arcades or cloisters, and entered by nineteen gates, surmounted by seven minarets. In the centre stands the Kaabah, which was the temple of Meccah ages before the days of Mohammed.

8

a base two feet high, and its roof being almost flat, it presents at a distance the appearance of a perfect cube. It is partly covered with black drapery, a mixture of cloth and silk with a golden zone running round its upper portion ; the hangings in front of the door are also embroidered. This Kiswah, as it is called, is renewed every year, and the origin of the custom must be sought in the ancient practice of typifying the church visible by a virgin or bride. . . . With memory thus refreshed, my readers may be better able to follow the curious ceremonies in which our Haji took part, especially the rite of Circumambulation.

For some minutes Burton gazed on this venerable object with interest and delight.   True, there were no giant fragments of hoar antiquity, as in Egypt ; no remains of graceful and harmonious beauty, as in Greece or Italy. Yet the view was strange, unique—and how few aliens had looked upon the celebrated shrine ! The mirage medium of fancy invested the huge catafalque and its gloomy pall with peculiar charms ; it was as if the poetical legends of the Arabs spoke truth, and that the waving wings of angels, not the sweet breeze of morning, were agitating and swelling the black covering of the Bayt Allah.[1] . . . Moreover, the plans and hopes of many a year were here partially realised, and our hero, as he stood a stranger in this Mohammedan sanctuary, felt for a moment all the triumph of a victory over conditions which had daunted every Englishman before him.

Moslems rarely contemplate the Kaabah for the first time without fear and awe, so the young Meccan had left his guest for awhile alone. Presently he returned, and the two entered the " Gate of the Sons of the Shaybah," raised their hands, repeated the Labbayk and other formulæ, recited certain supplications, and drew their hands down their faces.   Then they proceeded to the Shafei's place

---

[1] House of Allah.

of worship, the open pavement between the Makam Ibrahim and the well Zem Zem, where they said a prayer, accompanied by two prostrations, in honour of the mosque, and swallowed a cup of holy water.

The word Zem Zem has a doubtful origin. Some derive it from the Zam Zam, or murmuring of its waters ; others from Zam ! (fill ! *i.e.* the bottle), Hagar's impatient exclamation when she saw the stream. The produce of this well is held in much greater esteem than it deserves. Meccans advise pilgrims to break their fast with it, ignoring the fact that the holy fluid is apt to cause diarrhœa and boils, and has more than once been suspected of spreading cholera. Its flavour is a salt bitter, and the most pious Moslem can hardly swallow it without a very wry face.

At the Kaabah's eastern angle is inserted the famous Black Stone,[1] the touching or kissing of which is considered essential. Standing about ten yards distant, Burton repeated with upraised hands, " There is no God but Allah alone, Whose Covenant is Truth, and Whose Servant is Victorious. There is no God but Allah without Sharer ; His is the Kingdom, to Him be Praise, and He over all Things is potent." Afterwards he approached as near as possible ; but a dense crowd intervening, he recited more prayers and commenced the rite of circumambulation, or pacing round the Kaabah. This circuit has to be repeated seven times ; its conjectured significance is an imitation of the heavenly bodies, also symbolised by the circular whirlings of the Dervishes. After each course the pilgrim stood before the Black Stone, exclaimed " In the Name of Allah, and Allah is Omnipotent," kissed his fingers, and resumed his march.

Burton duly performed his seven circuits, repeated a prayer of portentous length, and then, aided by Mohammed

---

[1] When Allah made covenant with the Sons of Adam on the day of Fealty, He placed the paper inside this stone ; it will therefore appear at the Judgment, and bear witness to all who have touched it.

and half a dozen stalwart Meccans, cleared a path through the crowd and reached the stone, which he narrowly scrutinised for about ten minutes. He came away convinced that it is an aërolite.

This ceremony of touching or kissing the Black Stone, which, judging from the dense crowd around the shrine, must often be deferred perforce for hours, is the culminating act of devotion in the Meccan Sanctuary. On this occasion little further remained to be done. There were a few more prayers, followed by a second visit to Zem Zem, where another nauseous draught had to be swallowed, and where Burton was deluged with two or three skinfuls of water dashed over his head *en douche,* an ablution which causes sin to fall from the spirit like dust. Then our pilgrim turned towards the Kaabah, ejaculated sundry formulæ, and finally, quite worn out, with scorched feet and a burning head, left the mosque. Strictly speaking, he should have performed the rite called El-Sai, or running seven times between Mounts Safa and Marwah ; but fatigue, not to mention his lame foot, now sorely inflamed by the fiery pavements, put this further trial out of the question.

Mohammed the Meccan had miscalculated the amount of lodging vacant in his mother's house. Being a widow and a lone woman, she had made over for the season the letting of her apartments to her brother, a lean old harpy with the face of a vulture. He had lost no time in crowding the place with pilgrims, almost as densely as the Rais of the *Golden Wire* had crowded his craft ; and he regarded Burton with little favour when the latter insisted on having a room to himself. After some wrangling, he promised that on the return from Arafat a little store-room should be cleared out and appropriated to the guest's use ; but meanwhile the day had to be spent in the common hall in company with several Turkish strangers—large, hairy men, with gruff voices and square figures — who seemed to monopolise what little air and space there was. On the whole, our Haji was worse off at Meccah than at El-Medinah. The heat was stifling, for the city is so compacted together by hills, that even the simoom can scarcely sweep it, and the inhabitants are utterly ignorant of any art of therman-tidote. Moreover, the house, though larger, was far less cheerful. The hot, gloomy hall could not be compared with Shaykh Hamid's bright little parlour, where his guests lolled on cushioned embrasures, and gazed upon some of the brightest scenes in the city.

There being small temptation to linger in this oven-like abode, our pilgrim, accompanied by Mohammed and followed by Nur, who carried a lantern and a prayer-rug, repaired that evening to the mosque. The moon, now nearly full, lighted up the strange spectacle. There stood the huge, bier-like erection, black as Erebus, except where the moonbeams streaked it like jets of silver falling upon dark marble. It formed the point of rest for the eye ; the little pagoda-like buildings and domes around, with all their gilding and fretwork, vanished. One object, unique in appearance, stood in view—the temple of the one Allah, expressing by all the eloquence of fancy the grandeur of the idea which vitalised El-Islam.

The pavement round the Kaabah was crowded with men, women and children, mostly divided into parties ; some walking staidly, others running, while many stood in groups to pray. Here stalked a Bedawi woman in her long black robe, like a nun's serge, and her poppy-coloured face-veil pierced to show two fiercely flashing eyes. There an Indian woman, with semi-Tartar features nakedly hideous, and thin legs encased in wrinkled tights, hurried round the fane. Every now and then a corpse, borne on its wooden shell, circulated the shrine by means of four bearers, whom other Moslems, as is the custom, occasionally relieved. A few fair-skinned Turks lounged about. In one place a fast Calcutta Khitmugar stood with turban awry and arms akimbo, contemplating the view jauntily ;

in another, a poor demented wretch with arms thrown on high was clinging to the curtain and sobbing as though his heart would break.

The celebrated mosque pigeons flock mostly in the line of pavement leading to the eastern cloisters. During the day women and children sit with small piles of grain upon trays of basket-work ; for each a copper piece is demanded, and pious pilgrims consider it a duty to provide the reverend blue-rocks with a plentiful meal. These birds are held sacred not only in consequence of Arab traditions concerning Noah's dove, but as having been connected on two occasions with the Moslem faith ; first, when a pigeon appeared to whisper in Mohammed's ear, and secondly, during the flight to El-Medinah. Moreover, in many countries they are called " Allah's Proclaimers," because their movements when cooing resemble prostration.

That night Burton remained in the mosque until 2 a.m., hoping to see it empty. But as the morrow was to witness the egress to Arafat, many persons passed the hours of darkness in the sacred building. Numerous parties of pilgrims sat upon their rugs, with lanterns in front of them, conversing, praying, and contemplating the Bayt Allah. The cloisters were full of merchants, who resorted there to vend such holy goods as combs, tooth-sticks, and rosaries. Before leaving it was necessary to offer up a two-bow prayer over the grave of Ishmael, and this accomplished, not without difficulty on account of the crowd, our indefatigable Haji, profiting by the temporary somnolence of his two companions, succeeded in taking measurements of the Kaabah. He was sorely tempted to annex a strip of her ragged black curtain, but too many people were still awake. Later he obtained a piece through the agency of his host, who purchased it from the officials all the more easily as the venerable building was on the eve of donning her new attire.

Next day it behoved all pilgrims to hie to Muna and

Arafat, in order to join in the ceremonies peculiar to those localities. Mount Arafat is situated about twelve miles from Meccah, and is reached *viâ* Muna, a straggling village built in a low gravel basin surrounded by hills. The most striking functions that take place on these sacred spots are, the Sermon, delivered by a preacher seated on a dromedary in imitation of Mohammed, the Stoning of the Devil, and the Sacrifice of Animals. Muna, besides possessing the tomb, or rather a tomb of Adam, boasts of three standing miracles : the pebbles thrown by pilgrims at the Devil, who is represented by a trio of pillars, return by angelic agency whence they came ; during the three days of " Drying Meat " rapacious beasts and birds cannot prey there ; and, lastly, flies do not settle on the articles of food exposed so abundantly in the bazaars. Needless to add, these wonders were conspicuous by their absence on the occasion of our Haji's visit.

Burton and his party followed the road by which the caravans enter Meccah. It was covered with white-robed pilgrims, some few wending their way on foot, others riding. The barbarous Ihram was *de rigueur*, every man bare-footed and bare-headed ; and we read with little surprise that, during the six hours' journey under a burning sun, our traveller saw no fewer than five poor wretches lie down on the high road and give up the ghost. Nor on arrival at the plain of Arafat was there much rest after the exhausting day. Comforts were not lacking, for Nur and the young Meccan pitched a tent, disposed a divan of silk cushions inside, and placed at the entrance a large fire-pan with coffee-pots, singing a welcome to visitors ; but sleep was banished by Arab songs and shouts of laughter from Egyptian hemp-drinkers, not to mention a prayerful old Moslem who began his devotions at a late hour and concluded them at dawn.

Next morning was spent in visiting various consecrated sites on the " Mount of Mercy." Arafat, a mass of coarse granite split into large blocks, with a thin coat of withered thorns, is about one mile in circumference, and hardly two hundred feet in height. About half way up is a nook where Mohammed used to address his followers, and which is now occupied by the Khatib, or preacher, on the occasion of the Arafat sermon. Higher still is a large stuccoed platform, with a kind of obelisk, whitewashed and conspicuous from afar, commemorating the site on which Adam, instructed by the archangel Gabriel, erected a place of prayer. Close to the plain is the spot where the Egyptian and Damascus Mahmals stand side by side during the sermon; and yet lower a fountain, bubbling from a rock, supplies the pilgrims with water.

Even at an early hour Arafat was crowded with Hajis, who had hastened to secure favourable positions for hearing the preacher. As the function drew nearer, the general excitement increased. And certainly the *coup d'œil* was magnificent. First marched a grand procession of mace-bearers, of horsemen wielding long and tufted spears, followed by the beautiful Arab horses belonging to the Sherif of Meccah, a procession wherein about midway rode that personage himself, preceded by three green and two red flags. Then the Damascus Caravan, with its ensign of imperial power, all green and gold, flashing in the sun, and its host of white-robed pilgrims swept past to the holy hill. On joining the Egyptian Mahmal and its followers, the two camels, with their glittering loads, took up their prescribed positions on the slope. The Sherif, his retinue, and standard-bearers ranged themselves a little above; and the most picturesque of backgrounds was formed by the granite hill covered, wherever standing room could be found, with white figures waving their glistening garments. Burton, too restless to remain on Arafat, had lost all chance of a place whence he could profit by the discourse, and could only just distinguish the Khatib seated on his dromedary, and hear at uncertain intervals a chorus of cries, sobs, and shrieks from the vast and excited congregation.

The ceremony of Lapidation, though curious, is far less picturesque. Three rude pillars represent Satan, and at these pillars pilgrims are directed to throw a certain number of stones, repeating, " In the Name of Allah, and Allah is Almighty, I do this in hatred of the Devil and to his shame." As the fiend had maliciously chosen a very narrow pass wherein to appear and be thus commemorated, the place is exceedingly dangerous when crowded with a shrieking, fanatical multitude. Burton and the animal he rode narrowly escaped with life, while Mohammed, who ought to have known better, had to fight his way out of the crowd with a bleeding nose. Both must have heaved a sigh of relief when, the pebbles having been duly flung at the senseless little buttress, they could retire to a barber's shop to rest, and rearrange the Ihram. After about an hour the two men—Nur was usually missing when danger was in the air — raced on donkey-back to Meccah, an undignified return known as the El-Nafr, or the flight.

Here a piece of luck awaited our pilgrim. Shortly after his arrival, Mohammed entered his room in a state of excitement, exclaiming, " Rise, Effendi ! Dress, and follow me ! " The Kaabah, though open, would for a time remain empty, and thus afford an opportunity for a quiet visit which might not occur again. Hastily resuming the Ihram, Burton hastened with the young Meccan to the mosque.

What he saw shall be described in his own words :

" A crowd had gathered round the Kaabah, and I had no wish to stand bare-headed in the midday September sun. At the cry of 'Open a path for the Haji who would enter the house,' the gazers made way. Two stout Meccans, who stood below the door, raised me in their arms, whilst a third drew me from above into the building.[1] At the

---

[1] The only door is about seven feet above the pavement.

entrance I was accosted by several officials, dark-looking
Meccans, of whom the blackest and plainest was a youth of
the Beni Shaybah family, the blue blood of El-Hejaz. He
held in his hand the huge silver-gilt padlock of the Kaabah,
and presently, taking his seat upon a kind of wooden press
in the left corner of the hall, he inquired my name, nation,
and other particulars. The replies were satisfactory, and
young Mohammed was authoritatively ordered to conduct
me round the building, and to recite the prayers. I will
not deny that, looking at the windowless walls, the officials
at the door, and the crowd of excited fanatics below, my
feelings were of the trapped-rat description. This did not,
however, prevent my carefully observing the scene during
our long prayers, and making a rough plan with a pencil on
my white Ihram.

" Nothing is more simple than the interior of this
celebrated building. The pavement, which is level with
the ground, is composed of slabs of fine and various
coloured marbles, mostly, however, white disposed chequer-
wise. The walls, as far as they can be seen, are of the
same material, but the pieces are irregularly shaped, and
many of them are engraved with long inscriptions in the
Suls and other modern characters. The upper part of the
walls, together with the ceiling, at which it is considered
disrespectful to look, are covered with handsome red
damask, flowered over with gold, and tucked up about
six feet high, so as to be removed from pilgrims' hands.
The flat roof is upheld by three cross-beams, whose shapes
appear under the arras ; they rest upon the eastern and
western walls, and are supported in the centre by three
columns about twenty inches in diameter, covered with
carved and ornamental aloes wood. At the Iraki corner
there is a dwarf door, called Bab el-Taubah (of Repentance).
It leads into a narrow passage and to the staircase by which
the servants ascend to the roof : it is never opened except
for working purposes. The ' Aswad ' corner is occupied

by a flat-topped and quadrant-shaped press or safe, in which at times is placed the key of the Kaabah. Both door and safe are of aloes wood. Between the columns, and about nine feet from the ground, ran bars of a metal which I could not distinguish, and hanging to them were many lamps, said to be of gold.

" Although there were in the Kaabah but a few attendants engaged in preparing it for the entrance of the pilgrims, the windowless stone walls and the choked-up door made it worse than the Piombi of Venice; perspiration trickled in large drops, and I thought with horror what it must be when filled with a mass of furiously jostling and crushing fanatics. Our devotions consisted of a two-bow prayer, followed by long supplications at the Shami (west) corner, the Iraki (north) angle, the Yemani (south), and lastly, opposite the southern third of the back wall. These concluded, I returned to the door, where payment is made, and was let down by the two brawny Meccans."

After quitting the Kaabah, Burton returned to his lodgings, and endeavoured to mitigate the pain of the sun-scalds on his arms, shoulders and breasts by washing them with henna and warm water. Towards evening, he donned a gay, laical attire in honour of the festival, viz., the "Three Days of Drying Meat," and rode back to Muna. Though he had heard sundry details of the sacrifices in this place, he was unprepared for the ugly spectacle of fanaticism, greed and cruelty that met his eyes. During his absence had begun the wholesale slaughter of animals, a relic of Judaism preserved and caricatured by Mohammed, which renders Muna at times a veritable plague-spot. The Takruri might be seen sitting, vulture-like, contemplating the doomed sheep and goats, and no sooner was the signal given, than they fell upon the still quivering bodies and cut them up for eating. No doubt it is necessary that the poorer pilgrims should be fed; and, were just sufficient animals butchered to preserve the Takruri from starvation,

a good excuse might be made by Moslems for the practice;
but the supply so far exceeds the demand that the valley,
running with blood, soon becomes one huge, stinking place
of slaughter. Burton estimated the number of beasts slain,
September, 1853, from five to six thou an l—camels, sheep,
oxen and goats.   Camels, however, are killed only by the
Sherif and chief dignitaries.   It seems as if even this
fanatical people have some inkling of the barbarity of such
waste of life, for when the victim's face is directed towards
the Kaabah, preparatory to the cutting of its throat, instead
of their usual ejaculation, " In the Name of the Most
Merciful God ! " any mention of mercy is carefully omitted.
Still the practice continues ; and as no sanitary precautions
whatever are taken, each pilgrim killing his "offering"
where he likes, and as the basin of Muna somewhat
resembles a volcanic crater, an Aden closed up seawards,
cholera has originated amongst the heaps of decomposition
more than once, and has amply avenged the poor murdered
animals.[1]

At night fireworks were let off and cannon discharged
in front of the Muna mosque. Next day Burton, who had
to spend two nights in this horrible spot, rose before dawn
to visit the " dragging place of the ram," a small enclosure,
situated on the lower declivity of Jebel Sabir, commemorating the events recorded in Genesis, chap. xxii.[2] The usual
marvel is not lacking ; a block of granite in which a huge
gash several inches broad, some feet deep, and completely
splitting the stone in knife-shape, notes the spot where
Abraham's blade fell when forbidden to slay his son. Having
examined this wonder with due decorum our pilgrim after
strolling awhile about the hill in hopes of seeing some of the
peculiarly hideous Hejazi apes, said still to haunt the

---

[1] This odious rite, though a Sunnat or practice of the Prophet, is
not obligatory, its non-observance entailing merely a ten days' fast ; so
Burton was spared having to act butcher.

[2] Moslems claim Ishmael as hero of the story.

heights, returned to his tent, where he passed an atrocious day. The heat was stifling, nought moved in the air except kites and vultures, speckling the bright blue sky; swarms of flies, regardless that their presence was prohibited, and fetid exhalations from the bloody, saturated earth, rendered existence almost intolerable. It was truly a merciful deliverance when Masud's camels appeared at early dawn on Friday, and Burton and his party, every rite performed, were free to return to Meccah and hear the sermon in the Mosque.

This function concludes the Hajj, and though it does not present so picturesque a scene as that on Arafat, it appears from our pilgrim's description to be a very striking spectacle. The vast quadrangle, when he arrived, was crowded with worshippers sitting in long rows and everywhere facing the central black tower: the showy colours of their dresses were not to be surpassed by a garden of brilliant flowers, and such diversity of detail would probably not be seen massed together in any other building on earth. The women, a somewhat sombre group, sat apart in their peculiar place. The Pasha stood on the roof of Zem Zem, surrounded by guards in Nizam uniform. Where the principal Olema stationed themselves, the crowd was thicker; and in the more auspicious spots nought was to be seen but a pavement of heads and shoulders. Nothing seemed to move but a few Dervishes, who, censer in hand, sidled through the rows and received the unsolicited alms of the Faithful.

Apparently in the midst, and raised above the crowd by the tall, pointed pulpit, whose gilt spire flamed in the sun, sat the preacher, a venerable elder with a snowy beard. The style of head-dress called Taylasan covered his turban, white as his robes, and a short staff supported his left hand. Presently he arose, pronounced a few inaudible words, and sat down while a Muezzin, at the foot of the pulpit, recited the call to sermon. Then the

old man stood up to preach.   As he began to speak there
was a deep silence.   Later a general " Amin " was intoned
by the congregation at the conclusion of some long sentence.
And at last, towards the end of the discourse, every third
or fourth word was followed by the simultaneous rise and
fall of thousands of voices.

Burton added: " I have seen the religious ceremonies
of many lands, but nowhere aught so solemn, so impressive
as this."

The few remaining days at Meccah sped pleasantly
enough.   Young Mohammed presented his guest to
numerous friends and acquaintances, who always welcomed him hospitably with pipes and coffee.   The first
question always was, " Who is this pilgrim ? " and more
than once the reply, " An Afghan," elicited the language
of Afghanistan, the Pushtu, which was one of the few
that Burton could not speak.   Of this phenomenon nothing
was thought ; many Afghans settled in India and elsewhere, know not a word of their native tongue, and even
above the Passes some of the townspeople are imperfectly
acquainted with it.   With the Meccans our traveller could
of course converse easily.   They speak Arabic remarkably well, and Persian, Turkish and Hindustani are
generally known.   As regards the character of the inhabitants of this holy city, Burton sums it up as follows :

" The redeeming qualities of the Meccan are his courage,
his *bonhomie*, his manly suavity of manners, his fiery sense
of honour, his strong family affections, his near approach
to what we call patriotism, and his general knowledge ; the
reproach of extreme ignorance which Burckhardt directs
against Meccah has long ago sped to the limbo of things
that were.   The dark half of the picture is pride, bigotry,
scurrility, irreligion, greed of gain, immorality, and prodigal
ostentation."

Our indefatigable traveller made a few more enquiries
as to the possibility of proceeding eastwards, but he heard

on all sides the Bedawin were in such a ferment that they threatened an attack even upon Jeddah. Shaykh Masud, the old camel-owner, from whom Burton parted on excellent terms, seriously advised him to remain at Meccah some months longer, advice which so restless a man was utterly incapable of following. Apparently there was nothing to do but to return to Egypt and spend the remainder of his leave in hard study.

There remained one more curious rite to perform before quitting the Holy City—the Umrah, or Little Pilgrimage. Resuming the Ihram, Burton, with three companions, mounted asses which resembled mules in size and speed, and rode to the Great Mosque, to offer up a short prayer. The party then directed their course towards the open country, and after cantering about three miles, arrived at a small settlement, popularly called El-Umrah. Dismounting, the four men sat on rugs outside a coffee-tent to enjoy the beauty of a moonlight night, and an hour's rest in the sweet desert air, doubly delightful to olfactory organs half-poisoned by the smells of the town. Not so pleasant was a compulsory visit to the principal chapel, an unpretending building, badly lighted, crammed with pilgrims, and offensively close, wherein the night devotions had to be offered up, and gratuities distributed to the guardians and sundry importunate beggars.

And now our Haji's gravity was to be sorely tried. One Abdullah, Mohammed's eldest brother, a staid and highly religious man, who had accompanied Burton for this special purpose, insisted upon performing a vicarious pilgrimage for his friend's parents. Vain was the assurance that they had been strict in the exercises of their faith. Abdullah expected hard coin in exchange for his solicitude regarding the eternal weal of the old folks at home, and would take no denial. So at last he was permitted to act substitute for the "pious pilgrims, Yusuf (Joseph) bin Ahmed and Fatimah bint Yunus." Gravely raising his hands and directing his face to the Kaabah, he intoned, "I do vow this Ihram of Umrah in the Name of Yusuf, son of Ahmed, and Fatimah, daughter of Yunus. Then render it attainable to them, and accept it of them! Bismillah! Allahu Akbar!"

Remounting, the party galloped towards Meccah, shouting Labbayk, and on reaching the city, repaired again to the mosque to observe the Tawaf, or circumambulation of Umrah. This was followed by running seven times between Safa and Marwah, two small eminences with about the same right to be called hills as certain undulations in Rome. Although, on account of Burton's lameness, the rite, supposed to represent Hagar seeking water for her son, was, with the exception of sundry supplications, performed mostly by the donkey, it proved quite fatiguing enough for our pilgrim to feel most thankful when the fourth or last portion of this good deed, for which Allah is said to be grateful, concluded at a barber's shop with a very peculiar prayer: "O Allah, this my Forelock is in Thy Hand, then grant me for every Hair a light on the Resurrection day, O Most Merciful of the Merciful!"

There are various places of pious visitation at Meccah, whereof it is enough to say they are connected with the life of the Prophet. The Jannat el-Maala, or cemetery where Khadijah is buried, differs so little from El-Bakia, and the prayers and prostrations prescribed on entering it are so similar, that any lengthened description would be wearisome. It is open to men on Fridays, to women on Thursdays. Burton found the beggars even more importunate than those at El-Bakia; in fact, they were so utterly distracting, that after a very brief inspection of the tombs, he turned and fled from the sacred enclosure.

And now all the ceremonies of the Moslem's Holy Week concluded, it was time for pilgrims not otherwise detained to prepare for departure. In the house where our traveller lodged, blue china-ware and basketed bottles of Zem Zem water appeared standing in solid columns; and the Hajis occupied themselves in hunting for mementoes of Meccah ; ground-plans, combs, balm, henna, turquoises, coral and mother-of-pearl rosaries. The lower floor was crowded with provision vendors ; and the Turks, who were suffering severely from nostalgia, could talk of nothing except the chance or no chance of a steamer from Jeddah to Suez.

On parting, the hostess, who being a widow and elderly, had often emerged from her retirement for a chat with her son's friend, became quite motherly. She begged our traveller to take care of her boy, who was going as far as the seaport, and then laid friendly but firm hands upon a brass pestle and mortar, which she had long coveted and now insisted on annexing as a keepsake.

Nur preceded his master to Jeddah with the heavy baggage. About twenty-four hours later Burton and young Mohammed, mounted on stalwart Meccan asses, followed in his wake, and after an uneventful journey reached Jeddah safely. It was full time to consider such prosaic matters as $£$ *s. d.*—our pilgrim had exactly tenpence remaining in his pocket, a state of impecuniosity speedily remedied by a visit to the British Consul, who cashed a draft for him, and gave him a most hospitable welcome.

The exit of Mohammed the Meccan was truly ludicrous. This wily youth bought a large quantity of grain with some of Burton's recently acquired money, secured every article not his own on which he could lay his hands, and then departed with marked coolness. For his own sake it behoved him not to go empty away ; but his vanity had been sorely, sorely wounded. For our Haji had taken him one day on board the steamer *Dwarka*, bound for Suez, and perhaps the new sense of security had rendered Burton less careful of preserving his incognito ; anyway, a dark suspicion shot through the Meccan's mind :

" Now I understand," quoth he to Nur before his abrupt disappearance, " your master is a Sahib from India, he hath laughed at our beards ! "

9

CHAPTER VI

BURTON remained in Egypt, writing up his notes, until his leave expired, when he returned to Bombay. But he did not stay long with his regiment, the dry routine of which must have been especially distasteful after the exciting scenes so lately witnessed. His active brain soon sketched out fresh adventures. Africa, not overrun then as now with all sorts and conditions of men, presented a likely field for one who cared little for beaten tracts; and in the extreme east of that Dark Continent lay a forbidden city which afforded peculiar attractions to our Haji—Harar, the capital of Somaliland.

It was not difficult to obtain the necessary furlough. The Court of Directors had for some years past lent a willing ear to the plan of a Somali expedition. Berberah, the true key of the Red Sea, and only safe harbour for shipping from Suez to Guardafui, had long been coveted by John Company; and though many an obstacle had prevented the Indian Government from assuming control over this coast, our establishment of a Protectorate, in 1884, proves the wise foresight of such men as Lord Elphinstone, Sir Charles Malcolm, and others of their day. So when Burton placed himself in communication with the Governor of Bombay and requested permission to pave the way for a thorough exploration of the Eastern Horn of Africa, leave was readily granted, October, 1854.

With certain limitations. Our traveller's original plan had been to set forth with three companions, Lieutenants Speke, Herne, and Stroyan, use Berberah as a base of operations, thence move westward to Harar, and, finally, in a south-westerly direction towards Zanzibar. This being considered too risky, anyhow, for a beginning, Burton then proposed to make the geography and commerce his sole objects, including, of course, all relating to the capital city. And, since the authorities had judged it wiser for the four men to divide their forces, Lieutenants Herne and Stroyan were ordered to make their way to Berberah, enquire into the caravan lines, explore the maritime mountains, and make a variety of meteorological and other observations as a prelude to more extensive research, while Lieutenant Speke was directed to land at a small harbour on the coast, trace the watershed of the Wady Nogal, and buy horses and camels for the use of a future and larger expedition.

For Burton was reserved the post of danger—the task of penetrating the mysterious capital. In fact, he alone of the four men was able to attempt the feat, owing to his knowledge of Arabic, and to his having performed the Hajj. The region he intended to traverse, the town he intended to visit, were previously known by only the vaguest reports. No European had yet entered Harar. The more adventurous Abyssinian travellers, Salt and Stuart, Krapf and Isenberg, Barker and Rochet, not to mention divers Roman Catholic missionaries, had attempted it in vain. The Moslem ruler and his bigoted people threatened death to the infidel who ventured within their walls, some negro Merlin having, it is said, read decline and fall in the first footsteps of the Frank.

So Burton utilised his title of Haji by breaking the guardian spell. Since the Egyptian and Abyssinian occupation of the city, many travellers have followed in his steps; and they tell us that the ancient metropolis of a once mighty race is now altered almost beyond recognition But until it passes into the hands of some European power, any changes are likely to be for the worse rather than the better.

On the 29th October, 1854, Haji Abdullah, disguised as

a Moslem merchant, left Aden in a small sailing ship for
Zeila, on the Somali coast.   Three servants accompanied
him—El-Hammal, or the porter, a sergeant in the Aden
police, Guled, another policeman, and one Abdy Abokr, a
Widad or Moslem hedge-priest, who, from his smattering
of learning and prodigious rascality, was nicknamed " End of
Time."   After an uneventful voyage of two days, the
Sahalat entered the creek which gives so much trouble to
native craft, being exposed to almost all the winds of
heaven.   Zeila has no harbour, and even a vessel of 250
tons cannot approach within a mile of the landing-place.
At noon our party sighted their destination, the normal
African port, viz. a strip of sulphur yellow sand, with a
deep blue dome above, and a foreground of darkish indigo.
Its buildings, raised high by refraction, rose apparently
from the bosom of the deep.   Whitewashed houses and
minarets — Zeila boasted of six mosques, including the
Jami or cathedral—peered above a low line of brown wall
flanked with round towers.

Bad news awaited the travellers.   The crew of a little
bark which came scudding up the creek roared out that
friendly relations between the Amir of Harar and the
Governor of Zeila had been interrupted, the road through
the Eesa Somal was closed, all strangers had been expelled
from the capital by its chief, and, yet more serious, small-
pox was raging with such violence in the town, that the
Galla peasantry would allow neither ingress nor egress.
Musing over these fresh difficulties, Burton stepped into a
cock boat, landed at the northern gate, and after array-
ing himself in clean garments, presented his respects to
Governor El-Haji Sharmarkay.

The two men had met before at Aden, where Sharmarkay had received from the authorities strong injunctions
concerning the personal safety of their envoy.   Always
friendly to the British, he had been badly wounded in the
left arm while defending the lives of the crew of the brig

Mary Anne, wrecked on the Somali coast in 1825. As might be expected, his reception of Burton was most gracious; and after half an hour's palaver in a sort of cow-house, which, with peculiar taste, he preferred to his solid two-storied abode, he conducted his guest through the streets of Zeila to a substantial building of coralline, plastered with mud and whitewash.

A room was speedily prepared under his directions, in a style of rude luxury. The floor was spread with mats, cushions were propped here and there against the wall, and a cot, covered with Persian rugs and satin pillows, was added, in case the stranger might prefer sleeping indoors to passing the night on the flat terraced roof. Here, after supper Sharmarkay considerately left his guest to rest, and the latter by no means loth, soon fell asleep while listening to the familiar sounds of El-Islam, the chant of the Muezzin, the loudly intoned Amin and Allaho Akbar, from a neighbouring mosque.

Burton had plenty to do at Zeila. A journey of 180 miles to an unknown city, through a strange country, required an enormous amount of preparation and forethought. Twenty-six days were spent in buying camels, interviewing guides, sending for mules, arranging all the minutiæ of travelling in a land where money was hardly known and yet where everything had to be heavily paid for. Of course these wearisome preliminaries were interspersed with many delays which entailed hours of enforced leisure. These were spent much as follows. Devotions on the terrace at dawn (our Haji had to keep up his character for piety); breakfast at 6 a.m. of roast mutton and grain cakes; then visitors, who swarmed in, careless whether their presence was desired or not. At 11 a.m. dinner, consisting of mutton stews, maize cakes, sometimes fish, and generally curds and milk, was provided by good Sharmarkay. Coffee and pipes followed, and presently more callers trooped in to stare at or jabber to the stranger. These intruders were

either the *élite* of Zeila, such as the governor's son, the port
captain, or some of the principal merchants, people whose
society was bearable; or the Somal, who yelled, combed
their hair, cleaned their teeth with sticks, in short made
themselves so unpleasantly at home that Burton must have
often longed to kick them out. After the departure of these
free and easy folk he often strolled to a little mosque near
the shore, where games resembling backgammon were
played, or the Somal shot at a mark, threw the javelin,
and engaged in gymnastic exercises; at other times he
walked to the southern gate of Zeila and amused himself
by watching a camp of Bedawin stationed just outside.
While returning punctually before sunset, an hour when
the keys were carried to Governor Sharmarkay, he heard
the call to prayer, and noticed with some surprise that the
Somal, unlike the children of El-Hejaz, generally failed to
respond. Then came supper, followed by an hour or two
spent on his terraced roof to enjoy the view of the distant
Tajurrah hills and the white moonbeams sleeping on the
nearer sea.

It is curious to read in the book,[1] of which I am giving
a sketch, how Burton used to treat the wild people amongst
whom he travelled to stories from the "Arabian Nights."
These tales—translated by him thirty years later—were
always favourites, owing to the wonderful insight they afford
into the character of Orientals. Unfortunately for the bulk
of English readers, the literal translations are suitable only
for students, and the extensively bowdlerised ones in many
instances turn the stories into nonsense.

But the Somal were not easily shocked. In fact, like
most Africans they seemed decidedly given to levity. When
reproached with gambling and asked why they persisted in
a practice forbidden by the Prophet, they frankly answered,
" Because we like it." And one night, whilst encamped

---

[1] "First Footsteps in East Africa, or an Exploration of Harar."
Longman, Brown, Green and Longmans. 1 vol. 1856.

amongst the Eesa tribe, Burton overheard an old woman suffering from toothache groaning forth at intervals throughout the night the somewhat impious refrain : " O Allah, may Thy teeth ache like mine ! may Thy gums be sore as mine ! " Still they observe their Friday, as may be seen from the following description of their weekly assembling of themselves together :

" At half-past eleven a kettle-drum sounds a summons to the Jami or Cathedral. It is only an old barn, rudely plastered and whitewashed, posts or columns of artless masonry support the low roof, and the smallness of the windows, or rather air-holes, renders its dreary length unpleasantly hot. There is no pulpit ; the only ornament is a rude representation of the Meccan mosque, nailed, like a pot-house print, to the wall ; and the sole articles of furniture are ragged mats and old boxes, containing tattered chapters of the Koran in greasy bindings. I enter with a servant carrying a prayer-carpet, encounter the stare of three hundred pair of eyes belonging to parallel rows of squatters, recite the customary prayer in honour of the mosque, placing sword and rosary before me, and then, taking up a Koran, read the Cave Chapter (No. 18) loud and twangingly. At mid-day the Muezzin inside the mosque standing before the Khatib repeats the call to prayer, which the congregation, sitting upon their shins and feet, intone after him. This ended, all present stand up, and recite, every man for himself, a prayer of Sunnat or Example, concluding with the blessing of the Prophet and the Salam over each shoulder to all brother believers. The Khatib then ascends a hole in the wall, which serves for a pulpit, and thence addresses us with ' The peace be upon you, and the mercy of Allah and his benediction,' to which we respond through the Muezzin, ' And upon you be peace and Allah's mercy.' After sundry other religious formulæ and their replies, our Khatib rises and preaches El-Waaz, or the advice sermon. Though also a Kazi, or Judge, he makes several blunders in

his Arabic, and he reads his sermons, a thing never done in
El-Islam except by the *modicè docti*.   The discourse over,
our clerk, who is, if possible, worse than the curate, repeats
the form of call termed El-Ikamah ; then, entering the
Mihrab or niche, he recites the two-bow Friday litany with,
and in front of the congregation. . . . This public prayer
concluded, many people leave the mosque ; a few remain
for more prolonged devotions."

Towards the end of the month spent at Zeila Burton
fretted sadly at the continual delays.   Like most Orientals,
Sharmarkay, though willing enough to help, procrastinated,
and when the anxious traveller showed signs of losing
temper, all the effect produced was a paroxysm of talk.
However, at last, an Abban or protector was secured, one
Raghe, a petty Eesa chief, who, for the consideration of four
cloths of Cutch canvas and six of coarse American sheeting,
was induced to accompany the caravan to the frontier of
his clan, distant about fifty miles.   He promised, besides,
to introduce it to the Gudabirsi tribe, who in their turn
would pass it on to the Gerad or Prince of the Girhi, and
he, in due time, to his kinsman, the Amir of Harar.   This
matter settled, two women cooks and other servants were
engaged, five camels procured, and on the arrival of some
fine mules, ordered from Tajurrah about three weeks before,
all was ready for a start.

Raghe did not enter on his new duties very cheerfully ;
on the contrary, he warned his employer to prepare for
disaster.   The citizens of Zeila, persuaded that their guest
was tired of life, croaked in a similar strain.   The natives
up country, they declared, were savage, treacherous, cruel
exceedingly ; there were constant blood feuds between the
tribes, and massacres were incessant.   For these people are
not so anxious to plunder as to ennoble themselves by
taking life.   Every man hangs to his saddle-bow an ostrich
feather, and the moment his javelin has drawn blood, he
sticks it into his tufty poll with as much satisfaction as an

English officer feels when attaching a medal to his jacket.
Nor is the appearance of the Somal engaging in their
native haunts. Carefully selected, well scrubbed up, they
look picturesque enough in a fancy show in England, but
in the wilder parts of Somaliland their uncombed mop-like
heads, their scowling faces, their solitary garment—never
clean—would disconcert the most inveterate lover of the
noble savage. That the Eesa, the Gudabirsi, the Girhi, and
the Galla have their good points will be seen later; but
their virtues were kept strictly in the back-ground by the
ravens with whom Burton was surrounded.

Early November 27th, 1854, the mules and all the paraphernalia of travel stood ready at his door. The camels,
growling loudly, submitted perforce to their burdens;
and at 3 p.m. our little caravan sallied forth with an
escort of Arab matchlock-men, the Governor and his son.
After half an hour's march, adieus were exchanged, and
the soldiers fired a parting volley.

It was a curious company. Foremost strutted Raghe,
in all the bravery of Abbanship. Bareheaded, clothed in
Tobe[1] and slippers, a long horn-handled dagger strapped
round his waist, he grasped in his right hand a ponderous
spear, while his left forearm supported a round shield of
battered hide. He also carried a prayer-carpet of tanned
leather, and a wicker bottle for religious ablutions. Even
more comical were the two cooks, Samaweda and Aybla,
buxom dames of about thirty. Each looked like three
women rolled into one; a bustle as an article of attire
would have been utterly superfluous. Fat notwithstanding, they proved invaluable. During the march they
carried pipes and tobacco—for other folks' delectation,
not their own—they led and flogged the camels, adjusted
the burdens, which were continually falling awry; and,
most wonderful of all, never asked for a ride. At every

---

[1] A cotton sheet, an article which, like the Highland plaid, can
be worn in many ways.

halt it was they who unloaded the cattle, pitched the tent, cooked the food, and then bivouacked outside. No more about these culinary treasures; it makes an English housewife green with envy to think of them!

Strung together by their tails, five camels paced along under their burdens—bales of American sheeting, Cutch canvas, with indigo-dyed stuff, slung along the animals' sides, and neatly sewn up in a case of matting to keep off dust and rain—a cow's hide, which served as a couch, covering the whole. They carried besides a load of indifferent Mocha dates for the natives, and another of better quality for the expedition, half a hundredweight of coarse Surat tobacco, and two boxes of beads and trinkets. The private provisions were represented by about 300 lbs. of rice, a large pot full of flesh sun-dried and fried in ghee, salt, clarified butter, tea, coffee, sugar, a box of biscuits, Arab sweetmeats, and a little turmeric. A simple *batterie de cuisine*, sundry skins full of potable water, and a heavy box of ammunition, completed the outfit. The cost of all this, including the passage money from Aden, seems singularly small—£149.

Alongside the camels rode Burton's three attendants, attired in the pink of Somali fashion. Their fuzzy wigs shone with grease, their tobes had just been washed, their shields newly recovered with canvas cloth, and the spears poised over the right shoulder, freshly scraped and polished. Last of all came Burton, mounted on a snowy mule, which, with its bright-coloured Arab pad and wrapper cloth, looked fairly dignified; a double-barrelled gun lay across his lap, and a rude pair of holsters of native make contained his Colt's six-shooters.

The route to Harar chosen on this occasion was a winding road, which passes south along the coast to the nearest hills, and thence strikes south-westward among the Gudabirsi and Girhi Somal, which extend within sight of the city. The direct line is about 186 miles in length, of which about 150 are over the plains or desert, the remaining 36 being a remarkable ascent until the town is reached, at an altitude of over 7,000 feet above sea-level. But good Sharmarkay had objected to the nearer route on account of a recent blood feud with one of the tribes, and Burton had to respect the old man's wishes. Marching as described, the caravan made its way over a level country, here dry, there muddy, across boggy creeks, broad watercourses, and warty flats of black mould powdered with nitrous salt and bristling with salsolaceous vegetation. Such, between the mountains and the sea, is the general formation of the plain, whose breadth in a direct line may measure from forty-five to forty-eight miles. Near the first zone of hills the land becomes more fertile; thorns and acacias of various kinds appear in clumps, and after the monsoon it is covered with rich grass, a favourite haunt for game, as our British sportsmen have now discovered.

At eight p.m. our party reached a halting-place, where they lighted fires and passed the night. Early dawn found them *en route* through a Somali Arcadia, whose sole flaws were salt water and simoom. Whistling shepherds carried in their arms the younglings of the herds, or, spear in hand, drove to pasture long, regular lines of camels, that waved their vulture-like heads and arched their necks to playfully bite their neighbours' faces, humps, and hind legs. The huge brutes were led by a patriarch to whose throat hung a wooden bell, and most of them were followed by colts in every stage of infancy. Sheep with snowy fleeces and jetty faces flocked in crowds over the yellow plain ; and herds of goats resembling deer were driven by hide-clad children to the bush.

In the centre of this pastoral scene stood a kraal called Gudingaras, about twenty miles from Zeila. Here the two women rigged up a very cosy wigwam and made everything snug for the night. Before turning in, Burton astonished the natives by shooting a vulture on the wing, which not very remarkable feat so impressed a Nestor of the tribe, that he begged for a charm to cure his sick camel, and having obtained it, blessed the magician in a speech of portentous length, and then spat upon the party for luck. At Kuranyali, a little further on, the Abban, being amongst his own people, waxed so lavishly generous with his employer's goods, that there was no small difficulty in persuading the wild men to let the caravan depart.

Leaving the coast they now struck south-westward into the interior, across a low plain, towards a blue strip of hill on the far horizon. One evening a scare arose; they had come upon the trail of a large cavalcade supposed to belong to a rival and hostile tribe. The celebrated footprint seen by Robinson Crusoe affected him not more powerfully than did this dreadful discovery the poor timid Somal; and certainly they had reason for their fears, nine men and two women being a small party to contend against two hundred horsemen. Raghe kept well to the front, ready for a run. Burton, whistling with anger, asked his attendants what had frightened them—he had to be stern, else they might have all decamped and never been found again. The hedge-priest, in a hollow voice, replied: "Verily, O pilgrim, whoso seeth the track seeth the foe!" and, by way of raising yet higher the general spirits, proceeded to quote the dreary lines:

> " Man is but a handful of dust,
> And life is a violent storm."

Fortunately, the riders had bigger game to stalk; and about half an hour afterwards rough ravines, with sharp and thorny descents, a place of safety, where horsemen rarely venture, was reached by the terrified little band. Soon came fresh troubles. On quitting the maritime plain, and on entering the Ghauts, threshold of the Ethiopian highlands, the Somal were again dismayed, this time by the change of temperature. Stiff with cold, with chattering teeth, the wretched creatures stood and squatted all but inside the huge fires which had to be kindled to keep them alive.

Strange sights enlivened the march. Strangest of all, perhaps, the hills of the white ants. Owing to their extraordinary labours, the land in places resembled a Turkish cemetery on a grand scale; in others, it looked like a city in ruins. In some parts, the pillar-like erections were truncated, whilst many, veiled by trees and overrun with gay creepers, suggested sylvan altars. Generally they were conical, and varied in height from four to twelve feet. They were to be counted by hundreds. Burton remarked these curiosities for the first time in the Wady Darkaynlay; in the interior they are larger and longer than in the maritime regions.

Far inferior in ingenuity were the wigwams of the natives—huts like old beehives, about five feet high by six in diameter. The material was a framework of sticks, bent and hardened; these were planted in the ground, tied together, and covered with mats. Hides were spread on the top during the monsoon, and little heaps of earth raised around to keep out wind and rain. Many a British pig could boast of a more comfortable and salubrious abode.

On the 10th December Burton was obliged to halt for a day or two at a kraal belonging to the Gudabirsi tribe. Bad water, violent fluctuations of temperature—51° in the morning, 107° at midday—and incessant fatigue had so seriously affected his health that, very unwillingly, he had to give himself a short rest. The sick stranger created a prodigious sensation; all the population flocked to see him, darkening his hut with nodding wigs and staring faces. Men, women and children appeared in crowds, bringing milk and ghee, meat and diink, everything they imagined might tend to restore his health; and truly, if Burton remembered the bugbear tales croaked by the citizens of Zeila, he must have been surprised at the humanity of beings represented as little better than fiends. His attack

—one of colic—soon passed off, but only to return with greater violence a week or two later.

At this settlement Raghe, who on the whole had performed his duties satisfactorily, gave over the charge of the caravan to six Gudabirsi, sons of a noted chief. Beuh, the eldest brother and spokesman of the party, proved more valiant in speech than action; but he was a trustworthy guide, and, under his direction, a little further on our traveller first descried the dark hills of Harar looming beyond the Harawwah Valley.

On the 23rd December the little band entered the Barr or Prairie of Marar, one of those long strips of plain which diversify the Somali country. As this was neutral ground, where the Eesa and other tribes met to plunder when so disposed, it was deemed advisable to join forces with a small native caravan, which carried next to nothing worth stealing. However, no robbers appeared, and, barring a bloodless adventure with a lion, and the distant sight of a prairie fire, a broad sheet of flame which swept down a hill and for awhile threatened to ignite the entire Barr, nothing occurred to agitate even Somali nerves. All safely reached Wilensi, a long, straggling village belonging to the Gerad Adan, a powerful chief of the Girhi highlands, and, as already said, kinsman of the Amir of Harar.

The Gerad was away, but one of his wives ordered two huts to be prepared for the strangers' reception. This princess, a tall woman, with a light complexion, handsomely dressed in a large Harar tobe, received Burton in person, and supplied him liberally with boiled beef, pumpkins, and Jowari cakes. The inhabitants of Wilensi proved as friendly as their mistress, rather too friendly, in fact, for the result of their hospitality was that the caravan began to split up. Such dismal tales concerning Harar and its neighbourhood were circulated by the natives that some of the travellers declined point blank to proceed any further. Samaweda and Aybla hearing of small pox in the city, feared for their sable charms, while Beuh and a one-eyed man, nicknamed the Kalendar, utterly refused to stir from a place where they were so comfortable.

Burton, as usual, paid small attention to these stories, and after a short rest pushed on with his remaining attendants to Sagharrah, a snug high-fenced village—in the mountainous regions the people live in more solidly constructed abodes than on the plains—built against a hill-side. Here he met the Gerad, who for motives of his own received him politely. This scheming and ambitious man had set his heart on building a fort to control the country's trade, and rival or overawe the city, and he hoped the stranger might assist him with plans and advice. Nor did he neglect the main chance. Whatever he saw he asked for ; and, after receiving a sword, a Koran, a turban, a satin waistcoat, about seventy tobes and a similar proportion of indigo-dyed stuff, he begged for a silver-hilted sword, one thousand dollars, two sets of silver bracelets, twenty guns, and a scarlet coat embroidered with gold. True, he promised in return horses, mules and ivory, but his memory conveniently failed just when the moment arrived for keeping his word.

Again was Burton seized with internal pains, this time so severe as to threaten his life. For forty-eight hours he lay in his hut almost unable to move. And again the wild people treated him with the greatest kindness. The Gerad's handsome wife on hearing the news sacrificed a sheep as an expiatory offering ; the Gerad sent as far as Harar for millet beer ; even the Galla Christians who flocked in to see the sick Moslem, wept for the evil fate which had brought him so far from his fatherland. But to expire of an ignoble colic was not to be thought of, and a firm resolution to live effected its object.

On the 1st of January, 1855, our traveller feeling easier, rose, clothed himself in his Arab best, and requested a palaver with the chief. The two men retired to a quiet

place behind the village, where Burton read aloud a letter
of introduction from the Governor of Zeila. The Gerad
seemed much pleased by the route through his country
having been preferred to the more direct line, renewed the
subject of his fort, and declared he had now found the
builder, for his eldest daughter had dreamed the night before
that this Moslem merchant would settle in the land. The
project was discussed and matters were proceeding most
satisfactorily when a disagreeable interruption occurred.

Suddenly five men, envoys of the Amir of Harar, who
had been sent to settle some weighty question of blood
money, rode up to the Gerad. After sitting with the latter
about half an hour, during which time they inspected our
traveller's attendants and animals with solemn countenances,
and asked sundry pertinent questions concerning his business
in these parts, they drew the chief aside and informed him
that his guest was not one who bought and sold, but an
enemy whose only design was to spy out the wealth of the
land. They ended by coolly proposing to convey the whole
party as prisoners to Harar. Unwilling to lose his prospec-
tive engineer, and feeling safe on his own ground, the
Gerad curtly refused, and the five men having concluded
the business on which they came, mounted their gaily
caparisoned mules and presently departed.

But, as it was plain enough they might return with an
armed force behind them, some decided step had to be
taken at once. From sundry insinuations Burton believed
the envoys suspected him to be a Turk, a nationality more
hated at Harar than any other. After weighty consideration he determined to declare himself a British subject, to
start immediately before further mischief were done, and to
deliver in person to the Amir a letter from the Political
Resident at Aden. A few lines addressed to Lieutenant
Herne directing him how to act in case of a disaster were
left with " End of Time," who, too much of a poltroon to
proceed, remained at Sagharrah. Most of the luggage

kept the Widad company, a single ass carrying only what was absolutely indispensable.. And thus, amidst the lamentations of the villagers who declared that their departing guests would shortly be all dead men, Burton, the two policemen, and an escort of three Girhi started on their perilous enterprise.

Two o'clock in the afternoon next day found them within a couple of miles of the city. There on a crest of a hill it stood, a long, sombre line strikingly contrasting with the whitewashed towns of the East. The spectacle, materially speaking, was a disappointment; nothing conspicuous appeared except two grey minarets of rude shape ; but the near prospect of penetrating that grim pile of stones, which had proved impregnable to all but himself, must have made our traveller's heart beat high with exultation.

Spurring their mules, our party advanced at a long trot. The soil on both sides of the path was rich and red ; limes, plantains, and pomegranates grew plentifully in the gardens, for which the neighbourhood of Harar was then famous. In places appeared plantations of coffee, bastard saffron, and the graceful Kat, a drug largely used in these parts as a pleasant excitant, its effects resembling those of green tea without the consequent nervousness. About half a mile eastward of the town they came to a brook, called Jalah, or the Coffee Water. Burton's four companions (one of the Girhi had turned tail) plunged into the water, and while they splashed about like lively seals, their employer retired to the wayside and sketched the city.

A short ride then brought them before the dark defences of Harar. Groups of citizens loitered about the large gateway, or sat chatting near a ruined tomb. One of the Girhi, who acted as interpreter, advanced to the entrance, accosted a warder conspicuous by his wand of office, and, in Burton's name, requested the honour of an audience with the Amir. Whilst the man sped on his

10

errand, Burton and his attendants sat at the foot of a round
bastion, where they were scrutinised, derided, and catechised by a little mob of both sexes, especially by that
conventionally termed the fair.

In about half an hour the warder returned, and ordered
the strangers to cross the threshold. They guided their
mules with difficulty along a main street, a narrow, uphill
lane, with rocks cropping out from a surface more irregular
than a Perote pavement, until they arrived within a
hundred yards of a gate constructed of holcus sticks, which
opened into the courtyard of this African Saint James',
when all dismounted, the Amir's abode having to be
approached with due ceremony. Leading their animals,
our party entered, marched down the royal enclosure, and
were told to halt under a tree in the left corner, close to a
low erection of rough stone. Clanking of fetters within
suggested a state prison.

A crowd of Gallas, a powerful tribe near Harar, were
lounging about or squatting in the shade of the palace
walls. The chiefs were conspicuous by their zinc armlets,
composed of thin spiral circlets, closely joined, and extending almost from the wrist to the elbow. All appeared
to enjoy peculiar privileges, such as carrying arms or
wearing sandals. They took little notice of the strangers,
so our traveller had leisure to inspect a spot about which
many and vastly divergent accounts were current. The
palace itself was a mere shed, a single-storied, windowless
barn of rough stone and reddish clay, with a thin coat of
whitewash over the entrance. The courtyard, measuring
about eighty yards long by thirty in breadth, was irregularly
shaped, and surrounded by low buildings; in the centre
stood a circle of masonry, against which reclined sundry
doors, which had been removed and confiscated in consequence of the evil deeds of their proprietors.

At last the guide returned from within, motioned Burton
to doff his slippers at a stone step, or rather line, about

twelve feet distant from the palace wall. Our Haji kicked off his shoes, and in another moment strode into the chief's presence.

Sultan Ahmed bin Sultan Abibakr sat in a dark room with whitewashed walls, to which hung—significant decorations—rusty matchlocks and polished fetters. His appearance was that of a little Indian Rajah; an etiolated youth about twenty-four or twenty-five years of age, plain and thin-bearded, with a yellow complexion, wrinkled brows, and protruding eyes. His dress was a flowing robe of crimson cloth edged with snowy fur, and a narrow white turban tightly twisted round a tall conical cap of red velvet, like the old Turkish headgear of our painters. His throne consisted of a raised cot about five feet long, with back and sides supported by a dwarf railing. Being an invalid, he rested his elbow on a pillow, under which appeared the hilt of a Cutch sabre. Ranged in double line stood the "court," his cousins and nearest relations, with their right arms bared, after the custom of Abyssinia.

Burton entered exclaiming " Peace be upon ye ! " to which Ahmed replied graciously, and extended a hand bony and yellow as a kite's claw. Two chamberlains, stepping forward, assisted the stranger to bend low over H. H.'s fingers, which, however, he could not persuade himself to kiss. Burton's attendants then took their turn, and, these preliminaries concluded, the party were led to a mat in front of the Amir, who directed towards them an inquisitive stare.

In answer to enquiries concerning his health he shook his head captiously, and after a pause asked what might be the stranger's errand. Burton drew from his pocket the Political Resident's letter; but Ahmed, who of course could not read English, merely glanced at it, laid it on the couch, and demanded further explanations. Our Haji then represented in Arabic that he had come from Aden, bearing the compliments of his Daulah or Governor, that he had entered

Harar to see the light of His Highness's countenance, and concluded his little speech with allusions to the friendship formerly existing between his nation and the deceased chief, Abubakr.

Much to Burton's relief the Amir smiled, and after whispering for awhile to his treasurer, made a polite sign to the party to retire. Their *baisemain* repeated, they backed out of the audience-chamber with far lighter hearts than when they entered it. Marshalled by a squad of His Highness's bodyguard, they were conducted to a second palace, situated about a hundred yards from the first, and were told to consider it their home. And soon a further proof of royal favour appeared in the shape of a slight repast, forwarded from the chief's kitchen—a dish of holcus cakes, soaked in sour milk, and thickly powdered with red pepper, the salt of this inland region.

Hardly was the frugal meal concluded before the treasurer entered charged with Ahmed's commands that the strangers should call without delay on his Vizier, the Gerad Mohammed. Under his guidance Burton proceeded to an abode distinguished by its external streak of whitewash, at Harar a royal and vizierial distinction, where he found a venerable man, whose benevolent countenance belied sundry evil reports current about him at Zeila. He received our Haji courteously, and enquired his object in excellent Arabic. The answer of course was couched much in the same terms as that to the Amir, plus that it was the wish of the English to re-establish friendly communications and commercial intercourse with the city. Some interchange of civilities ensued, and then Burton withdrew to his palatial quarters for the night. Before retiring to rest, he sent a six-barrelled revolver as a present to his august host, explaining its use to the bearer, and then prepared to make himself as comfortable as conditions permitted. Few men could have slept very soundly beneath the roof of a bigoted prince whose least word was

death, amongst a people who detested foreigners, and who,
save for the title of Haji, would certainly never have
permitted a Frank to cross their inhospitable threshold
unpunished.

During their ten days' stay our adventurous party
were called upon by a strange medley of nationalities—a
Magrabi from Fez, who commanded the Amir's bodyguard,
a thoroughbred Persian, a boy from Meccah, a Muscat man,
a native of Suez, a citizen of Damascus, and many others.
The Somal, of course mustered in force, and among them
the Hammal found relations and friends. When free from
visitors Burton explored the town. It has changed much
since 1855, after its occupation first by the Egyptians, then
the Abyssinians; for, whereas he describes it as a long,
sombre line of houses, topped by two grey minarets, later
travellers speak of it as a great yellow city, crowned by
a whitewashed, circular church, erected on the site of the
old Jami, one minaret of which alone remains. In 1855
it measured one mile long, by half that breadth. The
material of both houses and walls consisted of rough stones,
the granites and sandstones of the hills, cemented with
clay; but the buildings were so mean as to be little better
than flat-roofed cabins, with doors composed of a single
plank. The only spacious erection was the Jami, a long
barn-like structure, with broken-down gates and two
minarets of truncated conoid shape. Narrow lanes, strewn
with rubbish heaps, upon which reposed packs of mangy
dogs, served as streets; while gardens, which give to most
Eastern settlements so green and pleasant an appearance,
seemed to flourish only outside the town. Harar then
abounded in mosques and in graveyards crammed with
tombs; she was proud of her learning, her sanctity, and
her dead; and these, except perhaps the climate, which
resembles that of Tuscany, completed the scanty list of her
attractions.

No long interval elapsed before another summons

arrived to wait upon the Vizier, who on this occasion was transacting business at the palace. Sword in hand, and followed by two servants, Burton walked to the royal precincts, and entering a ground floor room on the right of and close to the audience hall, found the minister reclining upon a large daïs covered with Persian carpets. He was surrounded by six of his brother councillors, two wearing turbans, the rest with bare and shaven heads. The grandees were solacing themselves in the intervals of their labours by eating kat, or, as it was there called, yát. One of the party prepared the tenderest leaves, another pounded the plant with a little water; of this paste a bit was handed to each person, who, rolling it into a ball, dropped it into his mouth.

The Gerad, after sundry polite inquiries, seated Burton next his right hand on the daïs, where, while the business of the day was being despatched, the guest ate kat and fingered a rosary. Perhaps the sight of this article in a stranger's hand stimulated the elders of Harar to keep up their reputation for sanctity; anyway, no sooner had they settled the affairs upon which they had been engaged when Burton entered, than the whole company waxed pious and controversial. One old man took up a large volume, and began to recite a long blessing on the Prophet; at the end of each period all intoned the response, "Allah, bless our Lord Mohammed with his Progeny and his Companions, one and all." This exercise, which lasted half an hour, afforded our Haji the much-desired opportunity of making a good impression. The reader, misled by a marginal reference, happened to say, "Angels, Men, and Genii"; the Gerad found written, "Men, Angels, and Genii." Opinions were divided as to the order of things, when the stranger explained that human nature, which amongst Moslems is not held a little lower than the angelic, ranked highest, because of it were created prophets, apostles, and saints. His theology won general approbation and a few kinder glances from the elders.

Prayers over, a chamberlain entered and whispered a few words to the Vizier, who rose, donned a white sleeve-less cloak, and disappeared. Presently Burton was bidden to the Amir's presence. Entering ceremoniously as before, he was motioned by the Prince to sit near the Vizier, who occupied a Persian rug to the right of the throne. After sundry enquiries concerning various changes that had taken place at Aden, Ahmed suddenly produced Burton's letter, eyed it suspiciously, and demanded an explanation of its contents. The translation into Arabic rendered, the Vizier asked whether this British subject intended to buy and sell at Harar—a natural question enough as the start from Zeila as a Moslem merchant was probably well known. The reply ran : " We are no buyers nor sellers ; we have become your guests to pay our respects to the Amir, whom may Allah preserve ! " [1] This appearing satisfactory, Burton, who had seen as much of Harar as he desired, expressed a hope that the Prince would be pleased to dismiss him soon, as the air of the town was too dry for his constitution, and, worse still, his attendants were in danger of catching the small-pox. Ahmed, ever chary of words, bent towards his Vizier, who briefly ejaculated, " The reply will be vouchsafed." And with this ambiguous answer the audience ended.

The medley of nationalities in this city has been already noticed, but the most curious people were the Harari them-selves. The small population of 8,000 souls was then a distinct race, having its own tongue, unintelligible to any save the citizens and nearest tribes. The men pock-marked and scarred with various skin diseases, were most unprepossessing. Generally their complexions were a yellowish brown, their beards short and scanty, their hands and feet enormous. However, their dress, a mixture of Arab and Abyssinian, had the merit of picturesqueness, and helped to conceal their ugly figures.

---

[1] In conversational Arabic " we " is used without affectation.

The women, on the contrary, were decidedly handsome. Burton mentions with admiration their small heads, regular profiles, straight noses, and even well-shaped mouths. But sadly free and easy were those dames of Harar, with their gaudy clothes, their hair gathered up in two large bunches behind the ears and covered with dark blue muslin. They chewed tobacco, they indulged in intoxicating drinks, and their lack of modesty was so glaring that a public flogging was occasionally indispensable. Perhaps they have improved since those naughty days—the circular Abyssinian Church *may* have reformed their morals.

Amongst the crowd who flocked to see the stranger, Shaykh Jami, one of the Ulema, proved most friendly. Jami had acquired a reputation as a peace-policy man and an ardent Moslem. Though an imperfect Arabic scholar, he was remarkably well read in religious lore; even the Meccans had shown their respect for him by kissing his hand during his pilgrimage to their sanctuary. His peace-preserving character was assumed only after the first flush of youth and enthusiasm had departed, for he commenced his travels with the firm intention of murdering the British Resident at Aden. Struck with the justice of our rule, he changed his mind in time, offered El-Islam to the officer, and prayed fervently for his conversion. . . . Eminently characteristic was it of Burton, reminding one comically enough of his brushes with the Oxford dons, that during the very first visit he paid this scholar he corrected him in a matter of history. A temporary huffiness ensued, but, fortunately, the good little theologian bore no malice.

The days became somewhat monotonous, as without her ruler's permission nobody might venture outside Harar, and Burton had already exhausted her limited list of lions. At dawn he and his men attended to the mules, and then discussed a meal of boiled beef and holcus scones, supplemented by plantains, stewed fowls, and other dainties presented by visitors. After breakfast, the house filled with people, noon was usually followed by a little privacy, the callers departing to dinner and siesta. Later the rooms refilled and the motley crew dispersed only at sunset. Before everyone retired for the night the mules had to be fed again—after a fashion—for the Amir's provisions for man and beast were remarkable neither for quantity nor quality, and the hungry animals more than once attempted a stampede from the courtyard wherein they were tethered.

Meanwhile the envoys, inimical from the beginning, were not idle. Alarming rumours began to circulate. It was reported that Burton and his men were transacting business for Haji Sharmarkay, the bugbear of Harar. The Vizier became uneasy and showed his feelings. Truly it was time to depart.

Shaykh Jami now proved a valuable ally. If not precisely in the minister's confidence he thoroughly understood how to serve both sides. Perceiving matters were becoming strained, and that for the sake of the public peace it would be wise to speed these parting guests, he begged the Gerad to allow our party to escort him on a short trip which he wished to take in the neigbourhood. The astute old Vizier seized upon this excellent pretext for ridding Harar of suspicious characters; and the result of Shaykh Jami's application was a hasty summons to the *levée* room. There Burton, with his usual presence of mind, clinched matters. He had perceived the minister was suffering from chronic bronchitis, and he now promised on reaching Aden to send the different remedies employed by Europeans. The chance afforded of some alleviation of his sufferings so delighted the poor old man that he wished our traveller to depart as speedily as possible, while the courtiers looked on approvingly, and begged no time should be lost. A final interview followed with the sickly little Amir, and a long conversation about the state of Aden, of Zeila, of Berberah, and of Stamboul. Ahmed expressed himself desirous of obtaining the friendship of the British nation, a people who built " large ships"; and, in return, Burton praised Harar in cautious phrases, and regretted that its coffee was not better known amongst the Franks. Finally, he requested the chief's commands for Aden, upon which the Gerad, evidently the leading spirit, gave him a letter addressed to the Political Resident, and told him to take charge of a mule as a present. Then rising, Burton recited a short prayer, the gist of which was that the Amir's days and reign might be long in the land, bent his head over the Prince's hand, and retired.

Three days later the whole party departed unmolested. Pious Shaykh Jami had insisted upon waiting for a lucky day, and, as in such a country delays are especially dangerous, he was left to follow when the auspicious moment arrived. The adventurous little band had lovely weather for their journey. When they started at early dawn a cloudless sky, then untarnished by sun, tinged with reflected blue the mist-crowns of the distant peaks, and the smoke-wreaths hanging round the sleeping villages, and the air was a cordial after the rank atmosphere of Harar. The dew hung in large diamonds from the coffee-trees, the spur-fowl crew blithely in the wayside bushes; never did the face of Nature seem to Burton so truly lovely.

At Sagharrah and Wilensi the travellers were received with shouts of delight. Everybody was well, including the fat cooks, and all the property was intact. Nothing remained to do except to get back as quickly as possible. And as Burton felt disinclined for the delay and worry which would be inevitable were he to personally conduct his caravan to Zeila, he appointed Beuh his deputy, the man promising on arrival at the seaport to forward the private property to Aden. This settled, our traveller prepared to ride on mule-back to Berberah taking only three attendants and a stock of provisions sufficient for four days, the supposed length of the journey, a mistake that very nearly cost him dear. So at the end of a week, enlivened by the promised visit from Shaykh Jami, who insisted on chanting religious exercises until the small hours of the morning, Burton started with his men on January 26th.

Little guessed he what lay before him. Desperate indeed was this ride to Berberah. One night drenched with rain while lying in a deserted sheepfold, wet saddle cloths the only bedding; twenty-four hours passed without one drop of water, half of which were spent riding under a burning sun over horrid hills denuded of vegetation, across plains covered with stones, and rolling ground abounding with thorns apparently created to tear man's skin and clothes. When at last, blessed sight, sundry pools appeared, they were brimful of tadpoles and nameless insects; but, prudence cast to the winds, men and beasts drank and drank until they could drink no more. The suffering had been fearful; we can hardly wonder that a wretched guide, whose incapacity had partly caused these disasters, declared that the white man had been sent as a special curse upon the children of Ishak.

The worst was over when the springs were reached, but Berberah yet lay three days distant. The descent from the Ghauts into the low country was a sore trial to exhausted men and animals. No sandy water-course here facilitated the travellers' advance; the rapid slope presented a succession of blocks and boulders piled one upon the other in rugged steps, apparently impassable to any creatures but mules. Nor on the return march was our party assisted by the natives. There was nothing to give in exchange for hospitality, so the churlish villagers refused even a draught of milk; indeed, on one occasion, they threatened hostilities. No pauper in England could find shops more religiously closed to him than did Burton and his men find the huts of the natives in the wilds of Somaliland; and soon not a biscuit, not a handful of rice or dates remained.

Very slowly, on the last day of this race with death,

did the wearied little band march along the coast. Almost impossible was it to prevent the mules from remaining altogether by the wayside, certain death to the poor beasts. At last a long dark line was seen upon the sandy horizon ; it grew more and more distinct ; the silhouettes of shipping appeared against sea and sky—Berberah, the goal ! At 2 a.m. our exhausted cavalcade crept cautiously round the southern quarter of the sleeping town, and, after sundry inquiries, Burton dismounted in front of his comrades' hut. A glad welcome, servants and animals duly provided for, and he fell asleep, conscious of having performed a feat which, like a certain ride to York, would live in local annals for many a year.

Thus far success had crowned his efforts, and well for him had he reposed on his laurels. But, deeming his exploration of Somaliland sadly incomplete, he planned a fresh enterprise. Preparations were made at Aden for a second expedition on a larger and more imposing scale ; and after no long interval he landed at Berberah at the head of forty-two men—a motley crew of Egyptians, Arabs, negroes, and Somal, armed with sabres and flint muskets. Lieutenants Speke, Herne, and Stroyan acted as subordinates. The camp was pitched close to a creek, which lay between it and Berberah, a site chosen in order that the expedition might enjoy the protection of the gunboat *Mahi ;* but, most unfortunately, she was suddenly ordered elsewhere—a cruel blunder, the cause of the following disaster.

Had Burton and his men been able to start before the *Mahi's* departure, all might have gone well. But they were forced to wait for the mid-April mail with instruments and stores from England, and the delay proved fatal. On the 18th of April, while the expedition was still waiting and watching for the steamer, a native craft scudded into the creek, and, having landed her passengers, would have sailed again the same evening. Luckily, our traveller, with his usual kind-heartedness, insisted on feasting the commander and crew ; little he knew he had entertained dusky angels unawares !

Between two and three a.m. next morning, one Mahmud rushed into Burton's tent, crying out that the enemy were upon them. Three hundred of the wild hill-men had swooped down upon the camp. Burton sprang to his feet, and hastily aroused his English comrades, who were all close by. Lieutenant Stroyan rose to defend himself, but was instantly speared ; Burton, Speke and Herne, with overwhelming odds against them, endeavoured to defend their position—a ricketty tent. The Somal swarmed like hornets, and it was by no means easy to avoid in the darkness, lightened every now and then by the flash of a revolver, the jobbing javelins and long, heavy daggers thrown under and through the openings of the canvas. About five minutes after the fray began, finding the frail structure was almost beaten down, and knowing that to get entangled in the folds meant certain death, Burton gave the word to escape, and sallied forth, sabre in hand, followed by his companions.

The outlook was not reassuring. About twenty men were crouching at the entrance of the tent, while many dusty figures stood further off shouting their war-cry and trying to drive away the camels.

Breaking through the crowd, our hero imagined he saw the prostrate form of Lieutenant Stroyan lying on the sand, and straightway cut a passage towards it through a dozen hillmen, regardless of their war clubs, which battered without mercy. Suddenly, an unseen hand thrust a javelin through his jaw. Escaping as by a miracle, dazed with agony, he fell in with some of his own servants, who, too cowardly to take any part in the conflict, had been lurking in the darkness. In spite of the shock of his horrible wound, Burton happily remembered the sole chance of escape—the craft anchored close by. One man showed a little more courage than the rest, and him he ordered to signal the little vessel to approach the shore. As day broke, exerting all his remaining strength, he reached the head of the creek and was carried on board.

The hillmen having decamped with their booty, his comrades soon joined him. Lieutenant Herne had escaped unhurt ; Speke had received eleven flesh wounds, none dangerous. The body of Lieutenant Stroyan, cruelly muti-lated, had to be committed to the deep during the return voyage to Aden. It was with heavy hearts our three brave Englishmen set sail for the near Arabian shore, and after two days filled with saddest thoughts, told their friends the news of their terrible disaster.

CHAPTER VII.

BURTON'S hurt was not one to be trifled with. The Somali lance had transfixed his upper jaw, carrying away four back teeth and part of his palate. He could hardly speak or eat. Skilled treatment was required without loss of time, and as no doctor at Aden cared to be responsible for so critical a case, our wounded lion returned, shortly after the disaster at Berberah, on sick leave to England.

One loving welcome was missing. His mother had passed away on the 18th December, 1854, while he lay so dangerously ill at Sagharrah. Doubtless it was her loss which suggested in his preface to " Zanzibar " the pathetic allusion to the gaps in the household circle which a wanderer finds on his return, to the graves that have closed over their dead during his absence:

" And when the lesson strikes the head,
The weary heart grows cold."

He mourned her in reverent silence, for we find no distinct reference to her death in any of his works. But, unlike many men who lead an exciting and stormy existence, his numerous battles with fate in no way dulled his family affections. At first he rarely mentioned her, but in after days he would often speak with tender admiration of her wonderfully unselfish and blameless life, adding those pretty words already quoted, " Nice to be able to feel proud of one's parents." The brave old father still lived, and Edward, lately returned on furlough from Ceylon, was spending a few months with his sister and nieces at Boulogne.

To obtain first-rate surgical advice and to be near his publisher, Burton temporarily established himself in London. There, under the care of a clever surgeon and a skilful dentist, the painful wound inflicted by the Somali lance soon healed. Thanks to his sober progenitors, he inherited healthy blood, for we never hear of his numerous hurts troubling him for long—of those after effects so common from sword or gun-shot injuries. With regard to this spear-thrust, penetrating as it did such delicate structures as the jaw and palate, he was particularly fortunate in experiencing no further inconvenience, for his old Commander-in-Chief, Sir Charles Napier, who received a somewhat similar wound, wrote years later of the almost intolerable agony which it caused him.

As soon as Burton could speak with ease he read a paper on Harar at a meeting of the Royal Geographical Society. The reception of this paper, written with much care and pains, was one of his many disappointments. He had performed a great feat, unique so far as entering Harar was concerned, and he was exceedingly anxious to direct attention to the importance of the Somali ports, Berberah in particular. But the hour for interesting the public in such matters was most unpropitious. The Crimean War was still at its height, all England absorbed in hearing of the horrible carnage, the heroic bravery, and alas! the sad bungling of that terrible period. The scenes at Scutari during the preceding winter had struck the whole nation with horror and despair; people thought and talked of nothing but the glorious soldiers sacrificed to the want of foresight of well-meaning but incapable men. So, even had our traveller's story been twice as interesting as it was, it would not have arrested much attention. Few persons cared to know about an obscure town in Eastern Africa, or trouble themselves about annexing .: protecting Somaliland while such deeds were being done in Europe. Burton saw this himself in 1855; but, strange to say, the same fatality pursued him on other occasions; in fact, he used to remark, with grim humour, that whenever he wished to gain the public ear some startling event, if merely a great poisoning case, was sure to take place.

A comical incident, illustrating the difficulty which they who know have in teaching those who don't, happened during the solitary evening devoted by the Royal Geographical Society to his paper. An ancient " Fellow," regardless of the trifling disqualification of never having been to the spot in question, declared with authority that on approaching Harar, Burton had crossed a broad and rapid river. Vainly did our explorer, well remembering the little bourn which had afforded so refreshing a bath to his tired attendants, reject this astounding piece of information ; the general opinion seemed to be that the ancient " Fellow " knew best.

Burton ran down to Bath to see his father, and then as health mended, began to work at his " First Footsteps in East Africa." The " Pilgrimage to Meccah and El-Medinah," in three large volumes, was just issuing from the press, and the season though a sad one, black the prevailing colour, was at its height. So what with literary work and meeting many an old friend, he had his time fully occupied. But there was a new influence to reckon with. Although he had his " Pilgrimage " to correct, his other book to finish, his chums to look up, not to mention the various amusements of town life in May, which must have seemed doubly entertaining after the wilds of Somaliland and the ungenial society of the children of El-Hejaz, soon, very soon the prevailing excitement made him restless. Volunteering was all the rage, every officer neither invalided nor superannuated, endeavoured to repair to the Crimea. It would have been miraculous had a man with Burton's military talents, talents which unfortunately had few opportunities of being turned to account, proved an exception. We remember his per-

11

tinacious attempts to get under fire in India, and his bitter
disappointment when luckier comrades were sent to the
front and he was left fretting his heart out in some place of
inglorious safety. And now, while on all sides he heard
about the war and nothing but the war, a hope flashed
across his brain that at last there might be a chance for
him in this great struggle of the nations, wherein whole
regiments were not merely decimated but destroyed, so
blundering, so brave, so butcherly were the battles. At
last, he could continue his literary labours no longer. With
military ardour fanned to boiling by the fiery enthusiasm
around him, he applied to the War Office for a post, however insignificant; and in spite of refusals, not only of an
appointment, but even of the promise of one (the Department in question was besieged as closely as Sebastopol), he
arranged to start at once for the Crimea, and trust his lucky
star to get into the fight.

Here, however, I must not fail to mention that Burton
did not approve of this war, on the contrary, he looked upon
it as an unmitigated evil to England. Considered with
regard to her foreign affairs, it lost her the alliance of
Russia, her oldest and often her only ally amongst the
Continentals of Europe. It barred the inevitable growth
of the " Northern Colossus " in a southern direction, and
encouraged the mighty spread to the south-east, India-
wards; at the same time doubling her extent by the
absorption of Turcomania. Twenty thousand gallant
Englishmen and eighty millions of money were sacrificed
in a vain attempt to humble Russia, to serve the selfish
ends of Louis Napoleon, and to set up the Sultan, who,
like Humpty Dumpty, was incapable of undergoing that
process. In this year of grace, 1896, when Lord Salisbury,
the greatest statesman of our age, is sorely exercised concerning what to do with the present sick man, who, like
many chronic invalids, has waxed most froward and in-
tractable, Burton's opinion of the mistake of 1854 may well
be quoted.

On the way out he stayed a few days with his brother and sister at Boulogne. Fearing at first he might be sorely disfigured by his terrible wound, both scrutinised the hero with eager interest, and both were most pleasantly surprised at his appearance. The two years which had elapsed since he left England for Arabia, years filled to overflowing with adventure, anxiety, and toil, had left but few traces on that handsome face and herculean frame. His hurt had healed so thoroughly as to be only just discernable. He looked what he was, in the prime of manhood. His thick brown hair, worn longer than our present monkey-fashion, was parted in the middle and waved about his temples; and his grand mustachios so admired by the old El-Medinah camel-owner, were supplemented by a bushy beard. Stalwart, erect, sound in wind and limb, in no particular had he the physique of one who had knocked at death's door more than once during the past twelve months.

There was much to do and talk over during those few happy days. Old memories were revived, old friends invited, old scenes revisited. His brother, who had not seen him since the stormy times at Oxford, had plenty to tell of hair-breadth escapes and hunting adventures in Ceylon. An ardent sportsman, Edward Burton was the crack shot of his regiment, and many were the elephants, tigers, cheetahs and smaller game that fell before his redoubtable gun. Poor fellow! Even a finer character than Richard, and that is saying much, he might have become one of the soldiers of the day, for he had great talents, had not his military career been cut short by an accident. During one of his hunting trips, some Cingalese villagers, Buddhists all, animated by bigoted feeling towards one who openly violated the precepts of their religion by taking beast life wholesale, fell upon him and inflicted serious wounds on his head with sticks and stones. For awhile no evil consequences ensued, but after a sunstroke received during the Mutiny, when he distinguished himself so brilliantly as to

11—2

be rewarded by a valuable appointment at Lucknow, his mind slowly gave way and never recovered.

These evil days were still in the future, and our two brothers arranged that their short meeting at Boulogne should herald another in the Crimea ; a meeting which, though Edward in his turn hastened to the seat of war, never came off, for reasons to be explained as we proceed. With an effort, for as usual the painful hour of parting was deferred to the last moment, Richard tore himself away. He left on this occasion an interesting souvenir of his pilgrimage—a red sausage-shaped cushion strung with turquoise rings, which he had bought at Meccah as a present for his mother and sister. These stones, the solitary relic of his Arabian feat belonging to his family, are now in possession of Edward Stisted Mostyn-Pryce, of Gunley Hall, Salop, only son of the younger of the two beautiful cousins whom Burton so admired.

Our traveller hurried through France, and embarked at Marseilles on board one of the Messageries Impériales bound for Constantinople. Very imperial was the demeanour of her officers, who took command, in most absolute style, of her passengers, going so far, indeed, as to severely wig an English colonel for opening a port and shipping a sea. The vanity of our usually urbane neighbours, excited to frenzy by the creditable figure they were cutting in the eyes of Europe, rendered them doubtfully pleasant company to any son of Albion. The only exception on this occasion appears to have been General MacMahon, then fresh from his Algerian campaign and newly transferred to the Crimea, where his fortunes began. In due time Burton sighted the Golden Horn, and, glad to be rid of the bumptious Gauls, lodged for a day or so at Missiri's Hotel, kept by a former dragoman of Eothen's.

At Stamboul he met Mr. F. Wingfield, who was bound for Balaclava as assistant under that most unfortunate of Commissary-Generals, Mr. Filder. They steamed together over the inhospitable Euxine, whose dingy waters veiled in dark vapour contrasted unpleasantly with the turquoise and amethyst hues of the lovely Mediterranean. After a three days' voyage the steamer reached Balaclava, and found the little port, dug out of dove-coloured limestone, stuffed to repletion with every kind of craft. This place, ever memorable as the scene of our rudest awakening, had greatly improved since 1854. Under a stern Provost-Marshal, whose every look meant " cat," some cleanliness and discipline had been introduced among the sutlers and scoundrels who populated the townlet. Store-ships no longer crept in with cargoes worth their weight of gold to our starved and ragged soldiers, and crept out again without breaking bulk. A fair road had been run through Kadikeui to camp and to the front, and men sank no more ankle-deep in dust or calf-deep in mud. In fact, England was, in the parlance of the ring, getting her second wind and settling down to her work.

Lord Raglan the gallant, the chivalrous, had been dead about a month, the great historical battles were over, and the only important event that remained to befall was the storming of Sebastopol. Burton had arrived too late, a fact which, in the excitement of the military blaze and blare around him, he failed at first to recognise. A week was spent with friends, frequent visits being paid to the camp and front. Of course he tried at once for a post. To begin with, he called upon the Commander-in-Chief, General Simpson, whom years before he had met in Upper Sind— the Jimmy who Napier declared was always in the dismals. But poor Jimmy, more than ever in the dismals, was fast sinking into his grave, and could do nothing for anybody. Undaunted by one failure, Burton then wrote to General Beatson, an old Boulogne acquaintance, and volunteered for the irregular cavalry known as Beatson's Horse. This time success crowned his efforts, and much elated was he to see his name appear in orders.

He did not know it, but his evil genius had presided over this appointment. General Beatson, a bluff Indian officer, about five-and-fifty years of age, was no indifferent soldier. In his subaltern days he had served in the Spanish Legion under General Sir de Lacy Evans, and after sundry hard knocks had returned to India and seen plenty of fighting. In October, 1854, he had been directed by the Duke of Newcastle to organise a corps of Bashi-Buzouks, who were to be independent of the Turkish contingent, which we know consisted of twenty-five thousand Regulars, under General Vivian. And this commission he executed to the best of his ability. But, owing to an incurable habit of telling unpalatable truths in the most emphatic language, he had become exceedingly unpopular with the authorities. Even Burton, who was certainly outspoken enough, attempted more than once, when placed on the Staff, to modify the tone of his chief's despatches. To little purpose. Maddened in an intolerable environment of ignorance and roguery, Beatson raved on, received wigging after wigging, ended one quarrel only to begin another, and made a deadly enemy of every official who crossed his path. This would have mattered little had he injured himself alone, but unfortunately his unpopularity extended to his corps, the luckless Bashi-Buzouks.

Finding the General unmanageable, Burton turned his attention to his soldiers. With his keen military *flair*, he was by no means satisfied with the condition of these men. Stationed on the slopes of a hill to the north of the Dardanelles country town at the mouth of the Hellespont, they had been kept carefully in the background, and it was very clear that just then they were only fit for some place of inglorious safety. The meaning of the name Básh Buzuk is equivalent to Tête Pourrie; it succeeded the Dillis, or madmen, who in the good old days represented the Osmanli irregular cavalry; and certainly it seems to have described its owners pretty accurately. Recruited in Syria, Bulgaria,

and Albania, the motley crew required plenty of first-rate
English officers to drill and discipline them ; and the War
Office, which had overmuch to do, and probably considered
the raising of the corps a mere whim, would not take the
trouble of appointing a sufficient number. Those already
in command were, for the most part, able enough. Burton
mentions as most companionable comrades Charles Wemyss,
an ex-guardsman, Major Lennox Berkeley, Lieut.-Colonel
Morgan, Major Synge, and several distinguished men in
the Indian army. But they seemed to have been half
paralysed by the apparent impossibility of reducing to
order four thousand recruits, some little better than semi-
barbarians. The soldiers were left dawdling on the hillside
wasting their time in drinking and gambling. There were
no morning roll-calls, no evening parades, nor was there
even drill until Burton arrived and infected all around him
with his inexpressible hopefulness and energy. He soon
persuaded the General to attend to all these matters, and
to establish a riding school for the benefit of sundry
infantry officers who were not over-firm in the saddle. A
school of arms was not forgotten—our soldier had in no
degree lost his enthusiasm for the sword and the bayonet—
and before long, in spite of the scanty sprinkling of officers,
the improvement in the men was almost miraculous. Les
Têtes Pourries were turned perforce into a body of well-
trained sabreurs, ready to do anything or to go anywhere.

But the war was too far advanced, General Beatson
had made too many enemies, for his Bashi-Buzouks to win
either pelf or glory. Perhaps had the interest in the
campaign not begun to wane, the value of this now very
creditable corps might have more than balanced the enmity
excited by Beatson's Horse and their commander. As it
was, his foes had it all their own way. Lord Stratford
nursed a private grievance against the General, and was
besides angrily opposed to the existence of " Irregulars "—
Irregulars being unknown at Waterloo. Even the two

Turkish Pashas, civil and military, stationed at the Dardanelles, were displeased to see an *imperium in imperio*, and
did their best to breed disturbance between the two corps.
The French, too, jealous of so fine a body of men, directed
their Consul to pack the local press at Constantinople with
the falsest stories. And so, while our English regiments
bravely endeavoured to capture the Redan, while the Mala-
koff was stormed and carried, and the allies at last found
themselves masters of the smoking ruins of Sebastopol, the
Irregulars remained pertinaciously stationed on a bare hill-
side, far away from the scene of action. It must have been
a bitter pill to Burton, after all the pains he had taken with
his troublesome recruits, to stand idle and watch the war
now drawing to a close without being permitted to fire a
single shot.

Perhaps the most interesting episode during his stay in
the Crimea relates to the fall of Kars, December 12th, 1855.
It illustrates the curious dash of Quixotism, and a certain
lack of comprehension of political exigencies, which at times
did much to mar his fortunes. He thought he saw his
way to a grand success, no less than the relief of a town
whose wretched inhabitants were suffering from cholera
and famine, combined with the horrors of a siege. Pelissier
and his Frenchmen were long-sighted enough to know the
culminating importance of this stronghold as a stumbling
block in the way of Russia; but, as the Emperor was
beginning to wish for peace, they managed to keep Omar
Pasha and his Turkish troops in the Crimea, where the
large force was compelled to be idle, instead of being sent
to attack the Trans-Caucasian provinces, in which they
might have done rare good service. And when for once
the Turkish commander was permitted to fight the Russians
before the walls of the wretched town, he was in no way
backed up by the allies, and consequently forced to retire.
Burton thought years afterwards that, had the affair been
managed differently, England might have struck a vital

blow at Russia, by driving her once more behind the Caucasus, and by putting off for many a year the threatened advance upon India, which is now one of our nightmares.

In early September, the state of Kars, whose gallant garrison was allowed to succumb to hunger, disease, and the enemy, was becoming a scandal. Rumour whispered that General Williams, who with General Kmety, a Hungarian, was taking a prominent part in the defence, addressed upwards of eighty officials to Lord Stratford without receiving a reply. But at last His Excellency appeared to be considering measures for the relief of the unhappy town.

In utter ignorance of the then state of politics and its rhyming synonym, Burton became violently excited on hearing that the Turkish contingent was to be sent to the aid of the garrison, if only sufficient carriage could be procured for the troops. After some delay, Lieutenant-General Vivian wrote to Stamboul that no carriage was then available. Breathlessly elated at the prospect of taking part in a great military feat, Burton hurried to Constantinople, obtained an interview with Lord Stratford, and submitted a project for the old man's approval. *His* corps was in perfect readiness to start at any moment, and *his* general could guarantee any amount of means of transport.

How vividly one can picture that scene. Our handsome soldier in his smart cavalry uniform, with his great dark eyes flashing with excitement at the thought of the doughty deed to be done by his men ; and on the other side the astounded face of the white-haired Ambassador, whose icy impassibility could change at times into furious fits of rage. And of the latter our hero was treated to a specimen.

" You are the most impudent man in the Bombay army, sir ! " shouted the irascible politician.

Not until some months afterwards did Burton learn the

full extent of his transgression. Kars was doomed to fall as a peace-offering to Russia, and a captain of Bashi-Buzouks had madly attempted to arrest the course of *la haute politique.*

After this fruitless visit to Stamboul, Burton returned sadly crestfallen to the Dardanelles, where fresh disasters awaited him. His Bashi-Buzouks, like the unfortunate Turks at Kars, were in a state of siege. A trifling squabble between the French infirmiers and the Irregulars had been magnified into a desperate act of mutiny, and all the covert ill-will which had smouldered so long exploded in a down-right act of violence. On the morning of September 26th, the Turkish Regulars were drawn out in array as though against the foe; infantry supported by guns pointed at Beatson's camp and patrols of cavalry occupied the rear. Three war steamers commanded the main entrance of the little town, outposts were established within three hundred yards of the Irregulars; and to make matters still more ridiculous, the inhabitants had closed their shops and the British Consulate was deserted. No greater preparations could have been made against the Russians themselves.

General Beatson's phraseology was at times too forcible, but he was a good soldier and could restrain his fiery temper when duty bade him. Seeing that terrible consequences might ensue if his men struck the first blow, he showed no signs of anger, and did his utmost to soothe the intense irritation of his insulted men, who, furious with the aggressors, requested permission to take possession of their guns. By means of a politic order, and with the assistance of his officers, he achieved a perfect triumph of discipline. Not a shot was fired, not a man unhorsed or hurt. About 4 p.m. the military Pasha, ashamed of his absurd attitude, marched his Regulars back to their barracks, and the affair apparently terminated.

The venomous Turk, however, forwarded to Constantinople a bitter complaint of the very order which had prevented bloodshed, viz. : " That the Irregulars should remain in their camp until the Turkish authorities should have recovered from their panic and housed their guns." The steamer *Redpole* was despatched in hot haste with an exaggerated account of the affair, furnished by the French and English Consuls, the latter of whom had evidently lost his head, for he actually requested reinforcements against these new and formidable foes. The result may be anticipated :

> " One against a multitude
> Is more than mortal can make good."

General Beatson was removed from his command, and directed to make it over to Major-General Smith, who appeared at the Dardanelles, September 28th, supported by a fresh body of Nizans.

The unlucky chief was suffering from the effects of an accident when the order arrived, and felt quite unfit for business. His subordinates, while knowing only too well that nothing could reinstate him in his former position, did their best. Burton, who was then Chief of Staff, and Major Berkeley, Military Secretary, collected as many officers as possible, went in a body to Major-General Smith, and in the most conciliatory terms laid the case before him. They declared unanimously all the reports circulated by the Turks and the French were false, and offered to show him the condition and discipline of their corps. That Beatson and his officers were in the right was confirmed by the favourable view expressed in the public press by that prince of war correspondents William Henry Russell and by General Smith himself. But now, whatever the latter might think, he could only obey orders until fresh instructions were received from Constantinople. While many of the Buzoukers acquiesced perforce in the new *régime*, Burton and Major Berkeley, after ascertaining matters were quite hopeless, that their chief was certainly superseded, felt they could no longer serve with self-respect, and sent in their resignations.

On the last day of September the luckless General and his two faithful friends left the Dardanelles for ever. Arrived at Buyukdere, a report was sent to Lieutenant-General Vivian, who presently came on board to enquire into the affair. Rumours of a Russian attack had induced a more conciliatory tone. The Commander of the Turkish Contingent seemed satisfied with the "Buzouker's" explanations, and even listened favourably to the latter's urgent request for permission to return to his corps. But nothing could be done without the Ambassador's orders, and the peppery old Indian had got into the Eltchi's very worst graces. So, after a conversation on the subject with Lord Stratford, General Vivian altered his tone, and directed a stiff official letter to the hapless Beatson, giving him not the slightest hope of revoking the order which had removed him from his command.

The remainder of General Beatson's history is soon told. He went to England and instituted civil proceedings against his enemies. Chief amongst them was a Mr. Skene, who from the inception of the General's scheme had shown himself most bitterly opposed to it, and had used all his influence to make the position untenable. The case broke down on technical grounds, but it was generally felt the Buzouker had vindicated his character, and had very successfully exposed the conspiracy against the Irregulars, which had ended so disastrously for him and his officers.

Having resigned his post, nothing remained for Burton to do in the Crimea. He was not likely to get employed again, the war being all but over ; so on the 18th October he left Therapia *en route* for England, just missing his brother, who had started from home a few days before.

This waste of time and energy with the Bashi-Buzouks had been a very disagreeable experience. Burton saw, for the present, no chance of promotion in his military career, and, in a fit of despondency, determined again to follow for a while the exciting life of an explorer or pathfinder. Once more he turned longingly towards Africa, Central and Inter-tropical, and resolved to devote himself to opening out as fully as possible the resources of the Dark Continent, the heart of which no Englishman had as yet penetrated. And save that the unveiling of Isis was not for him, we shall now see how after two failures—one at Berberah, the other in the Crimea, neither from any fault of his—his good star once more gained the ascendant, and he achieved the great success of his life.

CHAPTER VIII

ALTHOUGH during the excitement of the Crimean War little attention was paid to our traveller's pilgrimages to the holy cities of El-Hejaz, and his journey to Harar, when the interest in the campaign had begun to flag, his works created a decided sensation in scientific and literary circles. So as soon as he made known his desire to penetrate the heart of the Dark Continent, several influential friends, amongst whom may be mentioned Sir Roderick Murchison, Mr. Monckton Milnes, and Vice-Admiral Sir George Back, the veteran explorer of the Arctic seas, succeeded in obtaining for him the command of an expedition to the interior of that country. Assisted by the Royal Geographical Society to the amount of one thousand pounds, this expedition was organised for a threefold object : to

" Behold the lakes wherein the Nile is born,"

to correct certain geographical errors, and to survey as fully as possible the resources of Central and Intertropical Africa.

Nothing was then known about the Lake Regions, which were supposed to consist of a huge inland sea. The error probably arose from the fact that the three chief caravan routes from Zanzibar coast abutted upon three several lakes, which, in the confusion of African vocabulary, were thrown into one. The Mombas Mission map had lately appeared, whereon figured a slug-shaped monster, an impossible Caspian ; the existence of this water our traveller vehemently doubted, and, as we now know, he proved it to be a myth. But he did more. Amidst all the blare and glory of the great exploits since his day, it should be kept in mind that he and he alone was the pioneer to those vast tracts. This expedition of 1856-9, the longest and greatest of his journeys, unequalled for its mingled audacity and foresight, one which resulted in the discovery of Lakes Tanganyika and Victoria Nyanza, was the first successful attempt to enter Central Africa, and it smoothed the way for all the brave men who followed. Preceded only by a French officer, barbarously murdered shortly after he landed, Burton under immense disadvantages led his inadequately equipped caravan into unknown regions, discovered Tanganyika and the southern portion of Victoria Nyanza, and thus opened out the road to all who cared to tread in his steps. Subsequent travellers had merely to read his writings to learn all they required concerning seasons and sickness, industry and commerce, what outfit and material were necessary, what guides and escort were wanted, and what obstacles might be expected. And now, where two tired, fever-stricken wanderers tramped along, resting only in filthy huts amongst the most degraded savages, missions are busy, commerce flourishes, and civilisation is established for many an age to come.

As with the survey of Somaliland, the expedition owed much to the warm support of Lord Elphinstone. Burton was granted two years' furlough, Captain John Speke was permitted to accompany him, and a Dr. Steinhauser, then staff surgeon at Aden, one of our traveller's firmest friends, received orders to repair at once to Zanzibar. Unluckily, the doctor, detained by weather, did not arrive in time—a sad *contretemps*, a medical man on such a journey being almost indispensable. Nor did Lord Elphinstone's kindness end here. Knowing how much importance Orientals attach to appearances, especially to first appearances, he arranged that a sloop-of-war should convey the explorers from Bombay to the African coast, so that they might arrive with all the honours.

The voyage was pleasant but monotonous, the only excitement the first view of Zanzibar island. Truly lovely was the swelling coast-line set off by a dome of distant hills like solidified air. The sea of purest sapphire just creamed with foam the yellow sand-strip that separated it from flower-spangled grass and underwood of metallic green. The palms, springing like living columns, graceful and luxuriant above their subject growths, were hardly ruffled by the breeze; and, to add a new pleasure, as the sloop drew near, a heavy spicy perfume, grateful indeed after the briny north-east trade wind, was wafted from the celebrated clove grounds. Presently appeared the straight line of Arab town, extending about a mile and a half in length, facing north and standing in bold relief from the varied tints and forest grandeur that lay behind. Right and left the Imam's palace, the various consulates, and the huge parallelo-grammic buildings of the great, a tabular line of flat roofs, glaring and dazzling like freshly-whitewashed sepulchres, detached themselves from the mass, and did their best to conceal the dingy matted hovels of the inner town. Zanzi-bar city, like Stamboul, must be viewed from afar.

The harbour is a fine specimen of the true Atoll, or fringing reef, built upon a subsiding foundation. It was thronged, when the sloop sailed in, with an outlandish fleet of dhows, batelas, ganjas from Cutch, and many other queer-shaped native craft. The strange scene looked its brightest under the most brilliant sunshine, a good omen for the expedition, as at times the sun veils his face during six weeks in succession.

Zanzibar Island, so named from the Persian Zangi, and Bar, a compound term signifying Nigritia, or Blackland, contained in 1856 about three hundred thousand souls. The town population varied from twenty-five thousand to forty-five thousand during the north-east monsoon, when an influx of strangers was usually expected. It was com-posed of a motley crowd of Arabs, Hindoos, Indian

Moslems, a few Europeans and Americans, but principally of free blacks, of whom the Wasawahili, a hideous chocolate-coloured race, were the most numerous. Burton found the town fearfully dirty and unhealthy. The foreground was a line of sand disgustingly impure, corpses floated on the surface of the waters, and the shore could be described only as a huge cesspool. The spicy odours were soon overpowered by stenches unutterable, and even our traveller shrank from a thorough survey of the native town, a filthy labyrinth of disorderly lanes and alleys, here broad, there narrow, now heaped with offal, there choked with ruins, all reeking in a temperature of 80° to 89° F. with effluvia of carrion and negro.

In spite of these and other drawbacks he decided to make Zanzibar his headquarters. First, because it seemed the most favourable place wherein to undergo the seasoning fever which every new-comer must expect in this part of Africa, the houses being fairly comfortable, and a certain amount of necessaries procurable. Secondly, in this little metropolis—residence of the ruler and chief officials, not to mention the French and English Consuls—he could best begin and carry out the preparations for his great journey.

The dry season was judged by old hands unfit for prolonged travel, and Burton was strongly advised to spend the intervening time in learning something of the coast. So he determined upon what he called "a preliminary canter," a trial trip to the Zanzibar seaports, varied by an excursion to the mountain range which lies some eighty miles inland. But there was plenty to do first; clashing interests and silly prejudices had to be reckoned with. No sooner did his project become public than intrigues abounded. Houses that had amassed in a few years large fortunes by the Zanzibar trade, were anxious to let sleeping dogs lie. The Arabs got frightened at the possible opening out of the interior ; they knew Europeans had long coveted a settlement on the sea-board, and they had no wish to lose

12

the monopoly of copal and ivory. At last, sundry European merchants settled in the place, fearing competition
might result from any development of the resources of the
Dark Continent, went so far as to spread evil reports of our
travellers among the natives, Banyans, Arabs, and Wasawahili, which might have secured for Burton and Speke
the disastrous fate of their predecessor. But Colonel
Hamerton, the English Consul, backed up his compatriots
by every means in his power, and fortunately the Sayyid,
or Sultan of Zanzibar, proved more enlightened than the
people he governed. This ruler, a young prince of mild
disposition and amiable manners, received Burton graciously
in spite of " whispering tongues," took considerable interest
in the coming journey, and finally entrusted him with
several circular letters, recommending the two English
officers to the chiefs of the part of the country about to be
visited, and to the Jemadars commanding the garrisons.

However, two conditions were insisted upon by his
advisers. Colonel Hamerton had to swear that the expedition was to be conducted only by men whose goodwill he
could rely on, and that it was not a proselytizing movement
of the " Sons of the Book." Had the consul hesitated to
accepted these terms, the project would have been wrecked;
but we shall see how, owing to the later stipulation, Burton
lost a very valuable companion.

Two Portuguese boys, Gaetano and Valentino, had been
engaged at Bombay as body-servants; and now a guide,
one Said bin Salim, was added to the party. A court spy,
he was a pledge of respectability, able to announce, in virtue
of his office, that his masters were not malignants. He
spoke a little bad Arabic, but principally Kisiwahili, the
language of the negro races in and around Zanzibar, and
even occasionally used so far as Ugogo. Burton, who,
unlike some travellers, strongly objected to explore any
land where he did not understand the tongue, turned his
attention to the said dialect, which contains some 20,000

words. Like the Somal and the Gallas there is no alphabet, and our indefatigable linguist, who never seemed to find any jargon, however barbarous, devoid of interest, commenced a grammar intended to illustrate the intricate combinations and the peculiar euphony which appear to be the first object of Wasawahili speech.

The outfit on this occasion, besides private property, consisted of twenty muslin turbans, a score of embroidered caps, a broadcloth coat, two cotton shawls, and 25 lbs. of beads, as presents. The provisions were rice, maize, dates, sugar, coffee, salt, pepper, onions, curry-stuffs, ghi, tobacco, and soap and candles. Of course, quantities were vastly increased before starting on the great expedition, but even then our travellers practised a somewhat severe economy.

Never more so than in the matter of the *Riami*, an old Arab beden, which was to convey them on their coasting trip. It was a miracle that this worn-out old craft with sails in rags, its timbers worm-eaten, its crew a set of incapables, managed nevertheless to keep afloat. Perhaps our travellers would have hardly cared to sail in so crazy a tub had they not possessed a galvanised iron life-boat, the *Louisa*, named in memory of one of Burton's early loves. This boat, twenty feet long, was of American manufacture, and a triumph of good building. The Arabs could not sufficiently admire her graceful form, the facility with which she was handled, and above all things her speed. Buoyant as graceful, fire-proof, worm-proof, water-proof, she would have been a veritable godsend on Lake Tanganyika; unluckily, want of carriage on the coast compelled her owners to leave her at Zanzibar. But on this occasion, the *Louisa* was towed in their wake; and although she broke her halter more than once, as if disdaining the company of the old beden, when she did consent to follow, she must have imparted an agreeable sense of security to her proprietors. They were certainly uncomfortable enough without the addition of the fear of being drowned : ants lodged in their instrument cases, cockroaches dropped on their heads, and rats made night hideous.

On the 5th January our party bade a temporary adieu to Zanzibar. That is to say, they embarked on board their uninviting craft ; but, in those days, travellers had to be prepared for three distinct departures—the little start, the big start, and *the* start. After dawdling about for two nights and a day, the crew fished up their ground tackle and began their journey, making Kokoto-ni the usual departure point from the island, January 8th. On the 10th, Pemba, the Emerald Isle of these Eastern seas, appeared in sight. Here Captain Kidd, in 1698, buried his hoards of gold and jewels, the plunder of India and the further Orient. It looked peaceful enough when Burton landed, with its silent, monotonous, melancholy beauty, the loveliness of death which belongs to the creeks and rivers of those regions, a great green grave. Striking was its wondrous fertility—cocoas, limes, jacks, and the pyramidal mangoes growing in clumps on the rises, the castor shrub, rich in berries, spreading over the uncultivated slopes.

Here the *Riami* anchored for about forty-eight hours, during which time the *Louisa* was manned and rowed to Chak-Chak, the Governor's residence. In the Wali's absence, our party were most hospitably received by the collector of customs. He treated them to a feast of mangoes, pineapples, rice, ghee, and green tea, and next morning ordered that their casks should be filled with excellent water, besides sending in his own boat a quantity of fresh and dainty provisions.

The three days that followed were less prosperous. Heavy mists hid the shore so effectually that sometimes the old beden sailed south instead of north ; then a drizzle increased to heavy rain, and, lastly, the north-east wind blew great guns, which gale, on a coast of shoals and corallines, made navigation exceedingly dangerous. Said, the

guide, wept incessantly, and during the worst night added
to the general panic by literally screeching with terror.
The captain announced, at intervals, his vessel was doomed,
and, worst of all, the *Louisa*, like a treacherous friend, broke
loose, and did not reappear until found stranded at Mombasah.

All landed at this miserable settlement, once the capital
of the King of the Zing, concerning whom Arab travellers
and geographers have written a variety of marvels. The
halt lasted until January 28th. Not that there was much
to see save the spacious land-locked harbour, and a few
relics of the Portuguese occupation ; but our traveller had
business with the Mombas Mission, or rather with its only
remaining representative, Herr Rebmann, to whom he was
entrusted with a letter from the Evangelical Society in
London. The founders of this mission, more successful
from a geographical point of view than any other, were the
first to attempt systematically to explore and open out the
Zanzibar interior. In 1842, Dr. Krapf undertook a coasting
voyage to East Africa, visited Zanzibar island, and, journeying northwards, established his headquarters amongst the
Wanyika tribe, near Mombasah. He was presently joined
by Herr Rebmann who made three important journeys to
the highlands, where he re-discovered Kilima-njaro, the
mountain bearing eternal snow alluded to by Fernandez de
Enciso in 1530.

The Mission house, situated about fifteen miles from
Mombasah, was neatly and solidly built. Though well
constructed and pitched in the comparatively pure air of
the heights, it seems to have been terribly unwholesome,
as the missionaries died off so rapidly of typhus and remittent fevers, that in 1857 Herr Rebmann and his wife
were the sole survivors. Burton found the undaunted pair
surrounded by their servants and converts ; the latter, most
grotesque in garb and form, gathered to stare at the new
white men, while sundry hill savages stalked about, and

stopped occasionally to relieve their minds by begging snuff
or cloth. No time was lost before discussing the matter
which had prompted our traveller's visit, viz.—Whether
Herr Rebmann would consent to accompany the expedition
into the interior. At first the missionary seemed tempted
to indulge his wandering instincts, but on second thoughts
he refused. He was not strong; he naturally bargained to
do a little proselytizing on the way, and this Burton, bound
by his promise to the Sayyid, could not agree to. It was
very unfortunate, for the good German understood the
language of the tribes through whose country the expedition had to march, a language of which Burton's knowledge
was recent and Speke's nil. However, they parted excellent
friends, and our traveller, most chivalrous of men, had the
satisfaction a day or two afterwards of saving Frau Rebmann from an ugly fright by giving her timely warning of
a raid of savages in her neighbourhood. And here it may
be said that, owing either to their calm good sense, or their
inextinguishable thirst for knowledge, Burton always got
on with Germans, preferring them indeed to any other
nationality. In one of his works I find the following
eulogistic expressions concerning the change which this
great united nation has worked in Europe:—

"By an Englishman who loves his country, nothing can
be more enthusiastically welcomed than this accession to
power of a kindred people, connected with us by language,
by religion, and by all the ties which bind nation to nation.
It proves that the North is still the fecund mother of
heroes; and it justifies us in hoping that our Anglo-Teutonic
blood, with its Scandinavian "baptism," will gain new
strength by the example, and will apply itself to rival our
Continental cousins in the course of progress, and in the
mighty struggle for national life and prosperity."

The journey along the coast continued, halts being
made at every convenient point to acquire information
regarding routes to the interior, and the benevolent or

malevolent disposition of the various tribes. Six days
were thus occupied at Tanga, one of the most important
of the coast settlements. On the 5th of February sail was
hoisted at 5 a.m., and early in the day the *Riami* arrived at
Pangani port. This being the place which Burton had
decided upon as his starting-point to the highlands, it was
necessary to land with some ceremony. Said, in his best
attire, was sent to deliver the Sayyid's letter to the Wali,
and to the military commander of the garrison ; while the
English officers, thinking it undignified to follow too closely
in the wake of a " letter of introduction," remained on
board until evening, when they leisurely disembarked with
their luggage and Portuguese servants.

Quite a grand reception greeted them, too grand, for it
included a most hideous concert. Three monstrous drums,
bassoons at least five feet long, a pair of ear-piercing
flageolets, a horn and a very primitive cymbal, composed
the infernal orchestra. Dancing too was performed in
their honour, the soldiers capering about with all the pomp
and circumstance of drawn swords, while some pretty slave-
girls, bare-headed, with hair *à la* Brutus, pranced delicately
over the ground as if treading on too hot a floor. Perhaps
our travellers were overtired, perhaps too hard to please ;
anyway, privately describing the scene as purgatory, after
enduring it for half an hour, they insisted on being conducted to the upper rooms of the Wali's house, their
temporary headquarters.

Next morning they rose early, and repairing to the roof
found the views therefrom not to be despised. The river
vista, with cocoa avenues to the north, yellow cliffs, some
forty feet high, on the southern side, the mobile swelling
water, bounded by strips of emerald verdure or golden sand,
and the azure sea, dotted with little black rocks, appropriately dubbed devilings, wanted nothing but the finish of
art to bring out the infinite variety of Nature. With half a
dozen white kiosks and serais, minarets and latticed sum-

mer villas, Pangani port might almost rival that gem of creation, the Bosphorus.

The town, which then boasted of some nineteen or twenty stone houses of the usual box style, the rest being a mass of huts, each with its large yard, whose outer line formed the street, was surrounded by a thick, thorny jungle. This jungle harboured not a few leopards, and the river swarmed with crocodiles. Naturally, the felines when hungry pounced upon and devoured any unhappy negro who happened to cross their path, while the amphibious brutes helped themselves unceremoniously to exposed legs and arms. But when the stupid Pangani people were asked why they did not fire the bush which sheltered the leopards, and endeavour to kill some of the crocodiles that infested the stream, they declared the latter brought good luck, and the jungle as a refuge in case of need was too valuable to destroy.

Of course there was plenty of trouble in organising this trip to the interior. The citizens, hearing that Burton was bearer of a letter from the Sayyid of Zanzibar to Sultan Kimwere, their own ruler, who lived up in the hills at Fuga, wrangled desperately over the route to be taken, clamouring for one which traversed exclusively their own territory. Then the son and heir of the said Sultan, who happened to be visiting Pangani, sent an impudent message to Burton, requesting him to place in his hands the gifts intended for his father. And high and low, rich and poor, all began to angle for bakhshish, while the harassed travellers, compelled to husband their resources for the great task of exploring the Lake Regions, had discovered even before leaving Zanzibar that a thousand pounds would go a very short way towards the cost of such a journey. Double the amount would have hardly covered it.

So they had to content themselves with a walking-cum-boating trip to Chogwe, the nearest Baloch out-post upon the Upper Pangani River, pushing on thence for Fuga, the highland home of Sultan Kimwere. Preparations went on silently but swiftly. The *Riami* was paid off, Said and Valentino, one of the Goanese lads, were directed to remain in the Wali's house; and at last, taking advantage of a quiet interval, Burton and Speke, under pretext of a shooting-excursion, hired a long canoe with four rowers, loaded it with sufficient luggage for a fortnight, and started January 6, 1858.

Not at first with *éclat*. The turbulent Rufu, or Upper Pangani River, was lashed by a little gale blowing up-stream into a mass of short chopping waves. Partly owing to the wind, partly to the abrupt windings of the channel, the canoe grounded, then flew on at railway speed before a fresh puff, then scraped again. Finally, it succeeded in turning the first dangerous angle, and the travellers were at liberty to admire a novel and characteristic scene. Behemoth reared his head from the foaming waters, crocodiles waddling like dowagers, measured the strangers with malignant green eyes, deep set under warty brows; monkeys rustled among the tall trees, here peeping with curiosity almost human, there darting away amidst the wondrous frondage and foliage. Not a few of the trees were so covered with creepers that they seemed to bear leaves and blossoms not their own. Upon the watery margin large snowy lilies, some sealed by day, others wide expanded and basking in light, gleamed beautifully against the black-green growth, and the clear bitumen brown of the bank water. Occasionally the jungle folk planted their shoulder-cloths, their rude crates, and their coarse weirs upon the muddy inlets where fish abounded; but they were few and far between, and nothing broke the peculiar tropical stillness save the curlew's cry or the breeze rustling in fitful gusts amongst the dense and matted foliage. Often since that day did Burton think with yearning of the bright and beautiful Zangian stream, and wish himself once more canoeing with Speke, still his loved and trusted friend, upon the lovely bosom of the Upper Pangani River.

At sunset the crew poled up a little inlet near Kipombui, a village on the left bank well stockaded with split areca trunks. Out flocked its people, inquisitive as monkeys to see the strangers, and proving their friendly intentions by offering a dish of small green mangoes, there esteemed a great luxury. About midnight, when the tide flowed strong, the voyage was resumed. Soon the river dwindled to a sable streak between avenues of lofty trees, darkness visible reigning save where a bend suddenly opened its mirrory surface to the moon. A snorting and blowing close to the canoe's stern frightened its timid rowers, who dreaded a certain rogue hippopotamus which haunted that part of the stream, and whose villanies had gained for him the royal title of " Sultan Mamba " ; but a few shots sufficed to scare him up the miry, slippery banks leading to fields and plan-tations. Presently, all became quiet as the grave, and by two a.m. our party reached a cleared tract on the river-side, the ghaut or landing-place of Chogwe, where they made fast their boat, looked to their weapons, and covering their faces against clammy dew and paralysing moonbeams, lay down to snatch a couple of hours' sleep. The total distance rowed that day was thirteen and a half miles.

Chogwe being an outpost, guarded by a Jemadar and a detachment of Baloch, the strangers, thanks to their circular letters, were received with honour. Next morning they inspected the bazaar, apparently all there was to inspect, escorted by the chief of the mercenaries, a consumptive, miserable-looking wretch, and his twenty ragged soldiers. The position of this outpost, seven direct miles from Pangani, was badly chosen, being short of water, infertile, and malarious. The Washenzi savages, too, sometimes crept up at night in spite of the armed men, shot a few arrows into their huts, set fire to the matting, and, after other similar amenities, departed as silently as they came. However, commanding the main road to Usumbara, Chogwe afforded opportunities for an occasional something in the looting line, which may have comforted the Baloch for its many drawbacks.

Our travellers confided their project of pushing on to Fuga to the Jemadar, who promised his goodwill, of course for a consideration. He even undertook to start them next day and—kept his word. He detached four of his garrison as guards, hired out the same number of slave-boys as porters, for the journey had to be performed on foot, and a stalwart guide, a huge, broad-shouldered negro, with coal-black skin and straight features, which looked as if cut in jet, was engaged to join the party at Tongwe, the next station. The kit was reduced to the strictest necessaries— surveying instruments, weapons, waterproof blankets, tea, sugar, and tobacco for ten days, a bag of dates and three bags of rice. The departure took place at 5 p.m., not without commotion. Each slave, grumbling loudly at his load, snatched up the lightest of packs, fought to avoid the heavier burdens, and rushed forward, regardless of what was left behind. This nuisance endured until abated by a form of correction easily divined. At length, escorted by the consumptive Jemadar and most of his company, Burton and Speke set forth for Tongwe.

The route was redeemed from monotony by the attacks of the bull-dog ant. Suddenly, while stopping to drink at some pools in a partially-cleared portion of thorny jungle, the whole party began to dance and shout like madmen, pulling off their clothes and frantically snatching at their lower limbs. The bite of this wretch, properly called atrox, burns like the point of a red-hot needle; and while engaged in its cannibal meal, literally beginning to devour man alive, even when its doubled-up body has been torn from the head, the pincers will remain buried in flesh. The only point in favour of this formican fiend is that, unlike its *confrère*, the stinking ant, which to young travellers suggests carrion hidden behind every bush, it has no smell.

The night spent with the Jemadar and his men was

truly characteristic, a savage opera scene. One recited his
Koran, another prayed in stentorian tones, a third told
funny stories, whilst a fourth trolled out in minor key lays
of love and war. This was varied by slapping away the
mosquitoes which flocked to the gleaming camp fires, by
clawing at the ants, and by challenging small parties of
natives who passed by with loads of grain for Pangani.
By-and-by the Baloch, who kept careful watch during
early night when there was no danger, slept like the dead
during the small hours, the time always chosen by African
freebooters, and indeed by almost all savages, to make their
unheroic onslaughts.

At daybreak, bidding a temporary adieu to the Jemadar
and most of his band, our party pushed on for Tongwe, or
the Great Hill. They ascended the flank of its north-
eastern spur, and found themselves on the chine of a little
ridge, with summer breezes on one side and a wintry blast
on the other. Thence, pursuing a rugged incline, after
about half an hour they entered the "fort," a crenellated,
flat-roofed, and whitewashed room, fourteen feet square,
supported inside by smoke-blackened rafters. It was
tenanted by two Baloch, who complained dismally of
dulness, and even more of ghosts. Though several goats
had been sacrificed to propitiate an ungrateful demon, he
still haunted the hill, while at times a weeping and wailing
of a whole chorus of distressed spirits made night hideous.

Tongwe is interesting as being the first offset of that
massive mountain terrace which forms the region of Usumbara ; here, in fact, begins the Highland block of Zangian
and Equatorial Africa, culminating in Kilima-njaro and
Mount Kenia. It rises abruptly from the plain and pro-
jects long spurs into the river valley, where the Rufu flows
noisily through a rocky trough, and whence can be distinctly heard the roar of the Pangani waterfall. Its summit,
about 2,000 feet above sea level, is clothed with jungle,
stunted cocoas, oranges grown wild and bitter, the castor

shrub, &c., through which our travellers had to cut their way with their swords when seeking compass bearings of the Nguru Hills. Below, a deep hole in its northern face supplies sweet "rock-water"; and the climate, temperate even in the height of an African summer, must have appeared doubly delicious after the humid, sickening heat of Zanzibar island and coast.

Before leaving Tongwe there was business to do which required a vast amount of palaver. The Jemadar had furnished an escort; but his soldiers, enervated by long habits of indolence, could hardly be induced to quit even for a week their hovel-homes, their black Venuses, and their whitey-brown offspring. Hard talking, however, enabled Burton not only to persuade them out of a half-expressed intention of returning forthwith to Chogwe, but to secure three men as additions to his small party. One, Sidi Mubarak, usually known by his nick-name, Bombay, proved the veritable black diamond of the lot. This negro spoke a little Hindostani, was bright and willing, and though of a *chétif* frame seemed as fresh after a thirty mile tramp as when he started. He had enlisted as a mercenary, but a little persuasion and the payment of his debts induced him to renounce soldiering and follow the fortunes of the expedition. Bombay gave a comical reason for working well—his duty to his stomach, and certainly his idol kept him straight. Such a gem amongst guides could scarcely fail to rise rapidly: he began by escorting our party to Fuga as head gun-carrier, became later Speke's confidential servant, and finally in 1871, when Stanley went in search of Livingstone, Bombay was appointed chief of the caravan.

With this treasure in their train, Burton and Speke started for Fuga, February 10th. Their path was curious enough, the land brick-red, a common colour in Africa as in the Brazil : and its stain extended half way up the tree-boles streaked by ants with ascending and descending galleries. Overhead floated a canopy of sea-green verdure, pierced by myriads of little sun-pencils; whilst the effulgent dome, purified as with fire from mist and vapour, set the picture in a frame of gold and ultramarine. Painful splendours! The heat began to tell upon the men, and the result was a general clamour for water. Only one of the Baloch had brought a gourd; but the four slave boys whose instincts of self-preservation approached the miraculous, found a puddle, a discovery they carefully kept to themselves, leaving the rest to endure their thirst until a similar find some hours later.

A halt of thirty-six hours was made at Kahode, the village of a friendly but extremely greedy chief—Sultan Mamba. Recognising the Baloch, this worthy donned a scarlet cloak, apparently his only one, superintended the launching of his royal canoe, and, as our party landed, received them with rollicking greetings and those immoderate explosive cachinnations which render the African family to all appearance so "jolly" a race. Sad to tell, an indifferent character, even in these regions, was Sultan Mamba. Converted to Islamism during a sojourn at Zanzibar, dubbed Abdullah by his proselytizer, no sooner did he sniff once more his native air, than he fell away from prayer, ablution and grace generally, and reverted to the more congenial practices of highwaying and hard drinking. Nor was this all. An inveterate beggar, he asked for everything he saw, from a barrel of gunpowder to a bottle of brandy. He announced that his people had only three wants—powder, ball and spirits; and he could supply in return men, women and children—in plain language, slaves. On receiving two embroidered caps, a pair of muslins, and a cotton shawl, he hoped no doubt to see the brandy and gunpowder forthcoming by and by; for on parting he waxed quite pathetic, swearing he loved his new friends, and offering the use of his canoe on the return journey. But when they reappeared with empty hands, Sultan

Mamba, like many a white brother, scarcely deigned to notice them.

From Kahode two roads lead to Fuga. Though more than double in length, our travellers chose that along the Rufu, as they doubted whether their porters could climb the passes, the heat having become intense. Marching by the riverside, they had an opportunity of examining the rude bridges of the country—floors of narrow planks laid horizontally upon rough piers of cocoa trunks, forked to receive cross-pieces, and planted a few feet apart. The structure was parapeted with coarse basket-work, and sometimes supplied with jungle ropes knotted, by way of hand-rail. These the number and daring of the crocodiles rendered necessary.

At Msiki Mguru, a village built upon an island formed by divers rapid and roaring branches of the Rufu, Burton's sense of humour was much tickled. After a night passed in incessant struggles with ants and other sleep destroyers which shall be nameless—he was as yet uninitiated in the African secret of strewing ashes round the feet of the cartel or bedstead—he sallied forth at an early hour to inspect his hosts. They had welcomed him very hospitably, some of the women, black but comely, being far from shy ; but the latter when chaffed by the Baloch and asked how they would like the men in trousers as husbands, simply replied, " Not at all."

Later the same day our travellers resumed their march, following the left bank of the Rufu, a broad line of flat boulders, thicket, grass and sedge, with divers trickling streams between. The way had become comparatively populous, the paths crowded with a grass kilted and skin-clad race, chiefly women and small girls leading children, each with a button of hair left upon its scraped crown. The adults toiling under loads of manioc holcus and maize, poultry, sugar-cane, and water-pots in which tufts of leaves had been stuck to prevent splashing, were bound for a

Golio or market held in an open place not far off. Here
none started or fled from the white faces.

Ascending a hill and making an abrupt turn from north-
west nearly due east, the party found themselves opposite,
and about ten miles distant from a tall azure mountain-
curtain, the highlands of Fuga. Below, the plains were
everywhere dotted with haycock villages. Lofty tamerinds,
the large leaved plantain, and the parasol-shaped papaw
grew wild amongst the thorny trees. After walking a total
of sixteen miles, at about 4 p.m. Burton and his followers
were driven by a violent storm of thunder, lightning, and a
raw wind, which at once lowered the mercury and made
slave boys shudder and whimper into the palaver-house of
one of the little settlements. The shelter consisted of a
thatched roof propped by uprights, and guiltless of walls ;
the floor was half mud, half mould, and the only tenants
were flies and mosquitoes. Fires were lighted at once, and
all made themselves as comfortable as conditions would
admit.

Next morning dawned with one of those steady little
cataclysms seen to best advantage near the Line. But,
thoroughly tired of the steaming barn, the men loaded and
set out in a lucid interval towards the highlands. As they
drew near the rain shrank to a mere drizzle, gradually
ceased, and was replaced by that reeking, fetid heat which
travellers in the tropics have learned to fear. Everybody
had a good rest before attempting the steep incline that lay
in front ; the slippery way had wearied the slaves, though
aided by three porters hired that morning, and the sun,
struggling with vapours, was still hot enough to overpower
the whole party.

At 1 p.m. they proceeded to breast the pass leading
from the lowland alluvial plain to the threshold of the
Ethiopic Olympus. The path, gently rising at first, wound
amongst groves of coarse bananas, whose arms of satiny
sheen here smoothed and streaked, there shredded by the

hill-winds, hid purple flowers and huge bunches of green fruit. Issuing from this dripping canopy, the travellers ascended a steep goat-track, forded a crystal bourn, and having reached midway, sat down to enjoy the rarefied air, which felt as if a weight had been suddenly taken off their shoulders. The view before them was extensive and suggestive, if not beautiful. The mountain fell under their feet in rugged folds, clothed with patches of plantains, wild mulberries, and stately trees whose lustrous green glittered against the red ochreous earth. Opposite and below, half veiled with rank steam, lay the yellow Nyika and the Wazegura lowlands; and beyond the well-wooded line of the Rufu, a uniform purple plain stretched to the rim of the southern and western horizon, as far as the telescope could trace it.

Resuming their march, our party climbed rather than walked up the steep bed of a torrent. Standing at last on the Pass summit,[1] they perceived a curious contrast of aspects; the northern and eastern slopes bluff and barren, the southern and western teeming with luxuriant vegetation. After another three-mile walk along the flanks of domed hills, and crossing a shallow bourn which nearly froze their parched feet, they turned a corner, and suddenly sighted, upon the summit of a grassy cone opposite, an unfenced heap of haycock huts, a cluster of beehives with concentric rings—Fuga.

The Baloch formed up and fired a volley, and our travellers, thus duly announced, were conducted through frightened crowds to four tattered huts, standing about 300 feet below the settlement, and assigned by superstition as strangers' quarters. Even the Sultan's son and heir was expected to abide in this shelter until the " lucky hour " admitted him to the " presence." Cold rain and

---

[1] About 4,000 feet above sea level.

sharp mountain breezes rendered any accommodation acceptable. The hovels were cleared of sheep and goats,
the valuables housed, fires lighted, while, mindful of the
mingled inquisitiveness and vanity of these African chiefs,
Bombay started on a mission to Sultan Kimwere to request
an interview.

Before dark appeared three bare-headed ministers, who
declared in a long palaver that council must squat on two
knotty points. First, why had these strangers entered
their Sultan's country through the lands of a hostile tribe?
—an objection already suggested at Pangani; secondly,
when would His Highness's Mganga, or magician, find
an hour propitious for the audience? One of the Baloch,
with rare presence of mind, declared the English travellers
to 1 e 'ikewise Waganga, a piece of news which so impressed
the " Cabinet," that they bolted in hot haste to spread it
abroad.

They soon returned breathless with a summons to the
" Palace." The three black wisacres led the way, through
wind, rain, and gathering gloom, to a clump of huts half-
hidden by trees, and spreading over a little eminence
opposite to and below Fuga. Only three Baloch were
allowed as escort. They were deprived of their matchlocks ; but Burton and his companion, when requested to
give up their swords, refused point blank.

Sultan Kimwere, who described himself as the " Lion
of the Lord," was an old, old man, emaciated and wrinkled.
None could have recognised him as the " leonine, royal
personage, the tall and corpulent form, with engaging
features and large eyes, red and penetrating," that so
impressed Dr. Krapf in 1848. The poor old fellow, whose
hands and feet were stained with leprosy, was dying of old
age and disease, and lacked even strength to dress properly,
his clothes being as dingy and worn out as his miserable
body. He was covered, as he lay upon his cot of bamboo
and cowskin, with the doubled cotton cloth called in India

a "do-pattá," and he rested on a Persian rug apparently coeval with his person.

His palace was only slightly superior to an ordinary hut, and very unsavoury must it have been at that moment, crammed with dignitaries no cleaner than their prince. The traveller's errand was enquired, and the dusky assembly being sadly unlettered, Burton, contrary to etiquette on such occasions, had to read out the Sultan of Zanzibar's letter. He was then cordially welcomed to Fuga; but Kimwere had strong personal reasons for his unusual civility. Caring for little else save to recover health and strength, and hearing the strangers were able to scrutinize trees and stones as well as stars, he believed at once they were European medicine men, and before entering even on the question of presents, he directed them to compound forthwith a draught which would restore him that same evening to his pristine vigour. Vainly did Burton parry this preposterous request by the objection that all his drugs had been left at Pangani; the Sultan signified that the two physicians might wander over his hills and seek the plants required.

Half an hour passed in palaver, and then the travellers returned to their quarters. Kimwere's presents, which his amiable son had tried to intercept, were forwarded with due ceremony; while Burton found awaiting him a prime bullock, a basketful of Indian corn boiled to a thick paste, and balls of unripe bananas peeled and mashed up with sour milk. A truly English meal of indifferently cooked, tough, freshly-killed beef was followed by the heavy sleep of the gorged, which angry blasts, sharp showers, and groaning trees had no power to disturb.

The rainy season had set in at Fuga; during Burton's stay the weather was a dismal succession of drip, drizzle and drench. So clouded was the sky that not a star could be seen; it was simply impossible to take a single observation. The two Englishmen employed their leisure in roaming over the hills to gather as much information concerning the country as they could extract from the timid inhabitants. Fuga, a heap of some five hundred huts, contained at that time about 3,000 souls. It was forbidden to foreigners because the ruler's wives, to the unconscionable number of three hundred, inhabited a portion, and it also had the honour of sheltering the chief magicians, in whose lodges criminals sought sanctuary. The people of both sexes appeared industrious for Africans, the result of a cold climate, but they were wretchedly governed; the Sultan selling his subjects, men, women and children, old and young, singly or by families, and whole villages. Heavy taxes in kind also enriched the "Lion" and his family. It may be added, as some excuse, that the said family must have required a large revenue; each wife was surrounded by slaves, and portioned with a separate hut and plantation, while the sons alone numbered between eighty and ninety. Some of the latter had Islamized, but their sire remained a pagan.

It being out of the question to do much in such weather, and as Burton and Speke were daily expecting their seasoning fever, they remained at Fuga only two days and two nights. On Monday, February 16th, they took leave of and were formally dismissed by the Sultan. The old man was cruelly disappointed. Long had he hoped for a white Mganga, and now two had visited him and were about to depart without an effort to cure him. Doubtless Burton would have done his best had he brought his medicine chest, for he mentions, in his usual kind-hearted way, how sad it was to see the wistful, lingering look which accompanied the Lion's farewell—a farewell *à tout jamais*. But not all the College of Physicians could have restored to the centenarian his vanished strength, nor patched up for long his feeble and suffering frame.

Our travellers made Kahode the third night, where they found Sultan Mamba as disappointed in his fashion as the

Old Lion had been in his. No presents, no canoe; so his once loved friends mourning the absent *Louisa*[1] had to be punted over the deep and rapid Pangani on a bundle of cocoa fronds, to the imminent peril of their chronometers. From this point the party followed the river course downwards, in order to ascertain by inspection if the account of its falls and rapids had been exaggerated. The environment was far from genial. Burton wrote his notes amidst a general grumble. The slaves whimpered every time it rained or blew; one of the Baloch declared the rate of walking excessive; another asserted that he had twice visited the Lake Regions of the far interior, but had never known such hardships even in his dreams. More valiant men might have quailed before this wretched march. Wet, wind, thunder and lightning, a track slippery with ooze and mire, crossed at every few yards by thorn trees with spikes two inches long, overgrown with sedgy spear-grass, and constantly obstructed by huge half-exposed roots, which many a time caused a troublesome fall, must at times have bewildered even Burton's strong brain. No trip in a " bath-chair " was that return to the sea-coast.

Nor did matters improve much at Kizungu, an island settlement of Wazegura. There was plenty of palaver but nothing to eat. The escort went to bed supperless and in a vile temper ; their chiefs would have fared as badly had not a villager brought in after dark an elderly hen and a handful of rice. But here ensued a funny scene. One of the Baloch had purchased a slave ; by some grave error of judgment he had failed to tether this chattel securely, and so, on the very evening after making the investment, he had the exquisite misery of seeing his dollars bolting at a pace which defied pursuit.

At sunrise, our party, again on the tramp, stood by nine o'clock on an eminence to view the falls of Pangani. The

---

[1] She had to be left at Pangani owing to scarcity of porterage.

stream swiftly emerging from a dense, dark growth of
tropical jungle, hurls itself in three separate sheets, fringed
with flashing foam, down a rugged wall of brown rock.
The fall is broken by a midway ledge, whence a second
leap precipitates the waters into a lower basin of mist-veiled
stone, arched over by a fog-rainbow, the segment of a circle
painted with faint prismatic hues. The spectacle is grander
during the wet season, when the river, forming a single
horse-shoe, acquires volume and momentum enough to clear
the step that splits the shrunken supplies in the " dries " ;
for of all natural objects the cataract most requires that
first element of sublimity, size. Still, even at the date of
Burton's visit, the Pangani Falls with their white spray
and silvery mists, set off by a background of black jungle
and by a framework of slaty rain-cloud, offered a picture
sufficiently effective to save him from disappointment.

Resuming their march, our travellers, after a weary
stage of fourteen miles, found themselves once more within
the hospitable shelter of Chogwe. The Jemadar and his
garrison received the wanderers in most friendly fashion,
marvelling much at their speedy return from Fuga, where,
as at Harar, a visitor could never reckon upon prompt
dismissal. Sultan Kimwere had frequently detained Arab
and other guests a whole fortnight before his Mganga
would fix upon a fit time for audience.

A few days were devoted to rest and kitchen physic. The
Englishmen's feet, chafed by heavy boots which many a
time had been soaked, roughly dried, and soaked again,
were treated with simple remedies, flour and white of egg.
Their discomforts alleviated, our travellers refreshed by a
short interval of *dolce far niente*, paid the Jemadar and his
men for their services, and moved down to Pangani.
There Said, who had watched over their chattels with the
fidelity of a shepherd's dog, greeted them with joyful
demonstrations, while Gactano, who had accompanied the
party to Fuga in the capacity of cook-boy, was no doubt

delighted to jabber to his *confrère* about the wonders he had witnessed, and the dangers he had heroically encountered.

So far the trial trip had answered all expectations. One hundred and fifty miles had been covered in eleven days, a fair budget of details amassed, fancy maps corrected, and, most important of any, the correct measuring of distances in that part of Africa had been acquired. Prudence should have suggested another interval of *dolce far niente*, until the arrival of the expected vessel from Zanzibar. Unluckily, our travellers' sporting instincts, fired *en route* by the frequent appearance of hippopotami, drove them to indulge in a day's hunting, a day which, judging from the number of unhappy brutes that received their quietus, must have been long and fatiguing. I spare my readers the gory details. Even Burton grew tired at last of the easy work of reducing poor, foolish Behemoth to a heap of bloody bones; and it would have been well for both slayer and slain had the ugly monsters been left to snort and dive undisturbed in the warm and pleasant waters of the Pangani River; for the sporting trip, added to an imprudent geographical excursion, taken under a burning sun almost immediately afterwards, brought on the long-expected fever in one of its sharpest forms.

Both men were down with it, and a wretched fortnight ensued in the Wali's house. The symptoms of this " bilious remittent " read like those of virulent influenza *sans* the catarrh. It is preceded by general languor and listlessness, with lassitude of limbs and heaviness of head, with chills and dull pains in the body and extremities, and with a frigid sensation creeping up the spine. Then comes a mild cold fit, succeeded by flushed face, an extensive thirst, burning heat of skin, a splitting headache and nausea. During Burton's first attack he ate nothing for seven days ; and, despite the perpetual craving thirst, no liquid would remain on the stomach. Speke also was very ill, but less

so than his friend. Dismal indeed must have been those
last days at Pangani. The Jemadar seeing he could do
nothing for the sick men, took leave, committing them to
Allah. Sundry citizens intending to be kind and agreeable,
but failing as regards the latter point, strolled in asking the
silliest of questions. Repose was out of the question.
During the day gnats and flies added another sting to the
horrors of fever ; by night, rats nibbled the patients' feet,
impatient for their death. Unspeakably did the invalids
long for the arrival of the vessel promised by Colonel
Hamerton. Their windows fronted the sea and they spent
every hour of daylight in gazing at the passing sails and
exchanging regrets as one by one hove in sight, drew near,
and scudded by.

There had been a delay. The craft had sailed from
Zanzibar as arranged, before the end of February, but the
fellows who manned her could not pass unvisited their
houses on the coast ; they wasted a whole week, and did
not make Pangani until the evening of March 5th. The
sick Englishmen and their servants embarked at once ;
Speke walking to the shore, his companion, who could only
just bear the exertion of leaving his room, having to be
carried like a paralysed centenarian. On their arrival in
port the good consul sent both men to bed, where they remained nearly a week, not recovering normal health until
another month.

CHAPTER IX

A T noon, June 14th, 1857, the *Artemise*, an old frigate belonging to the Indian Navy, sailed from Zanzibar harbour with the Expedition on board.

Nearly four months had elapsed since Burton and Speke returned from Pangani. Their time had been occupied in buying outfit, which could be more economically provided during the trading season, and in arranging for escort and porterage. The Sayyid himself ordered Said bin Salim to the coast to engage men for the up-country journey; and had this " respectable person " executed the errand properly, he would have spared his employers much trouble and fatigue. Unluckily, the mongrel Arab was such an arrant rascal—a fact soon discovered—that he never performed any duty attended with the slightest risk to his precious self with zeal or thoroughness. So when Burton and his companion arrived at Kaole they found that out of the 170 men required only 36 were available. The Baloch told off by the Sayyid as guard, and the personal following, including the Portuguese lads and Bombay, amounted, all told, to 12 persons; and although the escort was presently increased by 36 soldiers, Burton knew his caravan was sadly undermanned. Porters were indispensable. Cotton, cloth, brass, wire, and various sorts of beads are a bulky form of currency, and the savage tribes amongst whom our explorers were to travel recognised no other, cowries not being then circulated in Ugogo and Unyamwezi. Besides these loads an abundance of ammunition was required, not to mention stores of all kinds. So, at the very outset, as I said before, the invaluable *Louisa* had to be left behind, to her owners inexpressible annoyance, and many a less important possession kept her company.

Hopeless chaos seemed reigning at Kaole, but the " strong man " was not dismayed. Soon after Burton appeared on the scene something like order was evolved. Asses were purchased, drivers persuaded to accompany them (African donkeys require strong measures to coax them forward on their daily stage of duty), and, better still, thirty-five additional porters who sensibly preferred travelling through the more dangerous tracts without the compromising presence of white men, were engaged to meet the caravan with the greater part of the luggage at Zungomero, in K'hutu, a safe rendezvous of foreign merchants. As regards credentials, our explorer was well provided. The Sayyid had given introductory letters to Musa Mzuri the principal trader in Unyamwezi, to the Arabs there resident, and to any subject who might be travelling in the interior.

Bidding what proved a last farewell to good Colonel Hamerton, Burton, who had been superintending operations from the *Artemise*, going to and fro from the frigate, justly deeming the disorderly natives would be more manageable within reach of her guns, landed definitively at Kaole, on the Zanzibar coast, June 27th. During a short delay there he was much amused while settling accounts with the collector of customs, one Ladha Damha, at overhearing a conversation between this worthy and his clerk. Our explorer had insisted upon their inserting in the estimate of necessaries the sum required to purchase a boat on the shores of Tanganyika.

" Will he ever reach it ? " asked good old Ladha, conveying his question through the medium of Cutchee, a dialect of which, with the inconsequence of a Hindu, he assumed the traveller to be profoundly ignorant.

" Of course not," replied the clerk. " What is he, that he should pass through Ugogo ? " a province about half way.

Thus cheered and fortified, Burton, accompanied by Said, Valentine, three Baloch, and three asses bought that morning at the custom house, started for Kiringani, whither Speke had preceded him with the bulk of the guard. Another day or two's delay ensued in that stifling village ; and our explorer, who perceived by the hang-dog look of the Jemadar in command of the escort that the man's spirits required some form of artificial stimulation, engaged a Mganga. This sage, after having been carefully bribed to foretell prosperity for the expedition, and prosperity only, graciously consented to display his prophetic gift. Taking a seat opposite Burton, the ancient demanded a second fee, then indulged in a solemn and dignified pinch of snuff. Presently he drew forth a large gourd containing the great medicine, upon which no profane eye might gaze; the vessel repeatedly shaken gave out a vulgar sound as if filled with pebbles and bits of metal. Placing the implement upon the ground, Thaumaturges extracted from his mat-bag two thick goat's horns connected by a snake-skin, decorated with bunches of curiously shaped iron bells. He held one in the left hand, and with the right caused the point of the other to perform sundry gyrations, now directing it towards Burton, then towards himself, then at the awe-struck bystanders; waving his head, muttering, whispering, swaying his body to and fro, and at times violently rattling the bells. When fully primed with the spirit of prophecy, he spoke out pretty much in the style of his brotherhood all the world over. The journey would be prosperous. There would be much talking but little killing. Before navigating the Sea of Ujiji, a sheep or a parti-coloured hen should be killed and thrown into the lake. Successful voyage ; plenty of ivory and slaves ; happy returns to wife and family.

At 4 p.m. June 29th, with all the usual noise and con-fusion attendant on a start, the expedition moved slowly onwards to Bomani. The route finally decided upon was the Arab line of traffic first laid open to Lake Tanganyika

by Sayf bin Said in 1825. Burton's caravan, organised
after the normal coast model, contained, as we shall see,
certain elements of success, but it was badly equipped and
undermanned. This was partly owing to want of funds
(Speke and Grant's cost £2,500, and Stanley's last,
£27,000), also to the then scarcity of porters on the coast.
Burton, too, had been unfortunate in his men. Said was
a dishonest old coward, the Baloch were unusually ferocious
even for Baloch, and the guide, Kidogo, who did not join
the expedition until its arrival at Zungomero, was unequal
to his duties. To sum all in Burton's own words, " There
was not a soul in the caravan, from Said bin Salim to the
veriest pauper, that did not desert or attempt to do so; but
with ten thousand pounds we might have gone anywhere
or done anything; as it was, we had to do what we could."

During the first week they crept along at a snail's pace,
so slowly, indeed, that they could hear the booming of the
Artemise's evening gun. It was judged safer to advance
with some deliberation, as the maritime tribes through
whose lands they were passing were treacherous to a degree.
Not long before M. Maizan had been cruelly murdered, and
dismal stories passed from mouth to mouth as the village
where the deed was done came in sight. They were unmolested, however; and as the country itself was uninteresting, plain, swamp and jungle, instead of any detailed
description, a sketch of a single day's march of this "porter
journey " may give my reader some idea of Burton's
tortoise-like progress towards the Sea of Ujiji.

At 5 a.m. all still silent as the tomb, even the watch-
man nodding over his fire. About an hour later red-faced
chanticleer—there were sometimes half a dozen of these
feathered camp followers, prime favourites with the porters,
who carried them on their poles by turns—flapped his wings
and crew a salutation to the dawn. At the first glimmer of
light the torpid Goanese, trembling with cold (about 60° F.),
built up the fire, and prepared breakfast for their masters.

This meal consisted of tea or coffee, when procurable, or rice-milk and cakes raised with whey, or a porridge-like water-gruel. The Baloch required more substantial food; chanting their spiritual songs that followed prayer, they squatted round a cauldron placed upon a roaring fire, and fortified the inner man with boiled meat and toasted pulse.

About 5 a.m. the camp was fairly roused, and low chatting arose from all sides. This was a critical moment. The porters might have promised over night to start early and make a long march, but, "uncertain, coy, and hard to please," they changed their minds like the fair sex, the chilly morning rendering them quite unlike the comparatively active men of the preceding evening. Were the weather too uninviting, or had they symptoms of fever, it were vain to expect a move. If, however, a difference of opinion existed, a little active stimulating would force on a march. Then a louder conversation led to cries of "Kwecha! Pakia! Hopa! Collect! Pack! Set out!"—and to some peculiarly African boasts, "I am an ass; I am a camel!" reminding one of the yet more spirited announcement of Dickens' raven; all accompanied by a roar of bawling voices, drumming, whistling, and the braying of horns. The personal servants struck the tents and received small burdens which, when possible, they shirked. Sometimes the guide, Kidogo, did his master the honour to enquire the programme of the day; if ill-tempered he omitted that ceremony. The porters stuck to the fires until driven away and compelled to unstack the loads piled before the tents, when they gradually shouldered their packs and poured out of the camp. Burton and Speke, if well enough to ride, mounted their asses, which were led by the gun-bearers; if unfit for exercise, they were borne in hammocks slung to long poles and carried by two men at a time. Most part of the journey, however, Burton was able to perform on foot.

All being ready, the Kirangozi, or guide, selected his load, ever one of the lightest, raised his flag, a plain blood-

red, emblem of caravans from Zanzibar, and, followed by a
porter tom-tomming upon a kettle-drum much resembling a
European hour-glass, proudly strutted in front of the shouting, yelling mob.   He was a striking personage ; how the
caravan could have dispensed with him so far as Zungomero
seems hard to imagine.   Robed in the splendour of scarlet
broadcloth, a narrow piece about six feet long with a central
aperture for the neck, and with streamers dangling before
and behind, his head decorated with the spoils of a black
and white tippet-monkey and capped with a tall cup-shaped
bunch of owl's feathers, he must have looked like some
worthy judge in full paraphernalia who had run mad in the
wilds.   His followers gradually forming into Indian file,
wound behind him like a monstrous land serpent over dale
and plain.   The bearers of cloth and beads, poised upon
either shoulder, or sometimes raised upon the head for rest,
packs that resembled huge bolsters, followed the ivory
carriers, whose place was immediately after the guide.   The
maximum weight of burden was about seventy pounds
avoirdupois ;   but in Eastern Africa, as elsewhere, the
weakest go to the wall, the sturdiest fellows were usually
the least loaded.   Behind the cloth and bead bearers
straggled porters laden with lighter stuff, hides, salt,
tobacco, iron hoes, boxes and bags, beds and tents, pots
and water-gourds.   In separate parties marched the armed
men, women and children, and the asses neatly laden with
saddle-bags of giraffe and buffalo hide.   A Mganga accompanied the caravan as chaplain and doctor ;   he never
disdained to act porter, but invariably claimed in virtue of
his calling little to carry and plenty to eat.   The rear was
brought up by the owners, hardest worked of all, who often
remained a little behind to superintend matters and to prevent desertion.

The costume of the guide has already been described ;
as regards that of his fellow Africans it was scanty save in
the item of ornament.   Some of the men wore a strip of

zebra's mane bound round the head with the bristly hair standing out like a saint's gloria : others preferred a long bit of stiffened ox-tail rising like a unicorn's horn at least a foot above the forehead. Other adornments were fillets of white, blue or scarlet cloth, and huge bunches of ostrich, crane and jay's feathers crowning the head like tufts of certain fowls. Massive ivory bracelets or heavy brass bangles encircled the arms, strings of beads the necks, while small iron bells strapped below the knee or ankle by the coxcombs of the party, tinkled like the heroine's of our nursery rhyme. All carried some weapon, the heaviest armed a bow, a quiver full of arrows, two or three spears, and a little battle-axe borne on the shoulder.

The normal recreations of a march were whistling, singing, drumming, and abundant squabbling — in fact, perpetual noise. On the road it was considered prudent as well as pleasurable to be as loud as possible, in order to impress upon plunderers an exaggerated idea of the caravan's strength. When friendly caravans met, the two Kirangozis sidled up in stage fashion with a stride and a stop, and with sidelong looks pranced until arrived within a short distance, then suddenly and simultaneously ducking, they came to loggerheads and exchanged a butt violently as fighting rams. This might be mistaken for the beginning of a faction, but if there were no bad blood it usually ended in shouts of laughter.

At about 8 A.M., when the fiery sun topped the trees and a pool of water or a shady place appeared, the planting of Kidogo's red flag and a musket shot or two announced a short halt. The porters stacked their loads and loitered in parties, drinking, smoking tobacco or bhang, and disputing eagerly with regard to the resting-place for the night. On long marches Burton and his companion then seized the opportunity of discussing the contents of two baskets, which were carried by a slave under the eye of the Goanese.

Plenty of nourishment was required. On sunny days
the heated earth, against which the horniest sole never
became proof, tried the feet like polished leather boots on
a quarter-deck near the Line. Throughout Eastern Africa
made roads were then unknown. Even the most frequented
routes were mere foot-tracks like goat-walks, one or two
spans broad ; while during the rains the path, such as it
was, got overgrown with vegetation. In jungly parts the
tracks were mere tunnels through thorns and under branchy
trees, which cruelly hindered the men by catching their
loads. In others they spanned miry swamps intersected
with rivulets, breast deep, with muddy bottoms and steep,
slippery banks. As to the mountainous regions, the unlucky porters had to swarm like apes up almost perpendicular precipices, leaving the unburdened blacks to drag
along the asses and assist their white employers.

The final halt was therefore well earned. But it always
gave rise to many quarrels. Each selfish body hurried
forward to secure the best bothy in the Kraal, or most
comfortable hut in the village. For these halts were
managed in various ways. Some tribes admitted strangers
into their villages, others refused at any cost. In a third
case, if unsociable natives were timid or fairly harmless,
caravans would seize the best lodgings by force ; while, in
a fourth, strangers judged it safer to pitch their tents in
clear, open spaces. However lodged, the more energetic
members at once applied themselves to making all snug for
the night ; some hewing down young trees, others collecting heaps of leafy branches, one acting architect, and many
bringing in huge loads of firewood. To the East African a
bivouac in the open appears an intolerable hardship ; and
when the sudden changes of temperature are considered, it
is not astonishing that any shelter, even that of a thick
bush, is preferred to none. A heap of thorns round the
camp completed the arrangements, and then all applied
themselves to the pleasant work of refection.

Burton's day, when he was not on the march, was spent chiefly under a spreading tree, seldom in his flimsy tent. His occupations were writing his diary, sketching, and attending to the business of his caravan. Cloth had to be doled out, porters persuaded to scour the country for provisions, " housekeeping " supervised, for provisions were an ever fruitful source of dissension. Food of some sort was generally procurable ; it varied from holcus, bean-broth, or leathery goat-steak, to " fixings " of delicate venison, fatted capon, and young guinea-fowl or partridge with sauce compounded of bruised rice and milk. Dinner was at 4 p.m. At first the Goanese declined to cook " pretty dishes," such as pasties and rissoles, on the plea that such efforts were impracticable on the march, but they changed their minds when warned that persistence in their theory might lead to painful results.

At eventide the travellers were treated to a little music, vocal and instrumental. Knowing something of Kisiwahili, Burton was highly flattered by the following composition, which his impudent blacks bawled out in his hearing :

" The wicked white man goes from the shore,
　　　Grub, grub !
We will follow as long as he gives us good food,
　　　Grub, grub !
We will traverse the hill and the stream with this wicked white man,
　　　Grub, grub ! "

" It is possible," said George Eliot, " that Brazilian monkeys see hardly anything in us." Evidently the black members of the procession wending towards Ujiji entertained but a poor opinion of their leader.

A travelling party of pedestrians and asses, mostly loaded, could hardly be expected to advance very rapidly. Nevertheless, from June 27th to July 14th the caravan had covered 118 miles, and succeeded in safely entering the province of K'hutu. This seems for Africa fairly rapid marching, as Stanley, whose caravans were invariably

14

better equipped than Burton's, mentions seven miles per diem his maximum rate of progress. At first K'hutu promised well, the dense thicket opened out into a fine park country, peculiarly rich in game, where the calabash and giant trees of the seaboard gave way to mimosas and gums. Large gnus pranced about, pawing the ground and shaking their formidable manes; antelopes clustered together on the plain, or travelled in herds to slake their thirst at the river. The homely cry of the partridge sounded from every brake, and numberless guinea-fowls looked like large bluebells upon the trees. Beasts and birds afforded good meals; but presently it became necessary to wade through bogs from a hundred yards to a mile in length; the land appeared rotten, and the jungle smelt of death. The weather was a succession of raw mist, torrents of rain, and fiery sunbursts. In spite of the latter, the humid vegetation dripped with dew until midday, and rendered the black earth, even when free from bogs, greasy and slippery. K'hutu was a home of miasma.

Small wonder that by the time our Englishmen reached Dut'humi, Burton had an attack of marsh fever, which prostrated him more or less for twenty days. Speke suffered even more acutely, having a sunstroke superadded that seriously affected his brain. The two Goanese, who might have assisted their sick masters, seized the opportunity to yield themselves wholly to maladies brought on by over-eating, threatening, indeed, then and there to give up the ghost. Burton's marvellous courage under physical suffering, rare even in a brave man, never shone more brightly than on this occasion. The odious slave traffic was in full swing. A raid took place during his illness at Dut'humi, and as soon as he was able to move, with his head still swimming and hands yet trembling from weakness, he headed a small expedition against the robber, rescued seven unhappy wights, including two decrepit old women, who thanked him with tears of joy, and restored them to their homes. This feat was all the more admirable as the caravan was causing him great uneasiness. Said, as treasurer, had proved a very Judas; thirteen months' supplies had disappeared in as many weeks, and the asses were dying so rapidly that at one time it seemed as though the expedition must come to a standstill.

Struggling on again through horrid K'hutu, they crossed a steep and muddy bed, knee-deep even in the dry season, and entered fields under the outlying hillocks of the highlands. These low cones, like similar formations in India, are not inhabited; they are even more malarious than the plains. The surface is rocky, and the woodage, not ceasing as in higher elevations, extends from base to summit. Beyond the cultivation the route plunges into a jungle where the European traveller realises every preconceived idea of Africa's aspect, at once hideous and grotesque. The black greasy earth, veiled with thick shrubbery, supports in the more open spaces screens of tiger and speargrass, twelve or thirteen feet high, every blade a finger's breadth; and the towering trees are often clothed from root to twig with huge epiphytes, forming heavy columns of densest verdure, and clustering upon the tops in semblance of enormous birds' nests. The ground ever rain-drenched, emits the odour of sulphuretted hydrogen; and that no feature of miasma should be lacking to complete the picture, filthy heaps of the rudest hovels, built in holes in the jungle, sheltered their few miserable inhabitants whose frames were lean with constant intoxication, and whose limbs distorted by ulcerous sores, attested the hostility of Nature to mankind.

Two days' tramp through the fetid flat brought our party to the nearest outposts of Zungomero, or third of the K'hutu lowlands. Here were several caravans with pitched tents, piles of ivory and crowds of porters; and here waited the gang of thirty-six prudent souls who had preceded our traveller through the more dangerous regions. Unfortunately, owing to numerous desertions, even more porters were required, so a halt of a fortnight was necessary in a spot described as a very hot-bed of pestilence. It was chosen by the Arabs and others as a rendezvous on account of provisions being cheap and plentiful. Grain was so abundant when Burton passed through in 1857, that the inhabitants existed almost entirely upon pombe, or holcus beer, a practice readily imitated by their visitors. Bhang and the datura plant, dear to asthmatics, growing wild, added to the attractions of the place. Its list of fascinations, however, ended here, for our traveller declared that Zungomero very nearly accommodated him with a wet grave. His only lodging was under the closed eaves of a hut built African fashion, one abode within the other. The roof was a sieve, the walls were systems of chinks, and the floor was a sheet of mud. Outside the rain poured pertinaciously, as if K'hutu had been Ulster, and the tangled bank of the Mgeta River, lying within pistol shot of his hovel, added its quota of fell miasma. To crown the general discomfort, the Baloch, expecting everything to be done for them by the porters, became almost mutinous because left to make shelters for themselves, and nearly caused a riot amongst the villagers by robbery and general misconduct.

Fortunately, the next station presented a sort of transformation scene. From central Zungomero to the nearest ascent of the Usagara Mountains is a march of only five hours. But at a station called the "Little Tamarind," not more than three hundred feet above the ghastly plains, there was a wondrous change. Pure, sweet mountain air, clear blue skies lending their tints to highland ridges, in lieu of pelting rain and clammy mists veiling a gross growth of fetor. Dull mangrove and dismal jungle were supplanted by tall solitary trees, amongst which the lofty tamarind rose conspicuously graceful; and swamps cut by a network of streams and stagnant pools, gave way to dry, healthy slopes with short steep pitches and gently shelving hills. During the first night, the soothing murmur of a stream mingled with the faint sighing of the zephyrs, while the moonbeams lay like sheets of snow upon the ruddy uplands. Burton never wearied of contemplating the scene, for contrasting with the beauty around him, still stretched in sight the Slough of Despond, unhappy Zun-gomero, lead-coloured above, mud-coloured below, wind-swept, fog-veiled, and deluged by clouds that dared not approach these delectable mountains.

Sad sights, however, presented themselves even here. The path which ran over a succession of short steep hills with a rufous brown soil, dotted with blocks and stones, and thinly covered with grass, had been traversed only twenty-four hours before by a caravan smitten with small-pox. The track was marked by many swollen corpses of porters who had fallen behind and perished unaided amidst these solitary wilds. The poor creatures, almost blinded by disease, had staggered along until strength departed, and then lain down to die. Near most villages, detached tents were set apart for victims of this horrible malady; but, on the march, if one fell, his heavily-burdened breth-ren could not have assisted him even had they the will. Burton's Moslems passed these melancholy remains with averted faces and exclamations of disgust; while one de-crepit old porter gazed at them and wept with terror lest he should share their fate.

At Zonhwe, near a little river of that name still in these East African Ghauts, the expedition again threatened to collapse. The instruments, except two valuable thermome-ters, had been broken or rendered almost useless; another ass had died, reducing the number to twenty-three, and the Baloch and porters contemplated a strike. The Jemadar accused Burton of starving his party. He was told not to "eat abominations," upon which, clapping hand to hilt, he theatrically forbade our traveller to repeat the words.

Burton at once used the same phrase half a dozen times, upon which the old scoundrel departed to hold a colloquy with his men.

The debate was purposely conducted in so loud a tone that every word reached the master's ears. One of the Baloch threatened to take "that man's life," at the risk of chains for the remainder of his days. Another opined that "in all Nazarenes there is no good"; and each complained he had no respect, no food, and, above everything, no meat. Presently they formally demanded one sheep per diem— men who, when at Zanzibar, saw flesh once a year. This being inadmissible, they asked for four cloths as daily pay, instead of one. Receiving a contemptuous answer, they marched away in a body, noisily declaring that they were going to make instant preparations for departure.

And depart they did—for one day. Next morning, as the asses were being loaded for the march, the Jemadar, looking more crestfallen and foolish than he had ever looked before, suddenly re-appeared, took Burton's hand, and declared that, so far from deserting him, he was deserting them. The company, too, professed themselves profoundly penitent. They had taken opium ; they had been tempted by the Evil One; they promised to reform. Burton gave them a lecture, and then, with incredible efforts, started his caravan once more on its disorderly way.

Fresh horrors presented themselves. Huts torn and half consumed, the ground strewn with nets and drums, cots and fragments of rude furniture, testified to a recent slave raid. Two wretched villagers were seen lurking in the jungle, not daring to revisit the wreck of their homes. It must be remembered, however, by those who blame the Moslem kidnappers so severely, that their depredations are rendered not only possible but easy by the constant internecine wars of the Africans themselves. Were the natives of the intertropical provinces united, they could soon drive every Arab maurauder in the land into the deep waters of

their own magnificent lakes. Instead of this, each separate
tribe is ever on the war-path, and, when victorious, as eager
in bartering their black prisoners as any slave dealer in the
land. Truthful travellers, one and all, gave a dismal account of the "perverse race of Kush." Nowhere is the
"noble savage" less worthy of the epithet. The name
of hospitality, except for interested motives, is unknown.
These people will refuse a mouthful of water to a man
dying of thirst; they will not stretch out a hand to save
another's goods, though worth thousands of dollars. Their
squabbling and clamour defy description; and after a cuff a
man will cover his face with his hands and cry as if his
heart would break. Marriage is a mere matter of buying
and selling; their greediness and voracity know no bounds,
and their propensity for intoxication was gratified with
pombe long before a drop of trade rum was ever brought
into the country. As for their faith, if indeed it can be
called such, it seems a loathsome form of demonology or
fetishism. A common spectacle in many parts of the
country through which our traveller passed was a heap or
two of ashes with a few blackened human bones; often
close to the larger circles, where the father and mother had
been burnt, a smaller heap showed some wretched child
had shared their fate. And the sorcerer and sorceress will
not only confess, but boast of and believe in their own
criminality, the offspring of mental imbecility stimulated
by traditional hallucination.

By-and-by, ants red and black reminded the expedition
of their existence. Men and beasts were rendered half mad
by the cruel stings. The red variety crossed the road in
dense masses like the close columns of an army. Both
kinds know neither fear nor fatigue; they rush to annihilation without hesitation, and are expelled from a hut by no
milder means than fire and boiling water. The black men
also suffered severely from the tzetze. This horrid fly, the
torment of Cape travellers, was known in the vicinity of

Kilwa as the " little sword." On the line followed by the expedition it was found extending from Usagara westward as far as the Central Lakes; its usual habitat the jungle strip which encloses each patch of cultivated ground. Possibly at some future day when the country becomes more populated, this pest may be exterminated by the introduction of some insectivorous bird, an importation which would prove one of the greatest benefactors that Central Africa had ever known.

Before describing the crossing of the Rubeho Pass, the third or westernmost range of the Usagara Mountains, a few words are necessary concerning this region. Extending from the western frontiers of K'hutu to the province of Ugogo —its diagonal breadth is eighty-five geographical miles : native caravans, if lightly laden, usually traverse it in three weeks. The Usagara chain is the only important elevation in a direct line from the coast to western Unyamwezi, and although holding but a low grade in the general system of the earth's mountains, it possesses peaks that rise from 6,000 to 7,000 feet above sea level.

From its mingling of lively colours, Usagara delights the eye after the monotonous tracts of verdure at Zanzibar and in the river valleys. The subsoil displayed in its deeper ravines is granite, greenstone, schist, or a coarse brown sandstone ; the soil is either an ochreish brick-red, or a dull grey, the *débris* of comminuted felspar which appears dazzlingly white under the sun's rays. Its vegetation is of a pleasantly varied character : it is a land of jungle-flowers and agreeably acid fruits, and in the plains the air is heavy with the jasmine's delicious perfume, with the odour of a kind of sage, and the fragrant exhalations of the mimosa flowers hanging like golden balls from their green-clad boughs. The tamarind, everywhere growing wild, attains a gigantic height. On the steep hillsides, which here and there display signs of cultivation, flourish queer parachute-shaped mimosas, with tall and slender trunks, crowned by domes of verdure rising in tiers one above the other like umbrellas in a crowd.

The climate for Africa is chilly. In the higher levels it recalls the Neilgherry Hills in Western India. Compared with Unyamwezi, these mountains are a sanitorium, and European travellers might do well, when they have the leisure, to remain there awhile until acclimatised. Certainly Burton mentions a formidable list of maladies then prevalent; but these may have been partly due to the uncleanly, careless habits of the natives, the Wasagara and their sub-tribes, who, like most of the races encountered by our traveller, were cruel, treacherous, cowardly and dirty.

The journey across Usagara might almost be described as pleasant but for the terrific pass which barred the way to Ugogo. Burton himself contemplated with dogged despair an apparently perpendicular path that ignored a zigzag, and the roots and boulders hemmed in with tangled vegetation up which he, Speke, and the starving asses were about to toil. Speke was so weak that he required the aid of two or three supporters. Burton managed with one. After rounding in two places wall-like sheets of rock, they faced a long steep of loose white soil and rolling stones, up which they could see the porters swarming more like baboons than human beings. Another danger of a different description threatened. As the Englishmen moved slowly and painfully onward, the war-cry suddenly rang from hill to hill, and Indian files of archers and spearmen streamed like lines of black ants in all directions down the paths. A predatory tribe had awaited the caravan's departure, and seized the opportunity of plundering a neighbouring village. One of the porters proposed a *sauve qui peut*, leaving his employers to their fate, employers ever held to be the head and front of all danger and evil fortune. His advice was not followed, though for no disinterested reasons, and the " braves " passed by, too intent on their work of destruction to molest the strangers.

Resting every few yards, then clinging to their guides and advancing step by step, Burton and Speke, after about six hours' labour, reached the summit of Rubeho. There they sat down amidst aromatic flowers and shrubs to re-cover strength and breath. The view disclosed a retrospect of difficulties happily overcome. Below the foreground of giant fractures, huge rocks and detached boulders emerging from a shaggy growth of mountain vegetation, with forest glens and hanging woods black with shade gathering in the steeper folds, appeared, distant already, large square villages of the Wasagara, streaked with lines of tender green that denoted the watercourses, and patched with black where grass had been freshly fired. A glowing sun gilded a canopy of dense smoke which curtained the nearer plain, and in the background the hazy atmosphere painted with azure the broken wall of hill traversed the previous day.

Revived by a veritable tramontana which blew icily down the Pass, our Englishmen advanced over rolling ground decked with cactus and mimosa, to a small and dirty kraal in a hollow flanked by heights. Here a halt was called. Speke had been taken so ill, that a cool, quiet night was an absolute necessity. Happily, the rest and fine air combined gave him strength to move next morning; and the scramble downhill to the plains of Ugogo was safely accomplished with no worse disaster than the loss of some baggage.

Ugogo, the reader may remember, was the ultimate limit applied to the prospects of our expedition by the worthy clerk of Ladha Damha at Kaole. Despite his melancholy predictions, the caravan succeeded in traversing this province almost unhindered. The natives, the Wagogo, are a mongrel race, many of whom converse fluently in the Kisiwahili, or coast tongue. Milk, honey and eggs were freely offered for sale, but all proved of the indifferent

quality we are accustomed to in a second-rate English
lodging. Speke, luckily, had so far recovered from his last
attack as to be able to supplement the larder by many a
fine brace of partridge and fat guinea-fowl; but as the
party proceeded they found game had suffered from the
frequent halts of caravans, and from the carnivorous pro-
pensities of the people, who, huntsmen all, leave their prey
no chance against nets and arrows, pitfalls and packs of
yelping curs.

Ugogo, though in parts rich in grain, is mostly an ugly,
arid province. Its plains, yellow with stubble, and brown-
black with patches of jungle based upon a brickdust soil,
give it a general aspect of a glaring flat, darkened by long
growths of acrid and saline plants. There are no rivers,
the periodical rains being carried off by large nullahs,
whose clay banks are split during the hot season into
polygonal figures, like piles of columnar basalt. On the
sparkling nitrous salinas and dun-coloured plains, the
mirage faintly resembles the effects of refraction in desert
Arabia. Towards the end of December begins the rainy
season, with the wind shifting from east to north and north-
east, and blowing steadily from the high grounds eastward
and westward of the Victoria Nyanza, which have been
saturated by heavy falls commencing in September.

By the advice of his guide, Burton chose the middle
route through the hundred miles of Ugogo, principally
because it was infested by only four sultans, or chiefs; the
other roads were guarded by more. Each chief levied
heavy blackmail for the privilege of passing through his
dominions; there was no regular tariff, but the sum was
fixed by the traveller's dignity and outfit. The most powerful of the quartet, one Magomba, was impelled by combined cupidity and inquisitiveness to enter Burton's tent;
pride and a propensity for strong drink restrained the three
others. His highness did not present a very imposing spectacle. Picture a black and wrinkled elder, drivelling and

decrepit, with a half bald pate furnished with a few straggling iron-grey corkscrews, his only covering a greasy loin-
cloth, his neck decorated with strings of beads, his skinny
shanks with large anklets of brass wire, and his big black
ears nearly split asunder with huge brass rings.   Nor was
his deportment superior to his appearance.   He chewed his
quid, expectorated incessantly, asked idiotic questions, and
begged for every article he saw.   He demanded as tribute,
cottons, domestics, cloths, beads, brass wire ; and on
receiving the goods in question, clamoured for more.   This
was extra trying, as before his august appearance on the
scene, his favourite spouse, hideous as himself, had put in
her claim ; and who could refuse a royal lady?   Truly thankful
must the highly honoured but sadly plundered strangers
have felt when these greedy highnesses departed and left
them free to resume their difficult march.   Certainly
another sultan proved just as rapacious, but as he lay in
his hut half stupefied with pombe, he spared the Englishmen a personal visitation.

Day after day passed with the usual incidents repeated
with exasperating monotony.   The Baloch gave way to fits
of rage, the porters lost their loads and often failed to find
them ; Said, cheating ever, quaked over dangers real and
imaginary ; grumbling and quarrelling never ceased.   The
plains of Ugogo were safely traversed and the caravan
entered Unyamwezi, then the African explorer's Land of
Promise ; but the pleasures of hope were sadly damped by
the folly, recklessness and ingratitude of the sable environment.   Bombay alone showed his masters any human
feeling.   On one occasion he saved Burton's life.   Our
traveller, feeling unusually faint and exhausted, had allowed
his party to precede him and then became too weak to
follow.   Good Bombay however soon missed him and
returned to his assistance, not only with refreshments, but
leading an ass on which the almost prostrate man was
brought into camp.   But there was no other friend among

the unruly crew, and Burton must have felt his heart lightened of half its load when on the 7th November, 1857, the 134th day after leaving the coast, he entered Kazeh, the principal station of Eastern Unyamwezi and the capital village of the Omani merchants.

The site of Kazeh was the pleasantest our travellers had yet visited. A plateau in the depths of the tropics made temperate by altitude of from 3,000 to 4,000 feet above sea level, studded with hills rising abruptly from fertile, grassy plains, and broken by patches of cultivation, by valleys, and by forests of rich growth. The houses too, Moslem modifications of the African Tembe, appeared far superior in comfort to any shelter Burton had hitherto enjoyed. But it was not merely the pleasant position and compara- tive luxury of Kazeh that delighted him ; how rapturously he hailed the change from the society of his surly Africans to that of the courtly Arabs he alone could fully tell. The Moslems received him like a brother, led him and his companion to a vacant house, supplied them with pro- visions, and, after leaving the strangers in accordance with a gracious Arab custom, a day to recover from fatigue, proceeded to show them such hospitality as only these people are capable of. Burton described his reception as "meeting with hearts of flesh after hearts of stone."

Musa Mzuri (handsome Moses), the principal merchant settled at Unyanyembe, to whose protection Burton and Speke had been commended by the Sayyid of Zanzibar, happened to be away on a trading trip. His agent, Snay bin Amir, a Harisi Arab, came forward to perform the guest rites. No record of the Tanganyika and the Victoria Nyanza Lakes would be complete without a notice of this remarkable man. Burton, who always recorded any assist- ance rendered by the talents of others, frankly acknowledged his obligations to his gifted host. From his instructive and varied conversation was derived not a little of the information contained in the "Lake Regions of Central

Africa"[1]—conversation which we must bear in mind only
Burton could understand, as Speke's solitary linguistic
acquirement was Hindustani. Snay had travelled three
times between Unyamwezi and the coast, besides navigating Lake Tanganyika and visiting the northern kingdoms of Karagwah and Uganda; and he was as familiar
with the languages, the religion, manners and ethnology
of the African as with those of his natal Oman. By
the aid of his distances and directions, Burton was enabled to lay down the southern limits of the Victorian
lake, and so prepared the way for Speke's flying trip.
But Snay bin Amir was not merely clever. Some of
the loftiest characters, nothwithstanding the comparatively low moral standard of their environment, have been
met with in China, in Japan, in Arabia, in far Thibet.
This Arab ivory merchant and slave dealer certainly appears
as an example. Sixteen years before Burton's visit to
Kazeh he had begun life as a confectioner at Maskat. In
1856 he had risen to be one of the wealthiest traders in
East Africa. Success only developed his excellent qualities.
His kindness and generosity never failed, though not one
member of the expedition could make the smallest return,
and several must have caused him a vast amount of trouble.
Burton in particular he treated like a brother—doctored
him, feasted him, lodged him, warehoused his goods,
engaged porters in place of deserters, and settled quarrels
innumerable. During two halts at Kazeh, one on the way
to Tanganyika, the other on the return march, he passed
every evening with his favourite guest, and during this
prolonged intercourse no evil feeling of any kind appears
to have betrayed itself. In appearance he was a middle-
aged man with a somewhat Quixotic look, high-featured,
sunken-eyed, tall and large-limbed.

---

[1] " The Lake Regions of Central Africa," two vols. Longman, Green,
Longman & Roberts, 1850.

Good Snay bin Amir, with your talents, your high sense of honour, your warm and generous heart, you deserved a kinder fate! For the second expedition commanded by Speke and Grant found the neighbouring villages ruined, and Kazeh itself on the verge of destruction. The merchants had refused to pay a tax imposed by a headman of Unyam-yembe, hence a war which ended in the slaughter of Burton's faithful friend, who, too proud to run from his horde of enemies, lay down when abandoned by his negroes, and gave up his brave soul to Allah.

During five weeks our traveller and his caravan re-mained at Kazeh enjoying the hospitality of the Arab residents. With work yet to do, it must not be supposed Burton delayed so long without compulsion. Twenty marches only would conduct him to Ujiji upon the Tanganyika, for, thanks to his clever host, no uncertainty remained concerning the route and the goal. But fatigue had told severely upon him and his followers, and the " bilious remittent " once more declared itself. Again the familiar symptoms, distressing weakness, hepatic derange-ment, perspirations, aching eyes, and alternate thrills of heat and cold made night and day wretched. The malady lasted a whole month. Snay was the principal doctor, but as his usual treatment—counter-irritants—failed in Burton's case, a witch, celebrated for her cures throughout the country-side, was summoned in consultation.

The cures in question evidently appertained to the nature of those in civilised Europe known with the prefix, an all-important one, of faith, and Burton, though a sanguine man, was by no means credulous. Besides, his lady-doctor seems to have been most decidedly ugly. A wrinkled beldam, black as soot, set off by a mass of tin-coloured pigtails, arrived, bearing the implements of her craft, a girdle of small gourds dyed reddish-black with oil and use. The invalid's nerves, in spite of his fever, must have been fairly strong to endure such an object in the room; probably he was borne up by inquisitiveness. I have said elsewhere that he had a warm corner for doctors, but that alone hardly explains his permitting himself to be experimented upon by a Mganga in East Africa.

After demanding and receiving her fee, a precedent which might be useful to our general practitioners, she proceeded to search her patient's mouth and to enquire anxiously concerning poison. The question betrayed the prevalence of crime in the country, and the people seemed ever to dread it. She then drew from a gourd a greenish powder, apparently bhang, and having mixed it with a little water, administered it like snuff, which caused a paroxysm of sneezing. This not very uncommon symptom after a nasal inhalation she hailed with shouts of joy. Here faith should have performed its part; the medicine had succeeded, the doctor was contented. To make the cure certain, she presently rubbed her patient's head with powder of another kind; then announcing that sleep would usher in recovery, she departed, with a promise to return next day. Alas! our College of Physicians could never hold forth the hand of fellowship to this sable sister. Her conduct was disgraceful. Having become comparatively wealthy, she absconded to indulge in unlimited pombe for a whole week; and although her patient had not benefited in the slightest degree by her treatment, she never even enquired after him during those seven rapturous but sadly unprofessional days!

We will leave our traveller housed within a stone's throw of his new friend Shaykh Snay bin Amir, and record the discovery of fair Tanganyika in the next chapter.

CHAPTER X

THE five weeks spent at Kazeh to rest and recruit having elapsed, Burton bade his good host a temporary adieu, and resumed his way to Ujiji. Fever had left him so weak that he had to be carried in a hammock, and six men were engaged by Snay bin Amir for this duty. Although at first even the comparatively easy motion of the manchila caused at times acute suffering, our traveller, after his prolonged confinement indoors, was charmed with the prospect, a fine open country and well wooded hills rolling into blue distance on either hand. A forced halt of two days at Yombo, partly to wait for Speke, who had been obliged to retrace his steps in order to superintend the arrival of supplies of cloth and beads from Zanzibar, partly to collect a gang of porters for their journey westward, was enlivened by evening chats with the feminine members of the population. The sunset hour in Unyamwezi, as in other parts of Africa, is replete with enjoyment to the natives. Every night there mustered a smoking party; all the womankind, from wrinkled granddam to maid scarcely in her teens, assembled to apply themselves to their long, black-bowled pipes. Seated in a circle, upon dwarf stools or logs of wood, they smoked with such intense relish, slowly and deeply inhaling the weed, and exhaling clouds from their nostrils, that it was quite a pleasure to watch them, especially as Yombo boasted of no fewer than three beauties, Venuses cast in bronze. Nor were they merely handsome. Natural good-nature, or the soothing influence of the narcotic, rendered these Wanyamwezi ladies unusually affable. When our traveller in his best Kinyamwezi, which he had acquired a smattering of from Snay bin Amir, paid his compliments and added a present of a little tobacco, they smiled sweetly, and accorded him the privilege of a seat in the—well! undress circle.

Certainly the Land of the Moon offers its children every element of comfort and enjoyment. Burton described it as the "garden of Central Intertropical Africa." Its general character is rolling ground intersected with low hills, and its aspect of peaceful beauty soothes the eye like a medicine after glaring Ugogo and the dark monotonous verdure of the western provinces. During the rains—there are but two seasons, wet and dry, which represent summer and winter—a coat of many-tinted greens conceals Mother Earth. In the hot season the land becomes grey, lighted up with golden stubble and dotted with trees. Villages rise at short intervals above their impervious walls of lustrous green milkbush, with its coral-shaped arms variegating the well-hoed plains; whilst in the pasture-lands frequent herds of many-coloured cattle, plump and high-humped, and mingled flocks of sheep and goats dispersed over the landscape suggest ideas of barbarous peace and plenty. The yield of the soil at the time of Burton's visit to this favoured land averaged sixtyfold even in comparatively unproductive years.

Pleasant though the face of the country might be, travelling along it was subject to all the perils consequent on lack of civilisation. From want of proper shelter and suitable food both Englishmen suffered from various strange and painful symptoms. Sudden fits of numbness of the extremities resembling paralysis, temporary but almost total blindness, severe attacks of inflammation of the eyes, tormented them successively. Speke nearly lost his sight from ophthalmia. The unruly caravan, too, never ceased from troubling. Partly because the Zanzibar goods had turned out or the poorest and most flimsy description, it became more disorderly and unmanageable than ever. Even the two most important functionaries, Said and the Jemadar, instead of helping to keep order, actually impressed upon the porters that Burton's days were numbered, consequently it was useless to take any thought about him. To prove the contrary, our traveller, ill though he was, left his hammock, and, mounting his ass, rode manfully on through some of the worst parts of the way. The exertion was terrible, for Maître Aliboron in Africa is guilty of the four mortal sins of the equine race ; he shies and stumbles, rears and runs away. The roundness of his flanks, the shortness of his back and his want of shoulder combine to make the native saddle unfit for anything but a baboon or a boy ; while the straightness and rigidity of his goat-like pasterns render the pace a wearisome, tripping hobble. Fortunately, after one long day's trudge, Burton was hospitably received by a wealthy Arab proprietor in the Wilyankuru district. The kind-hearted man escorted his weary guest to a comfortable room, supplied him with milk, meat, and honey, and placed a new cartel, or substitute for a bedstead, in the coolest apartment of his handsome Tembe.

Four short and eventless marches through thick jungle with scattered clearings led Burton to the district of Msene, where the dense wild growth lately traversed suddenly opened out and disclosed a broad view of admirable fertility. He was conducted to an uncomfortable building with its clay roof weed-grown like a deserted grave, and surrounded by dirty puddles and black mud. His stay was not a pleasant one. Msene, a mass of detached settlements, proved a terribly naughty place even for Africa. All its inhabitants from Sultan to slave made a point of getting intoxicated whenever the material was forthcoming ; and intoxication was by no means their worst or only vice. The said Sultan, during his few sober moments, paid the travellers several visits. His first greeting betrayed his motive—" White men, what pretty things have you brought from the shore for me ? " On more than one occasion a bevy of wives accompanied him. Of their conduct, the less said the better. Had it not been for the eternal difficulty with regard to porterage which detained the caravan in this den of debauchery for twelve days, Burton would have left at once. His men became so demoralised that even good Bombay on the morning of departure was lured away by some sable siren, while as for the guide and his followers, despite orders, they refused point blank to leave until forty-eight hours later.

This act of disobedience put the finishing stroke to Burton's patience. Kidogo, the splendid Kidogo, had become insufferable, and no milder sentence than prompt dismissal was absolutely necessary. Disregarding the interested entreaties of Said and the Jemadar, our traveller summoned the Kirangozi and his staff of slaves, informed them that their time was expired, and ordered them to return forthwith to Kazeh. This step was taken none too soon. The black rascals had openly boasted of their intention to prevent the expedition from embarking on the Sea of Ujiji.

At Wanyika there was a forced halt of a day to settle the ever-recurring question of blackmail. The principal chief of Uvinza considered himself Lord of the Malagarazi River, and enforced his claims by forbidding the ferrymen to assist strangers unless his demands were complied with. Forty cloths, white and blue, and other goods to the value of fifty pounds, were paid to this rapacious roitelet, who then accorded the expedition the privilege of embarking in wretched canoes that, when high and dry upon the bank, somewhat resembled castaway shoes of unusual size. Burton and Speke entered these craft gingerly, but were surprised to find the ferrymen so skilful, that not only was the human freight landed without accident, but all the luggage besides. The riding asses had to be flung into the river, which they easily crossed by swimming.

The route then lay through a howling wilderness, once

populous and fertile, but lately laid waste by one of the savage tribes, who rendered the face of the land as changeable as the patterns of a kaleidoscope. On the 5th February our party set out betimes, traversing for some distance boggy land along the river side. The hardships of this march induced two of the porters who carried the hammock to levant, and the remaining four to strike work. Consequently, the Englishmen who had been indulging in the luxury of a rest had to remount their asses. The 7th February found them toiling along broken ground, encumbered by trees and cut by swamps. Presently, diverging from the Malagarazi River, they passed over the brow of a low hill above the junction with the Rusigi, and followed the left bank of the tributary as far as its nearest ford. Later, they skirted a settlement containing from forty to fifty beehive huts, tenanted by salt-diggers. One is surprised to read of such an industry amongst the childish races of Uvinga, and yet more so to learn that they turned out quite a superior article. The principal pan was sunk in the vicinity of the stream; the saline produce, after being boiled down indoors, was, when dry, piled up and handmade into little cones, far surpassing in quality the manufacture of the coast towns. After watching these people for a while, Burton and his party resumed their way, and found themselves obliged to cross the next ford on the backs of negroes who were waiting for the purpose—a less costly mode than by canoe, but subject to the drawbacks often attendant upon cheapness, for all the goods and chattels got thoroughly soaked.

More fords, more swamps, more jungle, then the sinking of the land towards the lake become palpable. The caravan halted from fatigue upon a slope beyond a weary bog; a violent storm was brewing, and whilst half the sky was purple-black with nimbus, the sun shone stingingly through the clear portion of the empyrean. But these small troubles were lightly borne; already in the far distance appeared walls of sky-blue cliff with gilded summits, gleaming as a beacon to distressed mariners.

On the 13th February they started betimes, forcing a path through screens of lofty grass, which thinned out into a straggling forest. After about an hour's march they breasted a steep and stony hill. Arrived with difficulty, for one ass fell dead on the way and the others refused to proceed, the two Englishmen rested for a few minutes on the crest.

" What is that streak of light which lies below ? " inquired Burton.

" I am of opinion," quoth Bombay, " that is the water."

A few steps further and the whole scene suddenly burst upon our traveller's sight, filling him with wonder, admiration and delight. Nothing could be more picturesque than this first view of the Tanganyika Lake, as it lay in the lap of the mountains, basking in gorgeous, tropical sunshine. Below, and beyond a short foreground of rugged, precipitous hill, down which the footpath zigzags painfully, a narrow strip of emerald green, never sere and marvellously fertile, shelves towards a ribbon of glistening, yellow sand, here bordered by sedgy rushes, there clearly and cleanly cut by the breaking wavelets. Further in front stretch the waters, an expanse of the softest blue, varying in breadth from thirty to thirty-five miles, and sprinkled by the crisp east wind with tiny crescents of snowy foam. The background, a high and broken wall of steel-coloured mountains, was that day flecked and capped in parts with pearly mists, in others, standing sharply pencilled against the azure air, its yawning chasms marked by a deep plum-colour falling towards dwarf hills of mound-like proportions. To the south and opposite the long low point behind which the Malagarazi river discharges the red loam suspended in its violent stream, lie the bluff headlands and capes of Uguhha, while a cluster of outlying islets speckle a sea-horizon. On this vision of beauty Burton gazed and gazed again ; forgetting toils, dangers and the uncertainty of a safe return to those he loved, he felt willing to endure double what he had gone through for so glorious a guerdon. All his party seemed affected by some pleasant emotion. Even his surly Baloch made civil salaams.

The night following this eventful day was passed at Ukaranga, a collection of miserable grass huts. Early next morning, an open, solid-built Arab craft having been hired, our travellers coasted along Tanganyika's eastern shore towards the Kawele district in the land of Ujiji. Their view was exceedingly beautiful, the picturesque and varied forms of the mountains rising above and dipping into the water, were clad in purplish blue, tinted in places by Aurora's rosy fingers. Burton, who had heard of a town, a ghaut, a bazaar, rather marvelled at an utter absence of all those features which prelude a popular settlement. Only sundry scattered hovels surrounded by fields of sorghum and sugar cane, and shaded by dense groves of the dwarf plantain and the Guinea palm, appeared at intervals along the shore. Presently some rude canoes, evidently belonging to fishermen, woodcutters, and market people, cut the water singly, or stood in crowds drawn up on the patches of yellow sand.

About 11 a.m. the dhow was poled through a hole in a thick welting of coarse reedy grass and flaggy aquatic plants, to a level landing-place of flat shingle, where the water shoaled off rapidly. Such in 1858 was the ghaut or disembarkation quay of Ujiji.

Around the ghaut a few huts of humblest beehive pattern represented the port town. Advancing some hundred yards through a din of shouts and screams, tom-toms and trumpets, and mobbed by a swarm of black beings whose eyes seemed about to start from their heads with surprise, Burton passed a relic of Arab civilisation, the bazaar. It consisted merely of a plot of ground cleared of grass and flanked by a crooked tree, where, for some hours every day, weather permitting, a mass of standing and squatting negroes bought and sold with a hubbub heard for miles. He and Speke were then conducted to a ruinous Tembe, built by an Arab merchant, situated about half a mile from the village of Kawele, which at that time was the principal settlement of Ujiji. This habitation enjoyed the double attraction of proximity to provisions and a beautiful view of the lake. Well that our travellers had this lovely vision before their eyes, for, as usual, the natives were most depressing objects, morally and physically. Hideously tattooed, further disfigured by loathsome skin diseases, their villainously-shaped heads partially shaved, these odious beings were besides insolent, thievish, immoral, and continually drunk. Men and women alike staggered about with thick speech and violent gestures, after indulgence in their favourite inebriant, palm toddy; while, after bhang-smoking, their whoops and yells resembled the noise of some highly excited wild beast rather than aught human. Curious how many good temperance folk in England insist upon depicting the African as a model of sobriety when free from the temptation of trade rum. True, the latter has a more deadly effect on his physique; still, long before the poisonous mixture concocted by benevolent Hamburghers and others had reached Ujiji, the natives presented as distressing a spectacle as our denizens of Ratcliff Highway on Saturday night.

Burton's first care on settling in his new abode was to purify the floor by pastiles of assafœtida and fumigations of gunpowder, and to patch up the roof against the rainy season. Aided by a Msawahili artisan, he provided himself with a pair of cartels, and substitutes for chairs and tables. As further luxuries, benches of clay were built round the rooms like divans, but these turned out useless, being occupied in force every morning by fine white ants. The roof, too, did not repay the pains bestowed upon it; hopelessly rotten, it never ceased leaking during wet weather, and at last partly collapsed. The result of such excessive humidity was unfortunate ; a large botanical collection, accumulated during the journey from Zanzibar, was irretrievably ruined ; and as the return to the coast took place during the dry season, when the woods were bare of leaf, flower and fruit, it could not be replaced.

On the second day after arrival, Burton received a ceremonious visit from one Kannena, the headman of Kawele. This personage, a type of the people he governed, was introduced habited in silk turban and broadcloth coat, borrowed from the Baloch, and accompanied by two natives a quarter clad in greasy and scanty bark aprons. He was a short, squat negro, with a low, frowning brow and an apology for a nose. Believing Burton to be a merchant, and hoping to make a good profit by exchanges of wares, he behaved at first with remarkable civility, but as soon as he discovered the stranger " lived by doing nothing," he doffed his garments and good behaviour together, and became a veritable thorn in the flesh during the whole of our traveller's stay at Ujiji.

Important work yet remained undone. Burton desired to explore the northern extremity of his curiously elongated lake, and, seeing scanty prospect of success and every chance of an accident if compelled to voyage in the wretched native canoes, he attempted to persuade cowardly old Said to undertake a little coasting trip for the purpose of securing the dhow which had conveyed the party to Kawele. The little sneak, as usual, when scenting danger, shirked ; so his master being at that moment too ill to travel, Speke, supplied with an ample outfit and accompanied by two Baloch, besides Gaetano and Bombay, started on this important quest in his stead.

He was away nearly a month. Burton spent the time in almost complete idleness, eating, drinking, smoking and dozing. But every evening the lonely man sat under the broad eaves of his Tembe to enjoy the delicious sight of his lovely lake. Unlike the dismal Albert Edward, or dreary Victoria Nyanza, Tanganyika resembles the fairest glimpses of the Mediterranean. There are the same laughing tides, pellucid sheets of dark blue water, borrowing their tints from the vinous shores beyond ; the same purple light of youth upon the face of early evening, the same bright sunsets, with their radiant vistas of crimson and gold, opening like the portals of a world beyond ; the same short-lived grace and beauty of the twilight ; and as night closes over the earth, the same cool flood of transparent moonbeams pouring upon the tufty heights, and bathing their sides with the whiteness of virgin snow.

Speke returned March 29th. He had not found a boat, but declared he had discovered the Mountains of the Moon. This intelligence, being unsupported by proofs, hardly made up for his failure to obtain a substitute for the much-regretted *Louisa*. However, Burton, fortified by three weeks' rest and quiet, bestirred himself in right earnest to overcome the difficulties which beset the cruise to Uvira, at that time the *ultima thule* of lake navigation. Kannena, who had evidenced his ill-will in various ways, instigating his people *à l'Irlandais* to injure the only remaining asses, to break into the travellers' outhouses and steal their property, and, finally, to cut off the supplies of milk, seemed at first utterly unmanageable. When the plan was broached to him he discharged a volley of oaths, and sprang from the house like an enraged baboon. There was no alternative than to bribe heavily. This was done, and at length Burton's patience and sagacity triumphed ; the headman yielded every point. After receiving an exorbitant sum, capped by a six-foot length of scarlet broadcloth, which nearly made the surly brute grin with delight, he consented to act as guide and furnish the explorers with two canoes fully manned.

Preliminaries thus settled, two " motumbi "—craft little better than hollowed tree trunks, one sixty feet by four, the second about two-thirds that size—were duly engaged and provisioned. Supplies of beads, cloth and brass bracelets were also placed on board. The party consisted of our Englishmen, the Goanese lads, two gun-carriers, and two Baloch, besides Kannena and the crew.

Their departure was heralded by a hideous uproar. Several Ujiji dames, excited by the bustle on the shore, performed on the noisiest musical instruments. To these sounds, which not the wildest flight of imagination could wrest into the slightest resemblance to our National Anthem, even when rendered by Board scholars, Burton's canoe, on the 12th April, 1858, bearing for the first time on those fair waters

" The flag that braved a thousand years
The battle and the breeze,"

stood out of Bangwe Bay, and, followed by Speke's, turned the landspit separating the bight from the main, and made directly for the cloudy storm-vexed north. Beyond this headland the coast dips, showing lines of shingle or golden coloured sand, and on the shelving plain appear little fishing hamlets consisting of half-a-dozen beehive huts. It must have required all Burton's concentrativeness to take observations, for his progress, which varied from five to two and a half miles an hour, was accompanied by a long monotonous howl emitted by a soloist paddler, answered by yells and shouts from the chorus. There were frequent halts to eat, drink and smoke, but for these purposes only, as the black sailors refused to allow either traveller to put into a likely place for collecting shells and stones, or even to stop for a few moments to take soundings.

Each night was spent in one of the villages dotted along the coast. The canoes were drawn up on dry land and our Englishmen slept under apologies for tents. Arrived at Wafanya, the solitary point in Urundi then open to strangers, they prepared to cross the lake, which is there divided into two stages by the Island of Ubwari. The breadth of the western channel between this long narrow lump of rock twenty to twenty-five miles long, averages from six to seven miles. Just before starting the two Baloch, who had been stealthily watching their opportunity ever since quitting Kawele, deserted, and thus left the Englishmen entirely in the power of the natives. However, the crossing to Ubwari was accomplished with no worse incident than several severe drenchings, the frail craft requiring to be constantly baled to keep afloat.

They halted for a day at Mzimu, an Ubwari landing-place, and towards evening tumbled again into the canoes, rounded the island's northern point, and put into a little bay on the western shore, where they passed the night. Rest was sorely needed. This primitive boating would have tried a Hercules. There was no means of resting the back, the holds of the canoes, besides being knee-deep in water, were disgracefully crowded. Originally appropriated to Burton and Speke, four servants and the crew, Kannena introduced, in addition to sticks, spears, cooking-pots and gourds, a goat, two or three small boys, several sick sailors, a slave girl, and a large sheep. Curiously enough, despite these discomforts, our travellers' health gradually improved. Burton suffered from ulceration of the tongue, but he dated his slow yet sensible progress towards comparative vigour from the nights and days spent in the canoes and on the muddy shores of Tanganyika.

On the 23rd April a start was made for the opposite or western coast, a cruise occupying nine hours. The landing-stage, Murivumba, was infested by mosquitoes, crocodiles, and anthropophagi. The latter, stunted, degraded wretches, seemed less dangerous to the living than the dead. Nevertheless, one of Burton's men preferred squatting uncomfortably on the canoe's bow throughout the night to trusting his precious person amongst these hungry-looking cannibals. The rest of the party slept on a reed-margined spit of sand, where, having neglected to rear a tent, they were rained upon to their hearts' content.

Leaving at early dawn the man-eaters' abode, they stood northwards along the western shore; and before long the converging trend of the two coasts showed they were approaching their destination, Uvira. Twenty-eight hours later found the voyagers safely landed on a sandy bay where the trade of this place was carried on. Tanganyika here measures between seven and eight miles in breadth.

Crowds gathered on the shore to gaze at the new merchants and to welcome them with screams, shouts, horns and tom-toms. The captain of each crew performed with solemn gravity a bear-like dance, while the crews with a grin which displayed all their ivories, rattled their paddles against the sides of their boats in token of greeting. Meanwhile, Kannena visited the chief of the district, who at once invited Burton and Speke to his settlement; but the outfit was running low and the crew and party generally feared to leave their craft. Our Englishmen therefore pitched their tents —the best had been stolen by Kannena —on a strip of sand, whence they were speedily ejected by Tanganyika's foaming waters, which a blast or small hurricane lashed completely over the green margin of the land.

Burton, who was not the man to calmly accept Uvira as an *ultima thule*, now prepared for a final effort, namely, to explore the head of the lake. Opposite rose in a high broken line the mountains of inhospitable Urundi, apparently prolonged beyond the northern extremity of the waters. Especially anxious was he to reach the spot where the Rusizi, then an almost unknown river, joins the Tanganyika. At that date it was impossible to tell whether this stream was an influent or an effluent, and, as travellers were still darkly groping for the Nile sources, he could not turn his face homewards without either visiting the mysterious river or obtaining some reliable information concerning it. But a long palaver with three intelligent sons of a local chief dispelled at once both hope and un-certainty. They all declared they had seen it, and unani-mously asserted, a host of bystanders confirming their words, that the Rusizi enters into and does not flow out of the Tanganyika. Still desirous of laying down the extreme limits of the water northwards, Burton was again disappointed. Kannena flatly refused to advance another mile; and the ulceration of the tongue from which our explorer was suffering grew so severe, that articulation became nearly impossible.

May 6th was fixed for the return journey. All went well until the night of the 10th of that month. The party left Mzimu at sunset, and for two hours coasted along the shore. It was one of those portentous evenings of the tropics—a calm before a tempest. They struck out, how-ever, boldly towards the eastern shore, and the western mountains rapidly lessened to view. Before they reached mid-channel, a cold gust, invariable presage in those regions of a storm, swept through the deepening shades cast by heavy rolling clouds, and the lightning flashed, at first by intervals, then incessantly, with a ghastly, blinding glow, followed by a pitchy darkness that weighed upon the sight. As terrible was the accompaniment of rushing, reverberating thunder, now a loud roar, peal upon peal, like the booming of heavy batteries; then breaking into a sudden crash, which was presently followed by a rattling discharge, like the pattering of musketry. The waves began to rise, the rain descended, at first in warning drops, then in torrents; and had the wind steadily risen, the cockle-shell craft never could have lived through the short chopping sea which characterises the Tanganyika in heavy weather. The crew behaved gallantly enough; at times, however, the moaning cry, "O, my wife!" showed they almost despaired of reaching the shore. Bombay, a sad Voltairean in fine weather, spent that wild night in reminiscences of Moslem prayers; while Burton sheltered himself under his good friend the mackintosh. Fortunately, the rain beat down wind and sea, otherwise Tanganyika would have proved a veritable Charybdis to her discoverer.

Fresh trouble awaited him at Wafanya, where at length the canoes were landed. Hitherto Burton had been most fortunate in avoiding bloodshed. But at this village, while he was sleeping heavily after his terrible fatigue, a drunken brawl arose. An intoxicated native had commenced dealing blows in all directions; a general *mêlée* ensued, during which Valentino, crazed with fear, seized his master's revolver and fired it into the crowd. The bullet struck one of the canoe men below the right breast, coming out two inches to the right of the backbone; and, in spite of Burton's kindly care, the poor wretch succumbed to his injuries. This affair, which might have ended in a general massacre, had the victim been not a slave, but a free man, cost one hundred pounds for blood money, and originated one of the many false reports that "Haji Abdullah killed the man with his own hand."

Early on May 13th our travellers returned to their Tembe at Kawele, and received a hypocritical welcome from Said and the Jemadar. The rainy monsoon having broken up, the climate became truly delightful with fine, cool mornings, a clear, warm sun, and deliciously fresh nights. Burton, who believed his work mostly accomplished, would have found this rest a period of real enjoyment but for the anxiety which had haunted him ever since starting from Zanzibar, anxiety about ways and means. The outfit was reduced to a minimum. Not a line from Snay bin Amir had arrived in reply to many missives, and want began to stare our Englishmen in the face. Nowhere might a caravan more easily starve than in fertile Ujiji in 1858. Its heartless and inhospitable inhabitants would not give a handful of grain without return, and, to use a Moslem

phrase, "Allah pity him who must beg of a beggar." Travellers are agreed that in these countries "baggage is life."
Burton's was reduced to a few—a very few—loads of beads
and cloth, some of the former black porcelains, and perfectly
useless, and with this pittance porters had to be hired for
the hammock, seventy-five mouths to be fed ; in short, the
innumerable expenses to be defrayed of a return march of
260 miles to Unyanyembe.

Help was nearer than either Burton or Speke dared to
hope. Their good genius, Shaykh Snay, had not forgotten
them. On the 22nd May, musket shots announced an
arrival, and by noon the Tembe was surrounded with
bales, boxes, porters, one of the Baloch who had remained
at Kazeh, all despatched by this excellent friend. The
goods, furnished by thievish Hindoos, at Zanzibar, though
rubbishy, were sufficient to pay the way to Unyanyembe.
But our traveller perceived with regret that his new outfit
was totally inadequate for the purpose of exploring the two
southern thirds of Tanganyika, much less for returning to
Zanzibar *viâ* Lake Nyassa and Kilwa, as he had once
intended.

Immediately after the arrival of the second caravan,
Burton made preparations for quitting Ujiji. The 26th
May was the day appointed for departure. He long
remembered the sunrise that morning over Tanganyika ;
he felt some prophetic instinct that it was the last he
would ever behold, and it proved but too correct, for,
owing to the blackest treachery and ingratitude, he never
saw his lake again. Masses of brown-purple clouds covered
the quarter of the heavens where the sun was about to rise.
Presently the mist, ruffled like ocean billows and luminously
fringed with Tyrian dye, were cut by filmy rays, whilst from
behind their core the internal living fire shot forth its broad
beams like the spokes of a huge aërial wheel, rolling a flood
of gold over the light blue waters. At last Dan Sol, who at
first contented himself with glimmering through the cloud

mass, disclosed himself in his glory, and dispersed with a glance the obstacles of the vaporous earth. Breaking into long strata and little pearly flakes, they soared high in the empyrean, whilst the all-powerful luminary assumed undisputed possession, and a soft breeze awoke the waters into life.

Burton had soon to turn his eyes from this glorious picture. A jarring din became audible. His caravan was on the point of starting. A crowd of newly-engaged porters stood before the Tembe in an ecstasy of impatience, some poised like cranes on the right foot with the left sole placed against the knee, others with their arms thrown in a brotherly fashion round neighbours' necks, whilst others again squatted on their calves and heels, their elbows on their thighs and their chins propped upon their hands. The usual fights, difficulties, and delays over, the caravan was gradually got under way. This return march presented little novelty save that they followed a northerly route, crossing and skirting the lower spurs of the mountains which form the region of Uhha. Only trifling incidents enlivened the weary trudge. The " slavey " of the establishment ran away, carrying off his own property and his master's hatchet ; the Jemadar was rendered almost daft by the disappearance of half the "black ivory" he had invested in at Kawele; and a porter placed his bundle, a case of cognac and vinegar, deeply regretted, upon the ground and levanted. The hammock was rendered almost useless by the behaviour of its new bearers, who dashed it without pity or remorse against stock and stone. These men's ill-conduct capped even that of the "sons of water" on Tanganyika. Loud-voiced, insolent, all but unmanageable, they proved the most odious "beasts of burden" Burton had yet had to deal with. He adds, however, after his complaints (and here lay his secret of success), "in these lands the traveller who cannot utilise the raw material that comes to hand will make but little progress."

16

Avoiding the *détour* to naughty Msene, the expedition sighted at Irora the blue hills of Unyanyembe. There Burton received a packet of letters, and heard for the first time of his father's death, which had occurred at Bath on the 6th of September, 1857. He thus alludes to the sad intelligence: "Such tidings are severely felt by the wanderer who, living long behind the world and unable to mark its gradual changes, lulls by dwelling on the past apprehension into a belief that his home has known no loss, and who expects again to meet each old familiar face ready to smile upon his return as it was to weep at his departure."

On the 20th of June, after a journey of twenty-six days, the expedition re-entered Kazeh, and received a warm welcome from good Snay bin Amir. He led his friends to their old abode, which had been carefully repaired, swept, and plastered, and where a plentiful repast of rice and curried fowl, giblets and manioc boiled in the cream of the ground nut, and sugared omelets flavoured with ghee and onion, presented peculiar attractions to half-starved travellers. Here Burton decided to remain for three months at least. He wished to gain as much information as possible regarding the numerous tribes in the neighbourhood of Tanganyika and the Victoria Nyanza, and to commit it at once to writing ; also to prepare with deliberation for his return journey, which he hoped to accomplish by a different route. This would have been right enough— with one little trip superadded. I have often wondered what was the cause of the mistake Richard Burton committed at Kazeh. That it was a blunder, he himself confessed. True he had wearied somewhat of Speke's company—"Jack" was nourishing some mysterious grudge which rendered him at times exceedingly unpleasant, but that did not prevent a coasting voyage to Kilwa together some months later. Anyhow, while Burton was writing and studying with good Shaykh Snay, John Hannen Speke went alone to explore the Victoria Nyanza, one of the Nile sources, and we all know what followed.

It came about in this wise. The Arabs had mentioned during the first halt at Kazeh their discovery of a large lake lying fifteen or sixteen marches to the north ; and from their description, translated by Burton, his companion had laid down the water in a hand map forwarded to the Royal Geographical Society. All agreed in claiming for it superiority of size over the Tanganyika. There remained to ascertain whether the Arabs had not with Oriental hyperbole exaggerated the dimensions, and Speke, who found the merchants' society deadly dull, not understanding one word in a hundred of their language, and who was moreover, restless as a caged squirrel, seemed only too delighted to undertake this duty. Again one marvels why Burton unwittingly placed such a temptation in another man's path. As I have remarked elsewhere, he was singularly deficient in character-knowledge, and probably imagined that the honour of the discovery would be shared between him and his brother officer. Still, there was no need for hurry in finishing his notes ; the preparations for the return journey could afford to wait. The cause of such blindness must ever remain a mystery, but we can now see plainly enough that his great opportunity then presented itself, was neglected, and vanished for ever. Had he accompanied his lieutenant, the Geographical Society could not have passed him over as commander of the second Expedition ; the second might have given birth to another, and Lake Albert, Lake Albert Edward, glorious Ruwenzori itself, might have been discovered and mapped out by Richard Burton long before the " Cloud King " soared into view of Stanley's delighted eyes.

As usual, it proved no easy matter to start even a small party on this trial trip. Said bin Salim utterly refused to have any part or parcel in it. The Kirangozi and fifteen porters, especially hired for the occasion, showed an amount of fear and shirking hardly justified by the risks of treading so well known a tract. Even Bombay turned restive and had to be heavily bribed.

However, at last Burton, assisted by good Shaykh Snay, succeeded in equipping his companion with every essential for success, and as soon as the little band had departed, turned his whole attention to the geography and ethnology of the land.

Six weeks passed away and Speke returned in triumph. The dimensions of the Victoria Nyanza surpassed the most sanguine expectations. True, he had enjoyed merely a glimpse of this inland sea over the rushy shores whence the waters are year by year slowly and surely receding; but it had quite turned his head. He announced at once, as one with authority, that there and there alone were the sources of the Nile.

Burton demurred. One glimpse over an unknown water seemed insufficient proof to a scientific mind. He admitted with his usual sagacity that the altitude, the conformation of the Nyanza Lake, its argillaceous colour, and the sweetness of its waters, combined to suggest it might be one of the feeders of the White Nile. But its periodical swelling which floods considerable tracts of land, forbade belief in the possibility of its proving the head stream, or the reservoir of the great inundation. The true sources of the Holy River he believed to consist of a network of streams filled by monsoon torrents and swollen by melted snow flowing from the Lunæ Montes. This he wrote thirty years before Stanley counted sixty-two streams descending from the Rain King's rocky sides. But Speke would listen to no arguments whatever : any doubt cast upon what he considered nothing less than inspiration made him look upon his whilom friend as a worse enemy than before.

Here, then, in the heart of Africa, the trouble began. Two enormous lakes had been discovered—surely this was fame enough. To proclaim to the geographical *élite* that the expedition had sighted the Mountains of the Moon, and succeeded in the unveiling of Isis, was to a conscien-

tious man impossible. How many times had not the fountains of the White Nile been discovered and re-discovered
after this careless fashion? Burton's great brain fore-
shadowed all the facts we have so lately learnt; he believed
in the several lakes, in the Lunæ Montes, and this belief
rendered him very chary of attributing to the Victoria
Nyanza the unique honour which his companion was
determined to award it.

Before resuming the thread of my narrative, I must tell
how the difference between the travellers ended, and then
dismiss a painful subject. Gradually his imaginary exploits
became fixed ideas in poor Speke's feverish brain. At Aden,
where the two men remained some days, waiting for a home-
bound steamer, Burton was seized with fever. Speke could
not brook the slightest delay, betraying a nervous haste
which, as his leave had just been prolonged by the Bombay Government, seemed somewhat suspicious. Probably
Burton began at last to fear treachery, for on parting he
asked his brother officer to wait a mail or two, until they
could appear together before the Geographical Society.
Speke gave his word. Unhappily, Laurence Oliphant, Mr.
Harris's famous neophyte, was a passenger on the same
ship; and it is suspected that this wrong-minded man's
wrong-minded counsel determined for evil Speke's waver-
ing will. For the very day after his return, he called at
Burlington House and initiated the scheme of a new exploration. He was induced, moreover, " much against his
inclination," so he said, to give a public lecture; and when,
one fortnight later, Burton reached London, the ground
was completely cut from under his feet. There was to be
a new expedition adequately dowered, but Speke was to
be the leader.

It is impossible not to blame John Hannen Speke for
this breach of faith, although he believed implicitly in his
own theories, and considered Burton both unreasonable and
malicious for criticising them. But what can we think of a

society of intelligent men, formed for the express purpose of promoting the knowledge of our earth's surface, deliberately perpetrating such a barbarous act of injustice ! It seemed so stupid, so utterly inexcusable, that one cannot help suspecting private enmity on the part of a very influential member.   Like many another piece of jobbery, it brought little luck to its object.   Speke's life was henceforth unenviable.   He never succeeded in thoroughly exploring the Victoria Nyanza ; that was left for Stanley, who circumnavigated it in 1874.   After the first flash his popularity steadily declined ; and at last, nearly blind, with health wrecked by fever upon fever, he lost nerve during a meeting at Bath of the British Association, when a geographical discussion was about to take place with his sorely injured friend, and accidentally shot himself with his own gun.

To return.   The three months and a half at Kazeh passed pleasantly enough.   On the 5th September " Handsome Moses " came home from a long visit to Karagwah, and emulated good Shaykh Snay in kindness and hospitality.   Better still, he was able to supply our traveller with many interesting details of the almost unknown land he had just left ; also of Unyoro and the now celebrated Uganda.   The great Suna, lord of the latter kingdom, had died quite recently after shocking his pious Arab visitors by boasting that he was the god of earth as their Allah was the Lord of Heaven.   He did not seem, however, to have been much, if at all, worse than his descendant King Mwanga, the truly promising proselyte of the French fathers; on the contrary, there was a wild magnificence and generosity about the pagan which inclines an unprejudiced reader to prefer him to the papist.   Besides imparting interesting and original information, Musa Mzuri assisted Burton in his preparations for the return journey.   A fine she-ass and foal were purchased as a sure means of providing milk on the way.   Supplies of pink porcelain beads were laid in—pink porcelain happened to be fashionable in Africa at this date—and all the damaged surveying instruments, various MSS., maps and sketch-books, together with reports for the Geographical Society, were forwarded to the coast by an Arab caravan.

There is no doubt Burton turned his face homeward with regret, especially as he found himself obliged by lack of funds to traverse the same route. The accounts given by Musa Mzuri fired both Englishmen with desire to visit the northern kingdoms (Karagwah and Uganda); but for this *détour* not only money, but time would have been required. Their two years' leave of absence was nearing its close, and even had they possessed a sufficient outfit, they were not disposed to risk being cashiered. Burton had already spent fourteen hundred pounds of his own private fortune, besides the thousand pounds granted by the Geographical Society; and had he forfeited his com- mission by unnecessary delay, he would have found himself in a sore strait. So at last he faced the inevitable, and fixed September 26th for departure.

Good Snay bin Amir, recently recovered from an attack of influenza which had confined him to his sleeping mat for some days, superintended the start in person. He treated both travellers to a copious breakfast well cooked and neatly served ; and as the caravan covered only two miles the first day, he followed with Musa Mzuri next morning, to see the last of his Moslem brother. The latter thanked his kind hosts most warmly for their very good deeds and promised to report in person to the Sayyid the hospitable reception accorded by his Arab subjects. Richard Burton, we remember, liked not saying good-bye ; I suspect by no means the least trying farewell of his life was that spoken to the noble-minded friend who had done him such rare good service in the land of Unyamwezi.

The return journey was uninteresting. In consequence of a famine along the Usagara road previously traversed, our travellers crossed the mountains by the Kiringawana line. I will spare my reader a list of uncouth names of tribes and villages along this southern route ; and the remainder of the way is already familiar. Arrived at Kaole, Burton sent his followers to their homes, and started with Speke on a coasting trip to Kilwa, returning to Zanzibar on the 4th March, 1859. Both Englishmen left for Aden on the 22nd, and, as before said, soon afterwards followed each other to England.

In conclusion, no better word-picture of Burton's followers during this eventful journey can be presented than by transcribing *verbatim* first an East African's every-day conversation, then a sort of seventh day one on theology.

Twanigana, a commonplace African youth, then acting as Kirangozi, attired in a red waistcoat, had safely passed through Ugogo, and was feeling fairly happy and secure amongst the Usagara mountains.

"The state, Mdula ? " (*i.e.*, Abdullah, a word unpronounceable to Negroid organs.)

"The state (of health) is very ! and thy state ? "

"The state is very!" (well) "and the state of Spikka? "

"The state of Spikka is very ! "

"We have escaped the Wagogo," resumes Twanigana, "white man O ! "

"We have escaped, O my brother ! "

"The Wagogo are bad."

"They are bad."

"The Wagogo are very bad."

"They are very bad."

"The Wagogo are not good."

"They are not good."

"The Wagogo are not at all good."

"They are not at all good."

"I greatly feared the Wagogo who kill the Wanyam wezi."

"Exactly so."

" But now I don't fear them. I called them . . . and
. . . and I would fight the whole tribe, white man O ! "

" Truly so, O my brother ! "

And thus for two mortal hours, until Burton's *ennui*
turned into marvel.

Older and more experienced was Muzungu Mbaya; and
the theological conversation which follows arose from an
attempt made by one Gul Mohammed, a Baloch, to impress
upon a Hamitic mind respect for the Moslem revelation.

Picture Muzungu Mbaya seated before a fire, warming
his lean black legs, and ever and anon casting pleasant
glances at a small black pipkin, whence arose the savoury
steam of meat and vegetables. A concatenation of ideas
perhaps induced Gul Mohammed to break rather unseason-
ably into his favourite theme.

" And thou, Muzungu Mbaya, thou also must die ! "

" Ugh ! ugh ! " replies Muzungu, personally offended,
" don't speak in that way ! Thou must die, too."

" It is a sore thing to die," resumes Gul Mohammed.

" Hoo ! Hoo ! " exclaims the other ; " it is bad, very
bad, never to wear a nice cloth, no longer to dwell with
one's wife and children, not to eat and drink, snuff, and
smoke tobacco. Hoo ! Hoo ! it is bad, very bad ! "

" But we shall eat," rejoins the Moslem. " The flesh
of birds, mountains of meat, and delicate roasts, and drink
sugared water, and whatever we hunger for."

The African's mind is disturbed by this tissue of contra-
dictions. He considers birds somewhat low feeding ; roasts
he adores ; he contrasts mountains of meat with his poor
half-pound in pot ; he would sell himself for sugar ; but
again he hears nothing of tobacco. Still he takes the
trouble to ask :

" Where, O my brother ? "

" There," exclaims Gul Mohammed, pointing to the
skies.

This is a choke-pear to Muzungu Mbaya. The distance

is great, and he can scarcely believe that his interlocutor has visited the firmament to see the provisions; he therefore ventures on the query:

"And hast thou been there, O my brother?"

"Astaghfar ullah!" (I beg pardon of Allah) ejaculates Gul Mohammed, half angry, half amused. "What a pagan this is! No, my brother, I have not exactly been there, but my Mulungu (Allah) told my Apostle, who told his descendants, who told my father and mother, who told me, that when we die we shall go to a Shamba (plantation) where——"

"Oof!" grunts Muzungu Mbaya; "it is good of you to tell us all this nonsense which your mother told you. So there are plantations in the skies?"

"Assuredly," replies Gul Mohammed, who expounds at length the Moslem idea of paradise to the African's running commentary of "Be off!" "Mama-e!" (O, my mother!) and sundry untranslatable words.

Muzungu Mbaya, who for the last minute has been immersed in thought, now suddenly raises his head, and with somewhat of a *goguenard* air, inquiries:

"Well, then, my brother, thou knowest all things! answer me, is thy Mulungu black like myself, white like this Muzungu, or whitey-brown as thou art?"

Gul Mohammed is fairly floored; he ejaculates sundry *la haut!* to collect his wits for the reply.

"Verily the Mulungu hath no colour."

"To-o-oh! Tuh!" exclaims the pagan, contorting his wrinkled countenance, and spitting with disgust upon the ground. He was now justified in believing that he had been made a laughing-stock. The mountain of meat had to a certain extent won over his better judgment; the fair vision now fled, and left him to the hard realities of the half-pound. He turns a deaf ear to every other word, and devotes all his attention to the article before him.

CHAPTER XI

DURING the summer of 1859, Speke, by claiming most of the honours of the Expedition, became the annual Lion necessary to the London season; still, Burton was regarded very highly by the principal men of that day. In him they recognised true genius, and predicted his speedy rise. The Duke of Somerset invited him to Bulstrode, Lord Palmerston to Broadlands, Lord Derby to Knowsley; Mr. Monckton Milnes, afterwards Lord Houghton, and the present Lord Stanley of Alderley, were numbered amongst his intimate friends; while in literary and Bohemian circles he was much sought after and fêted. I have mentioned only a few of the men of mark who esteemed and admired him; there were many others, and it was generally believed that certain of these influential well-wishers intended to right the wrong done by the Royal Geographical Society, either by equipping another expedition and giving him the command, or better still, by procuring for him some suitable appointment in the Indian Service. Much good work remained to be done on the frontier, as we know from the life of the late Sir Robert Sandeman; but we shall see later, an unexpected step on Burton's part complicated matters and delayed for awhile all the benevolent designs for his welfare.

Society claimed only part of his time. His "Lake Regions of Central Africa," that pioneer work which has helped many another traveller along the same road, had to be written and re-written with numerous additions. A portion of the MS. was begun at Dover, where his sister and brother-in-law were spending the summer; for, as

usual, after a long absence, some months were devoted
to his relatives. Colonel Stisted had just returned from
India, where he had taken a conspicuous part in the first
Relief of Lucknow, leading his regiment, the gallant 78th,
under " Watty Hamilton," through blood and fire to the
Residency. Thus the military brothers had plenty to talk
over ; and what with long walks with his sister, to whom
the " Lake Regions " is dedicated, some pleasant dinners
at the Castle, and hard literary labour, Burton passed the
time agreeably enough. Still, everybody remarked he
looked ill and depressed. The sweets of success were
mingled with many bitters. Speke's strange breach of
faith affected him more than he would confess to ; so
affectionate a nature could not fail to keenly feel the
complete severance of a long friendship. Blue-eyed, tawny-
maned " Jack " was not easily forgotten by the companion
of his many wanderings. Years later, when the fatal accident happened at Bath, Burton's emotion was uncontrollable. Doubtless his low spirits were aggravated by
ill-health ; it could hardly be otherwise after the fevers,
privations, and hideous strain of mind undergone during
the expedition to Tanganyika.

Thus passed the summer of 1859. In late autumn he
joined his brother and sister in Paris, and paid flying visits
from their *pied à terre* to various parts of the Continent.
As usual, in the matter of leave he was treated most
generously ; and after spending some weeks at Vichy, a
favourite haunt, the waters correcting the tendency to gout,
which later became so serious, ransacking the libraries of
two or three capitals, and finishing his book, he resolved to
take advantage of a fresh extension, no sooner applied for
than granted, and direct his steps to the New World.
The transition state of the Far West, those broad lands
which lie beyond the Missouri River and the Sierra Nevada,
offered much to interest a traveller ; besides, by staying
a month or so at the Mormon settlements, Great Salt Lake

City in particular, he could gratify a psychological whim
for observing the origin and the working of a regular go-
ahead Western and Columbian revelation. The tour was
rough enough to please even him, for the railway between
the two oceans was only being prospected, and he could
still enjoy the excitement of journeying in break-neck
waggons and of receiving his mails by " pony expresses."

The man was ready, the hour hardly appeared propitious for other than belligerent purposes. Throughout
the summer of 1860 an Indian war was raging in Nebraska;
the Comanches, Kiowas and Cheyennes were " out," and
the Federal Government had despatched three columns to
the centres of confusion. Horrible accounts of murdered
post-boys and cannibal emigrants filled the papers; besides,
the Mormons themselves were regarded as little better than
a host of desperadoes.

" Going among the Mormons?" said an American to
our traveller at New Orleans; " they are shooting and cutting one another in all directions. How can you expect to
escape ? "

But, struck with the discovery by some Western wise-
acre of an enlarged truth, viz., that the bugbear approached
has more affinity to the bug than to the bear, Burton decided to risk the chance of the red nightcap from the bloodthirsty Indian, and the poisoned bowie-dagger, without any
inamorata to console him from the Latter Day Saints. So
he applied himself to the audacious task with all the recklessness of a " party " from Town precipitating himself for
the first time into " foreign parts " about Calais.

As the voyage across the Atlantic was considered unworthy of remark, the journey proper dated from St. Joseph,
Missouri, a town more generally familiar as St. Jo. The
route mapped out was to comprise Great Salt Lake City,
Carson in California, where gold had lately been discovered,
and San Francisco. It is all easy travelling now, but nothing could have been more comfortless, more exhausting,

than the then mode of transport.   True, the line Burton selected was not quite so bad as what was known as the Butterfield Express, which kept its passengers twenty-four days and nights in a kind of van, until, half-crazed by whisky and want of sleep, they had to be strapped to their seats.   Still, a so-called spring waggon, constructed with an eye rather to strength than easiness, drawn by partially broken-in mules, and crammed to suffocation with pas- sengers, mails and luggage, must have become terribly wearisome before the regulation nineteen days were over.

Very unpicturesque did our traveller look when he took his place in the ungainly vehicle.   An adept in the art of clothing himself appropriately, on this occasion he sacrificed smartness to comfort.   Picture the whilom Arab Shaykh in dark flannel shirt, with broad leather belt for revolver and bowie-knife, his nether garments strengthened with buckskin, the lower ends tucked into his boots, a good English tweed shooting-jacket made with pockets like a poacher's, and his head snugly but ungracefully ensconced in a large brown felt hat, which, by means of a ribbon, was converted every evening into a nightcap.   However, even in the Far West appearances have to be considered at times ; so his chimney-pot, frock-coat, &c., even his silk umbrella, were carefully stowed away in his portmanteau ready for sporting on state visits to Mormon dignitaries.

The prairie waggon started from St. Jo. early on August 7th, 1860.   The other passengers were Lieut. Dana, an officer in the United States army, his wife and child, a judge, a state secretary, and a state marshal.   All were equally friendly, and, unlike the famous coachful that drove to Land's End, remained so during the whole of the weary way.   After traversing some dusty streets the van was transported bodily by steam ferry over the Big Muddy, or Missouri River, and on landing in Kansas, bowled merrily along Emigration Road, a broad and well-worn thoroughfare, celebrated as being the largest natural highway in the world. This easy travelling was too good to last. By-and-by the waggon emerged upon the Grand Prairie, where its occupants speedily made acquaintance with "chuck-holes," gullies or gutters which rendered the vehicle's progress not unlike that of a ship in a gale of wind. The first stage ended at about 1 a.m. at Locknan's Station, a few log and timber huts near a creek well feathered with white oak and American elm, hickory and black walnut, where the sadly shaken travellers found beds and snatched a few hours' sleep.

In the morning they had to drive some distance before they could get any breakfast, which was obtained at last at a village dignified with the high-sounding name of Seneca, a " city " consisting of a few shanties. Ensued a chequered day, the driver drunk and dashing like Phaeton over the chuck-holes, but, on the other hand, a good dinner of ham and eggs, hot rolls and coffee, peaches and cream supplied by a young Alsatian, who, under the excitement of Californian fever, had recently emigrated. At the station which possessed this treasure Burton saw the Pony Express arrive. Before the railways, the Express-man was a functionary of some importance, generally a youth mounted on an active Indian nag and able to ride one hundred miles at a time, about eight per hour, with four changes of horses.

Next morning's experience was unmitigatedly unpleasant. The passengers, already sick and feverish from the jolting of their vehicle, found themselves landed in a horrible shanty where a colony of Patlanders rose from bed without a dream of ablution, and prepared a neat *déjeûner à la four-chette* by hacking lumps off a sheep suspended from the ceiling and frying them in melted tallow. As Burton remarked, had the action occurred in Central Africa, among the Esquimaux, or the Araucanians, it would not have excited his attention : mere barbarism rarely disgusts ; it was the unnatural union of civilisation with savagery that made his gorge rise. As a general rule the food was vile, unless the halt was at a station provisioned by a Frenchman or a German ; unluckily, the sons and daughters of Erin abounded, and although, as in their native land, pigs and potatoes were common enough, not once did our traveller tell of a good square meal provided by a native of the Emerald Isle.

At Alkali Lake the curious spectacle was presented of an Indian remove. Shifting their quarters for grass, an animated crowd of bucks and braves, squaws and pappooses, ponies dwarfed by hard living, were straggling over the plains westward. In front, singly or in pairs, rode the men, some bare-backed, others used a stirrupless saddle, and for the most part managed their nags with a thong lashed round the lower jaw and attached to the neck. Their lank, long hair, rusty from the effects of weather, was worn parted in the middle, and hung from the temples in two pigtails, a style which aids in giving to the coronal region that appearance of depression which characterises the natives of North America as a race of " Flat Heads," and, being considered a beauty, led to the artificial deformities of the Peruvian and the Aztec. They were an ill-looking lot. A few had eagles' or crows' feathers stuck in their lank locks, others wore dilapidated Kossuth hats or old military casquettes, and their ragged, untidy garments of every hue and shape strongly suggested a pack of guys ready for the bonfire. However, there was a *belle* of the party, a veritable Poucahontas, who had large languishing eyes and sleek black hair like the ears of a King Charles spaniel, justifying a natural instinct to stroke or pat it, drawn straight over a low, broad, Quadroon-like brow. The grandmothers were fearful to look upon, and the boys, usually even ragless, with beady black eyes, and mouths like youthful caymans, were not much pleasanter. These wanderers followed the coach for many a mile, peering into the hinder part of the vehicle, ejaculating " How! How! " the normal salutation. But this politeness did not throw the passengers off their guard. The Dakota of those regions were expert and daring kleptomaniacs, and after the leathern curtain had been lowered as a matter of precaution, the noble savages, so dear to romancist and poet, drew off begging pertinaciously to the last.

Burton tells a curious anecdote *à propos* of one of these people. At Platte Bridge, as he was sitting after dinner outside the station-house with his fellow-travellers, two Arapahas Indians squatted on some stones close by. He happened to mention the dislike amongst African savages to anything like a sketch of their physiognomies; and his hearers expressing a doubt whether the "Reds" were equally sensitive, he immediately proceeded to proof. Soon the man became uneasy under the operation, averting his face at times, and shifting his position to defeat the artist's purpose. When the sketch was passed round it excited some merriment, whereupon the original rose fiom his seat and made a sign that he also wished to see it. At the sight he screwed up his features with a grimace of intense disgust, and, managing to smudge the paper with his dirty hands, he stalked away, with an ejaculation which expressed his outraged feelings.

To the Indians succeeded the more commonplace spectacle of the Mormon emigrants. On the 16th August a train of waggons was observed slowly wending its way towards the "Promised Land." The guide was a nephew of Brigham Young's, or the "Old Boss," as his people called him, and the caravan seemed well organised, few of the pilgrims showing any symptoms of sickness or starvation. Burton recognised the nationality at once, even through the veil of freckles and sunburn with which a two months' summer journey had invested every face. British-English, he said, was written in capital letters upon the white eye-lashes and tow-coloured curls of the children, and upon the sandy brown hair, staring eyes, heavy bodies and ample extremities of the adults.

17

For it was an unpleasant fact that, after America, England principally replenished the Mormon settlements. In 1837 a company of Mormons began preaching at Preston with such remarkable success that within eight months they had baptised about 2,000 people. A few years later, Brigham Young and his apostles conducted another mission in our islands, and despatched hundreds and hundreds of converts across the Atlantic. Other missionaries, too, worked in England, and founded meeting-houses in several towns. But at present the rapid spread of education has closed to a great extent their favourite recruiting-grounds. A late popular authoress related, amusingly enough, how in her day a Mormon elder promised a silly old Worcester-shire gammer a white donkey to convey her to New Jeru-salem, and while she was waiting and watching in all good faith for her heavenly messenger, her deceiver departed with a choice assortment of younger and fairer proselytes. Now gammer's grandchildren would enlighten her as to the exist-ence of the Atlantic.

The formation of the land, changing from tertiary and cretaceous to granites and porphyries, showed that our passengers were approaching the Rocky Mountains. The coach was about to enter a very uncomfortable region for nervous travellers, the region of kanyons, or cañons, those deep, narrow, wall-sided trenches which countless ages of water have cut through the solid rock. On the 19th a real bit of the far-famed " Rockies," hardly to be distinguished from some fleecy, sunlit clouds resting upon the horizon, came in view—Fremont's Peak, a sharp snow-clad apex of the Wind River Range. This was just visible from the Sweetwater Valley, a charming vale tapestried with flowery grass and copses, where grouse ran in and out, and afford-ing delicious shade with its long lines of aspen, beech, and cottonwood, its pines and cedars, cyprus and scattered ever-greens.

But the sublimest scene of all was viewed from the

South Pass, a majestic level-topped bluff, the highest steppe of the continent, situated nearly midway between the Mississippi and the Pacific. This wonderful spot, 7,490 feet above sea level, and twenty miles in breadth, the great *Wasserschiede* betwixt the Atlantic and the Pacific, the frontier points between Nebraska and Oregon, is not, strictly speaking, a pass. With some of the features of Thermopylæ and of the Simplon, it is no giant gateway opening through cyclopean walls of beetling rocks; rather a grand tableland whose iron surface affords space enough for the armies of our globe to march over. Amongst the world's watersheds it has no rival, for here lie separated by a trivial space the fountain-heads that give birth to the noblest rivers of America, the Columbia, the Colorado, and the Yellowstone, which is to the Missouri what the Missouri is to the Mississippi.

From the mouth of the Sweetwater, about 120 miles, the rise had been so gradual that it was quite unexpectedly the travellers found themselves on the summit. At first a heavy mist veiled the noble range of mountains; but towards sunset, when the departing luminary poured a flood of gold on the magnificent chain of *Les Montagnes Rocheuses*, imagination could depict no sight more beautiful.

Pacific Springs, the station where, in the midst of this glorious scene, the passengers found accommodation, consisted of a log shanty built close to a pond of ice-cold water. It afforded the unusual luxuries of bouilli and potatoes; but its crazy walls and ill-fitting door utterly failed to keep out the cold, no trifling matter, as the mercury at dawn stood at 35° F. Uncomfortable though it was, Mrs. Dana and her child, dazed with fatigue, were only too thankful that their despotic driver chose to linger a little later than his customary time; and the other travellers took advantage of the delay to enjoy once more the lovely aspect of the mountains upon whose walls of snow next morning the rays of the rising sun broke with splendid effect. . . . All were

en route again at 8 a.m., and, beginning the descent of the
Western watershed, debouched next day on the banks of
the Green River. Here they entered Utah territory, so
called from its Indian owners, the Yuta, or those that dwell
in mountains. For its lowest valley rises 4,000 feet above
sea level, the mountains behind Great Salt Lake City are
6,000 feet high, and the Twin Peaks that look upon the
so-called Happy Valley soar to an altitude of 11,660 feet.

Perhaps the most exciting day of any was the 24th
August, when the coach rolled along Echo Kanyon. This
strange, red ravine, with its broken and jagged peaks
divided by dark abysses, its clear swift stream now hugging
the right, then the left side of the chasm, one gigantic
rufous wall, fretted and honeycombed, frowning at its
brother buttress across the gorge, measured from twenty-
six to thirty miles in length. A sublime scene, but not one
to be viewed from a mail waggon with the pleasure and
admiration it deserved. Even Burton confessed to entering
it in rather an uncomfortable frame of mind, especially as
the team was headed on this occasion by a pair of all but
unmanageable animals. Down they rushed along the short,
steep pitches, swinging the wheels of the vehicle within
half a foot of the high bank's crumbling edge. Had the mules
shied or fallen, nothing could have saved the passengers
from as grim a form of death as fancy can conceive—down,
down an almost perpendicular precipice into an icy river
roaring and raging over its rocks and boulders. But the
wild drive came to an end at last, and its emotions terminated in bathos. Burton might have passed a good
night, only his doorless apartment happened to be the
favourite haunt of a skunk.

The journey was now drawing to a conclusion. Next
day, after breasting Big Mountain, an eyrie 8,000 feet
high, our party sighted the Happy Valley of the Great Salt
Lake. Its western horizon is bounded by a broken
wall of bright blue peaks, the northernmost bluff buttress-

ing the southern side of the water, while the eastern flank sinks by steps and terraces into a river-basin yellow with golden corn. After a few minutes' delay to stand and gaze, Burton resumed his way on foot, while the mail-waggon, with wheels rough-locked, descended a steep slope. The distance from the city was only seventeen miles, and before long the rough road was exchanged for a broad smooth thoroughfare, and the town, by slow degrees, came into view.

It showed to special advantage after a succession of Indian lodges, Canadian ranches, and log-hut mail stations. The site, admirably selected for space and irrigation, admitted at that time of each householder being the happy possessor, not merely of three acres and a cow, that delusive promise of a dead and gone Ministry, but of from five to ten acres in the suburbs and one and a half inside the city. Gardens and orchards filled with fruit-trees and flowers looked their loveliest, and it was with a decided sense of prepossession in favour of their industrious owners that our traveller concluded his journey of 1,136 miles in front of Salt Lake House, at that date the only hotel in the town. The proprietor, a Mormon, welcomed the passengers very civilly, and his wife took charge of poor exhausted Mrs. Dana and her little daughter.

Thanks to his fellow-passenger, Lieutenant Dana, who knew several of the principal people in the place, Burton found no difficulty in seeing something of Mormon society. Amongst others, Elder Stenhouse and his wife, a lively little woman from Jersey, seemed only too pleased to give him as much information as possible; in fact, the Saints one and all showed themselves in their fairest colours to a clever guest unbiassed against their pet institution. And as a natural consequence, while Burton admitted there were many things in the inner life of Mormonism which no "Gentile" was allowed to penetrate, it is generally agreed that he represented these strange people in too favourable a light. Hepworth Dixon was equally fascinated by them. Perhaps their marvellous industry captivated the two distinguished visitors; moreover, if the city were a " whited sepulchre," it was scrupulously whitewashed; the streets, perfectly free from the horrible scenes of drunkenness and immorality which disgrace the capitals of Europe, were a pattern of what a Christian town ought to be. In commercial matters, even foreigners who traded with Mormons extolled their unvarying honesty. On the other hand, the Saints, though sober and industrious, lied unblushingly when anxious to screen any misdeed committed by one of their members; and this habit would naturally mislead any stranger, however intelligent. In the matter of the Mountain Meadow Massacre, which had taken place only three years before, the butchery of a whole train of " Gentile " emigrants from Arkansas, the Mormons cast the entire blame upon the Indians; and it was only in 1877 that one of their dignitaries, Bishop John Lee, was shot for complicity in the horrible affair.

Like most infant communities, this of Utah was directed by one master mind, Brigham Young, its priest and lawgiver. A brief account of an interview which took place between him and our traveller at the Prophet's private office will give readers who know little about this polygamous personage some idea of a remarkable man.

Brigham Young, then about fifty-nine years of age, looked forty-five. Scarcely a grey thread appeared in his thick fair hair, and his large, broad-shouldered figure only stooped a little when standing. Accused of leading a most dissolute life, he reached nevertheless the ripe age of seventy-seven, and then died of cholera caused by too plentiful a meal of green corn and peaches. His appearance was that of a New England farmer; and although he had worked as a painter and glazier, and is said to have boasted of having spent only eleven and a half days at school, his manners were courteous and simple.

He conversed with ease and correctness, had neither snuffle nor pompousness, and spoke not one word on the subject of religion. However, he soon showed some curiosity as to the stranger's object in visiting the City of the Saints, and seemed quite satisfied with the reply, viz., that having heard much about Utah, Burton wished to see it as it really was. Conversation then ran on two very safe topics, agriculture and the Indians. The latter, be it stated, were great pets of the Saints, owing to a startling ethnological prophecy in the "Book of Mormon," that many generations shall not pass away before the Red Men become a white and delightsome people. Still, as reports were afloat of these embryo angels being killed off in unnecessarily large numbers, Brigham Young was at some pains to prove the contrary. It is certain he was an unscrupulous man— what fanatic is not?—but he may be credited with considerable talent to have ruled the heterogeneous mass of conflicting elements in his new territory even as well as he did. Any question as to the number of his wives would have been awkward; but on another occasion, while Burton was standing with him on the verandah of his block, our traveller's eye fell upon a new erection which could be compared externally to nothing but an Englishman's hunting stables, and he asked what it was. "A private school for my children," the Prophet replied. It was large enough to accommodate a huge village.

His creation, Great Salt Lake City, situated in a valley surrounded by mountains and watered by a brackish river, called New Jordan, is built like most of the nineteenth century New World towns, in the rectangular style. Already a fair size, it possessed in 1860 a large population.[1] Every object bore the impress of hard work; a miracle of industry in the short space of thirteen years had converted a wild waste, where only a few miser-

---

[1] The Saints were accused of cooking the numbers.

able savages had gathered grass-seed and locusts to keep
life and soul together, into a fertile and prosperous settlement. Of course, the buildings were as yet neither stately
nor substantial. The Prophet's block glaring with whitewash, and the Bee House, where his plurality wives
resided, were, in common with other houses belonging to
lesser personages, constructed of sun-dried brick; and many
would have looked dull and mean but for their cheerful
surroundings of garden and orchard, filled with fruit trees
and bright English flowers—roses, geraniums, pinks and
pansies. The shape of these homesteads was mostly of one
pattern, the barn with wings and lean-to; and these primitive erections, despising uniformity, sometimes faced and in
other instances turned sideways to the street. However,
the lapse of thirty-five years has brought about a change
as vast as that effected by the Prophet. Now real brick
and timber are the common building materials, the town is
lighted by electricity, and, judging by some interesting
views which appeared this year in *Black and White*, the
public edifices, with the exception of the ugly Tabernacle,
are exceedingly handsome and imposing.

The Temple Block, then the sole place of worship in
the city, was in a very sketchy condition. The Latter Day
Saints had been unceremoniously turned out of Nauvoo,
Missouri, in 1845, and their church destroyed. Still, considering they had housed themselves pretty snugly, Burton
remarked they were preparing rather leisurely for their new
Zion, as little more than the foundations were visible; in
fact, it took altogether forty years in constructing. The
Block, ten acres square, standing clear of all other buildings,
was surrounded with a wall of handsomely dressed red sandstone, raised to the height of ten feet by sun-dried brick,
stuccoed over to resemble a richer material; and a central
excavation, yawning like a large oblong grave, represented
a future font, these people observing the uncomfortable
practice of baptism by immersion. An adobe erection, with

a shingle roof, served as Tabernacle ; and ordinary services were held in a kind of huge shed, with a covering of bushes and boughs, supported by rough posts, and open on the sides for ventilation. The Bowery, as it was called, seemed a cool and airy place of worship, but was destitute of any element of the sublime.

Burton prepared for a Sunday in Utah by a painful but appropriate exercise, reading the " Book of Mormon." He describes this volume as utterly dull and heavy, monotonous as a sage prairie ; and though not liable to be daunted by dreary works, he confessed he could turn over only a few chapters at a sitting. On the stroke of ten the " book written on golden plates by the hand of Mormon " was tossed aside, and its prodigiously bored student hied to the Bowery, where he took a seat on one of the long rows of benches. It was curious to see the congregation flocking in, some from long distances, in their smartest attire, many a pretty face peeping under the usual sun-bonnet with its long curtain, others surmounted by the " mushroom " or " pork-pie " ; poorer women clad in neat stuff dresses, richer ones in silk, even sporting gauze and feathers. By our traveller's side sat an extremely ugly English servant girl ; *en revanche*, in front was a charming American mother who had, as he remarked in Mormon meetings at Saville House and other places in Europe, an unusual development of the organ of veneration. Between the congregation and the platform whence the discourses were delivered was an enclosure not unlike a pen ; this was allotted to the choir and orchestra—a bass, a violin, two women singers, and four men performers, who rendered the songs of Zion more agreeably than might have been expected.

Worship began with a hymn. Then a civilised-looking man, just returned from foreign travel, was called upon by the presiding elder to engage in prayer, which he did, while two shorthand writers stationed in a tribune took notes. He ended by imploring a blessing upon the Mormon Presi-

dent and all those in authority. The conclusion was an
" Amen " in which all joined, reminding our listener of the
historical practice of " humming " in the seventeenth century, which caused the Universities to be called *Hum et
Hissimi auditores.*

Next arose a Bishop, who began with " Brethring," and
proceeded in a low and methody tone of voice, " hardly
audible in the gallery," to praise the Saints and pitch into
the apostates. His delivery was by no means fluent even
when he warmed, still he might have been listened to with
profounder interest, but for the entrance of the " Boss."
Every one was then on the *qui vive*, even to the elderly
dame who, from Hanover Square to far San Francisco,
placidly reposes through the sermon.

The Latter Day Prophet did not present an imposing
appearance. A man with a Newgate fringe, clad in grey
homespun garments, and a steeple-crowned straw hat
decorated with a broad black ribbon, ill accords with most
people's ideal of a " Seer." He expectorated too, which
was disagreeable. After a man in a fit had been carried
out pumpwards, and the Bishop had concluded his discourse, another hymn was sung, and then came a deep
silence. Mr. Brigham Young removed his hat, swallowed
a glass of water, and addressed his followers. His manner
was pleasing and animated, the matter fluent, *impromptu*,
and well turned, spoken rather than preached ; and, apart
from his " gift of tongues," a sort of gibberish which nobody understood, and which he spoke at times for motives
best known to himself, he is said to have often indulged in
real flights of eloquence. But the occasion in question
was not propitious ; at times he descended to twaddle.
" Mormonism was a great fact, religion had made him the
happiest of men, the Saints had a glorious destiny before
them, and their virtues were as remarkable as the beauty of
the Promised Land." Certainly he made his congregation
laugh when speaking of the joy caused by his spiritual

convictions, for, declaring he felt ready to dance like a Shaker, he raised his right arm and gave a droll imitation of Anne Lee's followers ; but this seems to have been the best part of the sermon. When he had concluded, more addresses followed from minor personages, several hymns were sung, and then came the blessing and dismissal. Burton returned to his hotel directly the ceremony was over, and applied himself, not to the dreary Mormon " Bible," but to writing the notes which were to form the groundwork of a future book.[1]

A sketch of a day in Great Salt Lake City, when our traveller was neither exploring the environs nor attending religious exercises, will give some idea how his time passed. He rose early and breakfasted at any hour between 6 and 9 a.m. Then followed a stroll about the town, enlivened by an occasional liquoring up with a new acquaintance, a practice which, much to the Saints' credit, was confined to the " Gentiles," the stricter Mormons disapproving of spirit-drinking, anyhow, in public. This nipping by the way disagreed frightfully with Burton ; he could take his bottle after dinner with any man, but nip he could not, and I never heard of his indulging in the vile habit except during this stay in America. Dinner, at 1 p.m., was rather a disorderly meal. Jostling into a long dining-room, all took their seats, and seizing knife and fork, proceeded to action with a voracity worthy of beasts at the Zoo. Nothing but water was drunk, except when some peculiar person preferred to wash down his roast pork with milk, a truly horrible mixture ; but the meal ended with a glass of whisky served in the bedroom, there being no bar. Supper, or dinner number two, took place at 6 p.m. When neither eating nor strolling about, Burton spent his time mostly at the Historian and Recorder's Office, opposite Brigham Young's block. It contained a small collec-

---

[1] " The City of the Saints," 1 vol. Longmans, 1862.

tion of volumes, and appears to have served as a sort of club almost entirely frequented by Mormons, and it afforded many an opportunity of hearing these strange people discuss their social politics and soundly abuse their enemies.

One afternoon quite a stir arose in the city. Enquiring what the excitement might be about, our traveller was informed that a large party of emigrants were just arriving. He set off " down town " at once to view the curious sight. In marched the silly souls through clouds of dust over the sandy road leading to the eastern portion of the settlement, accompanied by crowds of citizens, some on foot, others on horseback or in traps. The new-comers had donned clean clothes, the men shaved, and the girls, who were singing hymns, were habited in smartest Sunday dresses. The company, though sunburnt, looked well and thoroughly happy, and few except the very young and the very old, who suffer most on such journeys, troubled the wains. Around were all manner of familiar faces—heavy English mechanics, discharged soldiers, clerks and agricultural labourers, a few German students, farmers, husbandmen, and peasants from Scandinavia and Switzerland, and corre-spondents, editors, apostles, and other dignitaries from the Eastern states. Very bovine looked some of our com-patriots, many had passed over the plains unaware they were in the States, and had actually been known to throw away *en route* their blankets and warm clothing, under the idiotic impression that perpetual summer reigned in their pinchbeck Zion.

When the train reached the public square of Ward No. 8, the waggons were ranged in line for the final cere-mony. At one time Brigham Young used to welcome in person his new recruits; but in 1860, fearing assassination, he appeared in public as seldom as possible. However, on this occasion, his place was taken by Bishop Hunter, who, preceded by a brass band and accompanied by the City

Marshal, stood up in his conveyance, and, calling the Captains of Companies, set at once to business. In a short time arrangements were made to house and employ all who required work, whether men or women. Everything was conducted with the most perfect decorum. If any matrimonial proposal took place, it was in strict privacy, the Mormon dignitaries, accused on such occasions of undue flippancy, looking as grave and proper as judges on the bench.

Amongst the welcoming crowd figured a large number of the city dames. Less smart than on Sunday, they affected much the same style of dress as the Salvation Army lasses, minus the blood-red ribbons. A poke-bonnet was universally worn—why is the Poke a symbol of piety, Quakers, Salvationists, Mormons, Sisters of Mercy retiring alike inside its ungraceful shape ? A loose jacket and a skirt, generally of some inexpensive fabric, completed this comfortable but exceedingly plain costume.

The most interesting excursion was to the Great Salt Lake. One fine morning our traveller and two Americans set out down the west road, crossed a ricketty bridge which spanned the New Jordan, and debouched upon a mirage-haunted and singularly ugly plain. After fifteen miles of good road they came to the head of the Oquirrh, where pyramidal buttes bound the southern extremity of the water. Driving on, they presently emerged upon the shores of this " still and solitary sea," the sea of which the early Canadian *voyageurs* used to tell such wonderful tales.

Under a clear blue sky, the " Mare Mortuum " appeared by no means unprepossessing. As Burton stood upon the ledge at whose foot lies the selvage of sand and salt that bounds the lake, he fancied he looked upon the sea of the Cyclades. The water was of a deep lapis lazuli blue, flecked here and there with the smallest of white horses—tiny billows urged by the soft, warm wind ; and the feeble tumble of the surf upon the miniature sands reminded him of scenes far away, where mightier billows pay their tribute to the strand.   In front, bounding the extreme north-east, lies Antelope Island, rising in a bold central ridge.   This rock forms the western horizon to those looking from the city, and its delicate pink—the effect of a ruddy carpet woven with myriads of small flowers— blushing in the light of the setting sun, is ever an in- teresting and beautiful object.   The foreground is a strip of sand, yellow where it can be seen, encrusted with flakes of salt, like the icing of a plum-cake, and bearing marks of submergence in the season of the spring freshlets.

This singular reproduction of the Judæan Dead Sea is about the size of the African Chad.   Its water contains nearly one quarter of solid matter, or about six times and a half more than the average solid constituents of sea-water, which may be laid down roughly at three and a half per cent. of its weight, or about half an ounce to the pound. Of course, it is fatal to organic life, the fish brought down the rivers perish at once in the concentrated brine; and near the bathing-place a dreadful shock awaits the olfactory nerves.   Banks of black mud on examination prove to be an Aceldama of insects, &c., a horrible heap of mortal coils of myriads of worms, mosquitoes, flies, cast up by the waves, fermenting and festering in the burning sun.

Escaping with undignified haste from this mass of fetor, Burton reached the further end of a promontory where a tall rock stood decorously between the bathing-place and the picnic ground, and, in a pleasant frame of curiosity, descended into the New World Dead Sea.   He had heard strange accounts of its buoyancy.   It was said to support a bather as if he were sitting in an armchair, and to float him like an unfresh egg.   His experience differed widely; there was no difficulty in swimming, nor indeed in sinking.   But after sundry immersions of the head to feel if it really stung and removed the skin like a mustard plaster as described, emboldened by the detection of so much hyperbole, he proceeded to duck under with open eyes, and smarted for his pains. There was a grain of truth in these travellers' tales. The sensation did not come on suddenly ; at first he felt a sneaking twinge, then a bold succession of twinges, and lastly, a steady honest burning like what follows a pinch of snuff in the eyes. There was no fresh water at hand; he was, moreover, half-blinded, so scrambling upon the rock, our ardent investigator had to sit in misery for at least half an hour presenting to Nature the ludicrous spectacle of a man weeping flowing tears.

On another occasion, Burton visited Camp Floyd, where a detachment of the United States army were then stationed. He was conveyed thither, a distance of forty miles, in an American merchant's trotting waggon, drawn by a fine tall pair of iron-grey mules christened Julia and Sally, after the fair daughters of the officer who had lately commanded the district. With a fine clear day and a breeze which covered him with dust, he set out along the country road leading from the south-eastern angle of the city. The route lay over the strip of alluvium that separates the Wasach Mountains from the waters of New Jordan; it is cut by a multitude of streamlets rising from the kanyons, the principal being Mill Creek, Big Cottonwood, Little Cottonwood, and Willow Creek—these names are translated from the Indians—and from the road were seen traces of the aborigines, who were sweeping crickets and grass-seed into their large conical baskets—amongst these ragged gleaners Burton looked in vain for a Ruth !

The military not being permitted to approach the city of the suspicious and cantankerous Saints nearer than forty miles, were located in a circular basin surrounded by irregular hills ; and their huts clustered closely on the banks of Cedar Creek, a rivulet consisting chiefly of black mud. A more detestable spot could be found only at Ghara, or some similar purgatorial place in Lower Sind.

The winter was long and rigorous, the summer hot and uncomfortable, the alkaline water curdled soap, and the dust storms equalled the Punjaub. Here, as Utah was in a very unsettled condition, the Saints and the Indians vying with each other in breaking the eighth command-ment as frequently as possible, the unlucky Regulars had to remain, until at last hostilities broke out between the North and South and they were hurriedly recalled. Burton makes grateful mention of their kindness and hospitality. At that period the American army was composed chiefly of Southerners, and one of the most genial of his enter-tainers was a Captain Heth, a Virginian, whose family dated from the Dominion of Queen Elizabeth.   Naturally, all the officers detested the dreary fanatics whom they were expatriated to guard. " They hate us, and we hate them," was the universal cry ; and from the " chief imposter to the last ' acolyte ' " every Mormon was declared to be a miscreant.

Besides the trips to the Salt Lake and Camp Floyd, Burton spent some days exploring the most curious of the kanyons. One of the finest was already dotted over with saw-mills, Uncle Sam's pet decoration for his fairest scenery. Blemishes notwithstanding, the ravines presented a strange and impressive spectacle ; and as autumn was just tinting the trees and the first snow whitening the mountain peaks, the country looked its loveliest.

Three weeks exhausted the attractions of the saintly city. About the middle of September our traveller began to think of departing. He wished to see something of the gold diggings about Carson on the eastern foot of the Sierra Nevada, and as two State officials, one a judge, were shortly proceeding in the same direction, he hurried on preparations for his journey in order to accompany them. The mode of transit was by mail-waggon, much like that from St. Jo, only ruder and even more dangerous. The distance was 580 miles, and the time occupied nearly a month. The extremes of heat and cold surpassed any endured while crossing the Rockies, the food was invariably bad, ditto the accommodation, while the Indians in that part of the country had acquired such an evil reputation that Burton, before starting, cut his hair as short as a French soldier's. However, no disaster occurred of any importance, and the travellers jogged into Carson City unscalped, and little the worse for their fatigues. A few days were spent lionizing, the most interesting visit being to the gold diggings of Placerville, where Burton was initiated into the mysteries of gold washing ; then on November 1st he journeyed by coach to Folsom, thence by rail to Sacramento, and after about a fortnight spent at San Francisco, he made his way home *via* Panama.

His book, the " City of the Saints," describing this visit to Utah, which was published the following year, created a certain stir. For it reads almost like a panegyric. The Mountain Meadow Massacre is pooh-poohed, the existence of the Danites doubted, and the poultry-yard arrangement, cock-a-doodle-doo and six hens, mentioned in terms approaching admiration. This burly volume, written in the same careful, accurate style which characterises all Burton's works, would lose nothing by the omission of lengthy extracts from Mormon letters and sermons advocating the practice of " Abraham, Isaac, and Jacob," arguments based on very unsound theology. The experience of thirty-five years, too, has proved our traveller mistaken in predicting a great future for the Mormons and their peculiar institution. Their numbers do not appear to have increased, their capital is now overrun with " Gentiles," and even dotted with Protestant and Roman Catholic churches, and the Pacific Railway has given them the go-by. While as to polygamy, the present Mormon President issued in 1890 a proclamation declaring that the church no longer taught that doctrine ; and when, in 1896, Utah was at last thought worthy of admittance into the United States, President

18

Cleveland, while not abrogating existing plurality marriages, declared all future ones illegal.

It is startling to turn from Burton's encomiums on the
polygamous Saints to his—marriage! This step, upon
which much misplaced sentiment has been lavished, surprised both friends and relatives; those who knew him
best were perfectly aware that it surprised him most of
all. He was past forty, for some years he had had no
serious *affaire de cœur*, and he invariably declared in his
private circle, in answer to occasional enquiries, that he
intended to remain a bachelor—principally from inclination, and partly because his limited means and roving
habits were unsuited for matrimony. Fate, however,
decreed otherwise. For some time past he had been acquainted with a Miss Isabel Arundell, a handsome and
fascinating woman, then entering her thirtieth year. Her
father, Henry Raymond, who with his brother Renfric
carried on business as wine merchants in Mount Street,
was not very prosperous, and, as often happens in such a
case, had a numerous family. Isabel, restless amidst her
dull surroundings, admired Burton's career, admired Burton
himself, and naturally wished to marry one of the foremost
of the men of mark of the day. Even the fact of belonging
to an old Roman Catholic family did not deter her from
choosing a husband of totally different views from her own.
A quotation anent the Sweetwater River in the " City of
the Saints " will show what ensued. " Wilful and woman-
like, she has set her heart upon an apparent impossibility ;
and, as usual with her sex under the circumstances, she
has had her way." Burton made one stipulation—that she
should give him her solemn promise that if he pre-deceased
her no Romish priest should be surreptitiously introduced
to his death-chamber.

The marriage had to take place privately, possibly
because the bride's mother vehemently objected to any
daughter of hers espousing a Protestant ; and as she ruled

her household with a rod of iron, it may have been judged advisable not to let her know until the deed was done. So one cold morning, 22nd January, 1861, Burton, clad in a rough shooting coat, other garments to match, and with a cigar in his mouth, bravado to hide his deadly nervousness on taking such a step, awaited his bride on the steps of the Bavarian Chapel in Warwick Street, where the ceremony was duly performed by priest and registrar, according to the law for mixed marriages.[1]

Shortly afterwards our Benedict fell ill with severe bronchitis, and leaving his wife to break the news to her people,[2] and see how they were disposed to receive him, he went to Dovercourt, the home of a wealthy and generous aunt, for rest and careful nursing. Isabel meanwhile announced her marriage. Mr. Arundell was much delighted; but his wife, an irascible but excellent woman, never forgave her son-in-law. Almost the last time I saw her she exclaimed, in answer to some remark from her daughter, " Dick is no relation of mine."

Looking dispassionately at this match, it is clear that Burton committed as serious an imprudence as when he sent Speke alone to search for the Victoria Nyanza. The reader will see later how, in spite of much that was agreeable and attractive, Isabel, owing to a fatal want of tact and judgment, was unfitted for the path in life which she had insisted on choosing for herself—a far more important matter than mere pecuniary difficulties. These, however, were bad enough. When his wife's debts and his own were paid, Burton had only four thousand pounds remaining from his little patrimony, a sum which, prudently invested in a joint annuity, brought in about £200 per annum. Besides this majestic income there was his half-pay.

---

1 The presence of the registrar disproved the silly story, circulated after his death, that he had joined the Church of Rome as a young man at Baroda.

2 His sister was informed a few days before the ceremony.

What was he to do? Perhaps his best plan would have been to return to India, but as a lieutenant the prospect seemed a poor one. His influential friends were startled, not to say dismayed by this imprudent step, and wondered, no doubt, what piece of eccentricity he would treat them to next. No one came forward, and yet something had to be decided upon at once, for the pair, neither economical, could not live on £350 a year. On such occasions the "something" is rarely agreeable. A Job's comforter suggested the Consular service, and the post at Fernando Po being then vacant, no unusual occurrence, it was applied for and obtained with little trouble. But a fresh disaster happened as soon as the appointment appeared in the *Gazette*. Instead of having ascertained whether he could retain his commission or make some special stipulation concerning it, with true Irish hopefulness Burton had taken no precaution whatever, and found to his dismay his name erased from the Indian Army List.

However, the deed was done. The Arundells kindly offered their home as their daughter's headquarters during her husband's absence—Fernando Po was then quite unfit for Englishwomen—and our Benedict, after providing most liberally for her comfort, started for his new post with spirits revived at certain holiday prospects of explorations on the West Coast of Africa during the intervals of his consular duties.

CHAPTER XII

RICHARD BURTON, Consul at Fernando Po, a spot nick na ned the Foreign Office grave! Richard Burton, whose knowledge of Eastern languages and Eastern customs would have proved of incalculable value in India and Egypt, or upon the Red Sea littoral, banished to a distant and pestiferous island to perform duties which any man of average brains could have done equally well! And on and on in this dismal strain throughout at least a couple of pages, my reader may expect me to bewail our traveller's evil fortune, and to complain in usual stock phrases of the Government of the day which permitted such an anomaly.

But as I am writing a true and simple story of his life, dispassionate as any memoir compiled by a near relative can be, after much thought, much reading, and many consultations with his best friends, I am unable in the matter of this appointment to represent him as a martyr to an ungrateful country. At forty years of age, having contracted an imprudent marriage, he was compelled by pecuniary considerations to enter a new service; could his most devoted admirers expect he should immediately receive one of the plums? Later a big one did fall to his share, and had it not been for a disaster, alas! to some extent of his own causing, he might have attained one of the highest positions which the Foreign Office had to offer.

He started for his new post on the 24th August, 1861. His ship, the *Blackland*, being a cargo and passenger steamer, left him ample time to visit every port town, and see all the objects of interest, while she discharged her merchandise.

Each scene possessed for him the charm of novelty. Madeira, then crowded with consumptives, who have since deserted it for dreary Davos; Teneriffe, most picturesque of the Fortunate Islands; Bathurst, a miserable fever-stricken settlement whose sanitary officer was needlessly strict in questioning the health of the new arrivals from England; Sierra Leone, overrun by litigious niggers, one of whom summoned the captain; Cape Coast Castle, which so quickly drove poor L. E. L. to despair, and no wonder, from our traveller's description of the horrid hole; Accra and Lagos, one as pestilential as the other. At the latter Burton had a pleasant surprise. All the Mohammedan population, under the leadership of a Haji, turned out in force to welcome a brother pilgrim. Haji Abdullah was petted and honoured in a fashion most unusual, and he left his unexpected friends with regret for the Bonny River, otherwise known as the African Styx. Finally, after a day or two's delay in a settlement equal in point of nastiness to the old Fleet Ditch, he found himself at Fernando Po, his destined headquarters for the next four years.

The first night he felt uncommonly suicidal. The Consulate was situated in the lower part of Santa Isabel, close to the harbour, and in unpleasant proximity to a military hospital, whence dismal sights were often visible. It was built of wood with a corrugated iron roof, and every sort of evil odour floated unhindered through its glassless windows. But, after some months, matters improved. An epidemic of yellow fever which decimated the garrison and threatened to become chronic, determined the Spanish governor to imitate other colonists and try the effects of altitude. Barracks were built on the heights, and as the soldiers' health mended as if by magic, our consul, indisposed for voluntary martyrdom through remaining in his unsavoury quarters, felt himself also at liberty to migrate from the neighbourhood of the port to a frame-house constructed by a Spanish official, situated eight hundred feet above sea level.

Then life became worth living. His nigger servants, Krumen all, the only people who will do anything in this part of Africa, set to work to lay out a large garden, which soon supplied the household with excellent vegetables ; a delicious rivulet ran along a neighbouring ravine ; and the views of the distant Camaroons were so lovely that Burton quite fell in love with " Buena Vista," as the little place was appropriately christened. Possibly this happy state of mind may have been caused partly by seeing so little of it. His trips along the coast were almost countless, his jurisdiction as consul for the entire Bight of Biafra extending over a wide range, and there being many objects of interest within practicable distance. I use the last two words with intention. He complained, justly enough, that some people expected him to perform impossibilities—to explore at least one thousand miles of the Congo, to clear up the uncertainties concerning the Niger, &c., &c., quite forgetting that while he could obtain short intervals of leave, he had his official duties to perform, and was no longer his own master.

The first stay in the town consulate, which he compared to a big coffin divided by the thinnest of walls from Anti-Paradise, lasted only one week. A " nautico-diplomatico-missionary expedition was just starting for ' Christian Abbeokuta,' " and Burton was fortunate enough to be included. The amiable natives, in spite of sundry treaties, had been offering up human sacrifices ; and as our good little country by means of its hapless West African squadron was keeping watch over the morals of that and other native states on the coast, Commander Bedingfield and H.B.M.'s Consul at Fernando Po were instructed to read the Alake, or chief, a sermon upon his evil behaviour.

This trip suited Burton exactly. He had read much and heard more about the " Town under the Stone," and

the glowing hues in which the subject was depicted had
conjured up in his mind a host of doubts that could be solved
only by means of that accurate organ, the eye.   Sundry
small good books on Abbeokuta, written with the best
intentions, had been published by the Mrs. Jellabys of the
day, all *couleur de rose*, representing the African washed,
combed, clothed, scented, sober ; and our traveller, as usual,
wished to discover and propagate the truth concerning
West Africa as about every country he visited.   Of course,
the reality proved vastly different from the pretty fancy
pictures painted by persons who had never been near the
spot.   To begin with, Abbeokuta did not merit its prefix ;
only one in every five hundred of the population made even
a pretence of Christianity ; the natives proved a decidedly
low type of negro ; the town was a grisly mass of rusty
thatching and dull red-clay walls, scavengered solely by
pigs and vultures, and the climate was appalling.

The route to this agreeable capital was as bad as the
goal.   The travellers rowed from Lagos in two gigs belonging to H.M.S. *Prometheus*, manned by Krumen, across the
Ikoradu lagoon, tame and uninteresting, with its low
shores and clay-tinted water; through the Agboi Creek,
little better than a ditch; and thence, up the Ogun River,
to within sight of Abbeokuta, a distance of about eighty
miles.   Burton repaired at once to the Mission Compound,
where he lodged.   He found a church, schoolrooms, houses
and gardens, all belonging to the Church Missionary Society
—a veritable oasis in a dismal scene of dirt and squalor.
But, as with the Mombas Mission, the mortality amongst
the clergy and their wives had been awful.   Burton's kind
heart bled for his poor pretty countrywomen ; even those
who had recently arrived, owing to disgusting sights and
smells, bad food and water, and the hot, steamy climate,
looked like galvanised corpses.

Abbeokuta was governed in 1861 by an old, drunken,
and exceedingly hideous chief; and this was not the first

time that he had received a well-merited wigging from our Government. But hard words break no bones, and the wily old ruffian, who apparently expected an excellent joke, lost no time in summoning his visitors to the "palace." This building consisted of a narrow clay house, long and rambling, provided with two courtyards, each with its own verandah, and divided into rooms strongly resembling horse-boxes. In one of these, hidden for a while by an old brocade curtain, sat the one-eyed, toothless chief, surrounded by women and children. Presently, with much pomp, the hanging was drawn aside, as in some foreign churches from a lovely picture, and revealed the Alake, encaged like an inmate of one of the larger dens in the Zoo.

The palaver then commenced. The African believes, with Dickens' policeman, that "words is bosh," unless backed up by an execution or a heavy fine, and this fact we and other civilised nations have only lately begun to realise. Abbeokuta *did* catch it at last. The Alake looked fairly bright until the object of the visit was discussed; then, obstinate as a pig, he either hung down his head and pretended to sleep, drank spirits until he could hardly speak, or varied the programme by telling an unblushing lie. Nor were his "ministers" any better than himself; nowhere could be seen more villainous crania and countenances than among the seniors of Abbeokuta. Their calvaria, depressed in front and projecting cocoa-nut-like behind, the hideous lines and wrinkles that seamed their skin, and the cold, unrelenting cruelty of their physiognomies in repose, suggested the idea of some foul kind of torturers. It has been said—and a horrible saying it is—that cruelty is the key-note of creation; it is certainly the key-note of the African character. The sight of suffering causes these people real enjoyment. In almost all the towns on the Oil Rivers Burton saw dead and dying animals fastened to trees in every sort of agonizing posture. Young women were still lashed to poles and left to be devoured alive by buzzards — a charm to bring rain — and the scenes at Dahomey are familiar to everybody. This horrid characteristic is partly the result of their religion—the lowest form of fetishism — and partly the huge destructiveness in the Hamite skull.

It was, therefore, no easy matter to persuade the bloodthirsty old chief of Abbeokuta even to promise obedience for the future. Although Captain Bedingfield and our Consul spent a whole week in this delightful capital, and had more than one talkee-talkee, it cannot be said the results of their efforts were either permanent or satisfactory. True, a letter of apology was dictated to the acting governor of Lagos, and a new treaty, wherein the prince and his ministers declared they would do their best to stop the slave trade, also that no human being should be sacrificed by them, their people, or others inside or outside the town, or anywhere else in their territory, was legalized by the great men touching the pen with the finger tip. But the broad grins with which this action was accompanied augured badly. Hardly had the two commissioners returned to Lagos before a man was offered up to propitiate the tutelary deities, or demons, of Abbeokuta, and a woman was kidnapped from the house of an English trader.

Burton's next excursion was far more pleasant and profitable. There are few spots on the earth's surface where more of grace and grandeur, of beauty and sublimity, are found blended in one noble panorama, than at the equatorial approach on the West Coast of Africa. The voyager's eye, fatigued by the low flat shores of Benin and Upper Biafra, rests with delight upon a " Gate " compared with which Bab El-Mandeb and the Pillars of Hercules are indeed tame. To his right towers Mount Clarence, the Peak of Fernando Po, 9,300 feet above sea level; on his left is a geographical feature more stupendous still, where the Camaroons Mountain, whose height is laid down as 13,746 feet, seems to spring from the wave, and to cast its shadow half-way across the narrow channel, whose minimum breadth does not exceed nineteen miles.

In 1861 the topmost peak of this magnificent mountain had never been scaled, a fact which rendered our traveller all the more anxious to set foot on its summit. After a brief official visit in H.M.S. *Bloodhound* to the dull and deadly Brass and Bonny rivers, he was prostrated with fever, and the Camaroons furnished the best and nearest sanatorium. So, hastily collecting an outfit suitable for a month spent in a wilderness, he landed at a mission station on the coast, and soon made up a party. Mr. Saker, a Nonconformist minister, proved a valuable guide, M. Mann, a botanist, afforded great assistance in classifying and arranging the curious flora of the district, and a Spanish judge from Fernando Po, who was compared to a wild, young pig-sticking magistrate in India, kept everybody alive.

Ensued a right pleasant holiday. With the exception of one night spent in a native village, when the chief got drunk, rushed out of his hut at 2 p.m. with drawn dagger and began the war dance, all went smoothly. Our traveller mentions with almost boyish exultation how he was the first to reach the top, Mr. Saker not caring to risk life and limb, and M. Mann being poorly, and absorbed, moreover, in botanical studies. To record his claim, he heaped up a small cairn of stones, and in it placed a fragment from the facetious pages of Mr. Punch; in fact, the sharp, bracing air, the magnificent view, and the consciousness of success, raised his spirits to the highest pitch. He half lamed himself, however, having purchased in an evil hour a pair of loose waterproof boots, which began by softening and ended by half flaying his feet; and what with the state of these unlucky extremities and the effects of over-exertion, he had to remain in camp for a week. But no sooner was the skin healed than he returned to the charge, and made the interesting discovery that Camaroons is not an extinct volcano, as was generally believed. While descending one of the numerous cones, he emerged upon a Solfatara in full action, regular lines of smoke jets and puffs rising in rings and curls from the ground. Burton thought that, although the mountain lacks its pristine vigour of destructiveness, it knows as yet none of those varieties of form and character which denote permanently burnt out or even of temporarily quiescent volcanoes.

Anxious to turn this expedition to some useful account, our traveller subsequently published several articles in leading London papers, advocating the establishment in the Camaroons district of a sanatorium for the fever-stricken coast towns under British protection, also a convict station to supply the necessary labour. Why England insists on keeping all her burglars, poisoners, dynamiters, &c., clutched to her breast, rejecting with horror any proposal to dispense with their precious presence in the land even for their and her good, was ever an insoluble problem to a man unbitten by a spurious philanthropy which benefits nobody. But little attention was paid to his advice; Africa had not assumed the importance in the eyes of Europe which she has now, and meanwhile the healthiest district on the West Coast has fallen into the hands of the Germans.

Official trips to the Camaroons River and other places, varied by literary work, whiled away the remainder of the winter. It was well he had plenty to occupy his mind, for yellow fever was raging in the town, and the sights at the military hospital waxed more and more dolorous. In March it became necessary, for health's sake, to take a longer holiday. An opportunity presented itself of a trip to the Gaboon, then the principal centre of trade in Western Equatorial Africa; and as our traveller had visited numerous English colonies, he was curious to examine a specimen of our rivals'.

On landing at Le Plateau,[1] the capital of this colony, he was amused at a scene so characteristically French. The officers appeared eternally in full uniform; sisters of charity flitted about in their serge gowns and white gulls'-wing caps; the tricolour waved everywhere, even sometimes on English craft, which might carry their own colours no further than Coniquet Island. The *table d'hôte*, too, with its savoury dishes and abundance of claret and cognac, reminded him, anyway, of *les provinces*, and the hotel was far more comfortable than any he had lodged at since leaving England.

But at that time, even more interesting than the Frenchman abroad, was the Gorilla. Du Chaillu's book had lately appeared, and wonderful tales were current concerning an ape apparently all but human. It was said this industrious anthropoid constructed a bower for his spouse in the centre of the tallest trees by intertwining a number of the weaker boughs, under which the pair can sit protected from the rains by the mass of foliage thus entangled together, some of the boughs being so bent that they form convenient seats. Now was the occasion for verifying such stories, as the Gaboon was one of the animal's favourite haunts. So, bidding adieu to the luxuries of Le Plateau, Burton started up country March 19th, 1862, on a gorilla hunt.

It proved, however, one of his unlucky expeditions, and the perils of an unavailing search were greater than the object quite warranted. Our traveller was nearly drowned while ascending the Gaboon River,[2] knocked down another day by lightning,[3] and during his final march had a narrow escape from the fall of a giant branch, which grazed his

---

[1] Now Libreville.

[2] See "Gorilla Land; or the Cataracts of the Congo." Two vols. Sampson, Low & Co., 1875.

[3] The sensation was compared to the shock of an electric machine combined with the discharge of a Woolwich infant, both greatly exaggerated.

hammock.   And while he had ample opportunities of
studying the Fàn, a race of chocolate-coloured cannibals,
mere wild beasts in human shape, the far more interesting
gorilla invariably eluded his search.   He came upon remnants of the creature's meals, traces of his fights, several
of the " bowers," which proved only untidy heaps of stocks
and stones, but sight, much less shoot the anthropoid, he
could not.   As usually happens, details concerning the
animal's habits and appearance collected on the spot contradicted many a popular tale.   The gorilla does *not* stand
upright when attacked, and strike his opponent like a prize-
fighter ; he does *not* run on his hind legs alone, but on all-
fours, and he is essentially a tree ape.   Nor has he the
marvellous courage at first attributed to him ; on the
contrary, he bolts with remarkable alacrity when escape is
possible, and as for Mrs. Gorilla, while even a hen will
defend her chicks, this huge brute will fly, leaving son or
daughter in the enemy's clutches.   Curiously enough, as
soon as Burton had returned to the coast, the native hunter
who had accompanied him on the search shot a fine large
male and forwarded it at once to his employer.   It is, or
was, in the British Museum, but owing to having been
carelessly prepared, it gives a very imperfect idea of the
broad-chested, square-framed, portly old " bully-boy of the
woods."

A trip to the Lower Congo, which took place the following year, proved hardly more fortunate.   Very little
was known in 1863 about this mighty river, second in
volume only to the Amazon, whose sources worthy Dr.
Livingstone mistook for those of the Nile.   Discovered
in 1485 by Diogo Cam, hardly any particulars were circulated in England until Captain Tuckey's expedition
in 1816—a wide interval indeed.   This expedition succeeded in exploring the Congo some 162 miles from its
mouth ; but the scanty knowledge thus acquired was
dearly paid for, as nearly every officer died, besides several

of the mariners that accompanied the party. The river thus became a bugbear; but our traveller, believing that much of the mortality was owing to unsuitable food and treatment, determined to follow in poor Tuckey's steps, and, if luck permitted, to push on further.

As usual, he was comfortably conveyed to his starting-point by one of the squadron. What he would have done without those friendly ships, that did not "pass in the night," but anchored for awhile and took him on board, I know not, as he could ill afford to travel on his own account, half his pay being sent home to his wife. It was on board H.M.S. *Torch* that he had his first view of the tawny African monster. About eight miles south of the *embouchure* the green sea changes to a clear brown, which turns to red during flood time; and the huge mouth yawning seven miles wide, is a worthy outlet for a river measuring in length over three thousand. Exciting was the moment when the mighty stream celebrated in song by his favourite poet and hero, Camoens, appeared in sight.

> " Alli o mui grande reino está de Congo
> Por nós ja convertido à fé de Christo,
> Por onde o zaire passa claro e longo,
> Rio pelas antiguas nunca visto."

At French Point, Burton started up the river in a launch manned by a few Jack Tars from the ship and sundry natives. The first stoppage was at Porto da Lenha, twenty-one miles, the second Boma, fifty-two miles from the sea, and so far, the way was easy enough. But at Boma, a Portuguese outpost, our traveller heard that the river a little further on was supposed to be part of the dominion of a chief named Nessalla, without whose permission neither interpreter nor canoes were to be had. Nothing daunted, Burton, taking with him a box containing a fine spangled coat, a piece of chintz, and a case of ship's rum, hunted up the potentate in question, and obtained an audience. Nessalla, a grizzled senior, wearing a crown not unlike a nightcap, and a beadle's coat of scarlet cloth, received his guest civilly; and after abundant palaver it was arranged that the chief should lend a couple of his own canoes in return for the above-mentioned gifts, valued at about nine pounds, and wonderful to tell, although he had received the goods, he actually kept his word.

So, under royal patronage our traveller continued his struggle up stream. When nearing the second north-eastern reach the interpreter exclaimed, " Yellala folla," " the cataract is speaking," and all could distinctly hear the roar. The river now assumed the aspect of Niagara below the Falls, and the circular eddies boiling up from below and showing distinct convexity, suggested the dangerous whirls of northern seas. At Banza Nokki, a settlement ninety-seven miles from the coast, the party again disembarked and spent some days in this pleasantly situated village. On September 12th all started for the cataracts. Four days' march brought them to the goal. From a rounded hill, one hundred feet above the river, Burton viewed the Yellala, a wild waste of waves dashing over their stony obstacles. As far as eye can reach, the bed, which suddenly narrows, is broken by rocks and reefs; and the current, after breaking into foam for a mile and a half above, rushes down an inclined plane of some thirty feet, spuming and roaring like billows dashing against a cliff. The height of the trough walls, at least a thousand feet, add grandeur to the scene.

It was annoying, having arrived thus far, to be forced to turn back. Our traveller had hoped to reach at least the Isangila cataract, or the second Sangalla of Captain Tuckey and Professor Smith, the point where Henry Stanley, after his wonderful voyage, abandoned the river and struck overland for Boma. But the party was small, inadequately equipped, and the guide, who had agreed to push on as far as Nsundi, suddenly declared he would not go beyond the Yellala. Banza Ninga, the next stage, was

distant two or three marches, and neither shelter nor provisions were to be found on the way. Without the guide
of course further progress was impossible; so, very reluctantly, Burton retraced his steps, and after a quick and
pleasant run down stream found another good friend,
H.M.S. *Griffon*, just returned from landing mails along the
coast, and embarked without further adventures.

Compared with the feats of later travellers, this voyage
sinks into insignificance. But it deserves to rank amongst
that pioneer work which does so much to stimulate and aid
discovery. A paper describing the trip was read before the
British Association in 1864, and it proved that martyrdom
was not an inevitable result of canoeing up the Congo.
Later, a scholarly volume, "The Cataracts of the Congo,"
drew attention to the deplorable ignorance then existing in
regard to the length and source of this magnificent river—
ignorance which sundry travellers, by hastily rushing to
conclusions, increased rather than dispelled. After writing
very modestly of the little he had done to assist future
explorers, Burton concluded the account of his voyage with
these remarkable words: "I hope the Congo, one of the
noblest and least known of the four principal African
arteries, will no longer be permitted to flow through the
white blot on our maps, a region unexplored and blank to
geography as at the time of its creation; and that my
labours may contribute something, however small, to clear
the way for the more fortunate traveller." The school-
children of our day hardly know what that white blot
means. No one worked harder to do away with it than
Richard Burton.

Two months were spent quietly at Fernando Po. Consular duties, writing his notes, and attending to his garden
at Buena Vista, for by this time he had left the unhealthy
town, filled up the time and kept at bay nostalgia, a complaint in those latitudes by no means imaginary, and which
occasionally attacked even our cosmopolitan hero. Then

came a change. He had volunteered, so far back as 1861, to visit Abomey, the capital of Dahomey, but the measure not being deemed advisable at that moment, he was obliged to wait for another opportunity. Now arrived the welcome intelligence that Her Majesty's Government had appointed him Commissioner, the bearer of a message to King Gelele, couched in much the same terms as that to the Alake of Abbeokuta, protesting against the slave trade, and even more strongly against the abominable waste of human life at the annual customs. The pill to be administered to this doughty chief, a compound of threats and soft sawder, was to be sweetened by the addition of sundry gifts, of which more anon.

Burton told, amusingly enough, in his " Wanderings in West Africa," how his wife, on hearing of the appointment, begged to accompany him ; for, like d'Artagnan, she had *une idée*. It was nothing less than by means of a magic lantern representing New Testament scenes, and by pro-nouncing a few words in the vernacular, to terrify the king into abolishing human sacrifices, and becoming a Roman Catholic. Unfortunately, it was necessary to represent rather forcibly that her lantern would be considered the work of magic, the African's pet horror, and that the human sacrifices, so far from diminishing, might possibly include an English witch and wizard.

So, on the 29th November, 1863, *sans* wife or lantern, Burton embarked on board H.M.S. *Antelope*. Instead of the white sheet, slides, &c., some big deal boxes filled with presents, destined by the Foreign Office for the sable poten-tate, constituted the baggage, which, together with its temporary owner, arrived at Whydah, the port town of Dahomey, in first-rate condition. An attempt was made to land with all the ceremony befitting a Commissioner, but it must have been difficult to maintain a pompous demeanour in a surf boat, paddled in violently upon the back of a curl-ing breaker until the boat's nose, thrown high and dry upon

the beach, was snatched out by some sturdy negroes.
However, when our traveller stepped at last on *terra firma*,
an escort of twenty men saluted with muskets and preceded
him to the town, shouting and firing, singing and dancing.
The party was headed by a Kruman from the *Antelope*
carrying the Union Jack attached to a boarding pike, and
followed by five hammocks, and a special guard of six
Krumen, armed, and brilliantly, though not superabun-
dantly, clad in red caps and variegated pocket-handkerchiefs.
A Wesleyan native teacher, who kept a small shop, Rev.
Peter Bernasko, represented the clerical or Mganga element
in the procession.

A delay ensued of some days at Whydah. Permission
from the king was necessary to start up country, and these
black chiefs seemed to find a morbid pleasure in keeping
white men waiting on their will. Burton employed the
time visiting the dirty congeries of villages that called itself a town, crammed with fetishes, the most sensible, or
I should say the least silly, being a " Devil's Dish," or clay
pot daily filled for the turkey buzzards which scavengered
the place; as in all Yaruba settlements the houses were
scattered, and except round the principal market-place
there was far more bush than building. The environs
were then either marshes or fields, palm orchards or
bosquets of savage beauty. The fine and highly cultivated farms found near Whydah in 1845 no longer
existed.

By December 13th Gelele's royal permit had arrived.
The Mission now assumed large proportions. The heavy
baggage was carried by fifty-nine porters; thirty hammock-
men were added to the equipage, making a total of eighty-
nine mouths, not including interpreters and body-servants.
The only European besides the Commissioner was Dr.
Cruickshank of the *Antelope*, the reverend who still remained with the party being a " coloured person."

Sixty-five miles lay between port town and capital.

The journey may be described as one long dance. At Savi the natives turned out capering and taboring a welcome; and at Toli the scene could be compared only to the revelry of devils and witches as witnessed by poor Tam O'Shanter in Halloway Kirk. Indeed, when double flasks of gin were handed round to stimulate the performers to yet more violent exertions, Burton, who confessed to having been amused by the demoniac scene, retired fairly deafened by the noise. A little further on, the first detachment of Amazons appeared, four women armed with muskets and habited in tunics and white skull-caps, under the command of a hag wearing a man's straw hat, a green waistcoat, and a white shirt put on *à l'envers*. They, too, danced with a will. At Whegho, the war-chief pranced at the head of his half-dozen soldiers, while an enormously fat old woman howled an accompaniment; and at Kana, the king's country palace, more capers were cut, the performers bawling meanwhile :

" Batunu (Burton) he hath seen all the world with its kings and
    caboceers,
He now cometh to Dahomey, and he shall see everything here,"

Gelele was detained in his summer quarters by a grave and urgent matter, nothing less than a judicial enquiry into some shocking scandals amongst his Amazons. These ladies, unless required as wives for the king, on entering the army take vows of celibacy; but, like certain virgins in European countries, do not always keep them. At first it was feared he was too perturbed to receive the Mission ; however, after a short delay, he signified his intention of granting an audience during the intervals of his inquisitorial duties.

Early one morning arrived the monarch's chief physician, whom for brevity's sake we will call " Buko "—a close-shaven, white-woolled personage, neatly clad in light coloured shorts and a large silk shawl with silver ornaments. Politely enquiring at first about everybody's health, he soon disclosed his principal errand, viz., to obtain a list of the presents destined for his master; and he was particularly anxious to ascertain whether a carriage and pair of horses which Gelele had modestly begged from the English Government were yet *en route*. On being told this gift might be forwarded by-and-by, provided the king were amenable to reason, he then announced that the Commissioner's reception would take place that very day, and on the morrow permission would be given to proceed to Abomey. "Dress at once" he added, "the king is preparing for the audience."

Burton had no intention of sitting for hours in full uniform opposite a mud palace, the invariable result of punctuality on these occasions, so took his own time. At last the Mission wended its way to an open space, partially shaded by ragged trees, which for many generations has been the scene of these ceremonies. Shortly after the Commissioner and his companions had taken their places, each on his own particular stool, an invaluable article of furniture in Africa, appeared a table, fated, as Burton facetiously remarked, to be one of his best friends. It was a venerable European object, once intended for cards, but the rough hands of its new possessors had stripped off its veneer and seriously damaged its legs. Two or three natives puzzled their brains awhile how to open it, and by the time they had succeeded, another man produced from a calabash sundry bottles of wine, gin, and pure water. These refreshments were supplied to the two Englishmen and the Reverend with praiseworthy regularity. Hardly had they taken their seats on any occasion when, lo! the table.

Thus fortified, our traveller watched a procession of caboceers, or chiefs, and their followers. First walked under two umbrellas the king's half-brother, then his majesty's numerous cousins, and the Viceroy of Whydah.

The local bards, who are not less powerful in Dahomey than in other wild lands, were appropriately distinguished by wearing a human jawbone. Eight skulls, dished up on small wooden bowls like bread-plates, at the top of very tall poles, were carried along, followed by capering soldiers and drummers; in fact, the *élite* of the country filed past palacewards. After they had disappeared, Burton marshalled his own little *cortège*, which, preceded by the Union Jack, was conducted by a chief to the royal residence.

Gelele was then in the full vigour of manhood, from forty to forty-five years of age. His figure was athletic, upwards of six feet high. He had not his father's receding forehead, nor the vanishing chin so common in Africa, his strongly marked jaw, too, rendering the face jowly rather than oval; his sub-tumid lips disclosed white, strong teeth, the inner surfaces only slightly blackened by tobacco, of which he was immoderately fond. The most disagreeable feature were his eyes, red, bleared and inflamed; though his nose, while not wholly wanting in bridge, was distinctly cocked. His dress, fairly simple for a savage potentate, consisted of a straw cap with a human tooth, fetish against sickness, strung below the crown; a body cloth of fine white stuff, and drawers of purple flowered silk. The sandals were gorgeous—gold-embroidered upon a crimson ground, two large crosses of yellow metal being especially conspicuous. On one arm he wore an iron bracelet, and no less than five similar circlets on the other. On the whole, in spite of his scarlet eyes and *nez retroussé*, Gelele appears to have been a manly, stalwart personage.

A throng of unarmed women, the royal spouses, sat in a semi-circle behind the king, the Amazons forming a double file extending from the barn-like palace as far as the court-yard. Very homely were these wives, but their devotion to their lord was quite touching. If moisture appeared on the royal brow it was instantly removed with the softest cloth; if the royal lips unclosed over the pipe a plated spittoon

was moved within convenient distance ; if the royal hand
carried a tumbler to the royal mouth every black queen
uttered a blessing. Never was a king more coddled and
adored than in Dahomey.

Our Commissioner walked towards the throne along a
sort of lane hedged by squatting Amazons, and was greeted
by the occupant with sundry vigorous wrings of the hand, *à
la* John Bull.   Still grasping his visitor's dexter, the king
inquired after our Queen, ministers, and the people of England in general.   He then greeted Dr. Cruickshank, whose
dull naval uniform did not impress him, and finally recognised the Rev. Bernasko, who impressed him still less.

Stools were placed for the strangers near the throne, and
then began a grand drinking of healths.   This ceremony
was conducted in a fashion peculiarly African.   After bow-
ing and touching glasses, the king suddenly wheeled round
while two wives stretched a white calico cloth to act as
screen, and another pair opened small and gaudy parasols,
which completely concealed his figure from the vulgar gaze.
This custom originated partly from the idea that a monarch
is too god-like to require refreshment, and partly from the
fear of witchcraft, black magic having special power over a
person while eating or drinking.   The toasts concluded,
salutes were fired, Amazons rang bells and sprang rattles,
ministers bent to the ground clapping their palms ; prodigious was the noise.   In spite of the uproar, Burton's
quick ear detected that the number of salutes in his honour
were insufficient, and, as he would never tolerate any slight
whilst on duty, he complained to Gelele, who immediately
apologised and ordered more.

Quaint indeed were the figures assembled in the long,
swish-walled, thatched barn and courtyard which did duty
as Gelele's summer palace.   Quaintest of all were the
Amazons.   Enthroned on a lofty stool sat the captain-ess
of the late King Gezo's life-guards, an old porpoise wearing
a cap like a man cook's, adorned with two blue cloth

crocodiles on the top. To the left of royalty, under a tent umbrella, squatted a corresponding veteran-ess, also vast in bulk, for these she-soldiers invariably fatten when their dancing days are done, and some become prodigies of obesity. The flower of the host was the mixed company of young Amazons lately raised by the king, a corps composed of the finest women in the service, and most picturesquely attired. A narrow fillet of blue or white cotton bound the hair; the bosom was concealed by a sleeveless waistcoat, giving freedom to the arms and buttoning in front; and the body wrapper of dyed stuff, blue, pink, or yellow, extended to the ankles, and was kept tight round the waist by a sash with long ends, depending on the left. An outer girthing of cartridge box and belt, European-shaped but home made, of black leather adorned with cowries, rendered the garb most compact. All had knives, and the firelock, a Tower-marked article, was guarded by sundry charms, and protected from damp by a case of black monkey-skin. Like the Amazons of the poor extinct Guanches, these women at times showed undeniable pluck; but our traveller thought an equal number of British charwomen armed with the British broom might on an emergency prove equally formidable.

Needless to add, the reception ended with a general caper, the younger Amazons being prominent performers and executing agreeable imitations of decapitating their enemies.

Next day, pioneered by Buko, who rode under the shade of a white umbrella, the Commissioner and his companions began their march to Abomey. Having plenty of bearers, they were carried in hammocks along a broad road bordered in places by shady trees; and as from Kana to the capital the land is emphatically the garden of Dahomey, the journey might have been fairly enjoyable. But the train was brought up by a band, chiefly boys, with three drums, a couple of tom-toms, two cymbals, and a pair of gourd-rattles, and the horrid din never ceased for a moment ; while the uncanny spectacle of skulls and bones, which, as with us in bygone days, were considered suitable decorations for trees and buildings, was not precisely exhilarating. After passing several villages, a thin forest of palms rising from a tapestry of herbage and presenting a truly charming picture, and numerous fetish huts containing the most hideous assortment of idols imagination can portray, the party safely arrived at the Kana Gate, where they descended from their hammocks, whilst all the attendants bared their shoulders, removed their hats, and furled their umbrellas as if it were part of the king's palace.

The *enceinte* of Abomey is perhaps larger than that of any town in this part of Africa. Eight miles in circumference, it is surrounded by a deep ditch and clay walls pierced by six gates. The site is a rolling plain ending in short bluffs to the north-west, where it is bounded by a long depression, grassy and streaked with lines of trees ; the soil, a rich red clay, is extremely fertile, and groves of oil palms, maize, beans, cassava, yams, oranges, and other tropical produce grow in great luxuriance. There are three large palaces belonging to the king, several large squares, and a number of farms ; for, as usual in Yoruba towns, they build sparsely, so as to avoid the fires which annually devastated Lagos. In 1863 the population numbered only 20,000 souls ; it has since increased to 30,000.

Two guard-houses protected the Kana Gate, and beyond it were the remains of a broken-down battery. Burton passed along the southern wall of the Abomey Palace, remarking on its summit a few rusty iron skull-holders ; but there was only one human relic, a great alteration since the days of King Adahoonzon II., who excited the admiration of his subjects by taking off 147 heads to complete the " thatching of his house." He then reached the *Grande Place*, the scene of Gezo's displays and receptions, but neglected by Gelele, and soon afterwards arrived at the domicile of Dr. Buko.

These quarters left, as the French say, much to be

desired. Buko's home resembled a cow-house, or rather several cow-houses, one of which was devoted to the Mission. The latter is described as a barn 45 feet long by 27 deep. A thick thatch descended within a short distance of the ground, and rested on a double line of strong posts buried in the earth. The low ceiling was made of rough sticks plastered with native whitewash. The accommodation consisted of a small dark room, which Burton immediately provided with a window by the simple expedient of knocking a hole through the clay wall; a second dark, airless hole, which having luckily a lock and key to its door, served as a store-room; two more apartments on the same scale, and verandahs. Every corner was crammed with fetishes begrimed with dirt, and so maddeningly ugly, that the new-comer, regardless of their owner's feelings, unceremoniously ejected them into the courtyard. Buko may have had his faults, but he was a good-tempered host. Imagine the rage of the British landlady if holes were made in her walls, and her china dogs, shell-flowers, and hideous woodcuts were bundled into the area! Buko only laughed.

The trial of the Amazons came to an end at last—it is a relief to hear they were not condemned to be walled up alive [1]—and on Monday, December 21st, everybody turned out to witness the arrival of the king. After a wearisome delay, a long line of men carrying flags and umbrellas debouched from the open road, marched to an open space before the Komasi Palace, Gelele's favourite residence, and, like the courtiers in " La Mascotte," walked round three times. Party after party filed along, until preceded by his ministers, and, surrounded by about 500 soldiers, his majesty appeared, seated in a horseless carriage of bygone pattern, harnessed by natives. He went round twice at first, but performed the circuit again, carried in a Bath-chair on the heads of the porters. Apparently he was

---

[1] On this occasion some were banished, others pardoned.

still upset by the behaviour of his graceless " women of war," for amidst all this homage he looked exceedingly cross, thinking only of keeping, by means of a thick kerchief, the clouds of dust out of his nose and mouth. Burton, dazed with heat and noise—he had been kept waiting three mortal hours in the burning sun — probably looked the same, as he finally retired to his barn afflicted with a bad headache, the usual finale to a Dahoman parade.

Next day, Sunday, ought to have been one of rest. But Gelele could not curb his impatience to see the presents sent by the Foreign Office. An attempt to force Burton to open these boxes in one of the cow-houses was vainly made by Buko, who then, under protest, forwarded them to the palace. It was clear from his expression that the absence of certain highly coveted articles, notably the carriage and horses, had already been reported, and our Commissioner followed his gifts feeling rather doubtful as to his reception. After waiting half an hour in front of the Komasi House, he received a summons to enter, and, removing his cap, passed through the Gate of Tears into a deep, gloomy barn, so dark that he could hardly distinguish sundry women selling provisions on the right, and Gezo's immense wardrum chapleted with skulls on the left. The inner court resembled that of Kana, only the westerly side was a royal store-house for cloth, cowries and rum—the notes, silver and copper of the country. In the yard stood four fetish huts, each containing a whitewashed idol. The most remarkable figure, a sort of Janus made of dark clay, with glaring white eyes, and two pair of horns bending inwards, would have surpassed the most terrific picture of " Auld Hornie" that the magic lantern could have possibly produced.

The king soon arrived, and his presents were duly unpacked and displayed. They consisted of a circular, crimson silk damask tent, one richly embossed silver pipe with amber mouthpiece, two heavy silver belts, two silver-gilt waiters, and one coat of mail and gauntlets. The Commissioner and Mr. Bernasko also offered some simple yet suitable gifts; but it was clear enough that the non-arrival of the carriage and horses was unforgivable. Gelele accepted everything, omitting to say thanks.

The monarch having returned to his capital, and the peccadilloes of his Amazons having provided several extra victims in the persons of their lovers, who, poor wretches, did not get off so easily, the Customs commenced. These yearly Customs must not be confounded with the greater functions which, taking place only after a king's decease, far eclipsed the annual rites in splendour and bloodshed; they were simply continuations of the Grand Customs, established in order to periodically supply the departed monarch with fresh attendants in the shadowy world. These odious institutions were first heard of in Europe about 1708, although no doubt they existed many years before. It is said they are now abolished, but probably something of the kind is still practised in a very modified form and in strict privacy. The ceremonies, which are extended over a week, a combination of carnival, general muster, and fetishism, seemed so thoroughly part and parcel of the creed and education of the people, that to suppress them entirely would be much like abolishing our courts of justice, military reviews, and religious services all at one blow.

Early on December 28th, a discharge of musketry near the palace and a royal message informed the Commissioner that the Customs had begun, and his presence at the palace was expected. Delaying as long as possible, some time after noon he and his companions mounted their hammocks and proceeded by the usual way to the Komasi House.

On the road they remarked in the centre of the market-place a victim-shed, completed and furnished. From afar the shape was not unlike that of an English viiiage church. The total length was about 100 feet, the breadth 40, and the greatest height 60. It was made of roughly-squared posts, nine feet high, and planted deep in the earth. The ground floor of the southern front had sixteen poles, upon which rested the joists and planks supporting the pent-shaped roof. There was a western double-storied turret, each front with four posts, and the roof was covered with a tattered cloth, blood-red, bisected by a single broad stripe of blue check.

In the turret and the barn were twenty victims. All were seated on cane stools, and were bound to the posts, which passed between their legs, the ankles, the shins, under the knees, and the wrists being lashed outside with connected ties. The confinement was not rigorous; each victim had an attendant squatting behind him to keep off the flies; all were fed four times a day, and were loosed at night for sleep. They wore long white nightcaps and calico shirts— somehow suggesting· the sufferers of old in an *auto-da-fé ;* and the resemblance was rendered yet more striking by the presence of the principal Fetishmen, who sat under a tall pole hung with white rugs, the Bo-fetish guarding the present Custom. The reverend men did not regard the Commissioner with an over-friendly eye; but he casually remarked in his description of the scene, such is the way of reverend men generally with respect to those not of their own persuasion.

Arrived at the open space in front of the Komasi Palace, Burton found more preparations for the approaching function. Close to a shed intended as a royal reception-room, wherein sat Gelele, stood a larger shed, somewhat like a two-poled tent. At first he wondered why it was jealously closed, even the entrance veiled by a pair of white umbrellas; and discovered at last, after sundry enquiries, that it was supposed to contain not only some earthly relics of old King Gezo, but his ghost. Everybody bowed low on passing this singular tabernacle, even before paying respect to the living monarch. Presently the latter arose, and, with

his head bent slightly forward, and hands clasped behind
his back, delivered an oration in his father's honour. He
then performed on the drum a sort of "Dead March in
Saul," and, after retiring behind the white curtain to
refresh himself with a drink, returned like a giant refreshed,
and danced vigorously. Certainly the changes in his
demeanour were sudden and startling ; for, these capers
concluded, he bowed low, surrounded by his wives, and
accompanied only by a single cymbal, making melancholy
music, sang a dirge for the dead. Then, rising with uplifted
staff, and turning towards the larger shed, he adored in
silence King Gezo's ghost. Gelele was not quite a brute!

Burton very properly refused to be present at the human
sacrifices, and threatened, moreover, if any death took place
before him to return at once to Whydah. But, as he was
anxious to save at least half the wretches tied up in the
market-place, he attended every bloodless ceremony with
praiseworthy assiduity ; even when Gelele played ball with
and then drank from three skulls of chiefs slain by his
own hand, and Buko, like the old sycophant he was,
enquired whether so grand a sight had ever been seen
before, our traveller remained studiously attentive and
polite. It is pleasant to add he gained his object. Half
the victims in their *san benitos* were unfastened, placed on
all-fours before the throne to receive the royal pardon, and
finally released.

The remainder perished during the third night of the
Customs. The number does not seem great — not so
many, in fact, as we used to hang weekly at Newgate ;
but our traveller discovered before leaving Abomey these
public executions were little better than a blind. From
seventy to eighty persons, male and female, were put to
death *inside* the palace ; although Gelele so far regarded
the explicit instructions which he had received—that no
life was publicly taken during the daytime. Dismal indeed
to so kind-hearted a man as Richard Burton must have

been those hours of darkness, with the death-drum booming forth an announcement of each execution; and he powerless to prevent the bloodshed! True, some of the victims were the riff-raff of Dahomey, and, like our poisoners and dyna-miters, deserved no pity; others, like the Amazons' lovers, had been foolish enough to get convicted of *lèse-majesté;* but it was sad to think of the wretched captives taken in petty skirmishes with neighbouring tribes, whose only fault had been defending themselves and their lands. Next morning our traveller felt so sickened and disgusted that he debated whether to attend at the palace as usual or give himself a day's rest.

However, as the message from the English Government was still undelivered, it seemed safer to give the king no excuse for shirking an official interview, which indeed he seemed strongly disposed to do. So at 11 a.m. Burton wended his way as usual to the Komasi House, where was to take place the ceremony known as the Procession of the King's Wealth.

The walk was not a pleasant one. The shed in the market-place was empty; out of its tenants nine had perished. Four corpses, attired in their criminals' shirts and caps, were seated upon stools supported by a double-storied scaffold. At a little distance upon a similar erection were two victims, one above the other; and between these, from a gallows, a single body hung by its heels. Lastly, planted quite close to the path, was another gibbet with two corpses dangling side by side. Very little blood ap-peared on the ground, the men having been clubbed to death. Traces of the more private executions soon ap-peared. Close to the south-eastern gate of the palace lay a dozen heads, within the entrance were two more, and while helping to set up the crimson and gold tent in the palace yard, Burton perceived poles being planted for a scaffold.

Nobody seemed to care. Processions, dances, and a

grand feast marked the festive occasion.   One procession in this savage land was very like another, but this of the King's Wealth was distinguished by a curious number of old vehicles, some of which had been presented to former chiefs by the English Government when slavery formed an important branch of our commerce.   A blue-green shan-dridan, a cab-brougham with a lion on the panels, two American trotting waggons, a peculiar old sedan-chair, dating from the days of Beau Nash, a large green chariot of venerable appearance, belonging to the late Gezo, several old barouches, and last, but not least, a rocking horse with housings and bridle, on wheels, filed past, drawn, of course, by natives, the only live horse present being Gelele's little roan pony.   Dancing, singing, drinking, smoking — the Amazons all had pipes in their ample mouths—went on uninterruptedly for seven mortal hours; and when Burton left the vile atmosphere to walk home he got into something worse.   A most awful smell almost poisoned him; the wretched dead bodies had been exposed in the sun the whole livelong day!

Dancing, we have seen, was an all-important part of every Dahoman ceremony; consequently, strangers were expected to take part in it.   The king had repeatedly fixed a day for the Commissioner to perform before him, and had deferred the operation probably with the delicate motive of allowing him time to prepare himself for so great an event. But the day and hour arrived at last.   Burton collected his party in front of the semicircle of chiefs, gave time to the band, and performed a Hindustani *pas seul*, which elicited violent applause, especially from the king.   So charmed was Gelele with this novel step, that on another occasion he seized hold of the Commissioner's arm and pranced opposite him amidst the loudly expressed delight of his people. . . . Dr. Cruickshank executed an imitation of Dahoman capers, which no doubt, poor man, he had learnt by heart, and greatly pleased the spectators.   It was then the Reverend's turn. But he treated the company to a very different performance. Posting himself opposite the throne, placing upon another stool his instrument, a large concertina, he preliminarily explained the meaning of the hymn, and then bravely intoned the "Old Hundredth." So far so good ; his next choice was unfortunate :

> " O, let us be joyful, joyful, joyful,
> When we meet to part no more."

The prospect of the company of King Gelele and his people for all eternity was too much for our traveller's nerves, with the vultures perched before him on a large tree by the palace gate expecting a feast, that night being the second *nox iræ*, when Gelele and his Amazons intended to privately slay the remainder of the criminals and victims.

After spending six weeks at Abomey without being permitted to deliver the message of H.M. Government, Burton formally complained to Buko and insisted on being given an opportunity of fulfilling his official duties. Soon after this " wig " came a hasty summons to the Komasi House, and our traveller naturally expected it was on the business in question. On arriving he found Gelele half mad with vanity, showing off a number of prisoners recently captured from a neighbouring tribe. Four skulls, fourteen male captives, nine women and four children were paraded before the disgusted Englishman; finally the men were sold, and the women and children despatched to the royal harem. This was too much. Throwing etiquette to the winds, Burton declared that until he could deliver his message he would come no more to the palace.

Returning to Buko's domicile, he had his bags and boxes ostentatiously packed in the compound, while Mr. Bernasko repaired to the Komasi House to formally announce that unless an audience were granted at once, the Commissioner must leave Abomey next day. Ensued a general hubbub.

20

The ministers were summoned, they did not arrive quickly enough, Gelele lost his temper, and when they did appear he ordered his Amazons to drive them with blows and curses from his presence. The Customs concluded that night with a smash up of glass crockery, even furniture; and the King sent word to Burton apologising for not attending to business, as rage would prevent his sleeping. Delays, however, were coming to an end.

At 3 p.m., February 13th, when, almost in despair, Burton had resolved to walk to the coast, using his hammock-men as porters, Buko hurried him in full dress to the palace. For four hours he had the pleasure of sitting in a kind of simoom, with glare enough to dazzle an eagle, opposite the ragged palm-leaf fence of the Jegbie House, another of Gelele's favourite residences. At last he received a summons. Inside, besides our traveller and his companions, were two chiefs and Buko, who acted ward.

Gelele rose, shook hands, and perceiving there was something wrong, told Burton that he had heard of sundry complaints, strangely enough after they had been the best of friends, dancing and drinking together. The longed-for opportunity had come at last, and the Commissioner read his message. Condensed, it ran as follows: That Her Majesty's Government was resolved to arrest the slave traffic; that the horrors of the human sacrifices were to be mitigated; that an agent would probably be soon appointed to reside at Whydah, both as an organ of communication with the king, and as an aid in carrying out all views of licit trade. Finally, Burton, doubtless to the consternation of the bystanders, Buko in particular, told the savage monarch more plain truths than he had ever heard before, especially with regard to the barbarous and revolting Customs.

Gelele showed some temper, but was profuse in professions. Still it was evident he intended to ignore even in the smallest matters the wishes of our Government. The unexpected civilities of sundry official visitors to his court had filled him with an exaggerated idea of his own import-ance ; and not a dozen messages from the principal rulers in Europe would have deterred him from following in every respect his own sweet will. However, on parting, he shook hands with Burton, telling him " he was a good man, but too angry," finally bade him adieu, exhorting a speedy return.

Two more days elapsed. Then Buko appeared with the permit necessary for leaving Abomey, and sundry presents. Those intended for Her Majesty, of which Burton was enjoined to be especially careful, were :

Two miserable half-starved boys to act as pages.

A green and white counterpane of native manufacture.

A huge leather pouch to hold tobacco.

A large leather bag.

History is silent as to the reception of these gorgeous offerings from King Gelele of Dahomey.

CHAPTER XIII

PROMOTION in the Consular Service was certainly more rapid than in John Company's. Burton had performed his difficult and dangerous duties as Commissioner to Dahomey to the entire satisfaction of the Ministry then in office, and, in acknowledgment of his services, Lord Russell transferred him to a more important post. Having nearly exhausted every object of interest within practicable distance on the West African coast, our traveller packed up his books, manuscripts and lesser valuables, and bade adieu to picturesque Buena Vista with but moderate regret.

His new Consulate was at Santos, in the Brazil. Had Lord Russell consulted Burton regarding this choice, he could hardly have provided him with a more suitable *pied à terre* whence to explore fresh scenes and, to him as yet, untrodden ways. It was fairly paid, and, better still, there was a Vice-Consul who good-naturedly left his clever chief unfettered whenever the latter required a change. Here, anyhow for a time, Burton was the right man in the right place. His consummate knowledge of the Portuguese language and literature delighted even the Emperor, Dom Pedro ; while his known determination to have nothing to do with that log-rolling in the way of railway and other concessions, on which so many public officers have been made shipwreck, was especially valuable in upholding British prestige during the construction of the San Paulo line.

At Santos he was joined by his wife. Heartily tired of her position as grass widow, and charmed with the prospect of travel and excitement, she hastened from England as soon as her husband had settled in his new quarters. At first the aspect of her outlandish home dismayed her; and no wonder. Santos, a low-lying, enclosed place, nine miles up an arm of the sea, was so unhealthy that it seemed at one time doubtful whether she could remain with any degree of safety. Fortunately for herself, she was able to take refuge from the steaming heat and malaria on the coast in the chief town of the province, San Paulo, situated two thousand feet above sea-level. Owing to the number of British navvies employed on the new railway, Burton's presence was frequently required at the little capital; and during one of his visits he found an old convent to let in the Rua do Carmo, wherein, after having it cleaned, painted, and whitewashed, he installed his wife and household gods. Of course, all the shipping business had to be transacted at Santos, so he alternated between the two stations, while Isabel, surrounding herself with priests and nuns, did not lack for company.

As this was the first time Burton and his wife had a home together, this grim old monastery in the Rua do Carmo, a few words concerning their domestic life may prove interesting. He began characteristically. Hating idleness himself, it worried him in others, so he set his wife to lessons. A flimsy conventual education had been early interrupted by her father's pecuniary embarrassments; and it was advisable, besides, in such novel and often depressing surroundings, to keep a very excitable brain occupied. The results of these studies were rather disappointing. A certain amount of grammar, geography, and a smattering of languages he succeeded in imparting; but with this he had to be satisfied. For though she was far from dull, there was something which prevented Isabel Burton from becoming the cultured woman one might have expected after long companionship with such a man. The obstacle may have been too large a development of self-

confidence, or possibly a deficiency in the reasoning faculties; anyway, she never succeeded in mastering any subject.
That she helped her husband to write his books is a story
often repeated as with authority. While of course in-
correct, it arose from his habit of commissioning her to
see his MSS. through the press while he was away
travelling, and permitting her to add a preface or insert
a chapter; a permission of which she sometimes availed
herself too liberally, as in the case of his " Lusiads," when,
though knowing little or nothing of Portuguese, she described herself as the "editor." Still, it must be added,
in the matter of these books she was useful. Burton
depended much upon his writings for bringing in welcome
pecuniary additions to his moderate income, and Isabel
spent many an hour copying the MS., even acquiring the
knack of imitating his handwriting so accurately that only
his sister or myself could tell the difference.

On the whole, considering their unlikeness, this strangely
matched pair got on fairly well. Burton was too sensible
to kick against the pricks; he was married, so he made
the best of it. And he depended for happiness upon occupation, not matrimony. As time went on, he centred his
thoughts more and more on his studies, until he became
almost unconscious of what was passing around him. Ever
an indulgent husband, it cannot be said the *rôle* quite suited
him. Owing to Mohammedan leanings, he never thoroughly
saw the *raison d'être* of monogamy; home he soon tired of;
his rooms, while exquisitely neat, always suggested a
bivouac; women rarely understood him, his wife perhaps
least of all.

For to understand such a man it was essential to drop
self, and try to rise to his level; and this Isabel never did.
Though a Romanist, she need not have ranged herself with
the extreme or Jesuitical party, nor allowed her mind to
sink into depths of superstition almost incredible in Burton's
wife. He often looked, oh! so sad and weary when hearing

for the twentieth time how a leaden image had tumbled out of her pocket during a long ride, and then miraculously returned to its despairing owner; or, worse still, on being told it was mere pride and perverseness on his part that prevented his believing in apparitions of the nature of old white cows looming through a fog. Nor were his friends spared this style of talk; and some clever men, on hearing themselves mourned over as infidels, &c., were not so forbearing. Many a well-wisher was alienated for want of a little tact, and Burton had already enemies enough. However, he was very patient; so long as he was permitted to lead a fairly quiet life, he remarked little and grumbled less, even when his wife involved him in social and political difficulties which, immersed as he was in his studies, he could neither foresee nor avoid.

It seems hard to believe that our traveller remained eighteen months at Santos without any great adventure. True, he journeyed half over his own province, São Paulo, and paid sundry visits to Rio, where he and his wife spent a very gay Christmas. But this to him was little more than our trips to town or summer rambles over an adjoining county. At Petropolis he was most kindly received by poor Dom Pedro. This excellent and enlightened sovereign delighted in the society of clever men, especially when, like Burton, they were masters of Portuguese literature. He granted the traveller audience after audience, and rendered every assistance in his power when the latter proposed to explore part of the country in order to help the Government in opening out fresh means of communication, means which, at that date, were beginning to attract the interest of English engineers and capitalists.

So the strong man girded his loins and prepared for another feat. Having obtained leave of absence from England, and a Portaria or special licence from his Imperial friend and patron, he started for Minas Geraes. He intended first to study the resources still unexploited of this wealthy province, next to visit some gold mines worked by English companies, and finally to paddle down the São Francisco as far as the rapids of the little-known falls of Paulo Affonso.

The start was made June 12th, 1867. Isabel was to accompany him during the first or safe part of the journey, but her husband very properly considered the canoe voyage far too risky. On this occasion Burton covered more than two thousand miles, of which eleven hundred and fifty were by the slow progress of an ajôjo, a craft half canoe, half raft. The time occupied was only five months, but of course, as many years might be profitably devoted to the São Francisco alone, and even then it would be difficult to write an exhaustive description. In his " Highlands of the Brazil," published in 1869, wherein he gives an interesting account of his travels through part of the Empire, he was careful to collect for those who might follow in his steps ample details concerning the natural features, the geological remains, and the rock inscriptions hitherto unworked of a long-vanished race.

What he termed his " holiday trip," as distinguished from the exploration of the river, began from Rio. The first halt was made at Petropolis, Dom Pedro's own creation : once a tiny village, in 1869 it was a flourishing town. No small boon must it be to citizens of hot, unhealthy Rio to possess within five hours of their capital a resort where appetite is European, where exercise may be taken freely, and where they may enjoy the luxury of sitting in a dry skin. Beautifully situated amidst the Brazilian highlands, 2,405 feet above sea level, Petropolis is rendered yet more cool and delightful by the bubbling, clear, brown streams that pour down its principal streets. The way thither, a parapeted macadamised road over a pass some 2,900 feet high, commands in places one of the noblest panoramas in the world, jagged hills, huge rocks, plum-coloured peaks on a sky-blue ground, and in the distance

the lovely bay of Rio Janeiro. Were it not for the change
of government, continual political troubles, and the chance
of fever on landing at the capital, perhaps by now Petropolis
would be included in our holiday tours. But an instable
republic and yellow Jack combined are too much even for
the globe-trotter ; and as yet a trip to Rio is rarely under-
taken save by people who cannot help it.

Only twenty-four hours were spent in this tropical Ems,
and next morning the Burtons left by coach for Juiz de
Forá, in the province of Minas Geraes. A twelve hours'
drive brought them safely to a large untidy town, which,
however, at that moment was looking its smartest in
honour of its patron saint, Antony and his pig. The
principal church suggested the Black Hole, so crammed
was it with worshippers, and its peal of bells, judging from
the discord, must have been badly cracked by hard hammering. Burton passed most part of Sunday in the
extensive grounds of a château lately built at enormous
expense by a wealthy Brazilian, who had further succeeded
in planting an arboretum and orchard upon what was
twelve years before a bog on the right bank of the Parahy-
buna. It was certainly curious to find, surrounded by
virgin forest, an Italian villa garden with its lake spanned
in places by dwarf Chinese bridges, and to see the emus
in their dull, half-mourning plumage, caged up with silver
pheasants. The European and tropical plants were magnificent, one arum leaf measured five feet four inches long,
a contrast indeed to our insignificant cuckoo plant. The
owner of the place, Commendador Lage, had recently
given a grand reception to Professor Agassiz in these
identical grounds, on the occasion of the great naturalist's
scientific expedition to the Brazil.

While Burton · was wandering about the orangery and
helping himself to the delicious Tangerines, an English
engineer, Mr. Swan, employed in the construction of the
great line of railway between the valleys of Parayba and

the São Francisco, invited him to take part in a function about to take place of laying the first chain. Accordingly, a few days later the travellers wended their way to a small settlement close to the future railway, and ranched at a kind of cottage kept by a Brazilian. The dog-holes serving for bedrooms were foully dirty, the ground floor was foot-stamped earth, and the beds were covered only with bits of thin chintz, not pleasant with the mercury at 35° F. Still both husband and wife enjoyed their stay in the outlandish little place, and especially the ceremony at the Alagõa Dourada. It took place at the site where the Dark became the Golden Lake.[1] At noon the Burtons, heading a little crowd of spectators, proceeded to the scene of action, the peg was duly planted, Isabel giving the first blow and breaking the bottle. The inauguration passed off well ; flags flew, the band played its loudest, everybody drank with many vivas ! and hip ! hurrahs ! to the healths of the Brazil, of England, and especially to the prolongation of the Dom Pedro Segundo Railway ; many complimentary speeches were exchanged, and music escorted the strangers back to their "ranch."

In the two thick volumes already mentioned Burton gives a detailed description of the various towns of Minas Geraes through which he passed ; but as one dead-alive, over-churched place was very like another, we will pass on to a most interesting study of English life in the heart of the Brazil—Morro Velho, a gold mine worked by a British company.

This industry had created, as if by magic, a little English village, a veritable oasis amidst the dirt and squalor of Minas Geraes. Handsome stores, a parsonage, an epis-copal church, a hospital, neat cottages with gardens for the European miners, well-built Anglo-Indian bungalows for the superintendent and other officials, must indeed have

---

[1] So called because, after much of its waters had been drained off, enormous quantities of the precious metal were discovered.

gladdened the exiles' eyes. Nor was the national virtue of hospitality lacking. A specially-appointed guest-house lodged our travellers, and so right comfortably that a stay originally planned for a week lengthened into a month.

The site of this settlement, not far distant from Congonhas, was an irregularly-shaped basin about three-quarters of a mile long by half a mile in breadth. The narrow valley ended westward in an *impasse* formed by high ground; and although the surrounding country had been disforested, the romantic beauty of shape was still there, and on bright days the sun and atmosphere made the colouring a pleasure to look upon. No iron furnace blowing off sooty smoke by day and belching lurid flame by night marred the pretty scene; the power for the machinery that worked the mine was supplied by water-wheels, whose soothing song reminded the strangers of autumnal waves sporting on the Scheveringen shore.

Doctors, matrons, clergymen (there was a padre for the black folk) were not lacking. A library of 920 volumes occupied a neat erection, tiled and whitewashed. Another building, with two lines of benches and a boarded platform opposite a raised orchestra, served as a theatre, and the hospital was clean and spacious. The miners, for whom all these comforts were provided, numbered about 150 Englishmen, a few Germans, and 1,452 blacks, male and female. Concerning the latter, our traveller remarked that the sable mothers, when in an interesting condition, were treated with an amount of care and consideration for which many a Lancashire navvy's wife might look in vain.

Very few days elapsed before the Burtons explored the Eldorado which had created this oasis of industry amidst the lotus-eating Brazilians. Every arrangement was made for the safety of a trip into the bowels of the earth by the superintendent, Mr. Gordon. Not, however, that it was a dangerous one, no accident having occurred during the last two years. Clad in the oldest of garments, plus a stiff leather hat to guard the head from rolling stones, and with feet cased in the heaviest of boots, Burton and a travelling companion descended in the bucket, or kibble, and were followed in due time by Isabel and Mrs. Gordon. Every reader of that terribly - realistic mining story, " Germinal," can picture the plunge into darkness, the almost perpendicular ladders, up and down which the miners run like cats, the mighty timbers for strengthening the walls, the swaying, uncomfortable vehicle ; but as soon as the bottom was reached all resemblance to the French coal-pits ceased.   Indeed, even for a gold-mine the Morro Velho was unique.   Unlike the dirty labyrinths of low drifts and stifling galleries, down which men must crawl like one of the *reptilia* or *quadrumana*, the vertical height 1,134 feet, and the 108 feet of breadth, unparalleled then in the annals of mining, suggested a mammoth cave raised from the horizontal to the perpendicular.   The huge Palace of Darkness, dim in long perspective, scantily besprinkled with lights like glow-worms upon an embankment, was well ventilated, the air fairly pure, with no trace of sul-phuretted hydrogen except when just after blasting.

Distinctly Dantesque, wrote Burton, was the gulf be-tween the huge sides.   Even the accents of a familiar voice seemed changed ; the ear was struck by the sharp click and dull thud of the hammer upon the boring-iron, and this upon the stone, each blow delivered so as to keep time with the wild chant of the workman.   The other definite sounds, curiously complicated by an echo, were the slush of water on the subterranean path, the rattling of the gold stone thrown into the kibbles, and the crash of chain and bucket.   Through the gloom gnomes and kobolds glided about, half-naked figures muffled by the mist.   Here dark bodies, gleaming with beaded heat-drops, hung by chains in what seemed frightful positions ; there they swing monkey-fashion from place to place ; elsewhere they swarmed over scaffolds which even to look up at would make a nervous temperament dizzy. Certainly once seen, the Morro Velho was never likely to be forgotten.

Burton, always extremely interested in such matters, having already studied mining in California on his return journey from Great Salt Lake City, followed the whole process of reduction, from the raising of the ore to the final despatch of the results in small ingots to England. The Morro Velho was then more than paying its way, but it has probably long since been worked out, the life of a gold mine being seldom a long one. It was certainly an interesting example of what British capital and British energy can do; for it must be remembered those were days before the railways made transport comparatively easy; and the expense of bringing over men and machinery from England was simply double.

Leaving the little English colony with sincere regret, the Burtons resumed their way. They did not fail to notice, like other travellers in the Brazil, the gorgeous beauty of the forests. The dense curtain of many-tinted vegetation on each side of the Upper Pangani River had excited our traveller's admiration during the preliminary canter into the interior of Africa; but the variety and brightness of the Brazilian flora, which, shooting up the trees, form glowing clusters, charged with almost blinding points of colour, impart a brilliance rarely seen in any other part of our world. Gold and purple blossoms first attract the eye; then white and blue, pink and violet, crimson and scarlet, glittering like vegetable jewels. Most astonishing of all are the epiphytes, air-plants and parasites. The weak enwrap the strong from head to foot in rampant, bristling masses, and hide them in cypress-like pillars of green. Even the dead trees are embraced by these vigorous shoots that swarm up, clasp, entwine them, and stand upon their crests, the nearer to worship Sol and Æther; every naked branch is at once seized upon and ringed and feathered with alien growths. The moist heavy air is loaded with perfume, every variety of odour, from the fragrant vanilla to the Páo de Alho, which spreads a smell of garlic over a hundred yards around. The cry of the jay, the tapping of the woodpecker, combined with the chatter of the many-hued parrots and parroquets, give life to the strange and beautiful scene, which really might seem an ideal of Paradise were it not for a continual buzzing of overgrown wasps, and a nasty rustle caused by a magnificent assortment, from a naturalist's point of view, of the deadliest of deadly snakes.

A visit to Ouro Preto, the capital of Minas Geraes, a city so irregularly built and so utterly uninteresting that any detailed description of it would be a difficult task, followed by flying trips to sundry other obscure towns, terminated the holiday portion of Burton's journey. The remainder was real hard woik. Under hot suns, drenching rains, buffeted by furious gales, he had to cover eleven hundred and fifty miles in that craziest of crafts, a Brazilian ajôjo. Accompanied by his wife and a party of friends as far as Sabará, a town situated on the banks of the Rio das Velhas, he there concluded his preparations, and bought a boat for the voyage. The moment arrived for parting, one by one familiar faces faded in the distance, and on Wednesday, August 7th, 1867, our traveller was left to the contemplation of his very peculiar vessel.

"I never saw such an old Noah's Ark, with its standing awning, a floating gipsy 'pál,' some seven feet high and twenty-two long, and pitched like a tent upon two hollowed logs. The river must indeed be safe if this article can get down without accident!"

The ajôjo represents the flat boat of the Mississippi and the Arkansas, in days when men spent a month between the mouth of the Ohio and New Orleans. It is composed of two or three canoes, in the latter case the longest occupying the centre. The canoes are either lashed together by side ropes or connected by iron bars. Poles fastened to the gunwales support the platform, a boarding of planks laid horizontally. The awning of rough Minas cotton is made fast by five wooden stanchions, of which the two pairs fore and the one aft are supported, besides being nailed, by strong iron stays. The ajôjo occupied by our traveller did not lack a certain rude comfort, for under the awning was a boarded bunk for sofa and bed, a table, and a tall writing desk; while in the stern stood the galley, lined with bricks and provided with a small *batterie de cuisine*. Nor had he neglected to provide himself with a locked box, containing eatables, spirits, and tobacco. His crew on starting numbered three, an old man and his two sons; but others, pilots especially, were engaged during the course of the voyage. Mr. Gordon had sent one of the Morro Velho lads as personal attendant, and a mastiff, the gift of the same good friend, mounted guard. On more than one occasion, sundry poverty-stricken emigrants who wished to descend the river cheaply were granted a free passage, and at times the owners of fazendas along the banks availed themselves of a chance of a pleasant diversion by claiming Burton's hospitality.

Obstacles on such a stream and with such a craft of course abounded. Whirlpools, detached rocks, sandbars, shallow sharp curves, snags and timbers encumbering the river-bed, required a constant look-out, and though the crew seemed familiar enough with the dangers they had to avoid, the ajôjo often grounded twice or thrice in one day, and great was the difficulty of getting the clumsy old object off again. However, the " *Brig Eliza*," as Burton had christened his property, braved all these perils with an impunity which a well-appointed steam-launch might have failed to share.

Our traveller, who was exploring the Rio das Velhas, which, as everybody knows, flows into the Sao Francisco, partly with a view to assist emigration, opined that the land best fitted for settlers lies between Bom Successo and the Coroa do Gallo. Beyond the reach of the great planters who desire to sell square leagues of ground, some good, much bad, hereabouts proprietors were ready to part with four square miles, including a fine corrego, for less than had been paid for the ajôjo. The views are beautiful, the climate is fine and dry, there is no need for the quinine bottle on the breakfast table as in parts of the Mississippi valley. Except snakes, there are no noxious animals, and save at certain seasons few nuisances in the way of mosquitoes, flies, &c. The river bottom is some four miles broad, and when the roots of the felled trees on either side are grubbed up it will be easy to use the plough ; while the yield of corn and cereals is at least from fifty to a hundred per cent. There is every facility for breeding stock and poultry, besides washing for gold and diamonds ; limestone and saltpetre abound ; iron is everywhere to be dug. Still, emigrants will do well to remember that parts of the country on the banks of the Sao Francisco, unlike those on the Rio das Velhas, rival Dickens' immortal Eden, where Mark Tapley failed at last to be jolly. Besides, although conditions change slowly amongst an indolent population like the Brazilians, thirty years may have altered for the worse the refuge from the want and misery in the Old World which Burton thought so suitable in 1867.

The voyage was pleasantly varied by short visits to the towns and fazendas along the river. A lengthy *détour* was to the city of Diamantina, which took more than three days of cross-country travelling. Mr. Gordon, with admirable thoughtfulness, had sent four mules and one of his troopers to the point on the Rio das Velhas, Bom Successo, where Burton disembarked ; so, except for the vile roads, there were no great hardships to endure. It was a lonely journey, but I came upon a passage in his book which sounds as if he had been bored with too much company—not too little :

" My old longing for the pleasures of life in the backwoods—for solitude—was strong upon me. I sighed unamiably to be again out of the reach of my kind, so to speak—once more to meet Nature face to face. This food of the soul, as the Arabs call it, is the true antidote to one's *entourage*, to the damaging effects of one's epoch and one's race, and it largely gives to him who wishes to think for himself."

No one disturbed his musings, and he reached Diamentina without adventures, and apparently more sociable. The site of this town is peculiar, almost precipitous to the east and south-west, whilst the northern part is a continuation of broken prairie-land. Viewed from the Alto da Cruz, the city has a well-to-do and important look. It is described in some of our encyclopedias as a mean place, and, in fact, it was known at one time as the "village of the mudhole." But, in 1867, we read of numerous houses painted in many colours—pink, white, and yellow—with large, green gardens facing broad streets and wide squares, whilst public buildings of superior size, and a confusion of single and double church steeples testified to the wealth of the population. Its citizens were not only wealthy, but lavish in their hospitality; and the men were the frankest, and the women some of the prettiest in the Brazil. Burton had an opportunity of admiring the singular beauty of the latter, as he received an invitation to a ball given by a rich widow, where every neck sparkled with diamonds, and the *toilettes* were almost Parisian.

He visited at once the principal diamond diggings, known as the Jequitinhonha, after a river similarly named. Planks, rough ladders, and inclined planes led to the bottom of the long pit, whose southern extremity measured eighty feet deep by twenty broad. The mine belonged to a lucky Brazilian, who had purchased it for six thousand pounds and was making over fifteen thousand a year. Burton recognised in the Lavadeiro the drawing familiar to childhood copied from John Mawe into every popular book of travels—the thatched roof of the Mandanga mine, with a stream of water passing through a succession of boxes; the four inspectors in straw hats, perched on the tallest of stools, and armed with the longest of whips; whilst the white-kilted sable washers, in a vanishing line, bent painfully to their tasks, and one of them, in an unpleasantly light toilette, was throwing up his arms to signify "Eureka." But the reality presented many points of difference, and it is a pleasure to learn the whips were conspicuous by their absence. Indeed, the discipline seemed somewhat lax, as the miners, negroes, and half-breeds were said to help themselves liberally to the sparkling booty. A receiver of stolen goods always settled close to every new digging, and some mine-owners complained that almost all their finest stones disappeared.

Less important diggings at Sao Joao were also visited by our indefatigable traveller. He left the Diamantina region with regret. Socially speaking, it was the most "sympathetic" spot in the Brazil, at least according to his experience, and he had to urge the absolute necessity of punctuality before he could escape from its hospitalities. On bidding adieu to the flourishing little city, he struck the direct road to Bom Successo, aud reached the river after a ride of forty miles. Before resuming the baggage, he engaged another pilot, grim and angry-looking as a Kurd, oftener drunk than sober, but who thoroughly understood the difficult and dangerous stream. The trooper and his four mules were dismissed, and they carried back our wanderer's letters to Morro Velho, where his wife was staying with Mrs. Gordon on her way back to Rio.

At Guaicuhy, a miserable port town, the Rio das Velhas is absorbed into the Sao Francisco. The "River of the old Squaws" sweeps gracefully round from north-east to nearly due west, and flowing down a straight reach, about 550 feet broad, merges into the Francisco, which rolls from the east to receive it. Already a triumph was it to have reached the bosom of this glorious stream; our traveller contemplated with enthusiasm the meeting of the two mighty waters, declaring afterwards that he had seen nothing to compare with it since his visit to the Congo. Like the latter and the Nile, it floods during the dry season, and *vice versâ*. Its water is a transparent green, and as it winds through its verdant avenue, spreading out into bays, 1,800 feet broad, grand indeed are the curves described on the lacustrine lowlands. After Guaicuhy, the region is most fertile and beautiful; all along the banks appear charming patches of cultivation—melon, sloped cuttings of sugar-cane ready for planting, coffee, tobacco, and enormous quantities of maize and rice.

Hitherto, save for a burning sun, the weather had been fairly pleasant; but shortly after passing Sao Romao, a miserable townlet where our traveller spent a few hours, he wrote of drenching rains, from which the brig *Eliza* afforded very poor protection. And worse was to come. Off Januaria, another port town, a storm assuming almost the force of a cyclone nearly beat down the awning, and, although the ajôjo was snugly moored under the shelter of a high bank, threatened to reduce her to a perfect wreck. Later still Burton described the elements as devilry broken loose. A cold wind from the north rushed through the hot air and precipitated a deluge in embryo. Then the gale chopped round to the south and produced another and yet fiercer downpour. A treacherous lull ensued, aud all began again, the wind howling and screaming from the east. Thunder roared, lightning flashed from all directions, the river rose in wavelets, washing over the clumsy *Eliza* and menacing her with a speedy descent to the depths below. It was in fact the beginning of the wet season—of all the inexpressible discomfort of tropical bad weather. No refuge in the townlets along the banks was practicable, for all were situated on unhealthy marshy sites, were more or less ruinous and decayed, some even undermined by the huge relentless river. In such circumstances our traveller was confined for many hours at a time to his bunk, where he solaced himself with sundry pocket classics, the woe of his youth, the delight of his maturer age; with Hafiz and Camoens, Horace and Martial, he declared occupation was never wanting. I think it was poor Speke who reproached him with dragging his books into the interior of Africa; the truth was Richard Burton could dispense with society, but he could not live without his little library.

On the 22nd October the Sao Francisco, which for many miles had been as smooth and unobstructed as the Thames, began to display warning signals of the great rapids that lay beyond. A little below Boa Vista, the river, after a short and tolerably clear northern sweep, returns to the eastern direction, and enters upon that Cordilheira of broken, surging water which lasts for some thirty leagues. A special pilot had to be engaged, and thanks to this man's dexterity and courage, the first rapids, whose dangers were further exaggerated by the supposed existence of a Siren who lies in wait for even the ugliest boatmen, were safely passed. The excitement of racing along these wild currents delighted our traveller; and instead of landing at Boa Vista, the usual terminus of barque navigation, he determined to paddle the *Eliza* as far as Varzea Redonda. During the next six days his journal was full of hair-breadth escapes. One part of the river thus traversed has nine rapids, two whirlpools, and two shallows, all within the space of six to seven miles. Burton humorously confessed to " cold hands " at the sight of the infamous turnings, the whirlpools, and the pot-holes some fifteen feet deep in the water. Head on they dashed by the rocks, here bare, there shrub-clad, and more than once they prepared for the shock; often the pilot giving the canoe a broad sheer with a sweep of his heavy and powerful paddle, carried her safely through places where death might be touched on either side.

The *Eliza* swayed and surged as she coursed down the roaring waters that washed her platform; the spray dazzled the eyes as it caught the sun, and in many places the surface was literally fanged with murderous black stones. Once a strong blast struck the ajôjo—in an instant she was hurled against a rock. The pilot exerted himself in desperation, fighting indeed for dear life; his men kept their presence of mind, and, to everybody's surprise, the craft floated again down stream with only a scrape and a graze. That afternoon, however, the crew would work no more, but paddled to shore and anchored for the night.

This strange voyage terminated at Varzea Redonda. Here, after studying awhile the glyphs on the rocks, whose interpretation may lighten a dark place in the prehistoric age of the Brazil, Burton broke up his boat, paid off the watermen, and engaged horses and followers for his short journey to the Falls, a journey now performed by tram. The mastiff, who had often got his master into trouble by persistently biting the wrong people, was presented to one of the crew, and probably spent the rest of his life paddled up and down the river. On the whole, our traveller had got on very well with his boatmen owing to the quantities of spirits manufactured in the Brazil, they were somewhat drunken, but their employer remarked that often when well primed they worked all the better.

The approach to the great Brazilian cataract lacks the broad majestic beauty of Niagara before the Falls. In fact, the river becomes somewhat repulsive; narrowing suddenly, its waters, now dull yellow, swirl against jagged rocks, whose black and tawny sides contrast unpleasantly with patches of chalky, white sand. Burton prepared himself for a disappointment. Was Paulo Affonso worth journeying so many miles to see?

Yes, and many more! A deep hollow sound like the rumbling of a distant storm which seemed to rise from the bowels of the earth, grew so loud that the ground

appeared to tremble at the eternal thunder. Making his
way to the Mother of the Rapids, where all the waters
that come scouring down with tremendous rush are finally
gathered together for their mighty leap, a point which
displays most forcibly the formation distinguishing Paulo
Affonso from his great brethren, Burton crossed the eastern
channel and reached an island whence a path led to a
jutting rock, where he clung to a dry tree trunk and
peered fascinated into the liquid vastness below.

The gorge here measures 260 feet in depth. It is filled
with what seems like froth of milk, a dashing, dazzling,
whirling mass which gives a wondrous study of fluid in
motion. It is the triumph of momentum over the immov-
able. Here the luminous whiteness of the chaotic foam-
crests, hurled in billows and breakers against the blackness
of the rock, is burst into flakes and spray that leap half
way up the immuring trough. There the surface reflections
dull the dazzling crystal to a thick opaque yellow, and there
the shelter of some spur causes a momentary start and
recoil to the column, which at once gathering strength
bounds and springs onwards with a new crush and another
roar. Now a fierce blast hunts away the thin spray-drift,
and puffs it to leeward in rounded clouds, thus enhancing
the brilliancy of the gorge; then the stream boils over
and canopies the tremendous scene; or, in the stilly air,
the mists surge up, deepening yet more by their veil of ever-
ascending vapour the dizzy fall that yawns under the spec-
tator's feet.

Burton declared that at last the feeling of awe became
too intense to be enjoyable, and he returned to camp to
let the emotion excited by this life-in-death, this creation
and construction by destruction subside amidst the minor
cares of existence. He revisited the scene, however, next
day, and was fortunate enough on the last evening of his
stay in the neighbourhood to see the magnificent King of
Rapids by moonlight. The effect of the soft silvery rays on

the flashing line of cascade, while semi-opaque shadows, here purple, there brown, clothed the middle height, appears to have been almost indescribable.

Everything now seemed flat and stale. Two days of monotonous riding led to the Porto das Piranhas. The steamer had just left, but a hospitable reception awaited our traveller at the house of the agent to the Bahian Steam Navigation Company. After about a week's rest he descended the lower Rio de Sao Francisco, made his way to Bahia, and finally returned *viâ* Rio de Janeiro to Santos, which he nicknamed the Wapping of the Far West.

During four months rough voyaging with alternations of storm and rain, cold and hot winds, mists and burning suns, Burton had not suffered from an hour's illness. But soon after he got home he was seized by the most agonizing pains, pains resembling the peri-hepatitis or "little irons," which once nearly destroyed Speke's life on his return journey from Tanganyika. Of course, the Brazilian medico had to confess his ignorance, and could do nothing to allay the awful agony which defied all the usual remedies. Bleeding, blistering, every sort of powerful drug was tried with the sole result of making the patient worse, and but for a happy inspiration, to leave Santos for a village on the sea-beach—of course he had to be carried—Burton must have died. I have already mentioned his strange meekness under the hands of the most ignorant Sangrado ; the nearest show to anything like fight was to fly.

Aided by pure sweet air, his glorious constitution triumphed yet again. But the mystery as to the cause of the malady, the suddenness with which he had been prostrated, the hideous pain, had given his nerves a shake. He began to take a dislike to both Santos and San Paulo, and longed to get away.

Events favoured him. In 1868 Brazil and the Republic of Paraguay were at war. For the last three years a succession of details had been published by one newspaper and directly contradicted by another; so Lord Stanley, then Foreign Secretary, deemed it advisable to obtain trustworthy information respecting the nature and causes of the conflict. No one was better fitted for the post of military correspondent than the erudite soldier then acting consul at Santos. Accordingly, Burton was directed to make use of his sick leave by paying two visits to the battle-fields of Paraguay, a mission which suited him exactly, for the travelling fever was again upon him, and he intended to visit not merely the seat of war, but the chief towns of Uruguay and Argentina, to roam over the Andes to Chili and Peru, return *viâ* the Straits of Magellan to Buenos Ayres, and finally work his way to England. Determined, come what might, never to return to Santos, he broke up his little establishment, and sent his wife home with sundry MSS. under her charge for publication. And then, free as air, he started on what he called his second and grander holiday tour through South America.

At Rio, early in August, 1868, he embarked for Monte Vidéo. The voyage was wearisome, the steamer crammed with disappointed emigrants, all more or less noisy and quarrelsome; and it was a relief, after five days of their company, to descry a forest of masts lying under the "Town of the Mount," backed by a splay and high-shouldered hill, which, while only 465 feet above sea-level, towers like a giant over the ridgy and peakless coast-line.

There are two points of view of the little capital where she best shows her peculiarities. The first is seen when skirting the southern end of the new town. The thorough-fares facing west-south-west abut upon the water; after the gorgeous vegetable growth of Rio de Janeiro they look bald and stony, treeless and barren. The sky-line is fretted by miradors, gazebos, steeples, and here and there towers a gaunt factory chimney. Successively rise high in air a huge convent, a Dutch-tiled cupola, over whose ochred walls peep cypresses and black rows of empty niches, declaring it to be a cemetery; the English church resembling a shed to stable bathing machines, the hospital, three-storied, yellow-tinted, the theatre, and the substantial stone church of S. Philip and S. James. The other and prettier *coup d'œil* is to be obtained by ascending the Cerro; from the summit, looking east, is a bird's-eye view of the city, which, set after a fashion upon a hill, can hide neither her charms nor her blemishes. Most remarkable is the enormous amount of water; on one side the bay, on the other the La Plata, that sea-like stream which can hardly be called a river, rather a yellow flood, a muddy Mediterranean.

Here Burton spent about a week. Monte Vidéo was not at that time the safest of halting-places. Political assassinations had been rife, and blood-thirstiness was the rule. Soldiers in Uruguay are almost always negroes, and a stranger approaching their barracks even by day must ask leave to advance, otherwise an infuriated blue-tunicked anthropoid will charge bayonet blindly as a mad bull. Nor were the police much better. In short, our traveller did not think highly of this republic as an emigration ground for Englishmen. Matters may have improved since; but then nobody expected justice, nobody had the slightest confidence in the Government; executions, frightfully common in revenge for party misdemeanours, were unknown when the offence was murder, and yet there was an unpleasant prejudice against self-defence. A Mr. Flowers, who, to save his life from a ruffian in the act of stabbing him, shot the wretch, was punished by nine months' imprisonment. The climate, too, seems to exercise a pernicious effect on the British constitution. Exiles arrive full of life and energy, ready to work hard, fond of riding and field sports, then by degrees lose all energy, and do nothing but eat, drink and smoke.

En route for Humaita, the scene of the principal battles between the wretched over-matched Republic of Paraguay and the allied forces of Brazil, Argentina and Uruguay,

Burton allotted a few days, sometimes hours only, to the
most interesting towns on his way. Buenos Ayres was the
first visited.   Stout Captain Sancho Garcia, if resurrected,
could no longer exclaim, as in 1535, " Que buenos ayres se
respiran en esta tierra ! "   Our traveller found the atmosphere heavy with meat, tainted as well as fresh, besides a
dreadful stench of tallow and calcined bones. Between
October, '68, and April, '69, three hundred and ninety
thousand head of cattle were slaughtered in this horrible
town—enough to sicken a stranger of Liebig's Essence for
ever after.   Insulted Hygiene had just been avenged by a
sharp epidemic of cholera, and it is very evident, from the
description of the then state of the city, that the water and
drainage works were begun none too soon. With regard
to the inhabitants, Burton wrote in laudatory terms of the
higher and educated classes ; but for the lower he advo-
cated a permanent gallows in the outskirts.

After a short stay at Paysandu, famous for its ox-
tongues, he embarked on the Rio Parano, halting a day
or so at Rozario.   The cathedral, whose two round white
steeples of the pepper-caster order can be seen from the
river, stands without a rival, rare indeed in South America.
It was crammed on Sundays and *fêtes*, chiefly with women,
who, however, evidently considering variety charming, spent
their Sunday evenings in a circus-tent devoted to bull and
bear-baiting. Even dogs were loosed at ponies and donkeys,
and the more viciously the animals fought the better were
the dames and damsels of Rozario pleased.   More interesting is it to learn that here Burton first saw the hairless
dogs whose parent stock came from the Sandwich Islands.
These curious creatures, which are now occasionally im-
ported into England, resemble clumsy Italian greyhounds.
Their leaden-coloured skin is entirely bald save for a few
bristles.   The people dub them *remedios*, because they
cure rheumatics by sleeping upon the afflicted limb ; and,
having no shelter for vermin, they are applied to the feet

in bed as warming-pans or hot bottles, with the distinct
advantage of not getting cold. Doubtless the dogs, being
so lightly clothed, do not object to an arrangement equally
comfortable for both parties.

At Corrientes, built on the margin of her noble river,
there bending eastward and showing to the north a lake-
like expanse of water, were a number of Indians lounging
about in their native costume. Clad in ponchas, chiripá
kilts, and short, stiffly starched calzonzillas of white or
scarlet stuff, these curious people looked just ready for
a wax-work exhibition, or the Crystal Palace. The felt
or straw headgear distinguishes them from the wild Indians
of the Gran Chaco, who were paddled over every morning
by their squaws in canoes, which they easily managed in
spite of the current. But all wore rugs and blankets, ear-
rings and necklaces of beads ; many were ornamented with
the real tattoo, said to be ineffaceable, and a few affected
black patches round the eyes, signs of mourning. The
most comical, not to say startling, novelty, was that the
Romish priests had taught them to publicly display their
Christianity by the exceedingly uncomfortable operation
of pricking crosses along and across their noses. Notwithstanding this show of piety they seemed to have been
rather spiteful : " That man's throat should be cut," exclaimed an ancient squaw, mistaking Burton for a Paraguayan officer.

Again on board—Burton was now travelling in civilised
fashion on a brand new floating hotel with its plated silver,
its napkins stiffly starched, and its gilt mouldings upon
white panels clean as a new sovereign—he gazed with
rapture upon the magnificent spectacle afforded by the
confluence of the Paraná and the Paraguay, which at the
astounding distance of two hundred and fifty leagues from
the mouth, equal a hundred of the biggest rivers of Europe.
Compared with these majestic proportions, this mighty
sweep of waters, the meeting of the Rios de Sao Francisco

and Das Velhas seemed to the memory insignificant. Presently the steamer dashed amongst floating trees and rippling isles of grass and reed up the Paraguay, which suddenly narrows from a mile and a half to four hundred yards, and seems quite a small influent, the cause being the Isla del Atajo, a long thin island to the left, disposed with its length down stream. Soon after passing the latter, signs of war began to appear. At Cerrito the Brazilians had built workshops and storehouses for their army. Not far away lay stranded the wreck of an American hospital ship, which had been burnt with her eighty sick; then the steamer approached the spot where the ironclad *Rio de Janeiro* was blown up, including her captain and crew. Further on was the site of the great actions fought in May, 1866, a site which smelt of death, for there lay buried some ten thousand men, victims of cholera, small-pox and fever; in short, the vessel shot past ground whose every mile cost a month of battles,—Curuzu, Curupaity, Humaita.

The latter, an entrenched camp *sans* citadel, looked very warlike. Ironclads lay at anchor, little gunboats buzzed about like wasps; and on landing the military correspondent found the ground everywhere sprinkled with Whitworth's forty, one hundred and twenty, and one hundred and fifty pounders, costing each from £20 to £50. Very few had exploded, and a pointed stick soon told the reason why; they had been charged, not with gunpowder, but with one of its constituents—charcoal. Burton was so courteously assisted in his survey of Humaita by one of the Brazilian generals, who even lent the English correspondent his own chargers, that he succeeded in correcting a great deal of nonsense spoken and written about this "stronghold," once looked on as the key-stone of Paraguay. Readers interested in this almost forgotten campaign are referred to "Letters from the Battlefields of Paraguay," published in 1870.

On leaving Humaita, Burton pushed on to the front in

the *Linnet*, a British gunboat. In places the Paraguay and Tebicuary rivers were obstructed by floating torpedoes and fixed infernal machines, which, had they exploded, would have blown the little *Linnet* into fragments ; luckily, they were so carelessly constructed as to cause but small mischief. At Guardia Tacuára he had an opportunity of inspecting the Brazilian forces and of conversing with the principal officers. Here the thunder of the ironclads was distinctly audible ; and in places the river banks were dotted with the Paraguayan dead whom the allies had not taken the trouble to bury. But the unlucky Paraguayans, who were losing rapidly, refused to admit him to their lines ; and as the Brazilian authorities were opposed to any visit to their enemies, Burton judged it prudent not to urge the matter. Enough that his object was obtained ; his keen insight into military affairs and knowledge of the language of the people around him enabled him to expose many a newspaper blunder, and forward to Lord Stanley a full and true report.

Later, when the allied armies gained so decisive a victory that the Marshal President and Madame Lynch fled to the interior, and the war was practically ended, our traveller paid a short visit to the Paraguayan capital. Seated upon its amphitheatre of red bank which slopes gracefully down to its lake-like stream, it presents a picturesque appearance. The Paraguay river here measuring from 800 to 1,000 yards broad, sags to the eastward, forming a bay or port of still, dead surface ; and the bight is landlocked by a natural breakwater, a long green islet upon which cattle graze. Ships anchor in safety along the shore, and their presence adds not a little to the beauty of the scenery, which has all the softness and grace without the monotony of the fair, insipid shores about Humaita.

The huge, unfinished residence of the Marshal President, a kind of Buckingham Palace, built upon the abrupt riverine slope, offended our traveller's eye, being far too large for the town.   Some of the public buildings, however, are massive and handsome.   The old cathedral is coloured pink and blue upon a white ground, its material brick upon ashlar of boulders.   When Burton entered, there were so few voices and so many echoes that he confessed to feeling quite startled when stumbling suddenly upon a French Frère Ignorantin who was making fierce love to a Paraguayan *belle*.   The terrible palace of Dr. Francia, with verandahs eight feet broad, and its eighteen columns fronting the river, is another solid building ; but the new cathedral, erected in 1845, is described as the "normal barn."   Summed up, his opinion of Asuncion and her people was as follows :

" A large and expensively-built arsenal, riverside docks, a tramway and a railroad have thrown over Asuncion a thin varnish of civilisation, but the veneering is of the newest and most palpable ; the pretensions to progress are merely skin-deep, and the slightest scratch shows under the Paraguayan Republic the Jesuiticized Guarani."

Besides his careful and thorough survey of the Paraguayan battle-fields, Burton crossed the Pampas and the Andes to Chili and Peru.   Perhaps he might have lingered longer amidst the many interesting and beautiful scenes in South America, but whilst sitting in a café at Lima, he heard by chance of his appointment to the Consulate of Damascus.   No further delay was possible.   At once he turned his face homewards, and though twice nearly shipwrecked, he was fortunate enough to catch the steamer at Rio, and three weeks later landed at Southampton.

CHAPTER XIV

A FTER a short stay in England, rendered yet shorter
by the necessity for taking the Vichy waters in consequence of his severe attack of hepatitis at Santos, Burton
spent six pleasant weeks at his favourite spa. Time passed
quickly in the society of such men as Algernon Swinburne
and Sir Frederick Leighton ; and, his course over, our
traveller, with mended health and in splendid spirits, started
for Syria, arriving without accident on the 1st October,
1869. Three months later he was joined by his wife.

In 1869 the Consulate of Damascus was a fairly important post. The Consul, paid at the rate of twelve hundred
a year, was expected to maintain a suitable establishment,
which included dragomans, kavasses, and a good stable.
He had jurisdiction, or rather exercised a protectorate over
British subjects in the whole district bounded by the three
provinces Baghdad, Nablus, and Aleppo ; upon him de-
volved the responsibility of the mail for Baghdad through
the Desert, as well as the safety of commerce, of travellers,
the English residents, missions, schools—in short, of any
person who had the slightest pretension to be considered a
subject of the Queen. Only nine years had elapsed since
the great massacre in 1860 ; the elements of discord still
existed amongst the strangely heterogeneous population,
and it behoved all in authority to exercise the utmost tact
and vigilance. In the event of any dispute during the performance of Burton's multifarious duties, appeal could be
made to his superior, the Consul-General of Beirut.

When Isabel arrived, she found her husband living, as
was his habit when alone, at an inn. The said inn, as

might be expected, was far from comfortable, so the
Burtons allowed little time to elapse before they started on
a house hunt.   Nothing could be more romantic than was
Damascus in those days, untouched by the vulgarising
finger of Change (think of it now with gas and trams!) ; but,
like most romantic places, it was neither hygienic nor
secure.   Isabel, after her two years' sojourn in the old
convent at San Paulo, was not very fastidious ; still, she
could find nothing to suit her in the town itself.   We know
that, behind mean entrances, Damascus boasts of splendid
houses—houses with white marble pavements, their walls
frescoed and decorated with mosaics, not to mention arabesque ceilings gorgeous with purple and gold.   But their
attractions are sadly counterbalanced ; all are more or less
damp, cold in winter, suffocating in summer ; while in case
of an *émeute* or a fire, the inmates painfully resemble mice
in a trap, the town gates being closed at sunset.   So,
turning away from these " marble palaces," the new-comers
prudently decided on taking a straggling whitewashed cottage, once a fair-sized building, before it had been cut in
two and sold separately.   Situated on high ground, in a
Kurdish village named Salihiyyah, about a quarter of an
hour's ride from Damascus through fields and orchards, it had
plenty of light and air ; and, although the village or suburb
was large enough to contain a population of 15,000 souls,
its new residents could get out of it in five minutes for a
gallop over the open country without the troublesome
suite necessary in Oriental cities.   I must mention another
attraction which this quaint abode possessed for our
traveller : his bedroom window and the minaret of a
neighbouring mosque were nearly on a level, so he could
join the Muezzin in the call to prayer.   As during his
stay at Zeila, he delighted in hearing the familiar sound
again, which he often compared with the Christians' brazen
summons, grievously to the disadvantage of the latter.

Front and back, the cottage, which has been faithfully

depicted by Lord Leighton, looked upon gardens. Over the narrow road, amongst some apricot orchards, the Burtons erected a stable for twelve horses, with a room for their grooms. The building itself seems to have been thoroughly Oriental, though not palatial. A visitor was ushered into a square courtyard painted in stripes of red, white and blue, planted with orange, lemon and jessamine trees, with a fountain in the middle. On this courtyard opened a room with three sides, spread with rugs and divans, the niches in the walls filled with plants ; and here Isabel received on hot days, entertaining her guests appropriately with coffee, sherbet, narghilehs and cigarettes. The dining-room was also on the ground floor, while upstairs six rooms occupied two sides of the courtyard, and a sort of terrace the remainder. The terrace afforded a delightful lounge on warm evenings, a kind of be-flowered, be-carpeted housetop, whence an unobstructed view was to be had of Jebel Kaysun, the tall, yellow mountain which forms the background of Salihiyyah ; and, when the wind blew from the right quarter, a delicious whiff could be inhaled of the pure air of the Desert which lies beyond Damascus. When at last Isabel had thoroughly settled herself in this romantic abode, and collected a strangely assorted menagerie of pets that never ceased worrying and trying to devour each other (a favourite leopard did perform the not unnatural feat of slaying a woolly black lamb), she declared she was madly enamoured of Eastern life. But her description of the dismal sounds proceeding from every side—howls of wild dogs, cries of jackals prowling near the burial ground of Jebel Kaysun, varied by a free fight in the road below, or the loud wrangling of the Kurdish women, make one suspect she would have grown very weary of "the solemn mystery, the romantic halo of Oriental existence" had it been much prolonged.

Here, then, at Salihiyyah, the Burtons spent their winter

22

and spring. At times they seem to have been far from lonely—rather the other way. All English people, and most foreigners that visited Damascus, called upon them and were shown in return every sort of hospitality possible in the circumstances. On Wednesdays Isabel held a reception, a function which began soon after sunrise and continued until sunset. The native dames arrived first; one very early riser complained bitterly of having been refused admission, as her sorely taxed hostess had failed to dress at the first glimmer of dawn. Church dignitaries appeared decorously at about one o'clock—lunch time; and were followed by the consular corps, Turkish authorities, mission and school people. These receptions, I may remark, were an innovation. As a rule, the European society split into cliques, the Protestant missionary and school folk forming one, the consular corps and the French another, and the three religious houses a third. But Isabel, with dangerous originality, endeavoured to keep a *salon* where all creeds, races and tongues could meet without ill-feeling—a neutral ground upon which everyone was expected to be friendly; about as hopeless an experiment as the menagerie outside. Had these reunions been less intolerably prolonged, they might have proved safer; but, as it was, I am inclined to suspect that some of the enmities which dogged our traveller may have originated in petty squabbles, jealousies, and especially tittle-tattle, during those long, long days in the room looking on the striped courtyard. Could even the wise woman of the Proverbs have kept due guard over her tongue for twelve consecutive hours every week?

Nor were her more intimate friends wisely chosen. The chief of these, Jane Digby, who had capped her wild career by marrying her Arab camel-driver, seemed hardly a desirable *confidante*. Her unsuitability for this post, which appears to have been conferred upon her somewhat against her will, was speedily proved by Isabel's own confession. More Bedawin than the Bedawi, this eccentric woman aided her tribe by every means in her power (and be it remembered she was a very clever woman) in their endeavour to conceal the wells and extort blackmail from all Europeans who visited Palmyra. Hearing that the Burtons intended to journey thither, and that the Consul had no intention of paying the usual tribute, Jane, fearing the attempt if successful might deprive her people of a considerable source of revenue, resorted to stratagem. Professing herself anxious about the safety of her English friends, she offered one of her trusty clansmen as an escort to assist them in keeping clear of the Bedawi raids. The man, of course, was secretly instructed to lead the Burtons into ambush, whence they could be pounced upon by his tribe and kept prisoners until ransomed. Here, however, our traveller was not to be hoodwinked. He accepted the offer most politely, but as soon as the party was well *en route*, he deprived the spy of his mare and accoutrements, retaining both as hostages until the return journey to Damascus.

We must not be hard upon Jane. In the power of an Arab spouse and living amongst a savage tribe, she might have lost her life had she acted differently; but the close intimacy with a person so placed shows a painful lack of discretion on the other side. Inexplicable too, for while some women can hardly live without a friend to cry over, or be cried over by, as the case may be, Isabel's feeling towards her own sex was far from enthusiastic. I can merely suggest that, what with the strange existence, the continual excitement, the perpetual element of danger— for when there were no rumours of another rising there came a sharp epidemic of cholera, and at times the grave-yards and the jackals must have seemed unpleasantly near —Richard Burton's wife almost lost her head.

Winter and spring were pleasant enough in this

Damascus suburb, but the heat in summer—105° F. in the shade—rendered some sort of country abode indispensable. So quarters were found at B'ludan in the Anti-Libanus— a little Christian village, Greek Orthodox and Roman Catholic, which clings to the eastern flank of the Zebadáni valley. It lies some twenty-seven indirect miles across country—an eight hours' moderate ride on horseback, and twelve for baggage-laden camels. The house, romantically situated amongst the mountains, is described as little better than a large limestone barn, with a deep, covered verandah running along one side, and provided with ample stabling on the other. It had to be cleaned, whitewashed, and furnished; and, from the absence of any complaints, I believe it was fairly adapted to its inmates' mode of living, a mode simple in the extreme. The air outside was delicious, hot only for an hour or two about midday; and the views may be imagined from the fact that on the right of B'ludan rises Jebel Sannin, monarch of the Libanus, and on the left Hermon, king of the Anti-Libanus.

Amidst these wild scenes the Burtons led a partly Eastern, partly farmhouse, existence. Butter and milk were procurable from the Bedawi, sheep and kids from the passing flocks. Bread was home-made, and game abounded on the neighbouring hills. Isabel gave a most sentimental account of life at B'ludan—how she and her husband rambled over the hills at early dawn; how all the sick poor within seventeen miles came to be doctored; how the hungry, the ragged, the oppressed, crowded into the garden, asking the Consul to settle their differences, and assist them with gifts of food, clothes and money. It was sadly like acting Good Samaritan to snakes. *À propos* of her doctoring, she tells an amusing story. A dying peasant woman sent a piteous request for aid, and it was deemed advisable to soothe her last moments by administering a harmless dose, which the poor soul might imagine a sovereign specific. Next morning her son presented himself before our Lady Bountiful, informed her of his mother's death, and then, to Isabel's unbounded indignation, begged for a little more of the nice, white powder, as he had a bedridden grandmother whom he was most anxious to get rid of. Nor were her benevolent endeavours to relieve the victims of the cholera epidemic more gratefully received. She dispensed a pretty strong dose of opium mixed with some other drug, the prescription of an Anglo-Indian surgeon ; and when the " gift of God " failed, as in common with every other remedy it does at times, the amateur physicking was described in the *Levant Herald* as wholesale poisoning. Worse still, in return for all her charity to the repulsive paupers of B'ludan, she was insulted in the street by the Shaykh's son; and the quarrel that ensued, during which she spiritedly slashed the man's face with her riding whip, did Burton no good with the authorities. Rudyard Kipling, in one of his admirable Indian stories, gives a sad example of the danger of even kindly meddling with races of whose dispositions we know nothing ; and, evidently, Isabel's was a case in point.

Yes, she described existence at B'ludan, anyhow in the earlier days, as a little heaven below. We will now turn to Burton's opinion of it. " The *idea* of pitching tent on Lebanon is delightful. Pleasant illusions dispelled in a week ! As the physical mountain has no shade, so has the moral mountain no privacy : the *tracasserie* of its town and village life is dreary and monotonous as its physical aspect, broken only by a storm or an earthquake, when a murder takes place or when a massacre is expected. For the reasonable enjoyment of life, place me on Highgate's grassy steep rather than upon Lebanon. Having learned what it is, I should far prefer the comforts of Spitalfields, the ease of Seven Dials, and the society of Southwark." We may reconcile the two opinions as follows :

Burton had no trace of " Holy Land on the brain." Imagination carried to the extreme of viewing objects as they are not was never his foible ; and from prejudice he was entirely free. Really refreshing is it after reading high-flown nonsense about a little country, picturesque occasionally, but mostly barren and disforested—nonsense which has been freely ridiculed by Mark Twain and others, to follow our plain-spoken traveller in his journeys through Syria. No exaggeration, no sentimental reminiscences, no trite quotations. He admired the grand, weird parts of Moab, he remarked the beauty of Bashan, a comparatively well-wooded tract ; but Hermon he described as a common " hogsback," berry-brown, moreover, in September and October. Carmel he spoke of as a short, barren buttress crowned with a convent and a lighthouse, the *latter* decidedly useful ; the plain of Sharon was ruthlessly compared to our Bedfordshire fields, while as for the Cedars of Lebanon, he declared they presented so mean and ragged an appearance, that no English squire would have admitted them into his park. Yes, glowing language is sparingly used in our traveller's word-pictures of Syria ; but it *is* possible that with eyes still full of the might and majesty of the Chilian Andes, and the grace and grandeur of Magellan's Straits, he viewed the insignificant lines and dull tintage of the Libanus under somewhat unfavourable conditions.

Still, though not a lovely country, Syria is intensely interesting. In 1870 it was yet more so. On first arriving, Burton feared his occupation as an explorer would be clean gone; but he soon found that, while certain lines had been well trodden, hardly a single traveller, and no tourist, had ever ridden ten miles off the usual ways. Even now, few personally know how many patches of unvisited and unvisitable country lie within a couple of days' ride of great towns and cities, such as Aleppo and Damascus, Hums and Hamáh. And valid reasons exist for the apparent oversight. The unexplored spots are either too difficult or too dangerous for the multitude. To conscientiously visit even

the well-known places in Palestine occupies six months ;
but, when we come to unbeaten tracts, where there is
hardly a mile without a ruin, the certainty that the surface
of the antiquarian mine has been merely scratched, and
that long years must elapse before the land can be considered fully explored, must take possession of any sensible
brain.

Burton's first trip, however, was to the often-described
Palmyra, or Tadmor in the Wilderness.   He was accompanied by his wife, the Russian Consul, a French traveller,
the Vicomte de Perrochel, besides a numerous company of
servants, dragomans and kavasses.   Seventeen camels
carried baggage and water, while the twelve horses were
mounted by their owners and their following.   Had a small
detachment of the tribe, El-Meyrab, escorted the party,
there would have been no danger whatever from the
Bedawin that infest more or less all parts of Syria ; but as
matters were, Jane's luckless Arab disarmed, perched upon
a mule, and closely guarded by two picked domestics, must
have vividly suggested the skeleton at the feast.   I say
feast, because this picnic appears to have been most luxurious.   Carefully arranged halts, with coffee, lemonade and
other light refreshments always ready, well-cooked meals,
tents pitched with comfortable bedding inside at the end of
the daily march, proved so agreeable, that our travellers
spent quite eight days in covering the 150 miles that lie
between Damascus and Palmyra.

Arrived at their destination, Burton and his two friends
lost no time before exploring Zenobia's once magnificent
city.   All three men were anxious to collect as many curios
as possible, so they hired forty-five coolies to assist in digging, and commenced operations at a group of tomb towers
bearing W.S.W. from the great Temple of the Sun.   This
group marks the site of one of the two Viæ Appiæ which
entered Palmyra, the first on the high road to Damascus,
the second, the main approach from Hums and Hamáh,

Both are lined on either side with monuments, which here take the place of the Egyptian pyramids; and their squat, solid forms of gloomy, unsquared sandstone contrast remarkably with the bastard classical Roman architecture glittering from afar in white limestone. Although only a day and a half could be spared for excavations, Burton made a pretty good haul. To mention every object would weary most readers: suffice it to say that he and his friends exhumed from the complicated, chambered catacombs several ancient skulls differing *in toto* from those of the Syrian population of the present day, some remnants of statuary which had fallen from the entrance to the tomb towers, and most curious of all, deep down in one of the graves, a lock of hair stained yellow. This strange relic was shown later to a distinguished physiologist, who, after a careful examination, opined it had belonged to some Palmyrene beauty, and as it appeared to be dyed, evidenced the ultra-civilisation prevailing at the court of Zenobia.

Besides relic-hunting and riding about the neighbourhood, our party interchanged hospitality with the two principal Shaykhs. After one dinner given by Burton in his biggest tent, the strange company strolled together over the ruins by moonlight, returning when tired to camp, where the kavasses and camel-drivers treated them to a concert, dancing the sword dance to barbarous music, varied by weird howls. All this sounds highly romantic to dwellers amidst ordinary English scenes; but Palmyra appears to have had serious drawbacks. The water was detestable, tasting like that of Harrogate; the climate was vile, and the natives were horribly diseased. So, after a week, Burton, though loth to leave a place where so much buried treasure yet lay concealed, thought it advisable to expose his party no longer to the risks of fever and dysentery. Already husband and wife were more or less knocked up, and the Vicomte fared little better.

An oasis on the northern side of the Arabian desert seems
healthy enough ; but, may be, the camping-ground close to
the great colonnade was unwisely chosen. Future visitors
were advised to select a space amongst the trees near the
fountain, anyway a more sheltered spot, where the simoom
could not blow over the tents, a disaster which nearly
happened more than once during this short sojourn in
the wilderness.

Baalbek, situated only thirty miles N.N.W. of Damascus,
interested our traveller yet more, and he paid it repeated
visits. He was much concerned to find that, owing to
the supineness of the Turkish Government, the glorious
remains of city and temples were wantonly injured by
the natives, some of the great columns having been
more or less undermined for the sake of metal clamps
worth a few piastres. The keystone of the noble portal,
which began to slip in 1759, and which falls lower with
every slight earthquake, did not escape his keen eyes;
and in consequence of his urgent representations to Rashid
Pasha, Governor-General of Syria, a Mr. Barker, chief
engineer to the Government, was commissioned to inspect
it. The two men met and forthwith planned to underpin
the keystone with a porphyry shaft, the prop to be as thin
as possible, so as not to hide the grand old eagle, emblem
of Baal, the Sun God, that occupies the lower surface of
the middle soffit stone. Unfortunately, Mr. Barker, soon
after beginning work, was summoned to Damascus on some
trivial excuse; and the Governor, although he had given
his consent to carrying out the repairs, suddenly changed
his mind *à la Turque*, and employed his engineer in constructing a sort of goat-track road which led to nowhere.
So, after an ineffectual appeal through the *Times* to
English antiquarians, Burton in despair abandoned poor
Baalbek to the decay and desolation of the last fourteen
centuries.

His first visit duly paid to these splendid ruins, he

proceeded to examine the spot where lie the true sources of the Litani and the Orontes. In Syria and Palestine generally, great influents have ever since historic ages been confounded with sources; whilst the latter are those represented by the most copious, not by the most distant fountains. Moreover, Wasserschieds, *versants* and river-valleys were and are universally neglected, if, as often happens, the young spring is drawn off for irrigation; this will especially appear at the head of the Upper Jordan. Hence we have the historical, which is still the popular, opposed to the geographical or scientific source. Again, in highly important streams, like the Jordan, the historical may be differently placed by the Hebrews, the Classics and the Arabs. The Litani originates in a muddy, unclean pool, without perceptible current during the dries; an oval, whose longest diameter is at midsummer about one hundred feet. The true source of the Orontes issues from the foot of a grey Tell and is fed further on by many streams. This river, contrary to the rule of all waters in Cœle-Syria, flows north, and is known by the natives as El-Asi, or the Rebel. And it is a rebel to the last: the gusts of the Asi gorge, where it falls into the Gulf of Antioch, are, as sailors well know, fierce, furious and unmanageable, as are the headwaters.

The above paragraph I have quoted almost word for word from " Unexplored Syria." Not that the information is very interesting, or at present even novel; but for the following reason. The exhaustive survey set on foot by the originators of the Palestine Exploration Fund, a survey begun not a day too soon, as many ruins figured by the surveyors will soon have utterly vanished under the de-structive hands of Change, owes not a little to our versatile traveller's labours. In the two bulky volumes just referred to, published in 1872, we may see how hard he worked during his leisure hours with his friends, Professor Palmer and Tyrwhitt Drake, in ascertaining the altitudes of the

principal mountains, the true sources of the rivers, in correcting inaccuracies, in recovering lost sites. In the course
of one excursion alone, he prepared for local habitation on
the map of Syria the names of five great mountain blocks,
traced out their principal gorges, and determined the dis-
puted altitudes of the Anti-Libanus. The best atlases
then failed to name a single valley north-east of Zebadani,
or a single summit save one, and that a misnomer. Now,
the whole of Western Palestine is mapped on a scale which
includes every ruin as well as every spring, every water-
course, every wood, and every hillock; but it is rare to
find even a solitary reference to the man who helped
forward that work by his personal exertions, his influence,
and his advice.

His visit to Baalbek and the northern Libanus, not
omitting the Cedars, which, as aforesaid, inspired but scant
enthusiasm, was followed by a sister excursion to the
southern regions, long celebrated as a principal stronghold
of the Druses. At Shakkah, a village near the edge of the
Jebel Duruz Hauran, Burton and his two friends were
received by one Kabalan, a local chief, who had promised
an escort of ten horsemen to Umm Niran, a curious cave
containing water, situated in the volcanic region east of the
Damascus swamps. But, for this favour, instead of demanding a moderate fee, he insisted upon forty napoleons, an extortionate sum, which our traveller, with
his deep-rooted objection to being fleeced, refused to pay,
whereupon the old ruffian hung out his true colours, and
threatened to prevent the party from leaving Shakkah.
Burton merely laughed in his face, ordered the horses, and
departed for Tayma, another village about eight miles
further on. Kabalan, too surly to return even a parting
salutation, squatted baboon-like outside a fine old pagan
ruin and meditated his revenge.

But the travellers were not fated to set out *sans* their
escort, sorry as it proved to be. One by one, prompted no

doubt by inquisitiveness, sundry Druse youths dropped in to Tayma, mounted on their best mares, until at last there mustered six guns. During the first march they were rein-forced by their attendants, and thus the total amounted to the respectable figure of ten combatants—without paying forty napoleons.

Events proved that the escort might just as well have remained at home. Burton was much disappointed with these people. A brave and even desperate race in their own mountains, where they are everybody, a residence in or about a town where their numbers are insignificant appears to utterly demoralize them. Even at a few miles beyond their own habitations they are as fish out of water. Only one of the six young Druses who volunteered to accompany the three Englishmen during a short tour of discovery in their neighbourhood got so far as Damascus. Their be-haviour *en route* was womanish in the extreme. They called for water every half-hour, ate every hour, and clamoured for sleep every four hours. They complained of the heat and the cold, of the wind, of the dust, the mist and the dew. They declared the fatigue of a half-night's journey was intolerable, and often they would throw themselves into the shadow of a rock, pitiably sighing forth the words : " Mayyat laymun "—lemonade. After their first day's ride they turned black with sunburn, and one, perhaps the most inventive, fashioned an umbrella of leaves fastened to a long stick, which he kept strictly for his own convenience. The mares, soft and lazy as their masters, dropped their plates, and after the second day half of them fell lame. Altogether a curious experience of a race lauded in books of travel as singularly brave, temperate and moral, and whose religion is supposed to be unusually pure and advanced.

There was indeed no reason to remember the Druses of Shakkah with affection, for worse remains to be told. Kaba-lan did not lose much time in meditation. The day our party left Tayma he sent an emissary to the Ruhvah valley, mustered the Bedawin, and proceeded on the Englishmen's track. Fortunately, the latter discovered his treachery in time, adopted the tactics of hunted animals, and so saved their lives. The story runs as follows :

Burton, Drake and Palmer, with their uncomfortable crew of followers, started June 2nd on the tour already mentioned. A stiff sirocco was blowing, blurring the outlines of the far highlands ; clouds appeared to the north-east and north-west, and a distant rag or two of rain trailed upon the head of Jebel Duruz Hauran. After a good breakfast our party rode north-eastwards, amidst a scene wild enough to please a wizard. Lava torrents showed volcanic dykes, secondary craters, and blow-holes with barrows arbitrarily disposed at all angles. Stone heaps were placed as landmarks, and there were not a few graves. Some hares and a lizard or two darted away from the strangers ; men there were none. By the afternoon the cavalcade slowly ascended a hill-brow, whence they had their first view of the Safá, a volcanic block with seven main summits. A deeper blackness made it stand out from the gloomy plain, which seemed a rolling waste of dark basalt. But, in the far distance, extending from east to south-east, and raised by refraction from the middle ground which lay beyond and below the rolling volcanic foreground, glittered the sunlit horizon of the Euphrates desert.

It was interesting enough to rivet a stranger's attention, but, like many old travellers, Burton's eyes were everywhere. Amongst numerous half-effaced footmarks of sheep, goats, and shod horses appeared the fresh hoofprints of a dromedary. The rider was evidently bound for the north-eastern regions, where the Bedawin dwelt ; and our three wise men gave the ill-omened footprints all the significance they deserved. Existing plans had to be altered then and there, and the escort kept in profound ignorance of the route.

Not that any work was to be neglected. No indi-

vidual of that plucky trio had the slightest intention of
returning to Damascus until he had seen and done what
he went to see and do. This coolness seems marvellous
even to one familiar with Burton's feats of valour, and
with the noble heroism of the man murdered in the Wady
Sudr while striving to serve his country. That all three
explorers *were* perfectly cool is proved by Burton's minute
description of the hideous volcanic region through which
the party were riding—a landscape spoiled and broken to
pieces, blistered, wrinkled, broken-backed and otherwise
tormented; here ghastly white, there gloomiest black, and
scorching beneath the sun of a Syrian June. The aneroid
was duly corrected, the thermometer noted, the tape used,
all as leisurely as though no foe were on the track, no
mortal danger threatening of a cruel death should that foe
succeed in running down his prey. Physical disagreeables
also abounded. The road became simply a goat-path over
domes of cast-iron ovens in endless succession; the escort
wasted so much water that the masters had to go without;
and lastly, a furious gale arose, which filled the air with
acid, pungent dust, obscured all landmarks, and delayed
the little company several hours on their way.

However, pushing on in spite of all obstacles, they
succeeded in reaching the cave at Umm Nirán, a mysterious cavern occupying the eastern slope of a rounded
bubble of basalt, which opens with a natural arch of trap.
The hottest weather fails to dry this curious tunnelled
reservoir, which has evidently been enlarged by man,
possibly by one of the olden kings of Damascus. Burton,
regardless of the Jann supposed to haunt the spot for the
benevolent purpose of driving thirsty strangers out of their
wits, scrambled in on all fours, and reached the water in
about three minutes. The supply was sweet, and cool
enough to depress the immersed thermometer from 74° in
the air to 71°. The atmosphere of the place, which by the
way was tenanted only by a water-scorpion, felt close and

dank; and whilst the roof was an arid, fiery waste of the blackest lava, the basalt ceiling of the cave sweated and dripped incessantly. The taped length of this tank was 140 feet; according to the Arabs, it is supplied by springs as well as rain—probable enough, as all above the cave was dry as the Land of Sind, and, during summer sunshine, the hand cannot rest upon the heated surface.

After a comfortable bath our travellers passed the night in the open air, and made next morning for an extinct volcano in the neighbourhood, Umm el-Ma'azah. Thence they visited the so-called lakes, which at that moment contained no water. But now the party had to turn their attention towards the preservation of their lives. In one of the most dangerous spots, significantly named the Road of Razzias, the Druse escort suddenly became unwilling to proceed. A palaver was held. Every attempt was made to find out the Englishmen's plans, and, of course, all failed. During the night mares and men, with but one exception, disappeared.

Truly it was time to get home. Next day brought this desert excursion to an end. A gallop over the plain of thirty miles placed our heroes in safety, but not an hour too soon. The Bedawin had tracked them at last, missed them at the Umm Nirán by the merest chance, and had our party not ridden hard for their lives, must have speedily overtaken them. By peculiar good fortune Burton and his friends escaped from a murderous crew of ruffians numbering eighty to a hundred horsemen and some two hundred dromedary riders. His remarks thereupon are characteristic:

" I duly appreciated the compliment—can any unintentional flattery be more sincere?—of sending three hundred men to dispose of three. Our zigzag path had saved us from the *royaume des taupes*, for these men were not sent to plunder. The felon act, however, failed; and our fifteen days of wandering ended without accident."

In March Burton found time for a visit to Jerusalem. He travelled by land with his two friends, there being much they wished to do by the way, but he sent his wife by sea as the safer route. The Holy Week, which fell rather late that year, is not the best time for studying the topography and antiquities of this interesting city, especially if the complicated ceremonies of Latin and Greek, Armenian and Copt—some lasting throughout the night, and none of them worth seeing—must be attended. However, in this case there was a division of labour ; the wife went to the interminable services, while the husband worked equally hard in his own fashion. Assisted not only by Messrs. Drake and Palmer, but by Captain (now Sir Charles) Warren, and Clermont Ganneau, an Orientalist whose laborious studies were striking out a path beyond and beside older investigations, our sturdy Deist set himself to determine some of the more celebrated historical sites with almost boyish enthusiasm. Want of space forbids my enumerating more than a few of the changes then proposed in the topography of Jerusalem and its environs by these five clever men—changes rendered inevitable by the rapid increase of knowledge characteristic of our century.

According to Clermont Ganneau the Temple occupied not the south-western angle, the centre and the northern part, nor yet the southern portion, but the whole of the present Haram Enclosure, extending to the Birkat Israil. In this view he has been followed by Conder, who deemed it most improbable that any architect would neglect the obvious advantage of the summit of a hill for an uneasy slope ; or depart from the universal custom of selecting the highest ground for temple, fort, or city. The Pool of Bethesda he declared to be not the traditional Birkat Israil, but an underground piscina lately discovered within the *enceinte* of Sta. Anna ; this was verified in 1888 by Schick, who found the remains of the substructure. The Ecce Homo arch all five men recognised as of the Ælia

Capitolina period, erected probably in commemoration of the decisive victory over Bar Cochebas, and the third systematic destruction of the city. The young Frenchman further pointed out that the Tombs of the Kings—which must be sought for about Sion, the city of David, and thence to Siloam—are a monument of the later Asmoneans; while the curious crypt, popularly known as the Tombs of the Prophets, is merely the remains of an old Christian cemetery attached to one of the numerous monasteries founded upon the Mount of Olives. This last he proved by showing crosses over the loculi, and by a dozen or so of Greek *graphitæ*, mostly proper names of men and women, and belonging to a period as far back as the first year of official Christianity, that is to say, not far from Constantine. The so-called Holy Sepulchre he claimed as the " Monument of the High Priest," the fifth after the return from the Captivity, popularly known as John, son of Judas, but called in Nehemiah (xii., 2) Jonathan, son of Joiada. Needless, perhaps, to add that all agreed that every trace of the site of the rock tomb of Joseph of Arimathæa is utterly lost; even in the fourth century no reliable tradition concerning its position existed.

Clermont Ganneau also made sundry interesting discoveries in some enormous quarries near the city, known as the Royal Caverns. The entrance, not far from the gate of Damascus, looked like a mere hole in the wall; creeping through, a stranger found himself in endless artificial caves and galleries, most of them unexplored. By means of the magnesium light, for candles and matches were almost useless, Ganneau perceived a branch on the right, displaying characteristic traces of human labours, rock-rings for hanging lamps, and a very ancient stone-picture representing the man-headed, bearded, and winged Assyrian bull.

No *contretemps* seems to have marred Burton's stay at Jerusalem. He evidently enjoyed it keenly, and, save for the noise and confusion caused by the pilgrims, his visit was happily timed. He could inspect in person the able and honest labours of Wilson and Warren; he was delighted with the learning and originality of Clermont Ganneau, and during the whole of his sojourn he was able to enjoy the society of Drake and Palmer, men who shared his views and feelings, and with whom he could always work in perfect accord.

Leaving the fascinating city with much regret, not only for its own sake, but for that of the friends it harboured, husband and wife proceeded to Bethlehem, Jericho, the Dead Sea, in short, to most places of interest in Palestine. All went smoothly until they arrived at Nazareth, where they were joined by Tyrwhitt Drake. Here, strangely enough, a wretched village *fracas* proved the commencement of a run of ill-luck which culminated in the loss of our traveller's appointment, August 15th, 1871.

The Burtons and their followers, with two other parties, composed of Americans and Germans, had camped for the night in a grassy plain outside Nazareth, close to the Greek Orthodox church. Early next morning, a Copt who happened to be prowling about, bent on mischief, entered Isabel's tent, probably to extort money. She called for assistance, and he was promptly expelled by her servants. Unfortunately, just as the squabble was at its height, the Greek congregation filed out from their devotions, and, seeing a row, could not resist joining therein, of course taking the part of the Copt against the strangers. Matters soon began to look ugly, for Burton's followers numbered but six, while the assailants mustered about one hundred and fifty. The two Englishmen had rushed half dressed from their tents at the first alarm, and done everything in their power to soothe and calm the excited mob. Vainly: they were received with a shower of stones so dense as to darken the very air. A rich and respected Greek, carried away by fury and fanaticism, shouted, " Kill them all, kill them all ; I will pay the blood money ! " Burton's muleteer, in terror of annihilation, yelled in reply, " Shame, shame ! this is the English Consul at Damascus, and he is on his own ground." Further speech was smothered in the uproar, the fight waxed more furious, three of our traveller's servants were badly hurt, he was hit repeatedly, his sword arm injured, and although he stood perfectly calm, marking out the ring-leaders to arrest them later, he saw the odds were too great to contend against much longer. Pulling a pistol from his belt, he fired in the air as a signal for aid to the neighbouring camps. Happily, it was promptly responded to, and the white-livered ruffians turned and fled.

For this outrage no redress whatever could be obtained. The Greeks, with the mendacity so characteristic of their nation, declared it was not they who began the quarrel, a most improbable story, considering their superior num-bers. Worse still, a scandalous report of the affair was forwarded to Damascus, Beirut and Constantinople, signed and sealed by their bishop. This prelate, who was clearly not one of those excellent ecclesiastics who make our Tractarian clergy yearn for reunion with the Eastern churches, had been for some time past on unfriendly terms with the English Consul. He had purchased from the Turkish authorities a synagogue and cemetery which for the last four hundred years had belonged to the Jews of Tiberias, some of them British protected subjects; and the trans-action being a fraudulent one, Burton had been forced to protest against it, drawing thereby upon his devoted head the wrath of Monseigneur Niffon and his Orthodox congregations. Bishop and flock vied with each other in spreading abroad the most mischievous tales how the Consul and his party had directed a regular *fusillade* at harmless worshippers, ignoring the fact that not one pious soul could boast of a wound—how Burton and his wife had rushed into their church and torn down the pictures, finishing up with a "*pas de deux*" in the sacred building; in short, such a tissue of lies, that at last our ambassador at Constantinople telegraphed to know what it all meant. Apparently a trumpery squabble, it excited an enormous amount of dormant ill-feeling, and so proved the straw that shows the wind.

Nearly two years had passed away since our traveller's arrival in Syria. The time had been spent in able and honest work, work which exactly suited the man. His post required the exercise of constant vigilance and attention to the strangest variety of interests, while it allowed him occasional leisure for exploration and discovery. He was as happy as a man generally is when in his right place, and in after days he used to say the twenty-three months spent in Syria were amongst the pleasantest of his life. Most improbable, then, does it seem that he endangered his tenure of this valuable appointment by any unpopular act not absolutely necessary. Duty must be done; this he never shirked; but we know from his writings, from the testimony of his best friends, that his idea of duty was simple, straightforward, and utterly free from the slightest taint of fanaticism. I hope my readers will follow me attentively through the next few pages. The true cause of the terrible crash in August, 1871, the recall which was little better than temporary disgrace, has to be patiently sifted from a mass of nonsense and misrepresentation, and even from the minor agents which, unhappily, all more or less contributed to bring about the disastrous issue.

Certainly, he had made enemies of sundry Jew money-lenders. Not, as has been falsely stated, of the whole Jewish community—his behaviour in the matter of the cemetery and synagogue unjustly acquired by Bishop Niffon proves that; but there had been trouble with the usurers. In 1870-71, anybody having the smallest pretension to be called English could obtain a sort of official recognition, and rank thenceforth as a British subject, amenable only to the authority of the consular courts. The persons thus protected numbered forty-eight, and the majority do not appear to have abused their privileges. Three, however, were Jews, of whom Shylock was the prototype. When Burton arrived, one of this trio interviewed him without loss of time, and announced that he had three hundred cases of debt, amounting in all to nearly sixty thousand pounds, for the Consul to deal with at once.

Burton's reply was characteristic: " Sir, you had better hire a consul for yourself alone; I was not sent here as a bailiff, to tap the peasant on the shoulder in such matters as yours."

He soon discovered that the ignorant Syrian peasants were being ruined by hundreds. One poor wretch, ninety years old, had been imprisoned throughout an entire winter because he could not afford a napoleon; young men were thrown into jail for sums so inordinately increased by interest and compound interest, that it was impossible to repay even half; and, in some cases, whole villages were being sucked dry by these detestable vampires. No honest man could by any possibility aid or abet so crying an evil; consequently the money-lenders, furious because they received no assistance in their nefarious practices, wrote bitter complaints of their Consul to sundry leading Jewish families in England. And, enemies being usually more active than friends, the Hebrews whose part Burton had conscientiously espoused in the Niffon affair unfortunately remained silent.

Then arose a missionary trouble. An enthusiastic, self-ordained evangelical preacher, who, by the way, had not taken the precaution to master Arabic before expounding his version of the Gospel, and therefore pathetically entreated his hearers to lift up their dog unto the Lord, for a broken and contrite dog He would not despise,[1] insisted upon distributing Testaments and tracts in the

---

[1] Kalb—heart, kelb—dog.

bazaar, calling meanwhile upon the Moslems to forsake
Mohammed and be baptized. This rant amongst an in-
flammable population like the Damascenes could not be
allowed to continue. The regularly appointed missionaries
were most cautious in their methods of conducting their
labours, and lived on friendly terms not only with their
broad-minded Consul, but with the other Christian sects
and the irritable, intolerant Turks. The volunteer in
question was, to put the matter gently, a fanatic. " I
should glory in martyrdom," he announced when Burton
remonstrated with him.

" But we should not, nor would the many thousand
Greek and Roman Catholics that inhabit the neighbourhood," returned the Consul, who then and there took
measures to prevent a repetition of these zealous though
somewhat halting utterances. And he was only just in
time to save the man from insult or imprisonment, for the
matter having reached the ears of the acting Turkish
governor, that redoubtable official immediately ordered all
the books to be seized and burnt in the market-place.
Burton again exerted his authority, this time to prevent
the ignominious cremation; but the disappointed aspirant
to palm and crown, so far from being grateful for receiving
back his treasures intact, left Syria furious, and on reaching
London, loudly proclaimed his wrongs.

Although, besides the usurers and the irregular prose-
lytisers, Burton had an enemy in his Consul-General, who
preferred an easier life with a more commonplace associate,
I do not believe any one of these troubles was the true
cause of his recall. But on carefully reading the endless
papers and correspondence connected therewith, I find a
very curious circumstance. For the first time in his life
Burton was not on thoroughly friendly terms with the
Moslems. The Governor-General of Syria had become an
inveterate foe, and we hear of other annoyances connected
with men of a faith who formerly hailed him as a brother.

This will be explained by a strange story in his wife's memoirs. As related in her usual hazy fashion, when facts are concerned, three parts mirages of her own imagination, it seems at first fairly bewildering. Burton posing as a missionary, self-ordained like the Stiggins he had so lately snubbed! A marvellous tale indeed : let me try to make it intelligible.

During Isabel's stay at Damascus, a sort of religious intrigue amongst a sect of Mohammedans called the Sházlis was going on in the lower quarter of the town known as the Maydan. To entitle the movement a Christian revival would be exaggeration; it appeared rather a sort of hysterical, superstitious outburst, to which uneducated people of all nationalities are occasionally subject, and which is powerfully stimulated by the certainty of opposition. Stories like those of Lourdes, visions and revelations unutterable, were whispered from mouth to mouth; the seers worked themselves into a state of somewhat noisy exaltation, and before long a Roman Catholic priest of Teutonic origin appeared on the scene, to distribute crucifixes and devotional manuals amongst the enthusiasts. The latter soon numbered two hundred and fifty, held regular meetings in each others' houses, and at last publicly announced they were yearning for baptism and formal admission into the Church of Rome. Meanwhile, legends of the appearance of Isa bin Maryam in the suburbs of Damascus,[1] and accounts of the extraordinary behaviour of the neophytes, ended by attracting the by no means friendly attention of the Moslem authorities. Great was the consternation of the Ulema, or learned men, on hearing of heresy rapidly spreading in their midst ; and many a session did they hold in order to discuss what steps to take in such a strange and unusual dilemma. The sequel may be easily guessed. We are all aware that Moslems

---

[1] The second coming of Christ is to take place at Damascus, but Antichrist, or Dajsal, has to come first

are not noted for toleration towards their renegades ; a
number of the poor deluded wretches were arrested, and,
although nothing was known for certain as regards the
means adopted to make them acknowledge the error of
their ways, it was but too probable they were not over
tenderly dealt with.

Now this was a matter which in no way concerned our
Consul. Not a single English or Scotch clergyman was
mixed up in it, merely a German Roman Catholic priest.
There was already more than enough to do in protecting
the Protestant missions, the schools, the lives and property
of British subjects, without interfering with the religious
squabbles of the Turks. And Burton, who, in common
with his friend Drake, had the lowest opinion of Syrian
Christians, priest-ridden, steeped in superstition to such a
degree that they are the most arrant cowards in creation,
was about as likely to assist in increasing their numbers as
to join in a Shakers' dance.

But he reckoned without his wife. Isabel, anxious to
convert the Moslems by latter-day miracles as she had been
to Romanize his Majesty of Dahomey with her magic
lantern, threw herself open-armed into this revival. She
offered to stand sponsor to the two hundred and fifty 'verts
en masse, and she confessed to baptizing every dying person
she could get hold of. And while her husband, continually
absent exploring or attending to the duties of his consulate,
knew nothing, or next to nothing, about her dangerous proceedings, she impressed upon the people the belief that she
acted with his full permission and approval. All natural
enough. A zealous admirer and follower of Ignatius
Loyola (Isabel never made any secret of her Jesuitical
proclivities) could not be expected to resist the temptation of so wholesale a conversion—from her mortal enemy,
too, El-Islam. For she particularly disliked this creed,
partly from jealously of her husband's partiality, in contra-
distinction to his utter contempt for that of Rome ; and

partly on account of the sanction it gives to polygamy, an Old Testament practice of which Burton never seems to have thoroughly disapproved. We cannot be surprised at the terrible blunder she committed, but that it was a blunder, and a fatal one, there remains very little doubt. Enemies a man like Richard Burton could not fail to make, but he could hold his own against them; when he had to grapple with those made by his wife, he was overpowered.

So his good friends, the Moslems, gave him the cold shoulder. Doubtless they blamed Haji Abdullah's solitary spouse, for they behaved with singular moderation. Still, disagreeable reports got abroad of a probable attempt to assassinate him, and before long a warning reached the Foreign Office that, owing to Turkish fanaticism, the Consul's life was in danger. This, after so many other disagreeable reports, proved the last straw. Disputes with the Jews, the Greek bishop, and others, mattered little; but the English Consul must keep friends with the rulers of Syria. Can we blame the Foreign Office? Significant enough it is to any unprejudiced reader that the next appointment was in a Roman Catholic country.

The manner of the recall seems to have been unnecessarily harsh. Burton and his almost inseparable companion, Tyrwhitt Drake, were just setting off for a ride over the hills about B'ludan, little dreaming how never again would they wander together over the slopes of Lebanon, when a ragged messenger slipped a note into the former's hand. It proved to be from Mr. Kirby Green of Beirut, and it contained the startling intelligence that, by order of the Consul-General, he had arrived the previous day, August 15th, and taken over the Damascus appointment.

Hardly believing the evidence of their senses, the two friends leapt into their saddles and galloped into town without drawing rein. They found their worst fears realised. The post which Burton had been so proud of, the post he had worked to retain with unblemished honour, was not only taken from him, but already filled up. On the 19th, all hope having vanished of any mistake in the orders received from home, he sent a message to his wife : "I am superseded. Pay, pack and follow at convenience;" and then with an aching heart he started for Beirut to embark for England.

A cruel blow, one that required a strong brain to bear without reeling. At fifty years of age to be dismissed like some worthless domestic, without even a day's warning. The step may have been necessary—indeed, viewing it through the softening haze of five-and-twenty years, I think it was necessary. But so honest, so erudite, so heroic a servant of the Crown, should have been more tenderly dealt with in circumstances peculiarly cruel and distressing.

CHAPTER XV

LION-HEARTED though Burton was, the shock of this sudden recall told upon him cruelly. On landing in England he came at once to us at Norwood, and remained until his wife's return from Syria. My father had lately held civil and military appointments in Canada, so we had not seen our wanderer for several years. The pleasure of our long-deferred meeting was sadly spoilt by his dejected, heart-broken mood, a state of things we were quite unprepared for, as he had travelled so rapidly that he had not thought it worth while to write—in fact, a letter would have arrived the same time as himself. Never had we known him so wretched, so unnerved; his hands shook, his temper was strangely irritable, all that appreciation of fun and humour which rendered him such a cheery companion to old and young alike had vanished. He could settle to nothing; he was restless, but would not leave the house; ailing, but would take no advice—it was indeed a melancholy spectacle.

Natural enough! He was feeling not merely the loss of what we younger members of the family called a "beggarly Consulate" (our opinion of a Consul then tallied with Lady Augusta's in Charles Lever's novel), but he knew that, thanks to his wife's imprudence and passion for proselytizing, all further promotion was hopeless—Morocco, Constantinople would never be for him; his career was blighted. All this he saw at the time, and it proved only too true; but as the days went by his marvellously sanguine disposition reasserted itself, and, as his sister used to say, made him expect not only improbabilities, but impossibilities.

Presently Isabel arrived in London with the enormous amount of baggage the Burtons usually carried about with them, plus a pretty but useless Syrian maid. The books alone occupied a dozen cases, and curiosities of every description filled one large room. Her husband then left us for Montague Place, where the father and mother-in-law were still living (the latter had come to regard him as a necessary evil); but before he went we arranged to spend part of the following year together in Edinburgh. Prior to his sudden return from Syria, we had thought of passing twelve months in Scotland ; and as soon as we found he would enjoy the change, and seemed quite cheered up by the prospect of a visit to the northern capital, we departed to search for comfortable quarters in that romantic but fearfully cold and gusty town.

When Burton had recovered his spirits a little, he commenced a correspondence with the Foreign Office on the subject of his sudden removal from his Eastern post. He obtained, however, no satisfactory answer. He was in no way blamed, but the true cause of his recall was kept secret. The Press, which knew little or nothing of the attempt to convert the Shazlis, mostly blamed the Government for its rigorous treatment of so gifted a servant. But Lord Granville persisted in evading the main question, bided his time, and finally presented our luckless Benedict with a berth which ensured for the donor freedom from incessant complaints, and for the receiver a whole skin.

Unfortunately, a year elapsed between the two appointments, and a very lean year it proved to the Burtons. Neither, it may be remembered, was remarkable for economy; but Isabel, who held the purse-strings, used to get quite indignant when reminded of the duty of providing against rainy days.[1] However, unlike La Fontaine's Cigale,

---

[1] Burton left the management of his pecuniary affairs to his wife in order to have more time for study, but this arrangement worked so badly that at his death only a few florins remained out of £12,000 recently paid him for the " Arabian Nights."

she was not allowed to want. Each side of the family possessed its wealthy member, and the individuals in question, being as generous as they were rich, came to the assistance of our imprudent pair. A little ready money was, indeed, all they really required, as there was no necessity for housekeeping, that bane of small incomes, for the wife and her Syrian maid, who, by the way, became about as unpleasant in her line as Allahdad had become in his, lived with the Henry Arundells, while her husband paid long visits to old friends, and had his brother and sister's home always open to him.

Twice he stayed with us in Edinburgh. The first time was in February, and we were delighted to see that the Damascus trouble, which we feared had almost mortally wounded him, was skinning over. No one could have in a higher degree the invaluable form of common-sense which enables its possessor to speedily reconcile himself to the inevitable. The cherished appointment was irretrievably lost, but he had grieved long enough, and now it was time to turn his thoughts to some more profitable matter. A gleam of sunshine too had appeared after the storm. While racking his brains to find out how to keep himself and his wife until he was again employed, he had met a Mr. Lock, who was on the look out for a trusty emissary to report on some sulphur beds in Iceland. Mr. Lock had just obtained from the Danish Government the right of working the mines of Myvatn in the northern portion of the island, and he was anxious to know if this could be done with any certainty of profit. Passage-money, all expense of outfit, would be paid any way, and a big fee besides, if the property realised expectations. Burton, who had long been anxious to visit Ultima Thule, agreed with alacrity to undertake the survey; and, as Granton was his starting point, he spent part of his first visit in making preparations for the trip, and prolonged the second to his departure in June.

By May he was quite himself again, and seemed thoroughly to enjoy life. Many a walk did we take together down Princes Street and up Arthur's Seat ; and well I remember him swinging along in his grey ulster and high-crowned soft felt hat. Every trifle was noted by his keen eyes, and he appeared just as well amused while climbing the solitary hill with his sister and nieces as in the busy street where his friends were constantly exchanging greetings or stopping him for a chat. Seldom have I seen him better pleased with any place than with Edinburgh. In spite of its unattractive climate, he liked the town, the bracing air corrected a tendency to liver troubles, and he was flattered by the kindness and hospitality with which he was received. The 93rd Highlanders, stationed at the Castle, entertained in genuine Highland fashion ; and at our house he met most of the leading Scotch families who happened to be lingering in the northern capital. Lord Airlie was High Commissioner that year, and he and his handsome wife rendered the receptions at Holyrood even more popular than usual ; those romantic evenings when the grim old palace presents for the nonce so bright and picturesque a scene—women in their smartest gowns, men wearing their medals and ribands. Burton, while his brother-in-law donned his red collar and cross and star of the Bath, looked almost conspicuous in unadorned simplicity. The K.C.M.G. was given to him nearly fifteen years later.

We long looked back to these two visits. It was such a pleasure to know that his exuberant vitality had triumphed over his misfortunes. No doubt the complete freedom from any domestic worry helped not a little in the cure. Thoroughly contented, he was again able to sympathise with the pursuits and interests of every one of us, not neglecting even the family pets. Of course, his stay, like most of life's pleasant interludes, seemed far too short both to him and to ourselves ; and, as usual when he said good-bye, his hands turned cold and his eyes filled with tears. Only his brother-in-law was permitted to see him off. Such an amount of feeling was especially touching on the occasion in question, as this tour, which he was looking forward to with intense interest, was his first treat in the travelling line since the Damascus crash.

The somewhat uninteresting nature of the undertaking forbids a detailed account of Burton's visit to Iceland. Besides, that small white spot in the Arctic Sea, verging on the desolation of Greenland and lacking the grandeur of Nature in Norway, is now well-trodden ground ; and while travellers or students would do well to study " Ultima Thule," the general reader might resent too copious quotations from these erudite tomes.[1]   But the first impressions of such a man on viewing the stock sights are well worth recording, for Burton always insisted upon writing of things as they are, not as magnified or bedaubed by fancy.   If all travellers had been as truthful, how much less we should have to unlearn !

Thanks to the simple school-books of our early years, we were accustomed to draw for ourselves a delightfully exciting picture of Ultima Thule.   Even in more erudite and more recently published works, Burton suspected the colours were laid on too lavishly ; on arriving in the country he found the "touching up" had been even more audacious than he imagined.   " Giddy, rapid rivers " proved only three feet deep, "stupendous precipices" mere slopes, which the Icelandic ponies scaled with ease ; perils from Polar bears rather perils *to* the starved, numbed quadrupeds in question, which could hardly run away from the sportsman's gun.   The Hecla of our ingenuous childhood, a pillar of heaven upon whose dreadful summit white, black and sanguine red lay in streaks and blotches, with volumes of sooty smoke and lurid flames ascending skywards, is in

---

[1] Published by Nimmo, 2 vols., 1875.

sober reality a commonplace heap half the height of Hermon, rising detached from the plains, a pair of white patches representing its " eternal snows." Most disappointing of all were the Geysers : the Great Geyser merely hiccupped, the Strokkr required a full hour's poking up before it would treat the spectators to the tamest of displays, and the Little Geyser declined to give the slightest sign of its existence. No wonder our traveller dubbed them gross humbugs, adding, " if their decline continues so rapidly, in a few years there will be nothing left save a vulgar solfatarra." As to the " midnight sun," its rays had to be excluded from his uncurtained bedchamber by his landlady's flannel petticoat, a garment she kindly parted with for that purpose.

Still, though the wonders had been exaggerated, Burton, with his usual fairness, allowed there was much to see and to enjoy in Iceland. Mild east winds prevailed at Reykjavik ; after July 11th the sky was cloudless for a whole fortnight. The peculiar charms of the island, and it has peculiar charms, grew upon him. During such delightful weather there is much to admire in the rich meads and leas stretching to meet the light blue waves ; in the fretted and angular outlines of the caverned hills ; in the towering walls of huge horizontal steps which define the Fjords ; and in the immense vista of silvery cupolas and snow-capped mulls, which blend and melt with ravishing reflections of ethereal pink, blue and lilac into the grey and neutral tints of the horizon. There is grandeur, too, when the storm-fiend rides abroad amid the howl of gales, the rush of torrents, the roar of waterfalls, when the sea appears of cast-iron, when the sky is charged with rolling clouds torn to shreds as they meet in aërial conflict, when grim mists stalk over the lowlands, and when the tall peaks, parted by gloomy chasms, stand like ghostly hills in the shadowy realm. And often there is the most picturesque of contrasts : summer basking below, and winter raging above ; peace brooding upon the vale, and elemental war doing fierce battle upon the eternal snows and ice of the upper world.

Of course Burton did not spend much time in criticism and contemplation. Thoroughly equipped for work, he did work. His costume on occasions appears to have been more comfortable than beautiful. During his stay in Edinburgh, he had provided himself at Messrs. Hunter and Macdonald's with sou'westers at 2s. each, outer and inner hose at 3s. 6d., sailors' trousers for 10s., stout oil-cloth coats at 18s. 6d., and warm mittens, perhaps not quite so smart as those knitted by our Dorcases for Deep Sea fishermen, at 1s. 3d. Nothing could have proved more suitable for his many boating trips, or for fording the rivers. In spite of frequent drenchings and sudden changes of temperature, he never once caught cold. At times he rode the Iceland ponies, and was well satisfied with their agility, strength, and sure-footedness. Not a day was wasted. Every morning found him exploring either on foot, pony-back, or in a boat coasting about the island.

Foremost came the business on which he had been sent. To familiarise himself with the subject he first visited Husuvik, a port only ten miles distant from the mines of Krisuvik, then in full work. Having carefully surveyed these, he made his way, accompanied by the Messrs. Lock, a small party of workmen and nineteen ponies, to Myvatn, the concession he had to report upon. Various incidents enlivened the march. At one village where they halted the people were holding a fair, and were mostly in the state politely called excited. Mr. Lock, senior, had a narrow escape from a hideous matron, snuffy as our great grand-mothers, who tried to kiss him. Near Hrossaborg it was the sand that proved too lively. A dozen columns were careering at once over the plains, although rain had fallen during three days. One of these curious whirlwind bolts struck the caravan, but, unlike the powerful Shaytan of the

Arabian wilds, it did not even remove a hat. The journey ended pleasantly enough save for the loss of a carpet-bag or two and the disappearance of a homesick pony.

Three days were spent at the Solfatarras of Myvatn, lodgings being found at the house of a farmer whose alacrity in composing a bill of charges had won a wide reputation. It was not pretty scenery save to a capitalist's eye—a speckled slope of yellow splotches set in dark red and chocolate-coloured bolus, here and there covered with brown gravel, all fuming and puffing, and making the tender-hued Icelandic flora look dingy as a Sierra Leone mulatto. Burton worked hard. On one surveying expedition food, liquor, tobacco, all ran short; and after an eight hours' ride he regained his quarters with feet so numbed that he feared a case of frostbite. Pretty strong remedies were immediately applied, but it was not until morning that his circulation was restored.

As regards the results of the survey, the mass of mineral was enormous, and the reproductive process, which occupies a period of thirty years in Italian mines, is produced within three in those of Iceland. In short, the speculation seemed a very promising one. At that time nearly all the sulphur for Europe and America was drawn from Sicily; and Iceland being much nearer, and the chance of her ports being blockaded in case of war much slighter, it seemed well worth while to seek a new source of supply. But the scheme ultimately collapsed. The difficulties of transport, the vile climate, the countless obstacles that always hinder the establishment of a new industry proved too much even for British pluck and patience. And now, since Clarke's process, patented in 1888, enables us to make our sulphur from the refuse of soda manufactories, we hear no more about the mines of Iceland.

The speculation was unsuccessful; but the work had proved a veritable boon to our traveller. It had filled a dreary gap in his life—given him a fresh interest. The bracing summer marvellously benefited his health, and when on September 1st he embarked for England, he looked at least fifteen years younger.

At home a piece of good luck awaited him, all the pleasanter because long deferred. Some of his friends, dreading the effect that the misrepresentations of so many enemies might produce on the Foreign Office, feared he might either never be employed again, or else be offered some post so small and ill-paid as to seem hardly worth his acceptance. Lord Granville, however, was far too just and clear-sighted to make any such blunder. As I have already said, he waited until a good berth fell vacant, and on Charles Lever's death at Trieste, appointed Burton Consul in his stead.

As consulates go, Trieste was not to be despised. The emoluments amounted to £600 a year, besides £100 office allowance, and there was a vice-consul. It was unsuitable in some respects; a third class seaport seemed hardly the right place for a scholar who spoke twenty-nine languages, not including dialects, a man who occupied the proud position of premier linguist in Europe. *Ma che fare!* There were many advantages: the duties were light, the leave was unlimited, Isabel could convert whom she pleased; indeed, she tells us in print that she stood sponsor to a housebreaker. Naturally, at first we felt it hard that he should be condemned for life to dull, prosy office work, which anyone not absolutely idiotic could do as well; but now, on looking back dispassionately, I can but think that the enormous amount of liberty accorded him during those eighteen years proves that Lord Granville, far from bearing any ill-will against the luckless Haji, made up for the harshness of the recall by providing him for the rest of his days with what was practically a sinecure.

Trieste is not one's beau ideal of a home. Foreign towns rarely reach that level. Like many such cities, it presents a fair appearance from afar, a foul one on close

inspection.   Its death rate is at times appalling, and little
wonder.   During the winter the Bora pours down from the
north, bitterly cold, and sometimes so violent that the
quays have to be roped to save people from being blown
into the sea.   Cabs and horses have been upset, a train
has been overturned, and an English engineer was once
suddenly hurled into a ship's hold by this aggressive blast.
The summers are hot and debilitating, while, to add to the
unwholesomeness of the place, the Citta Vecchia, dating
from the days of Strabo, is unutterably filthy, a veritable
focus of infection, as its drainage, flowing into the harbour,
is wafted inland by the sirocco, and spreads around odours
which would have sickened Cloaçina herself.

Such as it was, the Burtons had to make the best of it.
Their earlier home was a flat, airily situated in a tall block
of buildings close to the sea.   It had one merit, for it was
perched so high that the smells failed to reach it.   At first
Isabel contented herself with ten rooms, but after a time
insisted upon twenty-seven.   Burton's own private apartments—he was too busy a man not to require a den to
himself—were gay with Oriental hangings, brass trays and
goblets, chibouques with great amber mouthpieces.   Signs
of the Crescent reigned paramount, crucifixes, madonnas,
relics, and so forth being strictly relegated to his wife's
side of the flat.   Glittering daggers and curious sabres hung
on the walls, and the favourites amongst his eight thousand
volumes were neatly ranged in plain deal bookcases in his
sanctum sanctorum.   Thermometer, aneroid, every kind of
scientific instrument, had each a little place of its own;
while clocks and watches, which, like most punctual men,
he delighted in, ticked cheek by jowl.   The office was in
the heart of the town, whither Jack Tar after a spree could
easily find his Consul, and where the Consul, if necessary,
could confer with his good-natured colleague, Mr. Brock.

Life at Trieste was simple and regular.   Burton rose
about 5 a.m., studied until noon, strolled from his rooms to

the fencing-school, thence to his Consulate. By evening he required a little relaxation; and not being of the tame-cat species, addicted to his own armchair in his own chimney-corner, he and his wife used to dine with a party of friends at the Hôtel de Ville, where they could obtain a fair dinner and a pint of country wine for a florin and a half.

So much for their town existence. But no lover of pure air could hope to remain well for long in a place which numbered as many stenches as far-famed Cologne. While exploring the neighbourhood, Burton pitched upon summer quarters, whither he could repair for hygienic surroundings. Opçina, the sanatorium in question, is one hour from, and twelve hundred feet above, Trieste. The visitor can drive all the way along a good road, and after his very moderate exertion be rewarded by a lovely view of the town, the sea, and all the picturesque points of land. Fairly good accommodation is afforded by an old-fashioned village inn, where the Burtons hired rooms by the year, and stayed for periods ranging from three days to a month, whenever their health required a change. This *pied à terre* proved most convenient; for the surrounding Castellieri—prehistoric remains, supposed to be Celtic—are eminently interesting to scholars and antiquarians; in fact, every spot of ground within a hundred miles of Opçina soon became familiar to our indefatigable traveller. Of Trieste he made a most careful study, as well as of the province of Istria, describing, in what he modestly called "a little guide-book," the ruins of the Roman Temple, Jupiter Capitolinus, the classical Arco di Riccardo (Richard of England, who was never there), the remnants of the Roman theatre and aqueduct in the old town, and the two Museums with their contents.

The Burtons often went further afield. Sometimes they would cross over to Venice, or pay a short visit to the fascinating Austrian capital. Certainly some of these trips were rather costly, the hotel bill during the Great Exhibition at Vienna amounting to £163 for only three weeks! Little cared they. Several legacies fell in about that time, and paid for many a tour. One especially interesting excursion was to Italy, the principal object being to study, on the spot, the Etruscan remains at Bologna. Here Burton remained some weeks, investigating the antiquities and collecting material for a small volume, partly of criticism, but mainly of original research, in which, from the hastily acquired data at his command, he has presented a complete and exhaustive account of this most ancient of the cities of Etruria. From the preface we learn that his stay was very enjoyable. The rich collections in the museums, and numerous trips to the sites which yielded them, made time pass pleasantly and profitably, while local notabilities vied with each other in treating their erudite guest with the most graceful attention and courtesy.

A desirable coincidence which occurred in 1875, of six months' leave and one of the legacies afore-mentioned, rendered practicable a winter tour through India. Our restless pair were only too glad to get away from Trieste during its most disagreeable season. Burton declared clean cold he could stand, dirty cold he could not. They started on New Year's Day, 1876, by an Austrian Lloyd steamer, bound for Port Said. What with old associations and the absence of any accident or annoyance, this ramble amongst familiar scenes was interesting enough to the former " lieutenant of blacks"; but as there was nothing remarkable about the journey, only the solid results thereof concern the public.

One of these was a most amusing book, " Sind Revisited," in two volumes; the other the inception of his last great expedition, to the ruined cities of Midian. The latter originated in almost fairy-tale fashion. Readers of the " Pilgrimage " may remember a description in its pages of a genial friend, Haji Wali, whom Burton met while sojourning in the Wakalah in Cairo; in fact, I have briefly alluded to him myself in chapter iv. In the course of one of many confabulations, the Haji, in an outburst of confidence, entrusted his cosmopolitan chum with a secret, which for a quarter of a century was destined to be kept inviolate. It happened by the merest chance : while the said pilgrim, who, in addition to strict observance of his religious duties, never neglected to secure the good things of the world wherein Allah had temporarily placed him, was returning from his second visit to El-Hejaz, he found gold close to the Gulf of Akabah. The caravan had halted for the night, he had strolled away from his companions, and, while walking along the dry bed of a torrent, he suddenly perceived sand of a curious colour. Scooping up a double handful, he secured it in his handkerchief, and carefully concealed it about his person. On arriving at Alexandria, he showed his *trouvaille* to an assayer, who, by means of his art, produced a bit of gold about the size of a grain of wheat. Ever since that day the Haji had been sedulously searching for some companion in whom to confide ; and, as soon as he had satisfied himself regarding the probity of his new friend, he proposed they should travel together to the spot and try their luck.

Burton, though brave, was not foolhardy. He saw at once that a journey amongst the wild tribes of Midian, with only one companion, would, if any suspicion of treasure-seeking got abroad, end in certain death for both. Moreover, he had set his heart on the far more romantic pilgrimage to Meccah and Medinah, where the risks, if as great, were less ignoble ; and so for a long while the scheme fell through.

Still, though many years slipped by, he did not forget the Haji's story. According to classical and Arab writers, gold has been found in Midian ; why then should it not be found again ? The land is scarred and honeycombed with ancient mines, and it seems improbable those bygone workers, with their comparatively rude tools and appliances, had extracted all the metal. Anyway, he decided that the matter was well worth investigating as soon as a favourable opportunity presented itself.

It came at last. Ismail, Khedive of Egypt, who, whatever his faults might have been, was always anxious to develop the resources of his country, happened to hear that long ago the site of a goldfield had come to Burton's knowledge. In the then critical condition of Egyptian finance, no chance of procuring supplies of the precious metal was to be neglected ; so, when our traveller was returning from India, *viâ* Suez, the Viceroy honoured him with an invitation to report on the matter *vivâ voce*. His reception was peculiarly gracious, and the first audience convinced him that this prince was a thorough master of detail, and that if he decided upon sending an expedition to Midian, he would do the thing liberally and well. Finally, after a few days' delay, Ismail came to the conclusion the mines were worth a search, and formally commissioned Burton to lead a caravan to the spot where the metallic sand had been discovered.

Nothing could please our traveller better. Now remained to find Haji Wali. A friend in the telegraph service was at once engaged in the quest, and a clue was soon discovered. An old man of that name, weighing some sixteen stone, was said to be living at Zagazig. Ensued a long correspondence. The Haji had four young children, his wife expected a fifth, he now numbered eighty-two winters ; and, under such circnmstances, it was not surprising that he seemed exceedingly shy of undertaking a long and uncomfortable journey. Fearing interminable delays, Burton swooped down on the old fellow in person, and by dint of many a " flattering tale," which none knew better how to tell than himself, he persuaded the octogenarian that, from a pecuniary point of view, it would be well worth his while to make the effort. As might be expected, even after his consent had been obtained, the ancient proved rather troublesome. Hardly had he arrived at Suez, than, declaring he had described everything, he asked to go home again, adding, with many a groan, there were pains in his head, in his side, and in his knees which utterly unfitted him for the fatigue of the expedition. Two bottles of bitter ale a day effected wonders; still Burton must have heaved a hearty sigh of relief when the venerable Haji's services were no longer required.

As on the occasion of the famous expedition to the Lake Regions of Central Africa, our traveller began with a "preliminary canter." Midian was to him virgin ground, so it seemed only prudent to prospect with a small band, before leading a numerous and expensively equipped company. The *reconnaissance* lasted three weeks, from March 31st to April 21st, 1877; but as I am about to describe in detail the second expedition, which covered four months, I will merely add that the first proved an entire success. The Land of Midian is still wealthy; turquoise mines exist, traces of gold are abundant, also of iron and silver. Eight boxes filled with metalliferous quartz, greenstone, porphyry and basalt, were carried back to Egypt for analysis, besides bags of gravel and sand for laboratory work.

The hot season necessitated a delay of six months before the survey could be resumed. Burton returned to Trieste, and never had that unsavoury seaport and its duties appeared more dreary and distasteful. Throughout the summer he was fairly haunted with memories of the Land of Jethro, with its sweet fresh breezes, its perfumed flora, its glorious colouring and its grand simplicity. The golden region appeared to him in many a nightly dream, in all the glory of that primæval prosperity dimly revealed by the recently interpreted Egyptian hieroglyphs. Again he beheld the mining works of the Greeks, the Romans, and the Nebathæans, whose names are preserved by Ptolemy, the forty cities mere ghosts and shadows of their former selves, mentioned in the pages of the mediæval Arab geographers; and the ruthless ruin that under the dominion of the Bedawin gradually crept over the country. And many a fair vision floated through his waking brain of a future Midian, whose rich treasures of various minerals would restore unto her wealth and prosperity after his second expedition had shown to the world what she has been and what she may be again.

At last the happy hour for departure struck. On the 19th of October, 1877, Burton left Trieste for Cairo. Six weeks sufficed for preparations. The Government magazines provided necessary stores, orders from headquarters threw open every door, and although a few delays and difficulties occurred, all was plain sailing compared with what it would have been in Europe. The Viceroy, who, it was said, paid all the expenses out of his own private purse, had determined that the expedition should not merely carry out the work of discovery by tracing the metals to their source, but that it should bring home specimens weighing tons, enough for assay and analysis quantitive and qualitive, both in London and Paris. So miners and mining apparatus were provided, with all the materials for quarrying.

The *personnel* consisted of an escort of twenty-five Soudanese soldiers, a few experienced miners and thirty quarrymen. The European staff mustered five—Burton, M. George Marie, an engineer, Mr. J. C. Clarke, a telegraph engineer, M. Emile Lacaze, an artist, and M. Jean Philipin, who, in addition to other duties, acted as blacksmith. The Egyptian commissioned and non-commissioned officers numbered thirteen, there was a small company of servants and camp followers, and last, but not least, fat old Haji Wali appeared on the scene, the "preliminary canter" having been too short to visit the spot where he had found the gold. A few mules were shipped; but camels could be procured on the spot, and there would be no difficulty as to expense, the generous

Viceroy having presented Burton with two thousand napoleons, besides all the stores.

Finally, the first week in December, 1877, the expedition departed by special train, under the immediate auspices of the governing family of Egypt. In spite of a heavy gale, which detained the party at Suez for a day or two, and which later sorely endangered the mules—Burton seemed more anxious about their limbs than his own—the gunboat safely reached her destination, off Fort El-Muwaylah, on the Midianite coast. A more disagreeable voyage would have been soon forgotten in sight of those glorious mountain walls which stand out from the clear blue sky in passing grandeur of outline, in exceeding splendour of colouring, and in marvellous sharpness of detail. " Once more," exclaimed our traveller, " the power of the hills was upon me."

No time was lost in disembarking the stores and properties, including sundry cases of cartridges and five hundred pounds of pebble-powder, which had been imprudently packed immediately under the main cabin. Implements as well as provisions were given in charge of an old Albanian, who acted as magazine man. This done, the steamer proceeded to a quiet little harbour a mile or two further, for the purpose of patching up her boilers, which had already caused no small trouble, and threatened to cause more.

Burton's landing at Fort El-Muwaylah was conducted with such ceremony as to be almost a function. The gunboat saluted, the fort answered with a rattle and patter of musketry; all the local notables received the expedition in line, drawn up on the shore. To the left stood the civilians in tulip-coloured garb; next were the garrison, some dozen Bashi-Buzouks, armed with matchlocks; then came the quarrymen, in uniform; while the black-faced escort held the place of honour on the right. The latter gave our traveller a loud " Hip, hip, hurrah ! " as he passed.

A whole day was spent in inspecting the soldiers and

mules, in despatching a dromedary-post to Suez with news of the arrival, and in conciliating the claims of rival Bedawin. Several of these gentry offered themselves as guides to the interior, of course for a consideration. Each wanted his camels to be hired and no one else's, each demanded extortionate sums, so extortionate indeed, that it was fortunate the Viceroy had proved liberal. Finally three Shaykhs were engaged, one hundred and six camels, and several dromedaries with their drivers. Half this number of quadrupeds would have sufficed, had not the wretched animals, one and all, been half-starved, and utterly unable to carry any great weight. Their greatest feast was a meagre ration of mixed beans, and their daily bread consisted of the dry leaves of thorn trees; no wonder they had hardly energy even to bite. In two or three days all was ready, and the caravan straggled off to Jebel El-Abyaz.

Straggled is the only word to use. Burton declared the first march reminded him of driving, or attempting to drive, a train of unbroken mules over the prairies. The escort, thinking solely of themselves and their property, seemed determined to follow their own sweet will, while each Desert craft sailed snarling and yelling along, steered after a fashion which proudly disdained the usual caravan file. Burton, mounted on an old white mule, appears to have performed the work of a sheep-dog in keeping his unruly party together.

Matters improved later. The lawless Arabs and Egyptians soon found their chief would stand no nonsense. His character, a rare combination of determination and gentleness, made him an almost ideal leader of semi-civilised races; and, as we have seen in other expeditions, it was rare indeed for him to lose all control over the men under his command. Prosperity attended them. The first part of the journey through Midian Proper lasted fifty-four days, during which time about 107 miles of ground were surveyed with the utmost care. The country through which they travelled was essentially a mining one, extensively but superficially worked by the ancients. Besides specimens of gold, silver, and iron, copper ore was discovered which sometimes yielded as much as forty per cent. of metal. Of the forty ruined cities, eighteen were visited during the exploration of Midian Proper, including the capital, Madiáma, the greater part whereof, originally built of gypsum, must, when new, have looked like a scene in fairy land. Its ruin was utter—foundations of walls, a bastion built in three straight lines overhanging the perpendicular face of a gorge, traces of furnaces now level with the ground, and sundry sunken, shattered catacombs were all that remained of the once wealthy and powerful worshippers of Baalpeor. A few old coins were picked up, some so glued together by decay and eaten out of all semblance of money as to be illegible ; others, after being treated with acids, fairly decipherable. Amongst the little collection was a copper coin thinly encrusted with silver, proving that even those days produced " smashers."

But now I hear the reader interrupt, " Tell me about Haji Wali and the torrent bed. Did he lead the caravan to the auriferous Wady, and did it contain gold ? " Well, it is my painful duty to relate that age had sadly deteriorated the once excellent qualities of my uncle's old friend. The pious pilgrim who had twice braved the perils of the way to Meccah and Medinah, now, like the old person of the nursery rhyme, would not even say his prayers. When informed by the Mullah it was the hour for devotion, he answered, " Wait a bit." Nor did he perform his earthly duties any better than his heavenly ones—his promises proving like the proverbial pie-crust, made only to be broken. The caravan had got about half way to the spot so long the centre of interest, when he suddenly insisted on returning home. Not for love of wife or children, but to look after his pecuniary affairs. And he stuck to his intention. Maddened by fear lest during his absence, in the height of the cotton season, the fellahs of Egypt would neglect to pay their debts, he malingered to such an extent that Burton feared the old fellow would kill himself out of sheer spite. So, after several attempts to detain him even a few days longer, he was permitted to leave the Expedition, then encamped at the Wady Sharma, and to ride to the Fort, whence a pilgrim-boat was about to start for Suez. On parting, the old man vowed he was dying and could hardly keep in the saddle. Little did he know that his whilom chum watched him amble away, and, almost pleased to be rid of the responsibility, laughed to see how rapidly he urged on his hapless mule as soon as he imagined himself well out of sight.

However, he had had the grace to leave a rude map of the spot. So many valuable mines had been discovered already, that it mattered comparatively little whether this particular site proved auriferous or not. But as the caravan was now so near, Burton thought it advisable to try by means of the plan to discover the place which had proved almost the *raison d'être* of the Expedition. And this he succeeded in doing. A rounded hill close to the Akabah Gulf, a dry watercourse between two tall bluff cliffs, a solitary mimosa, tallied with the description so often repeated of the scene of the *trouvaille*. At once the washing trough was prepared, a trench dug, and the gravelly sand manipulated. But to no purpose. Either some exceptionally heavy torrent had carried away the precious metal *en masse*, or, more probably, the workers having ascertained for certain the existence of gold elsewhere, would not put up with the delay and trouble of a sufficiently-prolonged search. That gold existed in the neighbourhood Burton heard on all sides. In camp men spoke freely of dust stored in quills carried behind the ear and sold at Suez. But neither promises nor bribes would persuade the poorest Bedawin who prowled about the tents to break through the rule of silence; and, after a fortnight had been wasted over this fruitless task, Burton gave the order to depart.

The exploration of Midian was divided into three principal journeys. The first, already partly described, concluded with a quartz prospecting trip along the Gulf of Akabah, whereon, the winds being chronically high and the gunboat's boilers hopelessly dilapidated, our party were very nearly shipwrecked. Between each excursion was an interval of rest at headquarters, Fort El-Muwaylah, which, being one of the defended stations of the Cairo Hajj, or pilgrimage caravan, seemed quite a gay and civilised spot after the solemn inland wildernesses. Here all enjoyed a halt of about ten days, preparatory to a march on the Hismá. Burton's heart was firmly fixed on this project, for he hoped to find an "unworked California" to the east of the Harrah volcanoes, virgin regions where granulated gold still lingers, unlike the mines on the coast, where machinery must take the place of the human arm. His Shaykhs and camel men, however, were by no means so enthusiastic, the region in question being the haunt of a tribe, the Ma'ázah, who from all reports seemed little better than cut-throats. Objections were silenced at last, and the party set out in force at 6.30 a.m., February 19th. Their Remingtons numbered ten, their camels fifty, and dromedaries six. Discipline had wonderfully improved, for the caravan now loaded in twenty minutes instead of five hours, and when no fear of danger delayed it, started in fifteen minutes after bugle-call.

Their route lay through East Midian. Having proceeded about six miles, they stopped for rest and refreshment by the side of a thready stream in the section of the Surr, which receives the Wady El-Najil. The banks were crowded with sheep and goats as in the days before the "hosts of Midian" received such an unmerciful thrashing from the hands of Gideon and his vindictive warriors; and the adjoining rocks possessed peculiar attractions for hares, hawks, and partridges. In these upland regions water is found almost everywhere, and is generally drinkable; hence the Bedawin prefer them to the arid and thirsty coast. Though mostly parched and stony, Midian has her bits of Arcadia. One is the great Wady Dámah, where our traveller saw not only flocks of sheep and goats browsing on the luxuriant herbage, but spots where a thin forest gathers and clumps of trees form quite a feature in the landscape. Again, in the Wady Sharma, the water scenery and consequent greenery is as fresh as Damascus. While there encamped, Burton used to wake every morning surprised by the home-like sound of a little runnel, babbling along its bed of rushes, stones and sand, accompanied by the musical rustling of several tall trees, which completed the fresh and delightful scene.

Next day was spent in northing, during which our caravan passed a broad tree-dotted flat of golden sand, bordered by an emerald avenue of dense mimosas forming line under the greenstone hills to the right, and the red heights on the left. Plants were rare; chiefly remarkable were the sorrel, and the blue thistle, or rather wild artichoke, a thorn loved by camels. Sometimes an impatient rider would leave the comparatively easy tracks in the valleys for a short cut over hills so steep as to induce even the three Shaykhs to dismount, anyway before commencing the descents. Views from the heights were lovely, especially the blue and purple screen of Sinai, which formed a splendid background. There was nothing to distract attention from the gorgeous aspect of Nature, for just then all traces of man had vanished; the Ma'ázah were up country, and another tribe had temporarily quitted their grazing grounds. On the night of February 21st, the caravan halted after a total march of eleven miles at the foot of a granite block wherein a gap supplied them with tolerable water.

All went well until February 23rd, when the enemy's

country appeared in sight. Burton and some of his officers were preceding the escort, who, on approaching the haunts of the bandits, had become so excessively nervous—starting at every sound—that it was necessary to show an example. While passing some black tents on the left bank of the Surr, where that stream enters a narrow rocky gorge, our traveller perceived about a dozen Arabs scampering over the sides of the Pass. The heights scaled, they emitted some unmelodious yells intended for a war song, and what was still more objectionable, they distinctly threatened to fire.

Dismounting at once, Burton looked to his weapons, and then, like one of Dumas' heroes, began to parley. But the ragged ruffians, who knew neither of the escort nor the numbers of the Expedition, explained in their barking voices that they would be satisfied with nothing less than plunder. And again they howled their war cry. Fortunately, at that moment the Soudanese soldiers, with their formidable guns gleaming in the sunshine, appeared on the scene, and immediately the Ma'ázah changed their tone, kissed Burton's hands, and declared, with one eye fixed on the Remingtons, there had been some mistake.

Still, it was a bad beginning. Next day a messenger, despatched in hot haste to obtain a pass from the principal men of the tribe, appeared officially heading five chiefs, who were followed by a tail of some thirty rowdy rascals. Two of these personages were mounted on horses, wretched animals stolen from another tribe, the rest on fine, sturdy, long-coated camels which looked Syrian rather than Midianite. So important an arrival was signalised with a certain amount of ceremony; bugler and escort, drawn up in front of the mess-tent which had to serve as audience chamber, saluted with all the honours.

During the palaver that ensued all was sweet as honey outside, and as bitter as gall within. The Ma'ázah, many of whom then saw Europeans for the first time, eyed their

25

hats curiously, with a facial movement which meant, " So now we have let Christian dogs into our land ! " When asked whence they had procured the two horses, they answered curtly, " Min Rabbina " (from our Lord), thus signifying stolen goods. However, in spite of their evident disinclination to have any dealings with strangers, they promised to escort the Expedition to their dens on the morrow.

That night was raw and gusty, the mercury sank to 38° F.; and blazing fires kept up within and without the tents hardly sufficed for comfort. Doubtless, Burton slept little ; anyhow, early morning found him engaged in a final struggle with his three Shaykhs, who were driven almost to desperation by the prospect of entering the robbers' haunts with their precious camels. Finally, after every available argument they could urge had been disposed of, they consented to proceed a little further; and at 7.15 a.m. the caravan and its brigand guides marched due eastward through the Pass leading to the enemy's country. The path was the rudest of corniches, worn by the feet of man and beast, and showing some ugly, abrupt turns. The ground, composed mostly of irregular rock steps, presented few obstacles to the horses and mules; but the camels, laden with the mess-table and long tent poles, must have had a troublesome time. Of course, the cautious beasts advanced leisurely, feeling each stone before they trusted it, so all arrived without the slightest mishap.

Burton and his European companions preceded as usual their noisy, braying company. On the Pass - top they halted to prospect the surrounding novelties. Looking down the long valley just traversed, they distinguished a dozen distances whose several plains were marked by all the shades of colour that the most varied vegetation can display. And in the far horizon appeared the eastern faces of the giants of the coast-range, glorious in all the grandeur

of their vast proportions. In fact, our traveller was standing on the westernmost edge of the great central Arabian
plateau, defined as El-Nejd, the highlands — an upland
running parallel with the " Lip-range" and with the maritime ghauts, and known as the far-famed Hismá. It probably
represents a remnant of the old terrace which, like the
Secondary gypseous formation, has been torn to pieces by
the volcanic region to the east, and by the plutonic up-
heavals to the west. Its length may be 170 miles. The
views on all sides were striking and suggestive. Facing
the spectators was El-Harrah, the volcanic area whose
black porous lavas and honeycombed basalts are still
brought down to the coast to serve as hand-mills; then,
southward, appeared a line of red ramparts and buttresses,
beyond which soared the sky-blue mountain-block that
takes its name from the ruins of Shaghab. Besides its
beauty, the land possessed another attraction, one ever
dear to Burton's heart—it had never yet been trodden
by European feet.[1]

Unfortunately, it proved impossible to penetrate this
then unknown region. The Ma'ázah chiefs and their
followers, after a display of rapacity and ill-temper far
from reassuring, suddenly sent off messengers in every
direction, a step which looked uncommonly like a general
call to arms. The chiefs then publicly declared they would
have no Nazarenes in their mountains, and privately consulted whether they should not raise a force of dromedary-
men to exterminate the strangers. And all this duly
reached Burton's ears.

It was most annoying. Not only had the "virgin
California" to be abandoned, but the Hismá also, a
region full of archæological interest. Besides, how dis-
concerting to beat a retreat before these unmannerly
brigands with their beggarly pop-guns, their wretched

---

[1] Since that time it has been explored by Mr. Doughty and others.

accoutrements! I think Burton did heave just one sigh
for the days when an Englishman might have forced his
way through black man's land without having every shred
of character torn to bits by those mock philanthropists who
make no distinction between men and semi-apes. However, under the circumstances, no alternative remained
but to turn back. So, at 4.30 a.m., February 25th, he
aroused his camp, gave orders to strike the tents and
load, an order obeyed with suspicious alacrity; and, after
some slight show of resistance from the robber chiefs, who,
as usual, wished to extort money, the caravan made its
way out of the enemy's country.

The time was not wholly wasted. When out of reach
of the Ma'ázah, Burton journeyed leisurely through South
Midian, surveying and collecting specimens on the way.
Ruins innumerable studded the land, ancient mines yawned
open to the sky. More enticing to the eye was the weird
and fascinating aspect of the southern Hismá wall, as seen
in the distance. Based on mighty massive foundations of
brown and green trap, the undulating junction perfectly
defined by a horizontal white line, the capping of sandstone
rises regular as if laid in courses, with a huge rampart
falling perpendicularly upon the natural slope of its glacis.
Further eastward the mass has been broken and weathered
into the most remarkable castellations, into likenesses of
cathedrals, spires, minarets, and pinnacles, of fortresses,
bulwarks and towers. Nor are the tints less remarkable
than the forms. When day warms them with its gorgeous
glaze, these curious shapes wear the brightest hues of red,
set off by lambent lights of pink and ruby, and by shades
of deep transparent purple. The even-glow is indescribably
lovely, all the lovelier because evanescent; the moment the
sun disappears the glorious rosy smile fades away, leaving
the pale grey ghosts of their former selves to gloom against
the star-spangled sky.

Burton's journey through Eastern Midian occupied a

month. It included his fruitless attempt to penetrate the Ma'ázah country, a visit to Shuwah and Shaghab, two of the ruined metal-working cities, and a partial ascent of the Sharr, a mighty maritime Alp, monarch of Midianite mountains. This successfully accomplished, the Expedition returned as usual to Fort El-Muwaylah for rest and fresh stores before undertaking its third and final march.

The latter, which lay through South Midian, would interest hardly any save a geologist or metallurgist. Burton, however, believed it was chiefly there that gold would be found, pending the exploration of the tract east of the Harrah volcanoes. The whole eastern counterslope of the outliers that project from the Ghaut section, known as the mountains of the Tihámat Balawiyyah, is one vast outcrop of quartz. The parallelogram between north latitude 26°, including the mouth of the Wady Hamz, and north latitude 27°, which runs some fifteen miles north of the Bada plain, would form, so he believed, a Southern grant sufficiently large to be divided and subdivided as soon as judged advisable. Free gold was noticed in the micaceous schists veining the quartz, and in the chalcedony which parts the granite from the gneiss.

Little now remained to do. After about three weeks' scrupulous survey of this rich, metalliferous region, during which all manner of fruitless enquiries were made concerning stone-coal, the Viceroy, having laid even greater stress on the search for black diamonds than for gold, our traveller felt his mission was accomplished, and that he could with a clear conscience turn the head of his old grey mule homewards. And as both Egyptians and Europeans were desirous of leaving a country which possessed for them few, if any, charms, once the signal for return given, there was but little delay. Ismail had already sent another gunboat, one with sound boilers, to convey the Expedition back to Egypt. A busy scene ensued on arriving at headquarters. The remainder of the stores, which, wonderful to relate, had been honestly dealt with by their caretaker, the old Albanian, were transferred to the ship from the fort. Twenty-five tons of specimens were gradually stowed away in her hold, and the three Shaykhs received such a handsome fee that they actually refrained from grumbling— much. At last came the exciting moment when the *Sinnar*, firing a farewell salute to Fort El-Muwaylah, started on her homeward way. Suez was safely reached April 20th, 1878.

Nothing could be more flattering than Burton's reception by the Viceroy. Directions were given for an exhibition of the trophies. It proved a great success, opened, as it was, by Ismail in person, and attended by all the members of his family. Experts from England and Australia pronounced a favourable verdict on the specimens, and our traveller was directed to draw up a general description of the province, to report upon the political and other measures whereby it could be benefited, and to suggest the means of profitably working the mines. Moreover, the Viceroy renewed his promise that Burton should receive either a concession, or a royalty of five per cent., on the general produce of the mines as a reward for his discoveries.

Apparently our hero had won both honours and affluence. Or, had he yet another disappointment to bear in his sorely disappointed life?

CHAPTER XVI

APPARENTLY Fate had decreed that never was Richard Burton to win fortune by exploration. The two expeditions to the mines of Midian, which promised so much, ended in utter failure. Ismail Pasha—perhaps the ablest, certainly the most extravagant, ruler Egypt had yet known—had been compelled to abdicate, and Tewfik, his son, reigned in his stead. The first results of the change of government, until the English had succeeded in reducing the financial confusion to some degree of order, were not particularly happy. Public works were neglected, the great improvements which could only become profitable long after their completion were more or less starved, and the burden of taxation became every day less endurable.

Ismail's downfall, every one knows, happened suddenly. When Burton left Egypt, after his triumphal return from Midian, the political horizon was certainly lowering, but he did not anticipate his patron's speedy deposition; nor, when the news reached his ears, did he fear that the policy hitherto pursued of developing the resources of the country would be reversed. So he journeyed leisurely through Germany for the purpose of examining various collections of arms to figure later on as illustrations in his " Book of the Sword," and, by means of his consular duties and literary work, managed to while away the time until he could ascertain personally how matters were progressing in Cairo.

Towards the end of 1879, having once more obtained a few months' leave, he again visited that city, and there did his utmost to induce the new Khedive to renew the works in Midian. But, after sundry fruitless attempts to gain the ear of the principal advisers of the Viceregal Court, Burton could not conceal from himself the unwelcome certainty that all his labours had been thrown away, and that the funds already expended might just as well have been flung into the Nile, for any good they were likely to do the old Black Land. Tewfik had become Khedive under circumstances of exceptional difficulty ; he could spend no money on schemes, however brilliant. In fact, the change of rulers had destroyed at a blow all our hero's hopes—not merely of his own fortune and advancement, but the nobler ones of restoring wealth and prosperity to an unfortunate country. Every effort to persuade the more powerful officials to listen to his plan for converting deficits into surpluses was received with worse than coldness ; the National Party opposed his scheme as the idea of a foreigner, and all agreed that, owing to the wretched condition of the Egyptian treasury, it was utterly impracticable. So, having wasted at Cairo nearly half a year of his life, Burton returned to his Consulate wearied out and disgusted.

After about eighteen months' work at Trieste, varied by a brief visit to London, our traveller made his final attempt to wring treasure from the many rich hoards yet lying in the bosom of Mother Earth. As in the case of the Icelandic sulphur mines, a Liverpool merchant required Burton's services. Mr. James Irvine, a large mine owner in the Gulf of Guinea, had just obtained important concessions in the valley of the Ancobra River ; and aware that Burton knew more about the Gold Coast than any other Englishman, requested that he, together with Captain V. L. Cameron, should inspect his new property and advise regarding the best means of extracting the precious metal.

Although the West Coast of Africa is not usually regarded as an agreeable touring ground, this offer was received with rapture by our versatile traveller. Delighted at the prospect of escaping from commonplace Trieste, utterly oblivious of many a bygone fever in those malarial districts, he eagerly consented, and on the 18th December, 1881, found himself once more on the familiar route. At Madeira he was joined by Cameron, who, like himself, was in high spirits and fully equipped for work. They voyaged leisurely per ss. *Senegal*, spending a day or two at Bathurst, Freetown, and other mouldy, mildewed pest-houses along the coast, which they briefly described as being in an advanced stage of decomposition. The latter part of the journey was not rendered more agreeable by a crowd of native passengers — daddy, mammy, and piccaninny — especially as these negroes were permitted to travel first class. Black daddies, whose conversation at every meal consisted of whispering into each other's ears, with an occasional guffaw like that of a laughing jackass, and whose pronounced kleptomania no surveillance could keep in check, especially excited Burton's ire. Nor did even the sable women find favour in his sight. Their language and manners seem to have been indescribable ; their appearance, thanks to frightful semi-European gowns of striped cottons, harlequin shawls, and scarves thrown over jackets which showed more than neck and bare arms to the light of day, he compared to devils seen in dreams after a supper of underdone pork, and would, he added, have scared away any crow however bold.

Barring these black nightmares, the voyage seems to have been pleasant. There was a little too much rolling occasionally, the *Senegal* being a ship sailors euphemistically term lively, and nobody, however industrious, can write or read with much result when this movement becomes too pronounced ; but the glorious Harmatan weather, with its cool, dewy mornings and evenings, and the pale round-faced sun gleaming through an honest fog, made our traveller wish that sundry friends who had marvelled at his pleasure in exchanging the bitter blasts of the Northern Adriatic for this genial temperature could have spent a day with him. Finally, after passing the hummocks of Apollonia, Axim, his destination, peeped up over the portbow at dawn on the 25th of January.

The first aspect of Axim is charming; there is nothing more picturesque upon this coast. Situated on a bay within a bay, it boasts of a noble forest as background; and consisting of a fort and subject town, it wears a baronial and Old World air, decidedly agreeable after the frowsy mean-looking settlements touched at *en route*.

The agents of the several Aximite houses soon came on board, hobnobbed with captain and passengers, and presently embarked with Burton and Cameron in the usual heavy surf-boat, manned by a dozen leathery-lunged " Elmina boys " with paddles, and a helmsman with an oar. The anchorage place lies at least two miles south-west of the landing stage, but since only one sunken reef prevents larger vessels from running into the bay, a reef which merely requires a buoy to mark its whereabouts, Axim can pride herself on possessing the safest harbour on this part of the African sea-board.

Our travellers and their belongings, duly housed by Mr. Irvine's agent in his little bungalow facing Water Street, spent a day or two inspecting town and fort, marvelling meanwhile at the unusual cleanliness of the natives, who, even on chilly mornings, never failed to take a bath in the sea. Then business had to be attended to. The King of Amrehía, who had granted the concession, had not yet signed the document enabling Mr. Irvine's representatives to take formal possession of the Izrah mine. So the potentate came in state to Water Street to affix his sign-manual to the legal papers; and as usual on such occasions, the interview consisted chiefly of compliments, presents and drinking. Nothing more about the king's costume need be said than that it was peculiar: better leave it to the reader's imagination.

Soon after this important preliminary, the two friends

started for the scene of their labours. The site of the Izrah Mine proved a fine one, situated about four geographical miles from the sea. The travellers also visited neighbouring concessions even superior ; but all had certain disadvantages, vile roads, and equally vile anchorage at the nearest points on the coast. Gold was abundant, but the blacks who delved for it were arrant thieves ; and as machinery was costly and the staff had to be liberally paid, the prospects of handsome dividends for English shareholders seemed somewhat doubtful. The two friends worked together most amicably : Cameron made an excellent route survey of the district, corrected by many and careful astronomical observations; Burton described the land as minutely as possible, searched, often under a broiling sun, for the shortest cuts to the sea, and studied separately the various gold-pits belonging to the different properties. He came to the conclusion that this Wasa country, Ancobra section, is far richer than the most glowing accounts have represented it. The land is literally impregnated with the precious metal, and there are, besides, signs of diamond, ruby, and sapphire. On the other hand, he could not help noticing the serious drawbacks already mentioned.

But now, to his sore discomfiture, Burton was reminded that even his iron constitution could not last for ever. Both he and Cameron worked too hard. Their mornings and evenings were spent in hammering quartz and gold washing, often in fetid pits half full of water ; their days in walking instead of hammocking. Deeming themselves seasoned travellers, they neglected such simple precautions as fires at dawn and sunset. And, as usually happens after any great imprudence committed in such a climate, the penalty was soon exacted. Both men fell ill on the same day—Cameron was prostrated by a bilious attack, Burton by fever and ague. The former resorted to chlorodyne, the latter to Warburg's drops (tinctura Warburgii), in which he had the greatest faith; but sickness left them so utterly prostrate that, after long and anxious deliberation, they decided on that not very dignified proceeding by which people live to fight another day. So, more dead than alive, our travellers embarked on the Ancobra river, and hastened back to the comparative luxury of Axim.

The rest is soon told. Cameron, the younger man, speedily recovered and returned to work. Burton, who could not shake off the fever, reluctantly confessed to a thorough breakdown, and so took the next steamer to Madeira, where he had little to do except to look after his own health. At the end of a month he was joined by his friend, who had completed the required survey single-handed, and the two men returned to Europe.

As may be guessed already, the Izrah mine and others, in spite of their rich store of metal, did not prove a success.[1] Two volumes, crammed with information, were the sole results of Burton's efforts. His expenses were paid, and with this he had to be content. His last long journey was over, and had left him neither richer nor poorer than when he started.

Acknowledging with his usual plucky good sense that his most vigorous years were past, he now turned his attention entirely to literature; for awhile, with scant success. Much time was devoted to a translation of the " Lusiads," followed up by a " Life of Camoens " and a Commentary.[2]

> " Englished by Richard Burton, and well done,
>   As it was well worth doing,"

said Gerald Massey. And certainly the man was equal to the task. None but a traveller can do justice to a traveller, and it so happened that most of his wanderings formed a running and realistic commentary on the " Lusiads." He

---

[1] " To the Gold Coast for Gold." Two vols.
[2] " Camoens." Six vols.

had not merely visited almost every place named in the "Epos of Commerce;" in many he had spent months, and even years. Only they who have personally studied the originals of the word-pictures of Portugal's greatest singer can appreciate their perfect combination of fidelity and realism with fancy and idealism. And another of our translator's qualifications was his thorough appreciation of the poem combined with ardent admiration for the poet. The gracious and noble thoughts of the "Lusiads" revived him as the champagne air of the mountain-tops; and the soldier-writer, whose motto was "Honour, not Honours," commanded the warmest sympathy of one whose life bore a strange resemblance to that of Portugal's noble and unfortunate son.

Unluckily, this was not the sort of work to bring at the time either fame or fortune. The general reader could hardly be expected to clamour at the libraries for an archaic translation of a classical epic. Not surprising, therefore, is it that this fine rendering of the "Lusiads," enriched by notes of the most varied erudition, fell almost stillborn upon the press. Now, as the truest copy of Camoens' immortal poem, it has become a standard work; then, like many books that finally attain this fondly-coveted position, it resulted in pecuniary loss to its writer.

Once more Burton's affairs began to look gloomy. His startling failure of health during his trips to the Gold Coast had revealed pretty plainly that he could no longer bear the strain of travels in pestilential climates. Moreover, in 1883 he was seized with a severe illness, suppressed gout affecting stomach and heart, which confined him to his bed for eight months. His last publication had not paid its expenses, no further legacies were expected just then, and a flat of twenty-seven rooms, even though situated in a dirty Austrian seaport, requires a certain amount of money to keep up.

But Richard Burton was destined to enjoy a brief season of sunshine before leaving a world which had often

proved so dark and dreary. Sanguine as he was, I do not
think he had any idea of the great good fortune life yet
held in store for him.   Hitherto his writings had brought
in at most sums such as two or three hundred pounds ; at
other times next to nothing; or, as in the case of the
"Lusiads," left him out of pocket.   Now, by a curious
chance, the birth of one of his brain-children attracted a
veritable shower of gold.   By a literal translation of the
"Arabian Nights," those wonderful tales first known in
Europe through the French rendering of Antoine Galland,
1704-1717, Burton realised what many persons would consider a little fortune, viz., twelve thousand pounds.

The history of this "revelation of Orientalism" is
romantic to a degree. With many intermissions it had
taken thirty-two years to write ; and laborious though
the work had often proved, it never failed to afford its
author interest and amusement.   During long years of
official exile to the deadly climates of East and West
Africa, the dull half-clearings of South America, it was
a faithful talisman against *ennui* and despondency.   From
disagreeable or commonplace surroundings the Jinn bore
away the translator to the land of his predilection—Arabia,
a region so familiar to his mind that even when he cast
his first glance on the scene, he tells us, it seemed a
reminiscence of some bygone metempsychic life in the
far distant past.   Again he stood under the diaphanous
skies, in air glorious as ether, whose very breath causes
men's spirits to bubble like sparkling wine.   Then would
appear the woollen tents of the Bedawin, mere dots in
the boundless waste, the camp-fire shining like a glow
worm in the village-centre, and the Shaykhs gravely
taking their places round the blaze, the women and children standing motionless outside the ring while their guest
rewarded their hospitality by reciting a few pages of their
favourite tales.   Even in wild Somaliland no one turned
a deaf ear to these fairy stories, and many a time did our

traveller keep the men of his caravan in good humour under trying circumstances by telling of mighty Harun-al-Rashid, or the immortal Barber.

The conception of this invaluable addition to English literature took place shortly after the " Pilgrimage to Meccah and Medinah." Burton arrived at Aden in the winter of 1852, and while lodging with the friend whose absence he so regretted on the journey to the Lake Regions of Central Africa, he came to the conclusion after many a confabulation with Dr. Steinhauser, who was as good an Arabist as himself, that, while the name of this wonderful treasury of Moslem folk-lore is familiar to almost every English child, no student ignorant of the language is aware of the valuables it contains. Even grey-beards at Oxford had to content themselves with selected, diluted, and abridged transcripts. Galland had gallicised the general tone and tenour to such an extent that even the vulgar English versions have failed to throw off the French flavour. Torrens attempted literalism, but his execution was of the roughest, nor did his familiarity with Arabic suffice him for the task; while Lane affected the Latinised English of the period and omitted nearly all the poetry. Clearly the work of bringing out a first-rate translation remained to be done. Burton was the first to confess that the coarseness of the original was a drawback; but students of " all sorts and conditions of men " can hardly avoid finding themselves at times face to face with unpleasant realities. Anyway, the friends agreed before parting to collaborate and produce a full, complete, unvarnished copy of " Alf Laylah wa Laylah," Steinhauser taking the prose and Burton the metrical part. They corresponded on the subject for years; but the doctor died in the seventies, and the survivor was left to complete the work alone.

It progressed fitfully amidst a host of obstacles. Burton had several large deal tables in his study, each devoted to a different set of books and manuscripts; and now that the "Lusiads" were finished and cleared off, the "Nights" became all paramount. He laboured incessantly at his gigantic task until 1880, when the process of copying began, and he felt himself within measurable distance of its completion.

Here, perhaps, the question suggests itself to an intelligent mind, what might be the traveller's motive for spending so much time and labour upon a collection of wonderful fairy-tales? And I explain with pleasure, for his object was most laudable. By preserving intact not only its spirit, but even its *mécanique*, its manner and matter, this Eastern Saga book seemed to be the work *par excellence* to place in the hands of men studying for the Indian Civil Service or qualifying as officials in Egypt, Persia, Syria, or even in those of our cleverest soldiers. With the aid of the writer's Annotations and his Terminal Essay, he believed an attentive reader might learn more of the Moslem's manners and customs, laws and religion, than is known even by the average Orientalist; while if he cared to master the original text, he would find himself at home amongst educated men in Egypt, Syria, Majd, and Mesopotamia, and be able to converse with them like a gentleman, not, as too often happens in Anglo-India, like a groom. Semitic studies alone teach how to deal with a race more powerful than any pagan, and strangely enough these are apt to be thrust aside for others comparatively useless. Does England forget she is at present the greatest Mussulman Empire in the world? Apparently, for of late years she has systematically neglected Arabism, and even discouraged it in examinations for the Indian Civil Service. Briefly, Burton believed if England wishes to govern her Moslem subjects wisely, she ought to know something of their literature.

And he was well qualified to be her teacher. No one else could give her the results of such enormous experience of Arab and Oriental life. His practical acquaintance with the East, his mastery of the languages and dialects, his indefatigable industry, all prepared him for a *tour de force* which has been well described as unprecedented. The necessity for the work was obvious; fortunately, the executor possessed every faculty for its successful accomplishment.

Volume I. appeared September 11th, 1885. The original edition—I say original, because a Library Edition has been issued since his death—consisted of ten volumes and six supplementary ones, which included explanatory notes and a Terminal Essay on the history of the " Book of the Thousand Nights and a Night." Hardly had the pages, yet damp from the press, time to dry before a veritable hymn of praise saluted the translator. The marvellous display of linguistic flexibility, the exquisite flow of language, the wonderful erudition displayed in the notes, captivated the critics as the voice of the charmer. Notice after notice appeared in " dailies " and " weeklies," one more courteous and appreciative than another. Nor was the foreign press far behind. From every city in Europe *literati* wrote complimenting the great cosmopolitan Englishman upon the wealth of learning contained in the latest translation of " Alf Laylah wa Laylah." Never had a writer enjoyed a nobler triumph, never had a writer deserved one more.

Naturally, after so many disappointments, so many failures, this unstinted praise fell like balm on a wounded spirit. He became brighter, happier, less of a pessimist. Professing himself truly thankful for the good word of the Fourth Estate, he acknowledged most gracefully the congratulations received from all sides :

" I seize the opportunity," he said, " of expressing my cordial gratitude and hearty thanks to the Press in general, which has received my Eastern studies and contributions to Oriental knowledge in the friendliest and most sympathetic spirit, appreciating my labours far beyond the

modicum of the offerer's expectations, and lending potent
and genial aid to place them before the English world in
their fairest and most favourable point of view."

Of course a few discords mingled with the generous
chorus of admiration called forth from all truly learned
men by Burton's great work. I notice the most blatant
screech, because it is necessary to clear up all miscon-
ceptions, not merely those concerning the object of the
work, but also the manner in which that object was carried
out. Sundry extra nice or nasty critics complained in somewhat Tartuffian strains of the coarseness of " Alf Laylah
wa Laylah." Wilfully ignoring the safeguards wherewith
Burton had almost prudishly invested his book, they pretended to be as shocked at this translation of an Arabian
classic, limited in issue and intended only for the select few,
as though it were destined to repose on the drawing-room
table side by side with—reader, forgive the sneer—the last
nauseous case from the Divorce courts. Now Burton had
taken every precaution, and they knew it, to ensure his
volumes reaching the hands, and the hands of those alone,
for whom they were penned. The work was printed, never
published, one thousand sets being issued to picked subscribers. In a circular forwarded with the first volume
the translator earnestly begged it might be kept under lock
and key; and although, later on, strong pressure was
brought to bear upon him to issue another five hundred
copies, he loyally refused either to break faith with his
subscribers or to add unnecessarily to the number of a
work suitable only for a small class of readers.

Never, by my uncle's special request, having even
seen the original, I have given the above summary of its
history from a somewhat cursory inspection of the edition
brought out by Mr. H. S. Nichols, and from reading the
reviews and laudatory letters written in 1886. About this
Library Edition I have something to say. The unexpected appearance of these twelve volumes in 1894 created

a considerable stir. Published almost in their entirety, with merely a few excisions absolutely indispensable, they were an unwelcome surprise to the original subscribers; and the sale of the copyright, by which the widow obtained three thousand pounds, regardless that a book for private circulation would be scattered broadcast over the country, coming as it did so soon after her somewhat theatrical destruction of the "Scented Garden," could not pass unchallenged. None of her husband's relatives sanctioned the proceeding; in fact, their consent was not asked. In all such matters Isabel Burton was guided by her own caprice. To any friends who have enquired whether Burton himself would have authorised the act, I have always given a decided answer in the negative; we have already seen by his refusal to issue another five hundred copies, even to his own subscribers, that it would have been utterly foreign to his original intention—viz., of placing the "Thousand Nights and a Night" in the hands of the few, the very few who could profit by them.

And now, leaving the subject of the wonderful translation of "Alf Laylah wa Laylah," I must add a few lines concerning the Burnt Manuscript. Reams of nonsense have been written about an act intelligible only to those who held the clue.

Burton had succeeded so well with the "Nights," and his literary friends had agreed that the insight he had given into Moslem life was of such priceless value to the country at large, that he determined on following up his work by one more translation of the same character. His original subscribers, delighted with their first treasure, gladly consented to inscribe their names a second time; and an acquaintance offered six thousand pounds for the whole, in order to save Burton and his wife from the almost intolerable worry of personally forwarding the book to every individual. The Arabic MS. in question, which had been translated by a Frenchman, but which, like the "Nights," could be done justice to only by a scholar and a traveller, is entitled: "The Scented Garden, Men's Hearts to Gladden, of the Shaykh al Nafzáwi," and was to be printed and circulated with all the same precautions as had been taken with its predecessor. When the work was *two-thirds* finished death struck down the writer. The fate of the fragment was truly strange. Isabel, who had described the "Arabian Nights" as her husband's *Magnum Opus*—Isabel, who knew exactly how he had been engaged until the last day of his life, and who was assisting him by every means in her power, took the papers from the desk in which he had carefully locked them, deliberately read through pages which probably she only half understood, and then, inspired by what seems to have been a fit of hysteria or bigotry, flung them leaf by leaf into the fire. As the MS. happened to be unfinished, and, as she told us herself, she could trust nobody to finish it for her, it was, comparatively speaking, valueless, and the sacrifice extolled merely by sundry unusually foolish women did not cost much. This act furnished food for thought, even to minds the least reflective. For it was a dangerous precedent. Men whose wives differ from them so vastly in religious views should leave special instructions with regard to their papers. Owing to irrepressible hopefulness concerning his own health, Burton had neglected this precaution: even when all could see that his life was hanging by a thread, he wrote to his sister in England making plans for the future, and only a few days before the end he told her gleefully of the progress of his last translation and of his little army of admiring subscribers. Little did he imagine how soon after that cheery letter his book would be ashes, he in Eternity! Much sympathy was shown us on this occasion, for every kind-hearted person realised the bitter pain the mad act caused his family and friends. Not so much on account of the destruction of the manuscript, insulting though it was, but on account of the wrong impression concerning the character of the work conveyed by a deed which the widow made no secret of, when she should have veiled it in absolute silence. But if the lesson to other great men similarly circumstanced be remembered, the lesson that bigotry is ever cruel and untrustworthy, the " Scented Garden," like certain sentient victims of Romish fires, will not have been burnt in vain.

To resume the thread of my story. Though Burton could ill afford the expense of a move before the publication of the " Nights," he found himself obliged by failing health to give up the flat and to take a house on the outskirts of Trieste. His last illness had left his heart so weak that the 120 stairs leading to his airy abode tried him cruelly. On the 16th of July, 1883, husband and wife migrated to their new home. It resembled one of those Palazzi which Italians loved to build in other times ; and it was said to have been erected by an English merchant in days long past when our wealthy commercial men yet patronised Trieste. A good entrance led to a marble staircase ; some of the rooms, numbering twenty in all, were magnificent in size ; but scorpions were unpleasantly numerous, and the blasts for which Trieste is notorious must have often suggested the cave of Æolus. The Palazzo evidently showed to best advantage in summer, for it remained fairly cool in the hottest months; its large garden and orchard overlooked the bay, and the views on all sides were lovely. It was quite the handsomest home the Burtons had ever owned. Unluckily, it did not prove a wholesome one. Burton, who like his father detested little rooms, a result no doubt of that craving for air caused by weak heart and difficult respiration, chose the very biggest in the house for his bedchamber, and the aspect happened to be north. Though warmed in winter by a large stove, the draughts from the ill-fitting window-sashes must have been bitter, and to keep himself warm he wore a fur-lined coat all day and slept at night, not between sheets and blankets, but

buffalo skins. A little den, where he could turn the
key on all intruders when extra busy, was also fitted
up for his use; but the big bedroom appears to have
been his favourite study. And it proved an unfortunate
choice. *Dove non entra il sole entra il dottore ;* and in
this case when the doctor entered he came to stay.
Never have I met a man with fewer fads than Richard
Burton; but a large room was to him a necessity. Many
years ago I well remember him say he could not write
in a garret with a sloping roof; and we used to be very
careful, however small the house might be wherein we
happened to be living, to give him the most spacious
apartment we possessed.

In May, 1885, the Burtons came to England, partly to
superintend the printing of the " Nights," partly for change
and amusement. It was delightful to see our hero so
happy over the success of his venture. Sixteen thousand
pounds had been promised by his subscribers; he calculated printing and sundries as costing about four thousand,
and the remainder was net profit. Except when his father
died, he had never possessed such a sum before; and at
the time it appeared inexhaustible. We were then staying
at Norwood, so he could easily run down from London
and tell us all his plans and doings. Bubbling over with
fun, he would pretend to make a great mystery as to the
Kamashastra Society at Benares, where he declared the
" Nights " were being printed—about as true as the
tales themselves—or he would try to alarm us by announcing that they might all be burnt on their arrival
in England. But we had perfect faith in him, and were
not to be taken in. At other times, after a trip to
Oxford, he would tell us about his fruitless attempts to
obtain for reference from the Bodleian Library the Wortley
Montagu MSS. of " Alf Laylah wa Laylah." These said
journeys to Oxford were very disagreeable; he grumbled
sadly about the discomfort of the Library, declaring that

few students save the youngest and strongest could endure
its changeable, nerve - depressing atmosphere. Nor as
regarded himself were his complaints unfounded. Oxford
invariably upset him ; and as that year the cold set in early
and found him unprepared, he contracted a severe chill
amongst the fogs of Isis, which, as usual, turned to gout.

It was deemed advisable by his doctor—he was then
trying the rhubarb and saline treatment for his complaint—
to winter abroad. So he settled himself for some months
at Tangier, leaving his wife in London. As often happens
when invalids quit their own country, he might just as well,
so far as meteorological conditions were concerned, have
remained at home. The highly-extolled climate of Morocco
did not appear to the best advantage. More than once it
rained for three days without a break, once it even snowed,
and as houses at Tangier are guiltless of fireplaces, the
temperature for delicate folk must fall at times to a depressing, if not a dangerous point. However, there was little
time to think about small discomforts. Burton's labours
were incessant, for only two volumes of the " Nights "
were printed, and he had the remaining fourteen to prepare
for the press. In spite of hard work and indifferent health,
he passed some happy days in the picturesque old town.
The Minister and his wife, Sir John and Lady Drummond
Hay, showed him much kindly attention ; friends and admirers flocked round him when he was disposed for society;
and when alone, with the white domes and the spreading
palms ever in his sight, he was able to peacefully finish the
greatest literary achievement of his life.

Sometimes he would stroll about Tangier, and listen to
the Rawi, or reciter, who yet flourishes in Moslem cities.
One at Tangier used to haunt the Soko de barra, or large
bazaar in the outskirts. Here the market people formed a
ring about the speaker, a stalwart man, affecting little
raiment, and noticeable chiefly for his shock hair, wild eyes,
and generally disreputable aspect. He usually handled a

short stick, and when drummer and piper were absent, he carried a tiny tom-tom, shaped like an hour-glass, upon which he tapped the periods. This bard opened the drama with extempore prayer; he spoke slowly and with emphasis, varying the diction with breaks of animation, abundant action, and the most comical grimaces. He advanced, retired, and wheeled about, illustrating every point with pantomime; and his features, voice and gestures were so expressive, that even Europeans, ignorant of Arabic, divined the meaning of his tales. All the stories Burton heard were purely local, but a young Osmanli, domiciled for some time at Fez and Mequinez, assured him that the "Nights" were still recited there.

It was at Tangier that Burton's last piece of good fortune came to pass. One day a telegram arrived from Lord Salisbury, conveying in the kindest terms the news that the Queen, at his recommendation, had made him a K.C.M.G., in reward for his services. Only his nearest relatives knew how keen was the pleasure afforded by this honour to one of the least worldly of men. Under all circumstances a loyal and chivalrous servant of the Crown, he now recognised with delight that he was not viewed with disfavour by his Sovereign. And the distinction was all the more acceptable because so unexpected. Though Conservative to the backbone, Burton was too proud and sensitive to vaunt his devotion to Queen and country, fearing lest it might be imagined he was trying to obtain by patronage what he preferred to win solely by his own exertions. Such unusual delicacy is apt to be misunderstood, and many people imagined his sympathies lay with democracy. Occasionally, perhaps, a combination of mental and physical pain made him irritable, unduly pessimistic, and inclined to consider himself ill-treated by the Government then in power; but hardly had the fit of gout, the pecuniary annoyance passed away before he resumed the easy, sweet-tempered mood most usual to him. His very last words uttered in public, on the occasion of the Jubilee, would prove, if proof be needed, he was no disappointed place-hunter, no votary of King Mob, but a true and loyal-hearted English gentleman.

" May God's choicest blessings crown our Queen's good works. May she be spared for many happy, peaceful, and prosperous years to her devoted people ! May her mantle descend upon her children and her children's children ! "

Once more did Burton wend his way homeward. We saw him oftener in 1888 than during any previous visit. Both brother and sister made every effort to meet as frequently as possible, almost as if they knew their next parting would be final. First he stayed with us at Folkestone, then we arranged to pass some weeks together at Norwood, and last of all we met again by the seaside. When he landed in June, we were horrified at the change in his appearance. We knew of course he had been ill and that his wife had engaged a resident physician, but he had not prepared us for the utter breakdown in health, writing rather about his plans than his sensations. By the autumn his loss of strength was yet more startling. His eyes wore that strained look which accompanies difficult respiration, his lips were bluish-white, his cheeks livid ; the least exertion made him short of breath and sometimes even he would pant when quietly seated in his chair. The iron constitution which had borne so much pain and labour was almost exhausted, and heart disease, a hereditary malady, was making rapid strides. Still, his splendid pluck never forsook him, he seemed to live on by sheer force of will ; and his wonderful faculty of concentrating his attention on outward objects, his favourite adage being " The wisdom of youth is to think of, the wisdom of mature age is to avoid dwelling upon, Self," enabled him to keep at bay that distressing melancholy which is often bred by an incurable disorder. Every morning, so long as the fine weather lasted, he and his sister took an early walk together, and talked over times and scenes long past. Strangely enough, my mother remarked that his memory, clear and retentive as to all concerning the present, failed slightly when he referred to his boyish days. The early portions of an autobiography partly dictated by himself are full of inaccuracies—inaccuracies proved on reference to our old family Bible.

The end was indeed approaching, and perhaps the most painful feature in the case was an ever-increasing restlessness ; even if a place suited him he could not remain in it with any pleasure longer than a fortnight. The bracing air of Folkestone afforded greater relief than any he had yet breathed, and we were most anxious he should give it a fair trial. Good English food, open fireplaces, the fresh winds from the Channel were preferable, we urged, to kickshaws, close stoves, and ill-smelling foreign towns. True enough, he answered, and forthwith took rooms at the Pavilion with his wife and doctor, lunching with us every day, and seeming for awhile fairly happy and amused. When he first arrived, autumn was not very far advanced, and the weather continued fine enough for him to take long drives in an open carriage to places of interest in the neighbourhood, especially to Dover, where, many years before, he had twice stayed with his sister and other relatives. Then, by degrees, the weary longing for change seized him again ; alarming insomnia set in, and it seemed he must travel or die. One gusty October morning, brightened occasionally by a pale gleam of sunshine which threw into bold relief the grand white cliffs of Eastern Kent, Richard Burton left his native land to return no more.

" I shall never see him again," exclaimed his sister, as she tearfully watched the outbound steamer. And she never did.

During the next two years the roaming was incessant. It seemed as though he dreaded a " straw death," and affronted all the perils of land and sea in hopes of escaping it.

One marvels how, with such delicate health, he could have endured the noise, fatigue and worry of the innumerable journeys ; and there is little doubt all combined to exhaust the small stock of strength that yet remained. Every letter we received was dated from a different place. Geneva, Vevey, Montreux, Berne, Venice, Neuberg, Vienna, Trieste, Brindisi, Malta, Tunis, Algiers, the Riviera, and finally Innsbruck, Ragatz, Davos and Maloja. On the way to the last he met with a carriage accident. As he was driving from Davos in a landau drawn by two grey horses one of the animals suddenly sprang over a low stone wall, luckily breaking the traces and leaving its fellow and the carriage on the other side. The scene of the disaster was a narrow road winding along the edge of a sharp precipice which dipped into the lake, and had both horses taken the leap to-gether, nothing could have saved our traveller from being hurled into the watery depths. Very lovely did he think the scenery at Maloja, and, for a time, very health-giving the air ; but by the end of August snow fell so incessantly that he longed to get back to Italy. The party started on the 1st September, 1890, spent a few days at Venice, and then very unwillingly returned to Trieste.

It had become absolutely necessary to resume for awhile his consular duties. During this last summer Burton had received more than one hint from the Foreign Office that his presence at Trieste for two or three months would be desirable. Marvellous was the amount of liberty accorded to the dying hero, but some pretence of work had to be kept up just for the sake of appearances. No one at home knew how very ill he was, and it is possible that other officials, who were remorselessly chained to their posts, may have grumbled at the favour shown their fellow consul. Burton recognised the justice of the mild reproof, and determined, with a mighty effort, to wander no more for the next ten or twelve weeks. His servitude was nearly at an end ; by March he would have completed his time, claimed his pension, and could live where he liked and devote his last days to literature. But oh! the five weary months that lay between, *could* he exist through them? As I have already said, it was agony to linger long anywhere, but here, besides the feeling of being fettered, was a strange horror of Trieste, well-nigh uncontrollable. Perhaps, like his Scotch mother, who exclaimed on entering the house in Bath, wherein later she ended her harmless and amiable life, " I smell death here," he had a presentiment of what awaited him in the Palazzo by the sea. However, brave and patient to the last, he tried to while away the autumn hours by working diligently at his translation of the " Scented Garden," and, as a treat, arranging with his doctor various little details of a winter tour, which he hoped to take by-and-by to Athens and other places in Greece. But his travelling days were done.

For a week or so before the fatal 20th of October, Burton suffered from a slight attack of gout, not sufficiently serious to prevent him from taking his daily walk, but painful enough to make him say he was beginning to lose the good gained in Switzerland and to feel once more the corroding climate of the pestilential seaport. These attacks were much dreaded by his doctor, for the heart had become so weak that its action was distressingly impeded by the flatulence that always followed in their wake. On the 19th he seemed neither better nor worse. He had worked at intervals during the day at his translation, and when dinner-time came he put away his papers with a strange sort of lingering care; he was always tidy, but on this occasion everything was arranged with singular neatness. He dined sparingly, laughed and talked in his usual fashion, and at about ten o'clock went upstairs to bed, accompanied by Dr. Baker, who generally assisted him to undress. No premonitory symptom of the fatal seizure seems to have been noticed by either; on the contrary, Burton assured his friend, when wishing him good night, that he felt unusually well and hoped to enjoy a fair night's rest.

Hardly had a couple of hours elapsed before he began to grow uneasy, and his wife, who slept in an adjoining room, hearing him groan and toss from side to side, went to fetch Dr. Baker. Still, the attack seemed a slight one compared with many others which had preceded it, so the doctor after examining the state of heart and pulse administered a remedy, and at his patient's urgent request returned to bed. At 6.30 a.m. Burton was no better, worse rather, and his physician was again summoned. Now the sick man evidently realised that his state was critical. Feeling his strength fast ebbing, he called out with rare presence of mind, " Isabel, chloroform, ether, quick! chloroform, ether!" Either drug taken internally is a powerful stimulant, and far more diffusible than whisky or brandy. But no time remained for further remedies. Suddenly the breathing became laboured, there were a few moments of awful struggle for air, then, conscious to the last, he exclaimed, " I am a dead man!" fell back on his pillow and expired.[1] The brave heart, so unmercifully tried, was stilled for ever. But not before all his work was nearly done, not before he had received unstinted praise, not before he had been loved and honoured, not before we who mourned him knew that his swift, painless death, before his matchless genius had begun to wane, was surely well.

So passed from our midst one of the heroes of our age. I would fain linger over his patient endurance of suffering, his indefatigable industry, his perfect composure face to face with Eternity, but painful as the task is, I must tell of the awful farce which was enacted about that death-bed.

In the letter mentioned below it was stated that Burton died suddenly at 7 a.m., October 20th, 1890. The terrible shock of so fatal a termination to what seemed an attack of little consequence, would have daunted most Romanists

---

[1] This account of Sir Richard Burton's death is taken from a letter written by Dr. Baker to Lady Stisted, 21st October, 1890. Later both he and Lady Burton's maid, an eye-witness, agreed in declaring that Sir Richard had expired before the priest's arrival.

desirous of effecting a death-bed conversion. It did not daunt Isabel. No sooner did she perceive that her husband's life was in danger, than she sent messengers in every direction for a priest. Mercifully, even the first to arrive, a man of peasant extraction, who had just been appointed to the parish, came too late to molest one then far beyond the reach of human folly and superstition. But Isabel had been too well trained by the Society of Jesus not to see that a chance yet remained of glorifying her Church—a heaven-sent chance which was not to be lost. Her husband's body was not yet cold, and who could tell for certain whether some spark of life yet lingered in that inanimate form ? The doctor declared no doubt existed regarding the decease, but doctors are often mistaken. So, hardly had the priest crossed the threshold than she flung herself at his feet, and implored him to administer Extreme Unction. The father, who seems to have belonged to the ordinary type of country - bred ecclesiastic so common abroad, and who probably in the whole course of his life had never before availed himself of so startling a method of enrolling a new convert, demurred. There had been no profession of faith, he urged, there could be none now ; for—and he hardly liked to pronounce the cruel words— Burton was dead. But Isabel would listen to no arguments, would take no refusal ; she remained weeping and wailing on the floor, until at last, to terminate a disagreeable scene which most likely would have ended in hysterics, he consented to perform the rite. Rome took formal possession of Richard Burton's corpse, and pretended, moreover, with insufferable insolence, to take under her protection his soul. From that moment an inquisitive mob never ceased to disturb the solemn chamber. Other priests went in and out at will, children from a neighbouring orphanage sang hymns and giggled alternately, pious old women recited their rosaries, gloated over the dead, and splashed the bed with holy water, the widow, who had regained her composure, directing the innumerable ceremonies.[1] One Englishman, and only one, had the courage to protest against this unseemly disregard for the dead man's wishes, thanks to my honest fellow-countryman. But it was of no avail. After the necessary interval had elapsed, Burton's funeral took place in the largest church in Trieste, and was made the excuse for an ecclesiastical triumph of a faith he had always loathed.

Even the demonstration at Trieste was not sufficient. The widow insisted on repeating the funeral ceremonies at home—on proclaiming once more her strangely won victory over Protestantism and infidelity. So her husband's body, after lying awhile in the Trieste cemetery, was conveyed to England and placed in an eccentric tomb in the Roman Catholic burial ground at Mortlake. Again the shaven priests intoned the mass, again the acolyte bearing the crucifix preceded the corpse to the grave, again was Truth trampled under foot in a vain endeavour to exalt a Church ever an enemy to Light. Poor deluded woman! After all it was but a barren triumph. No wreath from Royalty, silent or outspoken disapprobation from right-minded people. In spite of numerous and pressing invitations, only one member of her husband's family, a distant cousin, accepted: sister, niece, his favourite relatives, and many of his best and most sympathising friends, refused to countenance a Lie. The hero had been ever true to himself, and it behoved those who loved him to remain steadfast to the last.

It was a painful sequel to a noble death. But we must look to the future. Fifty years hence London's ever-advancing tide will have swept away every vestige of the shabby sectarian cemetery where Richard Burton lies. But his works will remain as a legacy to his country. So long

---

[1] Be it understood we did not blame Dr. Baker. He was employed professionally by Lady Burton, and had no authority to resist an outrage which, moreover, was utterly unexpected.

as the spirit of enterprise animates Englishmen his exploits will be honoured ; so long as genuine literature is appreciated his books will help to educate heroes yet unborn.

> While England sees not her old praise dim,
> While still her stars through the world's night swim,
>   A fame outshining her Raleigh's fame,
> A light that lightens her loud sea's rim
>
> Shall shine and sound as her sons proclaim
> The pride that kindles at Burton's name,
>   And joy shall exalt their pride to be
> The same in birth if in soul the same.

ALGERNON C. SWINBURNE.

APPENDIX

LIST OF SIR RICHARD BURTON'S WORKS.

A Grammar of the Játaki or Belochkí Dialect.   1849.

Grammar of the Mooltanee Language.   1849.

Critical Remarks on Dr. Dorn's Chrestomathy of Pushtoo, or
   Afghan Dialect.   1849.

Reports to Bombay :—

   (1) General Notes on Sind ;   (2) Notes on the Population ot
      Sind.   Printed in the Government Records.

Goa and the Blue Mountains.   1851.

Scinde ; or the Unhappy Valley.   2 vols.   1851.

Sindh, and the Races that Inhabit the Valley of the Indus.
   1851.

Falconry in the Valley of the Indus.   1852.

A Complete System of Bayonet Exercise.   1853.

Pilgrimage to Meccah and El-Medinah.   3 vols.   1855.

First Footsteps in East Africa.   1856.

Lake Regions of Equatorial Africa.   2 vols.   1860.

The whole of Vol. XXXIII. of the Royal Geographical Society.
   1860.

The City of the Saints (Mormon).   1861.

Wanderings in West Africa.   2 vols.   1863.

Abeokuta and the Camaroons.   2 vols.   1863.

Marcy's Prairie Traveller.   Notes by R. F. Burton.   1864.

The Nile Basin.   1864.

A Mission to the King of Dahome.   2 vols.   1864.

Wit and Wisdom from West Africa.   1865.

Psychic Facts.   Stone Talk, by F. Baker.   1865.

The Highlands of the Brazil.   2 vols.   1869.

Vikram and the Vampire ; Hindú Tales.   1870.

Paraguay.   1870.

Proverba Communia Syriaca.   1871.

Zanzibar: City, Island, and Coast. 2 vols. 1872.

Unexplored Syria, by Burton and Drake. 2 vols. 1872.

The Lands of the Cazembe, and a small Pamphlet of Supplementary Papers. 1873.

The Captivity of Hans Stadt. 1874.

The Castellieri of Istria: a Pamphlet. 1874.

Articles on Rome. 2 Papers. 1874-5.

New System of Sword Exercise: a Manual. 1875.

Ultima Thule: a Summer in Iceland. 2 vols. 1875.

Gorilla Land; or, the Cataracts of the Congo. 2 vols. 1875.

The Long Wall of Salona, and the Ruined Cities of Pharia and Gelsa di Lesina: a Pamphlet. 1875.

The Port of Trieste, Ancient and Modern. Journal of the Society of Arts, October 29th and November 5th, 1875.

Gerber's Province of Minas Geraes. Translated and Annotated by R. F. Burton.

Etruscan Bologna. 1876.

Sind Revisited. 2 vols. 1877.

Gold Mines of Midian and the Ruined Midianite Cities. 1878.

The Land of Midian (Revisited). 2 vols. 1879.

Cheap Edition of Meccah and Medinah. 1879.

Camoens. 6 vols. of 10. First publication, 1880.
    I. The Lusiads, Englished by R. F. Burton. 2 vols.
    II. The Commentary, Life, and Lusiads. R. F. Burton. 2 vols., containing a Glossary, and Reviewers reviewed.
    III. The Lyricks of Camoens. 2 vols. R. F. Burton. Four more vols. were intended to be issued.

The Kasîdah. 1880.

A Glance at the Passion Play. 8vo. 1881.

To the Gold Coast for Gold. 2 vols. 1883.

The Book of the Sword. One volume of three. By R. F. Burton, Maître d'Armes. 1884.

Arabian Nights. Printed by private subscription. 1,000 sets of 10 vols., followed by 1,000 sets of 6 supplementary vols. 1885-1886.

Iraçema, or Honey Lips, and Manoel de Moraes, the Convert. Translated from the Brazilian by Richard Burton. 1 shilling vol. 1886.

The Scented Garden, Man's Heart to Gladden, of the Shaykh al Nafzáwi. Printed for the Kama Shastra Society.

The Priapeia. Privately Printed. 1890.

Personal Narrative of a Pilgrimage to Al-Medinah and Meccah. 2 vols. Memorial Edition. 1893.

A Mission to Gelele, King of Dahome. 1 vol. Memorial Edition. 1893.

Vikram and the Vampire, or Tales of Hindu Devilry. 1 vol. Memorial Edition. 1893.

Arabian Nights, 12 vols. Library Edition. 1894.

The Kasîdah. 1894.

The Carmina of Caius Valerius Catullus. Privately Printed. 1894.

" The Uruguay " (translations from the great Brazilian authors), by Richard and Isabel Burton; the Book of the Sword, 2 more vols.; the Lowlands of the Brazil; Translation of Camoens, 4 more vols.; Personal Experiences in Syria; A Book on Istria; Slavonic Proverbs; Greek Proverbs; The Gypsies; Dr. Wetzstein's " Hauran " and Ladislaus Magyar's African Travels.

First Footsteps in East Africa. 2 vols Memorial Edition. 1894.

Besides which, Sir Richard Burton wrote extensively for " Fraser," " Blackwood," and a host of magazines, pamphlets, and periodicals; lectured in many lands; largely contributed to the Newspaper Press in Europe, Asia, Africa, and America (both North and South). to say nothing of poetry and anonymous writings.